:: :: :: :: ::

THE GIRL FROM GOD'S COUNTRY:
NELL SHIPMAN AND THE SILENT CINEMA

Kay Armatage

In *The Girl from God's Country,* Kay Armatage reintroduces film studies scholars to Nell Shipman, a pioneer in both Canadian and American film, and one of proportionately numerous women from Hollywood's silent era who wrote, directed, produced, and acted in motion pictures. Born and raised in British Columbia, Shipman became a contract actress for Vitagraph Studios, starring in *God's Country and the Woman* (1915) and *Back to God's Country* (1919), among other films. These action-packed adventure melodramas, in which the heroine is called upon to rescue her husband and defeat the villain, were immensely successful. Later, Shipman started up her own production company to make films centred on her screen persona, 'the girl from God's country.' By the mid-1920s, however, the formation of the large Hollywood studios and vertical integration closed down the independents, Shipman among them. Nevertheless, she continued writing until her death in 1970.

Through the use of social history, feminist film theory, and biography, Armatage creates a portrait of a woman film pioneer. Using Shipman's working life as a window to the profession, Armatage explores the position of women in modernism, the developing film industry, and cinematic practice of the 1920s. *The Girl from God's Country* also contextualizes Shipman's work within the development of Hollywood as a locus of artistic production as well as in relation to women filmmakers from Europe, Australia, Russia, and the United States. This book brings Shipman back to life.

KAY ARMATAGE is an associate professor in Cinema Studies and Women's Studies at the University of Toronto. She is co-editor of *Gendering the Nation: Canadian Women's Cinema* (1999).

The Girl from God's Country:
Nell Shipman and the
Silent Cinema

Kay Armatage

UNIVERSITY OF TORONTO PRESS
Toronto Buffalo London

© University of Toronto Press Incorporated 2003
Toronto Buffalo London
Printed in Canada

ISBN 0-8020-4414-X (cloth)
ISBN 0-8020-8542-3 (paper)

Printed on acid-free paper

National Library of Canada Cataloguing in Publication

Armatage, Kay
    The girl from God's country : Nell Shipman and the silent cinema /
Kay Armatage.

    Includes bibliographical references and index.
    ISBN 0-8020-4414-X (bound)   ISBN 0-8020-8542-3 (pbk.)

    1. Shipman, Nell, 1892–1970 – Criticism and interpretation.   I. Title.

PN1998.3.S55A7 2003   791.43'023'092   C2002-905658-6

University of Toronto Press acknowledges the financial assistance to its
publishing program of the Canada Council for the Arts and the Ontario
Arts Council.

This book has been published with the help of a grant from the Humanities
and Social Sciences Federation of Canada, using funds provided by the Social
Sciences and Humanities Research Council of Canada.

University of Toronto Press acknowledges the financial support for its publishing activities of the Government of Canada through the Book Publishing
Industry Development Program (BPIDP).

Contents

:: :: :: :: ::

Acknowledgments

I first have to acknowledge the help of Tom Trusky, director of the Hemingway Center of Western Studies, Boise State University, Idaho. He was unfailingly generous with his information about Nell Shipman, and his knowledge, assiduous research, and dedication in collecting have been invaluable. Not only is he really fun to work with, but I also know that he has offered equal assistance to everyone who is interested in Shipman. Alan Virta, head of Special Collections, Albertsons Library, Boise State University, responded immediately to each of my email inquiries, generously filled in blanks in my knowledge, and offered unsolicited information when he thought I needed it. The letters included in this book are from the Nell Shipman Archive in the Special Collections Department of Boise State University Library, and they are reproduced with the permission of Boise State University and the Shipman family.

Barry, Nell Shipman's son, and his wife, Beulah, were wonderful. They welcomed me into their home in Glendale, California, giving me food and a bed, and as Barry told stories to me and showed me through his memorabilia, Beulah typed excerpts from unpublished materials. Barry also gave me a copy of his screenplay, 'Silent Star,' based on his memories of his mother. Mrs Lloyd Peters mailed me a rare copy of her husband's memoirs of the Shipman years at Priest Lake. David and Marion Naar, of the Cape Charles (Virginia) Historical Society, sent me a copy of *The Story of Mr Hobbs*.

Leonard Ferstman, librarian at Innis College, University of Toronto, helped immeasurably with research. I would walk into his office with a helpless look on my face, and he would find stuff for me. Anthony Slide, archivist at the Academy of Motion Pictures, gave me time and information, and Margaret Herrick was extremely nice and helpful. I was also accommodated by the British Film Institute, where Karen Alexander was particularly helpful. Eve Goldin, of Cinematheque Ontario Library, was consistently gracious.

Caryl Flinn, Heather Murray, Kass Banning, and Joy Parr read chapters as they were available. They counselled me about writing style and gave freely from their personal libraries and their expertise. Janis Cole helped me to edit Nell Shipman's letters. Ian Birnie introduced me to Cari Beauchamp, who provided many tips about research as well as her insights into the period and the spirits of the Hollywood girls of the period. Meredith Brody drove me around Los Angeles, mapping out the historic sites for me. Charlie Keil gave me many email addresses of film historians. Warren Crichlow provided me with valuable references. Micah Rynor supported this work from the beginning, sending me clippings and acting as a volunteer personal publicist for me. Shelley Stamp and Amelie Hastings gave me the opportunity to present my last emotional gasps at a conference on women film pioneers.

I also have to thank my undergraduate student researchers. Working in an innovative program that allowed second-year students to assist in real projects, they helped with everything. Jennifer Little used her dad's office equipment to scan the letters, Joseph Bistray built a Nell Shipman web site, and Jennifer Chan and Wing Sze Tang supplied sophisticated abstracts of articles. Carmela Murdocca gave editorial assistance.

Sherril Grace and Sandy Kybartas were generous with their insights into Shipman's memoirs. Emily Andrew, formerly of University of Toronto Press, greeted the project with enthusiasm and supplied missing information about Canadian sources. Siobhan McMenemy, editor at University of Toronto Press, has also been consummately professional in her assistance. Barbara Tessman did a wonderful job of copy-editing and helped me meet a rigorous schedule.

I have also to thank my darling daughter, Alex Armatage House, who not only read passages and made astute comments, but also bore with me while I neglected grocery shopping for over a year.

⁛   ⁛   ⁛   ⁛   ⁛

THE GIRL FROM GOD'S COUNTRY:
NELL SHIPMAN AND THE SILENT CINEMA

Introduction

Simpering Lillian Gish with her lips pursed like a little posy; helpless melodramatic victim tied to the railroad tracks waiting for the hero to rescue her from the wicked landlord; sultry foreign vamp: these may be the popular stereotypes of women in the silent cinema, but they are by no means typical of all movie women from the period. Contemporary research is rewriting such inscriptions, as we discover a repressed image-bank of energetic modern women who drove automobiles, flew in airplanes, openly expressed sexual desire, and even rescued the hapless hero.

Nell Shipman, the Canadian-born independent filmmaker – one of the very few Canadians who were making feature films in the silent period, and certainly the first Canadian woman to make a feature film – was one of this twentieth-century breed of woman. She made a series of melodramatic adventure films in which she played the robust heroine known as the 'girl from God's country.' Snowshoeing and dogsledding across the great white North, she had to protect her husband, defeat the villain, and generally save the day, always with the help of a Great Dane and her private zoo of trained wild animals.

Shipman is known today as producer/director/writer/star of popular entertainments made in the period 1912–24. Three feature films and four short films are extant from this period, and a fragment of a sound film has recently been discovered. *Back to God's Country* (1919), *Something New* (1920), and *The Grub-Stake* (1923, re-released as *The Golden Yukon*, 1927) are features that have been restored by archives in Canada, the United States, and Britain, and three short films have been made available in video by Idaho State University, Boise. *The Story of Mr Hobbs*, also known as *The Clam-Digger's Daughter* (1947), an independent sound-era film, turned up in a private collection in 1996, but is missing the final reel.

As a subject, Shipman is significant for a number of reasons. In opposition to popular stereotypes of femininity in the silent era, recent scholarship in cinema and women's studies suggests that active, courageous, and independent women characters were by no means unknown. Contrary to common assumptions, current cinema history reveals that women in positions of creative power in the silent film industry were proportionately more numerous than they were again until the 1980s. Nell Shipman's productive career exemplifies both matrices of representation and participation in production.

The Silent Scream and My Talking Heart

I wrote my first paper on Nell Shipman as a conference address, intending it to be simply a summary of some of my recent research. I had titled it after Shipman's autobiography, *The Silent Screen and My Talking Heart.*[1] When I finally received the printed conference program, I found that technology had undermined me. I had phoned in my title to an answering machine, and it turned up in the conference schedule as 'The Silent *Scream* and My Talking Heart' (my emphasis). My first response was a mixture of amusement and dismay. However, upon reflection, I found that, as usual, technology had provided a new opportunity, for the 'scream' on my lips was just waiting to be released.

I had done some research on Nell Shipman years ago, when I first learned of her existence, and the Women and Film: International Festival (Toronto, 1973) had exhibited a print of *Back to God's Country*, Shipman's magnificent 1919 feature. But I abandoned my historical research almost as soon as I started it. I was swept up into what seemed more exciting and revolutionary – the feminist theory project, which in 1973–5 was in its germinal stages. Film theory was certainly a more comfortable terrain for me than history: my literary training was more suitable preparation for it, and an active participation in feminism required the ideological framework that Anglo-French Marxist film theory so unapologetically provided.

My return to history is the result of a number of different factors. When I was beginning to work in feminist film scholarship, in the *Women and Film: International Film Festival Catalogue* (1973), I wrote that the feminist film enterprise must be a three-pronged initiative. It must include an archival and historical element – the recovery of lost women filmmakers whose work had been overlooked in mainstream film history, and the continuing documentation of the work of contemporary women filmmakers as they emerged. Second, it must be analytical, providing an analysis of films made by women (at the time, we wondered whether certain themes, patterns, commonalities might emerge), and particularly of feminist films. Finally, it must include the critical/theoretical – that is, the development of appropriate theory to deal with women's films.[2] Because existing methodologies had been so stunningly successful in overlooking or negating women's films, clearly the methodologies operating to that time in film, as in the other arts, must be inappropriate for the study of women's films.

We all know what has happened since then. The third prong of the fork developed rapidly and productively into a veritable industry of theory. Books, journals, and articles poured off the presses, names and careers were made, university courses were inaugurated and ceaselessly revised in response to changing currents and eddies in the theoretical floodtide. New films and new kinds of films emerged in its wake. For nearly a decade we had 'feminist theory films.' Avant-garde in their formal strategies, in subject they deconstructed issues such as the mirror phase, the relation of language to the patriarchal unconscious, realism/illusionism, and spectator–text relations.

In film scholarship, there was some analysis of films by women filmmakers and some documentation of their work, extending in some measure as well the other two prongs of the scholarly pitchfork, documentation and analysis. However, in film studies the archival project and the continuing documentation/analysis of contemporary women's cinema did not develop quite so vigorously as the theoretical element.

In the other arts, the opposite was more the case. In literature and the fine arts, for example, recovery of lost writers or artists was the dominant tendency. Publishing companies such as Virago thrived on such reclamation, special galleries showcasing only women artists were founded (notably the architecturally splendid National Museum of Women in the Arts in Washington, DC), and myriad books and journals on newly reclaimed individuals, themes, and critical issues can now be found in any bookshop. Indicatively, two French large-budget feature films were made about women artists: one, starring Isabelle Adjani and Gérard Depardieu, about Camille Claudel, the sculptor who was Rodin's tragic muse,[3] the other about Artemisia Gentilischi, a Renaissance painter.[4]

The success of feminist scholarly work in literature and the fine arts is broadly reflected in the academy. Literature courses in universities, for example, routinely make a point of including women writers where they once were ignored. In cinema departments, on the other hand, courses have not been revised on a significant scale to include women filmmakers. At least this is the case in the program where I teach.

There remains now only one annual festival of women's films (in Creteil, France), the cinematic equivalent, perhaps, of the Washington gallery. But a festival is not an archive: the films shown are mostly contemporary and not otherwise available for viewing, study, or writing about. This is not, in the end, the equivalent of Virago publications or a special museum, for festivals cannot circulate or preserve the works, and thus cannot make them a permanent part of a body of knowledge.

The very different situation in the arts other than film is the result of differing histories. Film studies, newly founded as a discipline in the late sixties, was eager to construct critical methodologies specific to the medium. Labouring also under the stigma of studying the popular and commercial arts, progressive film scholars embraced the 'scientific' approach developing from Marxist semiotics, structuralism, and psychoanalysis in France. The other arts, which were already well established in both critical methodologies and institutional acceptance, did not embrace as readily as film studies the psychoanalytic/structuralist model, although by now such work has been generalized as cultural studies and applied to all the other arts. In the meantime, in literature and the fine arts, the more 'naive' aspects of the feminist cultural project – the historical and analytical – proceeded apace. In those disciplines feminist scholars began 'contest[ing] the canon'[5] fairly early on, producing a seismic shift in the definition of feminist criticism. As Jane Gallop outlines in *Around 1981* (1992), in literary studies feminist criticism moved in its first half-decade from a concentration on the examination of representations of women in the canonical (male-authored) literature to the recovery of texts by women writers and a taxonomy of women's literary traditions. By 1981, feminist literary criticism *was* the study of women writers.[6]

In film, on the other hand, where theory developed so prodigiously, rather than a general accretion of feminist film work in history and analysis, those elements of the project were developed in the 1970s and 1980s only in relation to what had become the mainstream of cinema studies. Women filmmakers were written about, but only certain women filmmakers: the makers of theory films, especially, and some directors who belonged to other traditions but whose strategies were embraced as theoretical. Of the older guard, the work on Dorothy Arzner represented at least one lost filmmaker retrieved. Marguerite Duras was written about extensively, as was Chantal Akerman, who came to prominence contemporaneously with feminist film theory. Of the younger women filmmakers who made theory films and who were written about, only Yvonne Rainer[7] and Trinh, T. Min-Ha remain active. The other women filmmakers from that period have all settled back into teaching or writing, and their films are more or less out of circulation.

The women filmmakers who were not written about are far more numerous. They included most of those women who were producing feminist work in traditional documentary or conventional realist dramatic fiction or unconventional but untheoretical art film. They also included most of those women who have been producing popular films throughout the history of cinema from 1896 to the present. Until recently, remarkably little was written about those women filmmakers, or any of the more 'correct' ones for that matter.

Early scholarship included several anthologies and catalogues or guidebooks such as *Women in Focus* (1974)[8] and *Women and the Cinema* (1977).[9] In the category of documentation, there is, of course, the mammoth Maya Deren project in two hefty volumes (1985 and 1988),[10] *Women Filmmakers: A Critical Reception* (1984),[11] as well as several memoirs, notably by Alice Guy Blaché[12] and Nell Shipman. From the same period, there are also several publications concerning Leni Riefenstahl and a few on Lina Wertmuller,[13] but they are by no means products of a feminist critical or historical practice.

In the 1980s a handful of texts included some discussion of the work of women filmmakers as examples of counter strategies to the classic realist text. In *Women and Film: Both Sides of the Camera*, E. Ann Kaplan wrote glowingly about the women filmmakers who bore the feminist theory seal of approval,[14] Kaja Silverman discussed Sally Potter and Patricia Gruben in *The Acoustic Mirror*,[15] and Teresa de Lauretis wrote about Lizzie Borden in *Technologies of Gender*.[16] There was a book on Ida Lupino;[17] Lauren Rabinovitz studied the work of Maya Deren, Shirley Clark, and Joyce Wieland in *Points of Resistance* (1991);[18] and Sandy Flitterman-Lewis examined Germaine Dulac, Marie Epstein, and Agnes Varda in *To Desire Differently* (1990).[19] Still, despite two decades of active feminist film scholarship, there were no historical surveys, no thematic studies of the sort that abound in literature, and only a handful of book-length studies of women filmmakers who have bodies of work. How do we account for this?

Feminist film theory developed out of studies of the classic realist text, and it remained embedded there for a considerable period. Needless to say, like anything else considered classical, that model was created and is largely perpetuated by men. Feminist film theory developed as a critique of the classic realist text, demonstrating the mechanisms of its complicity in the nurturing of the patriarchal unconscious. As a result, rather than studying the work of women filmmakers, feminist film theoreticians instead contributed importantly to the body of scholarship supporting canonical figures such as Sirk, Buñuel, Hawks, Hitchcock, Snow, von Sternberg, Walsh, Minnelli, and Pee Wee Herman (!), and the many genre directors involved in the production of melodramas, films noirs, musicals, and porn films.

Parenthetically, I should add that in Canada the situation has been somewhat different. The main thrust of feminist critical work here has been attention to women filmmakers, and Canadian ones at that.[20] But as Longfellow, Banning, et al. argued in the *Camera Obscura* special issue on female spectatorship,[21] Canada itself has been marginalized and has not made any major contribution to the development of feminist theory as it has marked the international academy. Nor, as far as I can see, has our work made much of a dent in the consciousness of male academics in Canada.

In Canada, it becomes increasingly difficult, rather than easier, to teach a historically oriented course on women's cinema. The majority of the primary film texts, whether from the twenties, the fifties, or the seventies, are simply not available. Important texts such as *La vie rêvée* (d. Mireille Dansereau, 1972) are not in distribution; any Canadian film prior to 1950 is available only for archival work in Ottawa. Jaqueline Audry, Nelly Kaplan, Marguerite Duras, Safi Faye, Ulrike Ottinger, and Chantal Akerman are some of the important international figures whose films are not available in Canada. To a certain degree, we must assume that this is due to a lack of demand from film scholars.

I do not sing this liturgy out of any sense of repudiation or retribution or to suggest that those nearly twenty years of theory were a waste of time. Far from it. I believe that film theory, and particularly feminist theory, was fruitful in just the way that theory should be: it initiated new subjects for academic study and new methodologies for analysing those subjects. Perhaps the greatest achievement of the theoretical project was the transformation of cinema studies into a truly scholarly enterprise. Nevertheless, I think it is time to reassess. That, at any rate, is part of the burden of my chant here, and hence the inadvertent and hilarious appropriateness of the mangled title of my paper, 'The Silent *Scream* and My Talking Heart.' Melodramatic as it was, it nevertheless described my anguished state.

In the late 1980s and early 1990s, that state was exacerbated by another trend in feminist scholarship. The turning of the field of feminist film theory and criticism towards popular culture as its principal object of study accelerated the pulling away from the cinematic practice of women creators as object of study, effectively evacuating the woman creative producer as a focus. Broadly speaking, there are no women creative producers in popular culture.[22] Before we counter with Rosanne, Oprah, Martha Stewart, Penelope Spheeris (*Wayne's World*, 1992), Amy Heckerling (*Clueless*, 1995), Beeban Kidron (*To Wong Foo, Thanks for Everything, Julie Newmar*, 1995), Winnie Holtzman (*My So-Called Life*, television series, 1994), French and Saunders (*Absolutely Fabulous*, television series, 1992–6, 2001–), Diane English (*Murphy Brown*, 1988–98, and other popular television series), let me unpack this area a bit with a short-term history of feminist film theory.

In the mid-seventies, feminist film theory engendered the Anglo-French structuralist movement, emphasizing the patriarchal unconscious as central to the operations of the cinematic apparatus. Although the explicit goal was the analysis of the construction of subjectivity in popular culture, scholarly attention remained focused largely on the classic Hollywood text. After a decade of what Teresa de Lauretis described as a major epistemological shift effected by feminist theory, cinema studies began to turn to Cultural Studies.

Three factors are germane here. One is the evacuation of auteurism as a methodological tool, repudiated for its humanist validation of the heroic Cartesian individual. Second, the universalized Eurocentrism of issues such as sexual difference and gendered subjectivity came under severe critique as the pressing questions of ethnic and other differences and culturally specific identity formations took hold. A third factor was a renewed interest in truly popular culture. Contemporary commercial cinema (rather than the classic Hollywood text of canonical auteurs) and commercial broadcast television became the principal objects of study. Feminist scholars took on rock videos, soaps, therapeutically confessional talk shows, sitcoms, *Star Trek*, and *Dallas*. They utilized the methodologies of feminist film theory and cultural studies to produce critical, resistant, or interventionist readings for the potential of simultaneous pleasure, recognition, and awareness of women's position within the structures of patriarchy.

This was all interesting work. Not only that, but it made feminism fun. Still I think what I am getting at is apparent. As long as the objects of study remain popular culture – commercial cinema and broadcast television – and the methodologies of analysis elide authorship to emphasize reception and readership, the woman cultural producer remains obscure. The plain truth is that women do not play a prominent role in the production of popular culture. They are present, as always, as 'luminous vehicles' (Patricia Mellencamp's phrase). A few women movie directors have made it onto the *Variety* top-grossers' list, and there are some powerful women sitcom writers, but women remain, in popular culture, primarily the 'bearer[s] of meaning, rather than the maker[s] of meaning,' to resurrect Laura Mulvey's ancient maxim.[23]

In *Feminism without Women: Culture and Criticism in a 'Postfeminist' Age* (1991) Tania Modleski offered a salutary critique of the challenges to feminism posed by the shifts from 'women' to 'gender,' from deconstructionist textual analysis to reception-based approaches, from feminine subjectivity to the study of masculinity and male feminism. Her book critiques many of the contemporary forms of feminist critical theory, from notions of performativity and masquerade in relation to gender to post-modern ethnography. Rather than the institutionalization of feminism heralded both positively and negatively in current meta-critical discourse, she argues that 'postfeminism' and postmodernism simultaneously evacuate both women and 'the feminist project,' which she defines as 'illuminating the causes, effects, scope and limits of male dominance.'[24]

Each chapter of Modleski's book centres on a particular text or genre of texts from popular culture – literature, television, commercial cinema. But here is the telling point: of all these exemplary texts, only two are by women creative producers, both of whom remain nameless in Modleski's text. She invokes *Crossing Delancey* (d. Joan Micklin Silver, 1988) to critique its use of racial stereotypes, and mentions *Three Men and a Cradle* (d. Coline Serreau, 1985) as the hypo-text of the misogynist Hollywood remake *Three Men and a Baby* (d. Leonard Nimoy, 1987). In neither case does she mention the woman director. The case of Coline Serreau is particularly interesting, for Modleski shows no curiosity about possible differences between the French and Hollywood texts, or about Serreau's two-decade career as a commercially successful writer/director of raucous male yuppie-bashing popular comedies. In her defence, it must be said that Modleski is utilizing methodologies that do not emphasize enunciation or authorial origins; instead, she takes pains to frame the feminist debates about essentialism in other ways.

Still I find myself troubled. I believe that the narrow definition of the feminist project as aiding us in 'illuminating the causes, effects, scope and limits of male dominance' has many serious consequences. One of the most pressing of these consequences is the retention of a focus on the cultural productions of the male creator, regressively reinstating the phallus as the primary signifier, and marginalizing – at best – or evacuating altogether the potential of women to achieve equality in the production of cultural meaning. This focus has produced a great lacuna in feminist scholarship. Indeed, Anthony Slide's *Early Women Directors* (1977, 2nd ed. 1984) addresses this lacuna in explicitly anti-feminist terms.[25]

In the 1990s, another trend in feminist film scholarship began to emerge. The past decade has seen the publication of a number of companions or encyclopedias of women filmmakers, as well as several memoirs and biographies. A Canadian text, *Calling the Shots*,[26] features interviews with twenty North American women directors, and *Gendering the Nation: Canadian Women's Cinema* (1999)[27] is the first study of women's participation as directors in a national film industry. The Women Film Pioneers Project (based in the United States) has also made great strides, inspiring scholars to pursue the history of women filmmakers and stars of the silent cinema, and helping to make available for study film texts that have been out of circulation, some of them almost since their moment of production. Many scholarly texts are underway and in press, and a new series of monographs on silent women pioneers is now in the planning stages.

Historians and Historiography

New historiographical approaches have emerged in the discussions integrating cinema history with film theory. As Tom Gunning writes, 'anyone can see that the apathy toward history evident in film theory in the early and middle seventies has been replaced by a mode of interpenetration ... Now ... film historians have appeared for whom film theory played a vital role and who are as interested in exploring what a fact is as in discovering one. Likewise theorists have realized increasingly the importance not only of the historian's facts, but of historical research and speculation in approaching issues of spectatorship, narrative structure, and the role of gender.'[28] Gunning goes on to say that 'It is no accident that much of the exciting new work being done in film history is being done by women. Recognizing their marginalized place in traditional discourses, these scholars have undertaken a rediscovery of women's experience of cinema which has led to a fundamental questioning of the established concerns of history and its dominant methods.'[29]

For many years feminist historians in all the arts have questioned dominant historiographical conventions. A repeated topic of debate has been the efficacy of simply interpolating female historical figures into mainstream history. Feminist historians have also argued that the conventional emphasis on the role of heroic figures and the master narratives of the past have been significant factors in obscuring the role of women in history. In *Old Mistresses* (1981), for example, Griselda Pollock discussed the theoretical problems of such simplistic historical interpolation of women artists into fine art history, and called for new critical methodologies as well as new historical categories.[30]

In a more recent update of this position, Irit Rogoff writes: 'Constructing a speaking position and a narrative voice from which to engage with the identity of women culturally constituted on the margins of modernism entails several acute paradigm shifts. Not only do the parameters of historical periodicity and historical value need to be shed, but the very interplay of voices and "telling" needs to be reworked.' However, with Pollack, Rogoff also cautions that 'the reconstitution of erased voices and their recuperations into existing narratives, structured as "probing models," achieve little more than a similar history gendered female. Perhaps it is not the materials and attempts of their alternative marshalling which we need to address but the modes of telling and retelling, the full consciousness that the narrative is endlessly and circularly retold, that the missing voices and erased identities cannot, should not, be robustly reconstituted.'[31]

Contrary to Rogoff's warning, I would argue that even if such 'reconstitution of erased voices and their recuperations into existing narratives' in the other arts has achieved 'little more than a similar history gendered female,' we are nevertheless richer for it. By now we not only have a treasure trove of women writers from the past, but we have also produced a more welcoming publishing climate for contemporary women writers from many geographical and cultural heritages, as well as new theoretical rubrics with which to consider them. When I read Rogoff's caution, 'that the missing voices and erased identities cannot, *should not*, be robustly reconstituted' (my emphasis),[32] I am reminded of B. Ruby Rich's ancient complaint about feminist film theory, that we are insisting on the absence of women subjects and spectators even in the face of our presence.[33] Indeed, we seem to be bent on *prohibiting* our presence in favour of 'uncertainty, ambiguity, and disorientation.'[34]

In cinema a number of factors combine to suggest a historical configuration with rather differently modulated significance for women historical figures and for feminist film historians. The novelty of the medium in its pioneering period, combined with its status as a popular entertainment growing alongside vaudeville and the 'legitimate' theatre – terrains already occupied by women – resulted in a period marked (albeit briefly) by the presence of women in positions of relative power.

It would be foolish to argue that cinema was anything like a 'free zone' for women, escaping the discrimination against women endemic to the other arts and the culture as a whole. But in its earliest days, at least, cinema had not yet achieved the deliberate exclusion of women found in the other more established arts such as poetry, music, and painting, in which women were systematically denied access to the educational and professional institutions that shaped the arts.

For the first thirty years, women pioneers in cinema worked in every nation that had a film industry. Although women were relatively numerous in authorial positions in the independent era of the silent cinema, by the late 1920s nearly all of them, on an international level, had become inactive. Women's evacuation from the film industry came about through a combination of three factors: the monopoly practices that accompanied the coming of sound; the rise of the large Hollywood studios; and the founding of the immediately powerful technicians' unions, which were dominated by organized crime and admitted only men to their membership. Between 1930 and 1970, only two women worked as directors in Hollywood, and as late as 1972 there were no women members of the Cinematographers' Union of America. All three of these factors came together just at the end of the silent period. This period is a site from which we can make 'trouble in the archives,' as Griselda Pollock writes, by 'contest[ing] the canon – the received and authorized version of the stories of modern art and its way of defining the visual image as the expressive site of an authoring self.'[35]

Nell Shipman is an exemplary figure, for her story parallels the entry, participation, and finally exclusion from cinema that was experienced by women filmmakers as a group in the first stage of film history.

Biography

Nell Barham Shipman was born Helen Barham in Victoria, British Columbia, in 1892, to a poor family of somewhat genteel British roots. Her father was a 'remittance man,' the colonial son of a British family with a proud heritage. Mother, father, brother Maurice, and Nell left Canada when she was an adolescent, settling in Seattle, Washington, where her brother returned to live after his stint in the First World War.

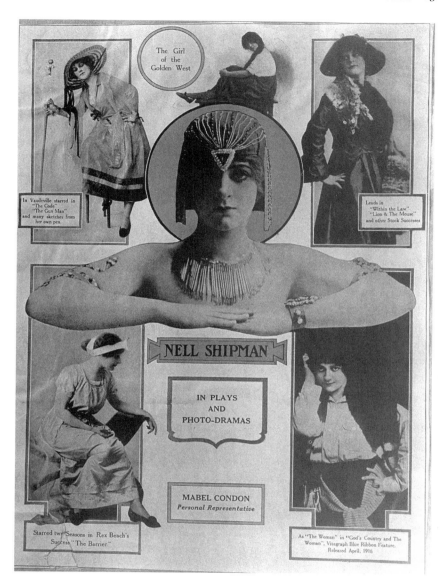

Nell Shipman, not yet typecast as the girl from God's country.

Although the family did not return to Canada, Nell Shipman remained sentimentally attached to her Canadian roots.

With her mother's permission, Nell left home at thirteen to become an actress with a small touring company. Eventually instead of bringing money to the family, Nell required help. In a show of support for women's career ambitions at a time when independent single women formed a very new social group, Nell's mother joined her daughter on the road, making her costumes, feeding her, and generally looking after her. By sixteen Nell had played every sort of vaudeville role and circuit. In 1910 at the age of eighteen, a leading lady, she became Canadian impresario Ernest Shipman's fourth wife. She bore a son two years later.

By 1912 she had already written and starred in her first film, *The Ball of Yarn*, which was so bad, she admitted, that even Ernie couldn't book it.[36] She directed her first film in 1914, 'an outdoor yarn' starring a handsome young leading man, Jack Kerrigan, in a buckskin suit.[37] In 1916 she starred in *God's Country and the Woman*, the James Oliver Curwood–Vitagraph feature that was to be Shipman's big break. The film's handsome budget of $90,000 reflected the stature of Curwood as a well-known short story writer specializing in western, wilderness, and animal tales, and Shipman's ascending trajectory as a star.

From the moment of her first association with Curwood, Shipman was known as 'the girl from God's country,' driving a team of sled dogs, canoeing, snowshoeing, and 'undergoing pages of Curwoodia drama.'[38] *Baree, Son of Kazan* (1918) was another Curwood adaptation, followed by *Back to God's Country* (1919), a melodramatic adventure set in the Canadian North. The film, in every frame a vehicle for Nell Shipman, features Shipman as the classic heroine, saving her invalid husband's life and bringing the villains to justice through her rapport with animals, her wilderness acumen, and her bravery and fortitude. *Back to God's Country* was an enormous critical and box-office success, reaping profits of 300 per cent and cementing Shipman's reputation as a star.

Despite the success of *Back to God's Country*, upon which she never ceased to capitalize, Shipman's partnerships with both her producer/ husband and James Oliver Curwood ended. She had taken up with Bert Van Tuyle, the production manager on *Back to God's Country*. She was so infatuated with Van Tuyle that she made him co-director of her movies and partner in her company, Nell Shipman Productions, formed in 1921.

Between 1922 and 1924, she lived in Upper Priest Lake, Idaho. Shipman, son Barry, and partner Van Tuyle – cast and crew – lived in the Idaho wilderness, making movies independently. They lived in a log cabin at a rented ranch, twenty-one miles from the nearest road and fifty miles from a railway line. To get out in winter, they had to dogsled and snowshoe across the frozen lake, a two-day walk in the best of weather, and nightmarish in the blizzards. In her autobiography, she describes a heroic real-life adventure, chasing Van Tuyle when he left the cabin raving in delirium from frostbite, herself barefoot for part of the journey because her socks had gotten wet and she knew better than to allow her feet to freeze.

By this time, Shipman was already known for her zoo of wild animals, including the famous bear, Brownie. There were also numerous 'untamable' animals such as elks, coyotes, wolves, a cougar, wildcats, skunks, eagles, and owls, and more easily domesticated animals such as raccoons, deer, porcupines, beavers, marmots, muskrats, rabbits, dogs, and cats. A map of Lionhead Lodge, the Shipman establishment at the tip of Priest Lake, indicates the prominence of the ten animal buildings, not counting eight malamute houses and a beaver dam. Nearly all of Shipman's films featured animals in prominent roles, functioning as romantic agent, comic relief, victim, or hero.

Shipman wrote, directed, and starred in at least three more feature films, *Something New* (1920), *The Girl from God's Country* (1921, now lost), and *The Grub-Stake* (1923, re-released as *The Golden Yukon*, 1927), using a skeleton crew, doing all her own stunts, wrangling the animals, and supervising the editing. Although Canada persisted as a fictional location for Shipman's narratives, she did not participate in the fledgling Canadian film industry. When the films were finished she would trudge across the lake to the nearest town and put on a vaudeville-type show at the local hall to raise money for her train fare to New York, where she would try to sell the films for distribution.

History: Just the Facts

An independent entrepreneurship in cinema was possible at the time. By 1908, 14th Street in New York City was well established as 'film exchange row.'[39] By 1912, New York City boasted 138 movie theatres,[40] and the following year saw the formation of many distribution companies with large syndicates. The Protective Amusement Company offered two features per week to one hundred syndicate-affiliated theatres. These companies made use of national distribution circuits developed for theatre and vaudeville in the late nineteenth century, circuits already supported by the communications-transportation infrastructure of telegraphy and railroads.[41] What rapidly became a vast North American circuit was propped on the low costs and almost limitless duplication of prints, and the virtually daily conversions of legitimate theatres to movie palaces. By 1923, even towns with populations under 10,000 would commonly have more than one movie theatre operating seven days a week.[42]

The process of selling your product in this climate was simple: you just put your film under your arm and kept going down 14th Street until one of the film exchanges offered to buy your picture. Until well into the silent period, even the price was standard: ten cents a foot.[43] By midway through the 1920s, however, independent production of this sort had become virtually impossible. Even earlier in the period, competition had been fierce; spying, sabotage, and theft were commonplace. With the financial and technological gearing up for sound, the film industry was interpenetrated by big business and organized crime. This new formation of the industry saw the rise of the studios and the monopoly practice of vertical integration of production, distribution, and exhibition. The exhibition and distribution circuits that remained unaffiliated with studios were rapidly closed down. All of the stalwarts of the silent cinema collapsed along with Shipman – Selig, Biograph, Vitagraph, and Essanay, as well as Solax (Alice Guy Blaché's company) and other tiny independents such as Kalem.[44] Shipman's cottage industry mode of production, as Peter Morris notes, was out of step with the new industrialization of Hollywood.[45]

History and Historians

The Silent Screen and My Talking Heart is Nell Shipman's autobiography, published in 1987, with a second edition in 1988 and a third in 2000. The book was written by Shipman herself – this is not an 'as told to' star bio – in 1968, when she was seventy-six years old. It is a sprightly piece of writing, replete with vivid detail, particularly of the travails of the Priest Lake winters. Although spotty in factual information, it has a high sense of drama and tension, as befits a work by a writer of numerous novels, articles, and screenplays over the course of nearly fifty years.

As an object and a work, the book is of great interest. Handsomely produced, it has close to fifty photographs, an afterword by Shipman's son Barry, and a note from Peter Morris, 'The Taming of the Few: Nell Shipman in the Context of Her Times.' The whole is the enterprise of Tom Trusky, of the Hemingway Center for Western Studies in Boise, Idaho, which is not far from Priest Lake, the scene of Shipman's most heroic and tragic episodes. Trusky has also managed to collect six of the surviving films from Shipman's career, as well as a collection of papers and letters, and he has in the works a complete filmography and an edition of her letters. Trusky's annotations in the autobiography attest to a great deal of research and information, and he has produced videotapes of the films now extant and in the public domain. *Back to God's Country* and *Something New* have been restored by the Canadian Film Archive and the UCLA Archive, respectively, and the British Film Institute has prints of *The Grub-Stake* and *The Clam-Digger's Daughter / The Story of Mr. Hobbs.*

As a scholarly enterprise, Trusky's is unique, for he is more interested in Nell Shipman than in her ex-husband Ernest. Thus far, Canadian historians have not shown the same interest in Nell, although she is clearly the more prolific, more creative, and ultimately more successful of the pair. Peter Morris has written substantially about Ernest Shipman, and it is from those writings that the researcher gleans, in tidbits and asides, something of the career of Nell Shipman.[46]

Of 'ten percent Ernie,'[47] as Shipman calls him, we learn much more. Ernest Shipman made his film career off his wife, failing first at vaudeville as her star began to rise, and finally getting into the movies as she accepted an exclusive contract with James Oliver Curwood. Curwood contracted with Nell Shipman that he would give her exclusive rights to his stories for screen adaptation if she would star exclusively in the films. Husband Ernie was to be the producer. As Morris notes, it was Ernie's 'big chance.'[48] Nell wrote the screenplays, tamed the wild animals, and starred in the films. David Clandfield notes that Nell is also 'credited with much of the work of ... staging.'[49] For example, the famous nude

scene in *Back to God's Country*, in which she skinny-dips under the water-
fall while the villain leers from the bushes, was clearly her idea and her
decision. In the autobiography, she tells of first wearing a flesh-coloured
cover-up, which she discarded when she saw how unattractive it looked
when wet, and conceived instead a mise en scène that allowed discreet
nudity. She also worked closely with cinematographer Joseph Walker
and the editor of *Back to God's Country*, as she did on all of her films.
When her marriage to Shipman ended, Ernest's contract with Curwood
came to a rapid close.

Here Clandfield's story continues in much the same vein as Morris's.
After mentioning Nell Shipman in connection with all of the creative
work on one film, *Back to God's Country*, Clandfield notes that in the
United States Nell had 'a successful career as actress, screen-writer, and
director, at a time when these last two professions included virtually no
women at all.' And then he carries on with his note on Ernest! Ernest
made seven films in all, including one that was never released.[50]
Although Nell suggests a rather different estimation, Clandfield calls
Ernest a 'successful theatre and film impresario,' noting that 'his entrepreneurial style consisted in arriving in a city, establishing a film company with local money for one or two films, and then moving on. In five
years he did this in Calgary, Winnipeg, Ottawa, Sault Ste. Marie, and
Saint John.'[51]

Shipman's portrait of Ernest adds some flesh to these bare bones:

> Men like Ernie made the '90's gay. A vanished breed. He had the bounce
> of a rubber ball, the buoyancy of a balloon, though the first can wear out
> under hard usage and the last suffer ill winds and the prick of evil fortune.
> He was one of the great cocksmen of his time, not immoral but amoral, not
> lascivious but lusty. If they named him dishonest he was always within the
> law's fences contractually and the ten percent he required of his minions'
> wages he considered a fair return for his efforts on their behalf.[52]

It was thanks to Ernie that Shipman began her screenwriting career.
Ernie was trying to break into pictures while Shipman was still recover-
ing from the birth of their son, Barry, in 1912 and thus unable to make a
living as an actress. When pregnant and unable to work, she had begun
to write magazine articles on the movies and the industry, so it seemed

natural to turn to writing screenplays. Ernest, she writes, 'scenting the golden future in store for even such shoddy entertainment, figured a day was coming when better-heeled motion picture makers would actually pay authors for the rights to their works.' Thus Shipman 'was thrown into the maelstrom of film writing' to support her family and to give her bounder husband another break.[53] There is no need to pursue this shabby portrait of 'ten-percent Ernie,' the 'successful impresario.' Like other independents, Ernest Shipman was squeezed out as the Hollywood giants seized control of the industry in Canada as well as the United States.

It is interesting that David Clandfield and Peter Morris, the pre-eminent Canadian film historians, give Ernest's career a solid summing up, while Nell Shipman's longer, more prolific, more varied, and more successful career is left undocumented. To be fair to Morris and Clandfield, we could argue that they both concentrated on the more faithfully Canadian of the pair. Ernest did, after all, return to Canada for his last failures, whereas Nell remained in the United States for both her failures and successes. Nell is lost in a strange limbo, it seems, for American scholars consider her Canadian[54] and Canadian scholars do not deal with her because she went to the United States. Thus, ironically for both feminist and Canadian film scholars, it is through the work of Tom Trusky, an American man, that we will be able to recover this almost lost Canadian filmmaker.

Biography: The End of the Story

Bert Van Tuyle's delusions of grandeur were the initial cause of the demise of Nell Shipman Productions. *The Girl from God's Country*, which Van Tuyle produced, went disastrously over budget, and Nell Shipman Productions was never able to recoup the loss. Van Tuyle was also a drunkard. Shipman stuck with him through the bankruptcy of the company, but finally let him go. After her production company collapsed and she left Bert Van Tuyle, Nell Shipman married artist Charles Ayers, and, for the duration of her career, supported herself and her family as a writer, mostly of novels and magazine articles.

At the personal level, she remained plagued by her disastrous selections of male partners. As Shipman pursued her obsessive attempts to revive her career in the film industry, her husband, Ayers, became afflicted with permanent artist's block due to the humiliation of being supported by his wife. She let him go. She then took up with a man who had as many aliases as he had creditors, and bounced around America with him for nearly twenty years. Shipman died alone, 'broke to the wide,' with the manuscript of the first volume of her autobiography waiting for publication.

Shipman's bankruptcy at the beginning of the sound era mirrors the demise of all the independent producers of the silent era, who were driven out of the industry by the rise of the major studios and their monopoly practices of production, distribution, and exhibition. Nell Shipman's career trajectory thus parallels not only the history of the silent cinema itself, but also represents in microcosm the history of women's participation in the industry. Shipman takes her place in history not as an unusual and uncommonly heroic individual, but as an exemplar of an industrial model that is of great interest in the current rewriting of film history.

For Shipman, then, we must recast the critical apparatus dramatically, from the female spectator to the female author, from the desiring body to the bear, the dog, and the raccoon, from the masquerade to the mukluk. And if we follow in Nell's snowshoed footsteps, we may make some gains in the recognition of female subjectivities of the heroic stamp, and with them the beginnings of women's cultural traditions in cinema.

Back to Nell Shipman

Rather than a psychological biography treating her family history or personal life, this book tells the story of Nell Shipman's working life, encountering her extant works, both film productions and writings, and situating them within a variety of contexts. Although there is a strong element of biography – of a sort – in this work on Shipman, it is not motivated by a desire to get inside the subject in a psychological biographical mode.

My resistance to personal biography is politically motivated and stems from long ago. When I was working on Gertrude Stein for my PhD dissertation, only a few of her works were in print – her own autobiographies and her little monograph on Picasso. By the time I had finished my dissertation on Stein in 1974, however, five Stein biographies were in print, at least one of them at the top of the non-fiction bestseller lists.[55] How could this be? How could a culture be so fascinated with her life in the absence of her work? This phenomenon seemed to capture exactly the problematic of women artists – that they were more interesting as personalities than as artists, especially if they were eccentric, alcoholic, or suicidal. In light of this political problematic, I determined to devote myself to the work – rather than the lives – of women creators.[56]

The tension for me at this juncture is the doubled fold of Shipman's work and her life. To set the work in a social, historical, economic, and institutional context is to continually encounter her personal as well as professional struggles, because she worked with her husbands and on a shoestring, on a seat-of-the-pants artisanal scale. Her years of failure are as much a part of her work as the films that she successfully – or not so successfully – produced. Hence my interest in her continued commitment, persistence, and energy, and even in their lapses – the vicissitudes of depression, homelessness, bankruptcy, loneliness, despair.

'What is it that history teaches. History teaches.'[57]

Since I started this project, I have been asked repeatedly why we should go back to Nell Shipman at this time. One important consideration is the renaissance in film history that was inaugurated in the early nineties with the work on so-called primitive cinema. Film historians brought new theories and new historiographical methodologies to the films of the nickelodeons, charting exacting trajectories of the increasing sophistication of cinema technology and film language. Other scholars argued persuasively to the contrary, that these films are characterized by particular usages of film language rather than simply primitive or nascent stages in an evolutionary scenario of the development of classic narrative. Connecting the 'cinema of attractions' (Tom Gunning's phrase) to the shock of modernity and its thrills of dislocation, destabilization of identity, and spatial and temporal rupture, this work connected forcefully with the rethinking of modernism and modernity that has characterized the postmodern period.

Current scholarship on films of the intermediate period (1905–12) gets traction from the new methodological tools of studies of popular culture, readership, and reception, while challenging assumptions and theories of the previous decade of scholarship. We are now blessed with a proliferation of work on the technologies and anxieties of modernity, ideology in the reformist era, and the shape-shifting of cinema and popular culture in the period.

The turn to history may also be motivated by the institutional problematic of the status of cinema studies as a discipline. Contemporary movies are being mined by new scholarly interests such as cultural studies and popular culture programs, both struggling for a toehold in the academy, while cinema studies, which in many universities has clung to a self-definition as a single new discipline, asserts its own methodological and linguistic specificity and – with increasing vigour – its own history.

Women filmmakers such as Nell Shipman are worth studying because we just do not know enough about them. For many years, we assumed that very few women worked in the film industry before 1970, as many of the texts examined in the introductory chapters attest. Moreover, especially in the first highs of 1970s feminism, women assumed that they were a new generation not only experiencing but also creating novel cultural meaning and lifestyles. We looked upon women from the past, especially those turn-of-the-century suffragists and reformers who had touted maternal instinct and moral purity, as if they lived in the dark ages. Now as we turn to examine the first decades of modernity, we are joyfully discovering that women then were very much like we are now – not only determined to change the world but also to have it all: sexual freedom, egalitarian relationships, children, professional work, class mobility, and material comfort.

However, the bright utopian hopes of modernity did not quite carry through. In North America, winning the right to vote around 1920 (except in Quebec) was followed by the depression of the 1930s and the postwar reassignment of women to the home in the 1950s; the women's movement got derailed in suburbia and valium. Meanwhile, the massive construction of women as consumers proceeded apace, with the influx of new and 'improved' domestic technologies (automatic washing machines, freezers, ironing machines, and mixmasters – my mom had them all),[58] the 'new look' marketed by the fashion industry, and the solaces of popular culture (television, the music industry, Wednesday matinees).

Similarly, the aspirations of the 1970s have not exactly panned out. In the late twentieth century, all but a few women hit the glass ceiling. The proportion of women in the academy rose no higher than about 20 per cent; women filmmakers have hit similar numbers only in the low-budget independent or government-supported wing of the film industry, and intermittently at that. Feminism ricocheted into post-feminism, prozac, and the consumption imperative that marked the 1980s and 1990s, whether it was power suits and computers or spas and designer potato peelers.

Changes in women's economic, social, and political status in the first two decades of the twentieth century uncannily parallel the experiences of women in its last three decades. New sexual freedoms and forms of relationships, political participation, opportunities for careers and pro-fessions, and women's comparative wealth were goals that were shared, although with different formations, by women from both periods. It seems appropriate that a new generation of young women scholars is now turning attention to women in the formative period of modernity.[59]

Ordinary women making their way in a new world, women of the early twentieth century were not necessarily outstanding historical figures or producers of cinematic masterpieces. I confess, however, that I did not start out with that sense. Long ago my intention was a reading of Ship-man's film texts only in light of current issues in theory: no history or biography for me. That intention was the result of a conviction – which I know now to be mistaken – that Shipman was unique, ahead of her time, one of the few women working in popular cinema at the time, and that her creation of heroic femininity and her commitment to the envi-ronment and animals were progressive and future-directed aspects that allowed her work to rise from the grave of the past to embrace the con-cerns of the present. It would be enough just to write about her, I thought, and the world would see her value.

Going back to Nell Shipman does not reveal her to be ahead of her time, however, or unjustly neglected in film history, a tragic genius, or an important contributor to change. Not lost masterpieces, her films and novels are generic popular works and low-budget pictures. She made her living in the movie industry – when she was able to – close to the lowest rungs of the cinema ladder, and there were other women working in similar capacities in similar genres and constructing similar capable heroines. Neither was it unusual to be interested in animals and nature in her day: in fact, the wilderness preservation and parks movements, along with animal welfare and theories of animal personality, were precisely of her time.

Moreover, along with her everyday heroism, in this study we have to face up to her ordinary human failings. She made bad partner choices and sometimes must have seemed like a maniac to her children, and her work is stained by racism. In other words, she was a lot like other women not only of her own time but of ours as well; she had the same aspirations, sexual appetites, hopes for love, creative and professional desires, and the same disappointments, anxieties, flaws, and failures. From my own point of view, in fact, she seems a lot like me.

Some chapters of this book place Shipman's works within the historical context of the time they were made, and others encounter issues that arise from the works. The general argument of the book is that Shipman's work is worth going back to not because she was unjustly ignored in the history books, unique, ahead of her time, or a lost genius, but because her work in popular genres welcomes a variety of methods of reading and unfolds issues of modernity, generic conventions, and cinematic practice. It is the study of the work of these ordinary women that will reveal the most for our understanding of the history of the film industry and women's position within it.

'Get 'em in a tree, throw rocks at 'em, get 'em out of the tree'

This was Shipman's description of a scenario: 'Get 'em in a tree, throw rocks at 'em, get 'em out of the tree.'[60] And the phrase, I am not ashamed to say, is an approximation of the methodology I have used here to write about Shipman's work. Working with the films in chronological order of production as the organizing principle, I have discussed issues, theories, and historical contexts – the multidisciplinary rocks I threw at 'em – as they arose from the texts. I have tried to situate the films not only in the context of the historical period in which they were made, but within various reading strategies both current and from the theoretical past. Fighting for a middle ground between heroic fantasies of empowerment or resistance and the (un)pleasures of negativity, while acknowledging the scholarship of writers whose discourse emphasizes liminality, ambiguity, and paradox, I have resolutely tried not to make spurious or extraordinary claims for the works or to press them into the various fashionable moulds of theoretical cinematic discourse. I have approached Shipman's works as rich texts, amenable to many different approaches, all the while insisting on my own affection and admiration for the woman and the work.

To get Shipman's films up in the tree, the first two chapters survey the available scholarship on women filmmakers of the silent era and situate Shipman in the context of women directors in North America and from abroad. 'Women Directors of the Silent Era: The Scholarship' places Shipman in the context of an international complement of women filmmakers in the silent era. It surveys the current literature in the field, beginning with the earliest text, Anthony Slide's *Silent Women Directors* (1972), which includes only U.S. directors. This chapter updates Slide's text, arguing that women directors were also relatively numerous in the silent era on an international scale. 'Women with Megaphones' narrates the beginnings of Shipman's career in films, and attempts to establish her in the context of other women filmmakers that she might have known.

For the first thirty years, women pioneers in cinema included Olga Preobrazhenskaya, Esfir Shub, and Elizaveta Svilova in Russia, Lotte Reiniger and Leni Riefenstahl in Germany, Lottie Lyell in Australia, Alice Guy Blaché and Germaine Dulac in France, Lois Weber, Mabel Normand, Alla Nazimova, Mrs Wallace Reid, Dorothy Gish, and many others in the United States. I have no intention of arguing that these figures were either individual geniuses who have been unjustly omitted from the historical pantheon, or that they were the 'first' to do whatever they did, although many feminist texts take that approach. That historiographical argument has long been discredited in feminist theory, as Griselda Pollock and Irit Rogoff attest. For my purposes, it is important to offer a localized synthesis of knowledge that until now has been either widely scattered or overlooked because of its naive historical claims. My argument here is that because women directors were proportionately numerous in the silent era, through knowledge of their widespread activities we can counter faulty historical assumptions about both their absence on the one hand and their uniqueness on the other. While charting the universal trajectory of independent pioneering work of women in all countries in which a film industry existed and their eventual evacuation from cinema production with the coming of sound, these two chapters challenge the virtually ubiquitous attempts to situate women as unjustly forgotten and ignored or the 'first' to do whatever.

Chapters 3 through 7 throw rocks at Shipman's films. The rocks include industrial, cultural, and historical contexts, along with textual issues specific to individual works. Socio-historical questions of modernity and technology in relation to women are pelted repeatedly at the films, along with the wilderness movement and women's history of participation in animal welfare reform. Anthropomorphism, ecofeminism, miscegenation, national identity, sexuality, femininity, and maternality frequently pepper the assault.

Some of the big rocks are the various genre conventions that resound through Shipman's work: animal and wilderness literature and films, road movies, melodrama in several modes, conventional figures such as the tragic mulatta, and, always, the construction of the heroine. Theoretical boulders include notions of performativity, control of the discourse, formations and representations of racial identity, and forms of cinematic visuality and spectatorship.

'*Back to God's Country*' recounts production conditions and analyses gender representation in *Back to God's Country* (1919), Shipman's best-known film. The chapter continues with an analysis of national and gender identity in relation to the landscape, wild animals, and the indigenous and immigrant people. This section operates through the comparative examination of remakes of the film from different periods, as *Back to God's Country* was remade three times in Shipman's lifetime. A 1927 version (d. Irvin Willat; sc. James Oliver Curwood; lost) with the same title must have been humiliating for her, as its release came so soon after her own bankruptcy. *God's Country* (d. Robert Emmett Tansey, 1946) is related to Shipman's text in title only, but sheds interesting light on the early work. Much later, a Hollywood studio production starring Rock Hudson and replicating exactly the plot of the earlier film, *Back to God's Country* (d. Joseph Pevney, 1953) exhibits telling differences in construction in relation to gender identity, the landscape, and the treatment of indigenous and ethnic 'others.'

'*Something New*' deals with two industrial films that kept Shipman going while she was waiting for the profits from *Back to God's Country* to roll in. *The Trail of the Arrow* (1920) and *Something New* (1920) were both bankrolled by automobile manufacturers as promotional projects. This chapter situates the driving heroines of the two films in relation to the history of women and automobiles in the socio-cultural context of modernity and the struggle for women's equality, and in the early popular cinema that featured the intrepid adventures of the serial queens. Taking up the metaphors of modernity, travel, and visuality, the chapter also investigates formal cinematic issues of the gaze through the car windscreen and the woman protagonist's expressions of sexual desire.

'The Girl from God's Country' relates the conditions of production, reception, and institutional consequences of Shipman's great epic production that is now lost. In The Girl from God's Country (1921), Shipman created dual roles for herself in an episodic melodramatic adventure that was designed to be a blockbuster but instead sent her company to the verge of bankruptcy. She created a scenario that pitted a snooty white society woman against a humble northern woman of mixed white and native descent, playing both roles with equal gusto. This chapter takes up issues of stereotypes particularly of 'Indian' characters in cinema of the day and examines related melodramatic conventions of the 'tragic mulatta.' As the film is now lost, the chapter concentrates on the novel that Shipman wrote later featuring the same mixed-race heroine in a different plot, Get the Woman.[61]

'The Grub-Stake' looks at the last feature film that Shipman made before her company went bankrupt. An old-fashioned 'meller' set in the Klondike, the film is the only one of Shipman's scenarios that fashions a mixed family setting for the heroine. Like other melodramas, Shipman's films tend to evacuate the mother, except when Nell plays the heroic mother to her own son. Youthful fathers who exhibit fond affection for their rampantly oedipal daughters, old uncles, or avuncular prospectors stand in for the family in Shipman's films, in which the heroine is almost always the solitary woman in a world of men. The chapter deals with The Grub-Stake (1923) in relation to theories of the maternal melodrama, the construction of motherhood, and Shipman's vision of egalitarian heterosexual marriage, concluding with a consideration of Shipman's characteristic solitude onscreen and the question of spectatorial relations that attend to the display of the heroic feminine body.

'Bits and Pieces' looks at films that Shipman made in the wilds of northern Idaho as she struggled to keep her company alive. Shoestring productions featuring herself, her family, her neighbours, and the zoo of wild animals that were her trademark, these films are simple stories set in the wild. Interrogating Shipman's deployment of animals in the films, and situating them within a history of animal and wildlife movies, the chapter encounters philosophical and theoretical notions of anthropomorphism in relation to Shipman's work and situates the films as well within the debates about animal personality and cruelty to animals, particularly in relation to the participation of women in animal rights movements and ecofeminism.

Chapter 8 gets Shipman down from the tree by offering edited excerpts from letters, interspersed by commentary and narrative, that Shipman wrote over the course of one year, 1939. The letters offer a portrait of a committed filmmaker who, although she has not made a film in fifteen years, shows no signs of giving up, and every sign of indefatigable optimism. 'Tissue-Paper Tower' is about Shipman's post-bankruptcy attempts to re-establish herself in the film industry. Living in New York with a new partner (her fourth), Nell writes to her grown son approximately every five days. She tells of the projects she has under way, her negotiations with investors, bankers, studios, and her hopes for the rebirth of her career. In that year, she and her husband move six times. Their addresses include a rooming house, a hotel, a penthouse (with blessings heaped upon the landlady who accepted their deposit in the form of a cheque), and the street ('We've learned the art of the one-toothbrush move'). Her reliable old Underwood typewriter has been pawned, and she eventually has to write on the back of old movie call-sheets. By the end of the year, her hopes have been revived, the typewriter is on its way home again, and there is new letterhead trumpeting Nell Shipman Productions. There is still no sign of production, however. The letters from 1939 present a particularly telling account of Shipman's optimism and commitment, the stock in trade of the independent filmmaker to this day.

'Naked on the Palisades' is the end of the story. In 1947, Shipman finally produced another film, a fragment of which was discovered in England in the fall of 1996. This short chapter looks at the production conditions and the authorial tropes that echo through Shipman's work, and re-examines the questions of who Nell Shipman was and why she is worth going back to.

In most of her films, Nell Shipman played the leading role, always of the heroic stamp. Husbands or lovers were either absent or incapacitated: they fell ill, were injured, or were simply 'artistic.' She invariably had to save the day, for what with the travails of the wilderness and the melodramatic villainy of the antagonists, there was always a day and a life that needed saving. Her amazonian beauty, the easy presence of her body (cross-hatched with equal parts of hysteria, display, strength, and bravery), her great sense of moral justice, and the connection with animals and nature: these are the signs of her essentialized femininity, and simultaneously the source of the heroism that allows her to resist conventional narrative inscriptions of the woman protagonist as victimized and rescued. These are not simply Meaghan Morris's 'imaginary acts of piracy,'[62] but Irit Rogoff's 'endless negotiations ... the circularity of advance and retreat, of point/counterpoint negotiations,' which allow historical 'parameters to expand while changing [women's] position in relation to [them].'[63]

The negotiations between contradictory forces are not only immense but endless: Shipman had her fifteen minutes and then refused to quit. The conflicting forces include the requirements of genre versus transgressions of social mores; the heroic character that Nell Shipman created as her exemplary persona versus her humiliating failure as a producer in the film industry; and her staunch commitment to her work and her own career versus her infatuations with male partners who alternatively exploited and failed her. As Rogoff writes, 'Nothing better exemplifies the contradictory nature of modernism – its weaving together of a valorized and radical concept of production with a traditional and unrevised legacy of the symbolic order – than the work of women within it and of their historiographic position in relation to it.'[64]

Out of the uncertainties and failures, out of the negotiations between an essentialist construction of feminine subjectivity and heroism, between generic convention and control of the discourse, between anti-racism and proto-feminism and ideological complicity, finally emerge dramatically different models of femininity played out in a gendered narrative of industrial production. The work leads down many trails, and that is why going back to Nell Shipman is worthwhile.

:: :: :: :: ::

chapter one

Women Directors of the Silent Era: The Scholarship

Why Study Women Filmmakers?

We may well ask, especially now, after thirty years of feminist film scholarship, whether a study of women filmmakers as a group in any era is
needed. One recent response to this question can be found in the
Gwendolyn Foster's introduction to *Women Film Directors: An International Bio-Critical Dictionary*:

> *Women Film Directors* evolved from a compelling urge I have had since I stud-
> ied women's literature and film at Douglass College to reclaim the legacy
> of women directors. As a student of film and literature, I saw a huge dispar-
> ity between feminist scholarship in literature and that in film. In the field
> of literature, feminists were successfully and actively involved in reclaiming
> women writers, but in film scholarship, most feminists were involved in crit-
> icizing films directed by men. They had, as I had, accepted the assumption
> that women had not directed any films until the 1970s ... It became obvious
> to me that remedying the paucity of scholarship on women directors was
> compounded by an unavailability of the films made by women in the early
> days of cinema, many of which had been lost, neglected, or destroyed.
> While women of the pen could reasonably hope that their manuscripts
> could survive the test of time, women filmmakers have had no such luxury.[1]

I shared these observations and urges in the early seventies. After getting my feet wet in cinema scholarship, one of my first questions was
'Where are the women directors?' When I began to look for answers to

that question in 1972, I found only one very partial study of women film-makers, a woefully incomplete filmography of the work of 150 women directors over the history of cinema.[2] And to this day, while there have been several books on individual women filmmakers, as well as a number of companions or encyclopedias, there is still a relative paucity of books that give a broad picture – either historical or contemporary – of women's creative production in film.

A dearth of scholarly attention to the work of women filmmakers perpetuates an institutional climate in which women film directors lack critical and theoretical support. If a body of scholarly work existed, it could help to ensure that films by women directors were studied in educational institutions, prints were kept in circulation, and generations of students became an informed and committed audience for films by women. Gwendolyn Foster underlines these arguments: 'it is painfully obvious that women directors, apart from a select few, remain invisible to the public and film critics and maybe, equally important, to one another.'[3]

There are practical reasons as well for insisting on the necessity of attention to films by women. In the absence of high box office returns, especially outside the Hollywood industry, where national cinemas are regularly subsidized by government cultural funding, such scholarly and even journalistic support might help to ensure that women filmmakers continue to produce.

On the other hand, there are substantive arguments against an isolationist gender approach to scholarship. Treating women filmmakers as a group may mask the differences among women by suggesting that women are a unitary category marked only by gender. Cultural traditions, sexual preferences, and racial identities are obviously equally compelling categories, and equally affect the examination of gender. Especially for the current generation of women carving out their careers in the contemporary commercial film industry, there is also the ever-present fear of ghettoization, pigeonholing women as concerned primarily with gender relations or feminist themes.

In addition to such arguments, since the early 1970s film theory has mounted a formidable challenge to an auteurist approach. Arguments against auteurism centre on a combination of the reification of the heroic Cartesian individual genius with the untheorized critical tools of pre-structuralist textual analysis. The auteurist search for 'unities' of theme and style in the 'body of work' produced a profile of an individual unalienated consciousness, flying in the face of the psychoanalytic emphasis on the workings of the unconscious (i.e., the split subject) and also obstructing the progressive social analysis offered by the methodologies of semiotics and structuralism. Auteurism also promoted the canonization of those filmmakers considered worthy of the 'pantheon,' who, by definition, were those directors who had made a significant number of films over a long career (Hawks, Ford, Hitchcock, and so on).[4] Even Peter Wollen's salutary reclaiming of auteurism for semiotics and structuralism chose Hawks and Ford for revisionary consideration.[5] Since few women directors had substantial bodies of work, they continued to languish outside the purview of auteurist methodologies.

The first feminist response to this scholarly dilemma was the emphasis on gendered spectatorship in the critique of the canonical Hollywood text. As the decades advanced, attention to gendered spectatorship broadened to include the 'gynetic' genres such as the women's film, melodrama, and television soap operas. Critical methodologies came to include the study of reception and address, arguing the empowering strategies of such genres for women spectators or the industrial implications of such gender-specific enunciation. These approaches amassed a significant theoretical toolkit packed with instruments capable of taking apart and rebuilding virtually any problematic construction as a productive retrofit for feminist readers. Nevertheless, as I suggested in the introduction, these tools were not crafted finely enough to include any but a few films by women directors. The creative production of women filmmakers continued to be overlooked, resulting in a considerable lacuna not only in historical knowledge but also in the instructional resources necessary to bridge that historical gap.

In *Streetwalking on a Ruined Map: Cultural Theory and the City Films of Elvira Notari*, Giuliana Bruno takes up the question of the female authorial voice. Echoing Kaja Silverman's challenge to Roland Barthes's pronouncement of the death of the author, Bruno argues that Barthes actually wished to annihilate the paternal author, not the possibility of female authorship. Bruno articulates a double authorial construction, for just as the death of the author announced the beginning of readership, feminist scholarship that centres on women figures constructs authorship not only for the woman director but for the woman writer as well: 'As has been true for other female directors, the constitution of [the woman director's] authorship has been a pure function of feminist criticism.'[6]

Using Kaja Silverman's notion of constituting authorship through a process of identification, Bruno retheorizes authorship as an intersubjective and interchangeable relation between mother/daughter and author/reader: 'Writing is mapped as a transitional site. Authorship becomes the locus of interaction, a scene of libidinal exchange, where encounters as well as separations and "little deaths" are staged ... The intersubjective predicament is another way to say, "In a way, I *desire* the author: I need her figure (which is neither her representation nor her projection), as she needs mine."'[7] Bruno also argues the necessity for this relation on political grounds: 'The constitution and analysis of [the woman director's] authorial text are part of the general effort to rewrite history by empowering the female subject, texts, and readings ... Insofar as she was somewhat exceptional in her early and productive engagement in the male-dominated field of filmmaking, giving room to the authorial subject is a "political" gesture for a feminist scholar. Because [women filmmakers'] authorship was suppressed, disregarded, and forgotten, not allowing for the authorial subject would only have continued the suppression.'[8] With renewed resolve, Bruno declares, 'For this reason, I will continue the story of Elvira Notari.'[9]

Gwendolyn Foster dedicates *Women Film Directors* to 'those women who have taken up the camera to instruct, enlighten, entertain, and speak their minds on issues that are of great consequence to them.' She claims for them an 'immense contribution' that is 'a legacy rich in personal insight, hard work, careful study, and, often, sacrifice' and offers her book as 'a testament ... to the continuing voice of women as a force for change and enlightenment within the cinema today.'[10]

I will make no such heroic claims for the accomplishments of Nell Shipman or women filmmakers in general. While some women in silent cinema were consciously progressive and even feminist, and some made significant contributions to the development of film language or achieved a place in film history, there were many, like Nell Shipman, who were simply scrabbling their way in a potentially lucrative new industry that was, in its earliest days at least, accessible to women.

Scholarship on Women Directors of the Silent Era

Because American universities employ the largest complement of feminist scholars, and their presses constitute the largest academic publishing industry in the world, much of the scholarly work on women filmmakers of the silent era concentrates on the pre-Hollywood and Hollywood establishment. The first text off the mark, however, was definitely not the product of feminist motivation. On the contrary, in the introduction to *Early Women Directors*, Anthony Slide expressly challenges feminist film scholars for their lack of historical research. The passage is worth quoting at some length, for it flames with sarcasm:

> The present striving by women to achieve their rightful place in all levels of society – a striving commonly referred to as Women's Lib. – has sparked a number of books and a deluge of articles on women in film, women's place in films and the film industry, and the image of women that the cinema has created. The careers of several women directors have been the subject of much analysis and discussion, most of it regrettably far too biased to be worthwhile.
>
> This outpouring of words on women in films has ignored one period of film history – the early years. Few women writers seemed willing to undertake the research necessary to uncover the facts concerning women directors before the coming of sound. It was far easier to protest about discrimination against women than to accept that there were more women directors at work in the American film industry prior to 1920 than during any period of its history. It would also seem that women's rightful place was in the home, cooking, and bringing up children, rather than researching film history in the Museum of Modern Art, the Library of Congress or the New York Public Library.[11]

Despite Slide's anti-feminist motivations, it must be said here that *Early Women Directors* is absolutely reliable in its historical accuracy. Slide holds an appointment as an archival scholar at the Academy of Motion Picture Arts and Sciences, where he has worked steadily and meticulously for some thirty years. He has published a library cart-load of books, in which he tends to offer factual information and extremely conditional opinions.

Early Women Directors is the ur-text for all later scholarship on women in Hollywood in its formative years. Slide is scrupulous in his acknowledgments when descriptions of the films come from contemporary notices, and when he does venture a critical judgment, he usually supports it with a quote from a contemporary source. For example, he writes of Nell Shipman's *Back to God's Country*: 'Old-fashioned, quaint, and creaky by today's standards, it was obviously not too well oiled when it was first released. *Variety* (January 2, 1920) commented, "The picture is a meller of the real old-fashioned kind, and after reading the story and seeing the picture it seems that the James Oliver Curwood tales make better reading than they do screen material."'[12] However, such critical judgments are rare in Slide's text, which concentrates on biographical information and industrial details such as conditions of production, marketing, box office returns, and contemporary reception. His bibliography consists largely of articles published contemporaneously with the films, and memoirs published later. It omits entirely the feminist accounts that he describes as 'far too biased to be worthwhile.'

In separate chapters, *Early Women Directors* profiles Alice Guy Blaché, Lois Weber, Margery Wilson, Mrs Wallace Reid, Frances Marion, and Dorothy Arzner. The chapter entitled 'The Universal Woman' contributes notes on nine others who were associated with Universal Studios.[13] In a final chapter Slide briefly mentions more than a dozen other American women filmmakers from the period.

It is worthwhile to précis Slide's introduction to the text, for he presents a broad outline of women's participation in Hollywood in the silent period, beginning with the assertion that 'During the silent era, women might be said to have virtually controlled the film industry.' He not only marks the presence of at least thirty women directors, but also notes that 'the stars were all women – the number of male actors who achieved any real prominence may be counted on the fingers of one hand – and many such stars had their own independent producing companies ... In the field of screen-writing, women wielded tremendous power. In 1918 alone, some forty-four women were employed in the film industry as scenario writers.' The top writers were all women: 'How many male screen-writers from the silent era are remembered today?' He also mentions the gossip writers who 'shape[d] the tastes of a generation,' three women cinematographers, multitudinous studio managers, editors, and even 'the women who hand-painted each frame of a Pathe-color film, for they were contributing their share to the art of the cinema.' He has also unearthed records of a women-financed production company, the American Woman Film Company, founded in 1916, whose intention was 'to produce motion pictures of the highest moral and artistic tone,' and of the Mandarin Film Company (1917), 'the only Chinese producing concern in the country,' whose president was Marion E. Wong.[14] Slide's introduction concludes: 'Women's predominant place in all areas of silent film production should be self-evident. As directors, women also left their mark on the silent film. Women directors were, quite obviously, not that unusual; a 1920 volume on careers for women devoted a full chapter to the woman film director. How many career guides for women today would offer even a paragraph for such a vocation? There were more than thirty women directors in the American film industry during the silent era ... Many of these women were the equal of, if not a little better than, their male colleagues. All of them, without a doubt, were pioneers in the true sense of the word.'[15]

It is not necessary to rehearse here the details of the lives and careers that Slide outlines. Each of these directors will doubtless be written about at length by a new generation of women scholars. Current research has already seen the publication of books on Dorothy Arzner,[16] Frances Marion,[17] and Lois Weber.[18]

There is as yet, however, no significant book-length study on women in the silent cinema on an international scale, although several books encompassing filmmakers across the history of cinema include studies of pioneering women working outside the American context. Germaine Dulac (France) is treated at length in both Sandy Flitterman-Lewis's *To Desire Differently*[19] and Andrea Weiss's *Vampires and Violets*.[20] Lynn Attwood's *Red Women on the Silver Screen*[21] is concerned primarily with the representation of gender relations and images of women in the Soviet cinema rather than with women directors, and does not dwell substantially on women directors. The book offers a few pages on Esfir Shub and Olga Preobrazhenskaya, both of whom directed films in the 1920s, but their work is discussed primarily in relation to their portrayal of women characters. Andrée Wright's *Brilliant Careers*[22] offers a panorama of important women figures in the Australian film industry, including producers, writers, and actors, as well as directors.

For substantive and wide-ranging information about women filmmakers of the silent era on an international scale, however, one still has to dig through the various dictionaries and studies of national cinemas to glean tidbits (and sometimes dubious claims) about the participation of women creative producers in the silent era. One must always be wary, for such companions cull almost exclusively from secondary sources, often other survey texts, whose scholarly accuracy may not be reliable. For example, as I read through the various notes on Nell Shipman, I found rumour, speculation, and plain old mistakes (some of which I perpetrated in the early stages of my research), even in recent texts. Descriptions abound of films that remain inaccessible for viewing, and second-hand assessments are credited as fact. Repeatedly, one finds claims for 'the first woman' or 'the only woman' or 'the originator' of any given situation, only for such claims to be undermined later when thorough and balanced scholarship is published. This is a hazard, but it is a joyful one: we must celebrate the early attempts along with more recent and more comprehensive scholarship, and we must expect – indeed, hope – that our work will continue to be superseded by new generations of researchers.

Some of the companions, surveys, and encyclopedias are useful for the silent era researcher, and others are less so. I will briefly comment on the existing texts in the field.

Sharon Smith's *Women Who Make Movies* (1975) was a brave and pioneering effort in its day, as it was the first attempt to amass information in an area that, except for Slide's *Early Women Directors*, had not received any kind of scholarly treatment. Smith's notes on individual women directors tend to be brief, and often amount to only a partial filmography. Where she does treat individuals at some length, she favours biographical details and attempts to establish inventions or firsts. A sample from the note on Alice Guy Blaché: 'Unresolved to this day is the question of who actually made the first film with a plot line. Blaché claimed that distinction, and actively campaigned for it, but film historians generally have credited her countryman, George[s] Mélies, or the American, Edwin S. Porter.'[23]

Unlike Slide, who underlines his film evaluations or descriptions with referenced sources, Smith rarely seems to have actually seen the films she discusses, and she does not distinguish her text with citations. The earliest films were unavailable for viewing and many have been lost. This is the case with her note on Guy Blaché's *The Good Fairy in the Cabbage Patch*: 'based on the mythical French tale of where babies come from, it shows a young husband and wife coming upon a cabbage patch where a fairy waits to present them with a child. The film, which probably ran for about a minute, launched her career.'[24]

Certainly Smith had not seen Shipman's *The Girl from God's Country* (1921), as that film is lost. Smith describes it as Shipman's 'most famous film,' which it definitely was not, although 'the girl from God's country' was Shipman's publicity tag-line from 1916 on, when she starred in *God's Country and the Woman*. Shipman made *The Girl from God's Country* later, after the success of *Back to God's Country* (1919), which in turn had capitalized on the success of the earlier film, *God's Country and the Woman*. In the Shipman note, Smith makes other scholarly errors as well. She mistakenly claims that Shipman pioneered in photographing her films, gets dates wrong for the films she lists, and gives directorial credit to Shipman for some films that she did not direct and for others that were never produced.[25]

I do not mean to nit-pick here, but Smith's errors in relation to a subject I know well cause me to doubt the reliability of the rest of the book. In fact, my old paperback copy, bought immediately after publication, is filled with my marginal notes either correcting or adding notes from my own knowledge, gleaned largely from the research in preparation for the Women and Film International Festival, which we had mounted only the year before.

This is unfortunate, as Smith has made a significant historical discovery (if it is accurate) in her note on Egyptian actress and producer Aziza Amir, whom Smith credits with 'found[ing] the first Egyptian film company in 1927; Amir acted and produced.' Smith notes other work by Egyptian women actor/producers – Assis, Bahija Hafez, and Mary Queeny – in the twenties and thirties.[26] These women remain unnoticed in the other compendiums of women filmmakers: are we to assume therefore that the later scholarship corrects Smith's errors in this case? More reliable research is clearly necessary.

To be fair, Smith's is a ground-breaking book, published well before there was any significant historical research in the field. Moreover, as one reviews the later scholarship, it becomes apparent that, with few exceptions, Smith had dug up all the women filmmakers from the silent era – plus some – who are noted in the later texts.

In *Women Filmmakers: A Critical Reception* (1984), Louise Heck-Rabi entered the research arena with a highly selective study of eleven women filmmakers, including three from the silent era: Alice Guy Blaché, Germaine Dulac, and Lois Weber. She includes chapters on Dorothy Arzner and Leni Riefenstahl as well, directors whose careers began in the silent era but were largely carried out after 1930. In her preface, Heck-Rabi echoes the laments of other scholars on the paucity of published research. In preparation of the paper that became the first draft of the book, she 'sadly ... discovered that documentation equals reputation. [She] could study and write only about those women film-makers whose films reviews and biographies were available to [her].' In selecting subjects for more comprehensive consideration, she was lim-ited to those for which documentation was 'at least adequate, if not bounteous.'[27]

There were other criteria for selection as well: 'Subjects chosen had to have a reasonable number of works in their filmography (no one-shot deals, however excellent ...). Also, the filmography had to be a valid and memorable entry into the history of filmmaking. The woman herself was to be individual, in the richest meaning of the word, with her films bear-ing the impress of her personality.' Happily, Heck-Rabi was able to dis-cover several 'common denominators of temperament, training, or talents', based not only on her study of the eleven subjects of the book, but 'upon the total galaxy of women employed in films':

These are the characteristics that I believe women filmmakers tend to share:

1. Most are married or work in collaboration with men. The fact that men open doors into the film industry for women is well known ...

2. Most are of short stature, are considered attractive, restless, energetic, dynamic.

3. Most have had previous training in the arts, especially dance.

4. Most have made, or want to make, films about women, or from a woman's point-of-view ... Having guts is the basic ingredient, never mind stature or knowing men who will help you.[28]

After these brashly naive beginnings, Heck-Rabi's text significantly extends both Slide's and Smith's. Her chief contribution to the scholarship is the extensive filmographies appended to each chapter and the many quotations from contemporary sources, biographies, and current scholarship. She provides the most comprehensive scholarly treatment to date, buttressed by cautious judgments. For example, here is her summation of Lois Weber's career:

> Undeniably a strong scriptwriter who may never have completely mastered the technical prowess required of photographing creatively, Weber managed to show stamina, staying power, and a sky-high ambition to make her moralistic stories come alive in motion pictures. Her storylines were strong: when consonant with public taste, her achievements were good investments and good ideologies. Never idolized or acclaimed as an actress or director, and never judged by her peers to be more than a zealous, competent worker, Weber nevertheless did write and produce many more films than we shall ever be able to identify and view, all of them suffused with her own style and personal conviction.[29]

Later research reveals that Heck-Rabi is simply wrong about the esteem in which Weber's contemporaries held the director, for we now know that Weber was, for a period, one of the highest-paid directors in Hollywood. However, Heck-Rabi's scholarly reluctance to make heroic claims must be appreciated, as it has resulted in the most balanced and dispassionate study of Leni Riefenstahl that I have seen. Its chief contribution is an extensive survey of scholarship that does not succumb to the 'percussive dissonance' of the embattled positions of writers on this controversial filmmaker. The chapter on Dorothy Arzner also stands as the most comprehensive until Judith Mayne's book, taking in not only biographical and industrial reminiscences and a variety of contemporary responses, but noting also the psychoanalytic/structuralist/semiotic rubric advanced in Claire Johnston and Pam Cook's studies.[30] In all, Heck-Rabi's contribution is her excellent research. She not only incorporates a wide range of sources, but quotes extensively from them to provide a vivid smorgasbord of information.

A few years later, Barbara Koenig Quart's *Women Directors: The Emergence of a New Cinema* (1988) gave short shrift to women directors of the silent era, dispensing with the 'antecedents' Guy Blaché, Weber, and Dulac in a few pages. Her assessment of women's position in the silent period is considerably more cynical than Slide's or Heck-Rabi's, who both suggest that women in Hollywood were not only respected but powerful. Quart offers quite a different picture:

> Women directors could have some impact as long as they could create their own companies, and also as long as conditions were fluid enough within existing studios to allow actresses or women screenwriters to try their hand at directing. Given the enormous need for product in the very early years, the generally low cost of production, and the much smaller scale of filmmaking, there was little to lose. Universal Pictures, where most of the women directors – like Cleo Madison, Ruth Stonehouse, Ruth Ann Baldwin – were concentrated, was perhaps more disorganized than others, less regularized. It paid very little, and in effect anyone off the street could try her/his hand.[31]

Although Quart admits the possibility that Guy Blaché, Weber, and Dulac were 'remarkable women who made remarkable contributions to early cinema,'[32] she relentlessly emphasizes the downsides of their stories. Noting Alice Guy Blaché as 'arguably the inventor of the film that tells a story,' Quart deals with Guy Blaché's career and hundreds of completed films in one sentence: 'Soon after [marriage and children], she started to direct great numbers of films again with great success, under her own company, Solax, where she was noted for her intrepid behavior, burning cars for effects, having characters hang from bridges, using a tigress.' Quart follows that sparse account of Guy Blaché's successful career with a paragraph charting her demise:

> After the firm dissolved, the marriage did as well. From 1920 on Alice Guy Blaché could no longer get work in the United States. She tried returning to France but was no longer young, had no prints of her films, and was unable to make a new start. She tried to track down her old footage and found that almost nothing had survived, though since then, small numbers of her films have been discovered in private collections. And though in her later years she tried also 'to assure herself of the place she felt she had earned in the history of film,' when she died in Mahwah, New Jersey, at 95,

there were no newspaper obituaries, as Louise Heck-Rabi notes, in the state where the second half of her career took place. Also, as Guy Blaché anticipated, the 'directing and producing credits for her films [were] falsely assigned to her co-workers' and her name, unintentionally or purposefully, was omitted from the histories of French and American film.[33]

After reading this paragraph, I could hardly bear to go on to Quart's account of Lois Weber's demise. Those tragic details include box-office failure, marriage breakdown, company bankruptcy, nervous breakdown, attempted suicide, eking out a living by running an apartment building, virtual disappearance until a failed attempt at comeback, dying alone after a long illness, and screenwriter/director Frances Marion paying for her funeral.[34] Predictably, Quart is not merciful. The paragraph outlining Weber's career is equally matched in length by the paragraph detailing her pitiful end. A sample: 'Weber died in 1939, alone, impoverished, forgotten.' Quart's one-sentence summation of Weber's significance offers Anthony Slide's characteristically restrained judgment that she brought to cinema 'an intelligence and a commitment that was rare among filmmakers.'[35]

Quart's treatment of Germaine Dulac is a smidgen more celebratory, but the overall tone of the writing is unreserved cynicism. In this Quart offers a salutary corrective to the excesses of some feminist writing of the sort that Slide found 'far too biased to be worthwhile.' Nevertheless, I find myself quite ambivalent about Quart's approach. I too find offensive those treatments that exaggerate the achievements of women filmmakers (although I disagree with Slide that those accounts are tantamount to worthless), and it is undeniable that the stories of many of the women directors of the silent cinema – Nell Shipman's among them – have bleak endings. The scholarly project must acknowledge the fact that, virtually to a woman, these directors were forced out of the industry, many of them while still in their prime. Still, it seems equally excessive to dismiss their careers or to unduly emphasize their tragedies over their achievements.

The fates of the European women directors seem not quite as grim as those in the American industry. It is true that Germaine Dulac's last film was made in 1929, the turning point for women in film history, when she was forty-seven years old. However, Dulac was never primarily a 'commercial' director, as Quart would have it, working just as often in the avant-garde and documentary. One of her most renowned films of the late twenties was *Germination d'un haricot* (1928), a time-lapse film exploring the scientific potential of cinema. Here is Quart's rendition of Dulac's end: 'When work was no longer available to her, she shifted her filmmaking energies into other film-related work – cine clubs to shape audience response, the founding of a film school, a film magazine, work on documentaries and newsreels – until her death in 1942.'[36] Contrary to Quart's dismissive account, however, Dulac was highly esteemed in the French film community precisely for organizing cine clubs, founding a film school, and publishing a film magazine – no small feats, any of them. Moreover, she did not just 'work on' documentaries and newsreels; she was head of the Actualités division of Gaumont Studios until her death at age sixty. Like some other European women directors, Dulac worked in various aspects of the French film industry during both the silent and sound periods, and was not lost from history. Quart's account is not only a tad too brisk; it also distorts Dulac's story by constructing it as precisely parallel to that of the American directors.

The culmination of Quart's account of these 'antecedents,' however, somewhat redresses this imbalance:

> Remembering these particular early directors – with all their creative boldness and originality, physical daring, tireless hard work and productivity – makes the near-total exclusion of women from filmmaking from the beginnings of sound film, essentially until the 1970s, even stranger and more disturbing than it already is. There are individual reasons why these particular directors' careers were abruptly terminated when they were in their prime in their 40s; and men suffered a similar fate at a time of rapid technological change, shifting audience composition, important changes in the whole nature of the film business. The situation takes on a different coloring for women, however, because it happened to every woman director (excepting Arzner), and from those endings no further beginnings issued.[37]

Reel Women: Pioneers of the Cinema, 1896 to the Present (1993) is the result of Ally Acker's research for a film series, Reel Women: Pioneers of the Cinema. Acker is a practising documentary filmmaker and, consistent with conventional documentary methods, much of the text is based on the oral histories gathered in 'interviews with "great women" in the movies who had been around the business a long time.'[38] As a result, references to other sources are relatively sparse, filmographies are seldom complete, and the bibliography is brief. The book is distinguished by Marc Wanamaker's wonderful collection of photographs of women at work in film in every capacity, as well as posters, publicity stills, and other memorabilia. Like the collection of photographs, *Reel Women* covers women working in many capacities, including directors, writers, editors, animators, and stunt women, and the producers, wives, secretaries, and muses who are best known for their partnerships with more famous men. This wide-ranging purview is enabled by a structure of cascading sections, including 'Short Takes' (shorter notes) and 'Previews' (brief samples) as well as longer individual entries. As the section titles indicate, the book is written in a lively, journalistic style.

Like most of the American-based scholarship, *Reel Women* is dominated by women directors who made their careers in the United States. In the introduction, 'The Feminization of Filmmaking,' Acker sets out her critical and theoretical project: 'And what about the woman who did succeed in Hollywood? How did her *female* vision reflect her artistic creation? What did women filmmakers bring as *women* to movies? Is there such a thing as a "female gaze" in moviemaking? And once she succeeded in entering the industry, did the woman filmmaker change the system, or did the system change her? Did gender even enter the picture? And, maybe more importantly, have the movies of Hollywood undergone a visible transformation because of her appearance on the scene?'[39]

Although the essentialist naivety of Acker's theoretical model is evident in her emphasis on her search for a 'female vision' or 'gaze,' nevertheless, for our purposes, the study of women directors of the silent era, *Reel Women* is a useful resource. As Acker writes, '[she] wanted to deal with "pioneers," women who blazed trails and forged paths where certainly other women, and in many cases, other filmmakers in general, had not gone before. Women who in some way pushed over boundaries that had not been crossed before.'[40] Although long individual notes profile only Alice Guy Blaché and Lois Weber, these entries offer valuable biographical details, career profiles, and lengthy descriptions of selected films. Other women directors of the silent era are covered at some length in the chapter 'Reel Women Actresses Turned Director/ Producer,' with individual notes on Mary Pickford, Mabel Normand, Nell Shipman,[41] and Lillian Gish, as well as 'short takes' on five of the Universal directors noted in Slide's *Early Women Directors.*

In light of Acker's emphasis on Hollywood pioneers, it is not surprising that the section 'A Reel Female Gaze: Select Foreign Reel Women' includes notes on only Germaine Dulac and Musidora from the silent era. These notes are buttressed with 'short takes' on Leontine Sagan (inexplicably included in 'The Silents' section, although her first film, *Maedchen in Uniform,* 1931, was a sound film) and Esther (Esfir) Shub. The section includes only a handful of contemporary directors, all but two of them European.[42]

The Women's Companion to International Film (1990) is by far the most comprehensive compendium, and remains so to the present.[43] In addition to entries on women filmmakers, it includes notes on national cinemas, actresses, men directors, film movements, theoretical concepts, individual feminist scholars, technical production terms, and critical terminology. The brilliant concept of the *Companion* is that women scholars – seventy-nine of them, working actively in the field of cinema research – wrote the entries. The contributors were given choices about what they would cover and were allowed to suggest important figures from their national contexts. Thus the text offers not only expertise, but also a diversity of subjects, approaches, and opinions. Notes on individual women filmmakers aim especially for a complete filmography, although bibliographies are limited to a few key references. The entries are severely edited both for space and for economy of writing style. Thus the *Companion* packs a remarkable amount of information – over 600 entries – into its 437 pages of text.

In the brief preface, the editors situate national cinemas firmly within an international context: 'In the West, cinema is often equated with Hollywood: and while acknowledging the fascination of Hollywood and the cultural dominance of the U.S. film industry, the *Companion* seeks to encourage users to consider these within an international framework.'[44] As the most comprehensive text to this day, and the only one published outside the context of American-based scholarship, the *Companion* is remarkable for its truly international knowledge base. The notes on national cinemas are especially useful. Not only is virtually every national cinema covered, but within those entries one can often find mentions of women filmmakers about whom not enough is known or who have an insufficiently large body of work to warrant an individual entry.

The *Companion* aims for comprehensive coverage of women directors from the past. As a text that refuses to privilege the Hollywood industry, it omits many of the directors from the silent era already adequately covered in Slide's *Early Women Directors*. Individual entries are dedicated to Dorothy Arzner, Lillian Gish, Alice Guy Blaché, Nell Shipman, and Lois Weber. Entries on silent era directors from other countries include Germaine Dulac, Musidora, and Marie Epstein (France); Mary Field (Britain); Lottie Lyell and Paulette McDonagh (Australia); Elvira Notari (Italy); Olga Preobrazhenskaya, Esfir Shub, and Elizaveta Svilova (Russia); Lotte Reiniger and Leni Riefenstahl (Germany); and Anna Hofman-Uddgren (Sweden).

The note on Sweden's national cinema is worth quoting, as it tells a tale that is by now painfully familiar:

> As for the role of women in Swedish silent cinema, this field was dominated by Anna Hofman-Uddgren, not only Sweden's first woman director but also one of the country's film pioneers, who managed to get Strindberg to agree to her filming his plays *Miss Julie* and *The Father*. Another woman director of silent films – in this case of short comedies and farces – was Pauline Brunius, later to be the first woman director of Sweden's national theater. With the coming of sound, however, cinema became a more complicated and costly business, the playful pioneering spirit was lost, and as a result opportunities for women to work behind the camera virtually disappeared.[45]

For my purposes here, a compendium of women filmmakers of the silent era on an international scale, it is worth noting, in contrast to the *Companion*, Gwendolyn Foster's caveat about the comprehensiveness of the international information in her *Women Film Directors*: 'Filmmakers were chosen on the basis of availability of information. As an American-based film scholar, I have no doubt been limited, to some extent, to a Western, Eurocentric tradition and knowledge base. Therefore I expect I have inadvertently been unable to include all international women film directors in this book.'[46] Nevertheless, Foster's text is the product of substantial scholarship. It includes fairly lengthy notes on each of the directors, as well as a good selection of bibliographical references and virtually complete filmographies. Its scholarly and theoretical methodology is current and comprehensive, and from this text one can glean reliable information.

Foster's introduction sets out her terms. In contrast to Heck-Rabi's highly selective criteria for inclusion and brash declarations about the commonalities among women directors, Foster is clear in her assertions of their diversity: 'There is no "typical" woman filmmaker. In creating *Women Film Directors: An International Bio-Critical Dictionary*, I first wish to stress that the various directorial visions showcased within this volume are as diverse as the practitioners themselves. There are as many different kinds of women making films today and yesterday as there are different approaches to the cinematic art ... The types of films [women directors] make vary widely in subject matter, budget, and intended audience.'[47]

Foster's introduction makes a wide sweep through the available literature. She reviews nearly every previously published compendium, as well as the major developments in feminist film theory since the 1970s. She attends to psychoanalytic, lesbian, and women of colour scholarship; she treats individual articles and authors as well as virtually every important anthology of feminist writing on film; and her list of references for the introduction alone takes up 2.5 pages. Moreover, her assessments of the contributions of these texts are not only eminently perspicacious but intellectually generous as well. This is an extremely useful book, despite its many oversights.[48]

Omissions are unfortunate but understandable in the current scholarly climate, in which the research imperative has forcefully accelerated work in the area of lesbian, women of colour, and indigenous filmmaking. It is ironic, however, perhaps especially to Canadians, that the emphasis on colonized and marginalized subjects has not broadened to include the massive colonization of Canadian film culture by the hegemonic American industry. Many important Canadian women directors are omitted here. Precisely because Foster's volume is the most recent, it promises to be a widely used text: therefore it may have the effect of the continued 'forgetting' of Canadian women filmmakers.

Contemporary filmmakers are not, of course, the focus of this chapter, or my book as a whole. However, when omissions of significant contemporary women directors from one country outside the United States can be spotted so easily, one is perforce reminded of Foster's caveat in her preface: 'I expect I have inadvertently been unable to include all international women film directors in this book.' And then, returning to the question of women directors of the silent era, one finds somewhat limited entries in that field as well.

Foster covers many of the well-known women directors of the pre-Hollywood and Hollywood era. Of the American directors profiled in *Women Film Directors*, all had been previously noted in Slide's *Early Women Directors*. Foster builds on scholarship that followed Slide's early text, and the entries on these American women directors tend to be more comprehensive than Slide's and to incorporate valuable feminist methodologies. However, with earlier researchers, Foster also laments the continuing dearth of advanced scholarship on such directors. Her note on Lois Weber begins: 'The paucity of scholarship on Lois Weber is stunning. Amazingly, no one has yet written a book-length study of the work of one of the most important pioneers of American cinema. Feminists have also overlooked the contribution of Lois Weber to the formation of "women's cinema," the melodrama, and social drama.'[49] In sharp contrast to Heck-Rabi, who had to rely on second-hand judgments for her much more qualified comments, Foster benefits from the recent restorations of Weber's films, now readily available on video for educational purposes. As a result, unlike earlier writers, Foster is in a position to offer critical readings of heretofore unseen works, and she wades confidently into the task. This is perhaps the most important contribution this entry makes to knowledge of Weber's work.

All of Foster's profiles evince impeccable and comprehensive scholarship, but little is new in the notes on the American directors. There is one significant discovery of a formerly unknown women director, however. Eloyce Gist was an African-American woman who wrote and directed evangelical films in the 1920s and 1930s. Foster credits her discovery to researchers Gloria Gibson-Hudson[50] and Mary Dean.[51] Unfortunately there seems to be insufficient research to warrant a separate entry on Gist, for she is mentioned only in passing in Foster's introduction.[52]

Foster's text profiles a dozen silent era women directors from the rest of the world, almost as many as from the United States. Most of these women are already known, and all of them are included in *The Women's Companion*, although Foster's notes somewhat flesh out the earlier texts. With few exceptions, the stories told here are consistent with current knowledge: relative success with independent or studio productions in the teens and twenties, and then shut out in the sound era.

In *Lois Weber: The Director Who Lost Her Way in History*, Anthony Slide offers his explanation of the truncated careers of women in the film industry. Contrary to feminist accounts, he argues that in the silent era women were hired 'because they were as reliable as any male and because there was no inbred, discriminatory thinking that certain types of jobs within the film industry were more appropriate to a man than a woman.'[53] While this utopian view of the film industry may be attractive, I find it implausible to conceive any institution as utterly free of the prevailing contradictions of women's position in modernity. Slide's assertion, absent the nuances of feminist analysis, also leads him to blame Weber for the demise of her career. He explains that both Weber and Alice Guy Blaché 'ultimately failed to hold onto their careers because of their sex.'[54] It was their 'emotionally draining divorces' that did them in: 'Weber never fully recovered from the breakup of her marriage. In that sense,' he argues, Weber and Guy Blaché 'were very much women of their day, bound by the Victorian view of the sanctity of marriage, in which women were the secondary partners.'[55] Later he suggests that 'the primary motivation behind Weber's decision to close the studio was ... a personal one. She was about to make a last-ditch effort to save her marriage to Phillips Smalley.'[56] When the attempt proved futile, 'Weber discovered that without the strong masculine presence of Phillips Smalley at her side, she could not continue directing.'[57] Thus, it seems, it was Weber's emotional frailty – which Slide equates with femininity – that forced her out of the industry. As his title suggests, Weber lost her way.

After 'a decade of uncertainty,' in which Weber made several more films that were not successful, despite favourable reviews, she shifted studios from Universal to United Artists. She was hoping to direct a serious version of *Uncle Tom's Cabin*, but the famous Duncan Sisters, who were already cast in the leads, prevailed with their own brand of racial comedy. Never a comic director, Weber was taken off the production.[58] She was then hired to direct *The Angel of Broadway* (1927), produced by Cecil

B. DeMille. Although Universal offered her a new contract in 1933, she was abruptly pulled off the production of *Glamour* (1934) and William Wyler was assigned to the film. Shunted to the minors, Weber contracted with Seven Seas Corporation to direct *White Heat* (1934), but the film did little business and 'none of the reviewers thought it pertinent to mention the name of the director.'[59]

Slide does offer something of an institutional explanation for Weber's unemployment. By 1928, her 'hundreds of well remembered screen plays' had been forgotten. The memory of the film industry is notoriously short ... Major Hollywood stars fell by the wayside. What chance did a director have whose heyday was ten years earlier? ... There was little room for directors of either sex who had been around since the cinema's infancy.'[60]

There is one significant exception to the trends noted in this chapter: a remarkable study of the career of screenwriter Frances Marion. For many years Slide's *Early Women Directors* and Smith's *Women Who Make Movies* were the only texts that mentioned Marion. Now, however, we have Cari Beauchamp's magnificent tome, *Without Lying Down: Frances Marion and the Powerful Early Women of Hollywood* (1997). Beauchamp's text weighs in at nearly 400 pages, not counting 47 pages of endnotes, 5 pages of bibliographical references, and 12 pages of filmographical notes, including credits. Written by a professional journalist rather than an academic, *Without Lying Down* gives us countless anecdotes, descriptions, background information, conversations, and details of Marion's life. Imbued with a palpable sense of the biographer's empathy with her subject, the vivid quality of Beauchamp's writing makes *Without Lying Down* a great pleasure to read. It offers a bountiful view of the daily lives of women working in early Hollywood, and touches on all the most famous stars as well as other screenwriters, producers, gossip columnists, and minor players in the industry.

In addition to details of Marion's life and career, Beauchamp's text fleshes out the academic portraits of many of the other women who were making their careers in Hollywood not only as writers and stars but also as directors. It tends to emphasize the conflicts these women experienced between family, home, husbands, and careers, what Mary Roberts Rinehart referred to women's 'double burden.'[61] Yet Beauchamp notes that several of them found time to participate in the historic New

York march for women's suffrage (1915), while harbouring 'a nagging suspicion that women were "trading superiority for equality."'[62] Beauchamp also underlines the inspiration, comfort, and support these women gave to each other. Lois Weber, for example, was known for supporting other women and gave Marion her start in films. Beauchamp mentions as well Elsie Janis, who directed four films for Weber's Bosworth Productions in 1914.[63] Finally, *Without Lying Down* is comprehensive in its wide-ranging research and as meticulous in its scholarship as any text in the field.

Another woman director of the silent era is the focus of an altogether different sort of book. In *Streetwalking on a Ruined Map: Cultural Theory and the City Films of Elvira Notari* (1993), Giuliana Bruno has written a superb work of scholarship and theory circulating around the work of Italian filmmaker Elvira Notari. Notari was the driving force of Dora Film (Naples, 1906-30) and director of approximately sixty feature films and over a hundred shorts and documentaries. Bruno writes: 'Unearthing the documentation on Dora Film, I was confronted with a ruined and fragmentary map. Elvira Notari's extensive production has not only been forgotten but lost to the historical archive. Only three complete feature films remain. The fragmentary textual body, and the silence surrounding this work, called for an "archeological," intertextual approach.'[64]

In her text, Bruno takes on the challenge of studying the work of a director whose films are no longer extant. She provides a complex theoretical methodology for treating filmic fragments, stills, and scripts and other writings such as novelizations, along with ephemeral documents such as posters, magazine and newspaper articles, and industrial contracts. Integrating methodologies from art history, cultural anthropology, architecture, feminist film theory, psychoanalytic theory, and the history of medical discourse and the body, Bruno produces an intertextual metahistory of intellectual discourse. In the process, she examines historical and thematic issues in the films of Elvira Notari, as discursively allegorized into industrialized society with the onset of the cinema, the medical industry, and the arcade.

Bruno not only reconstructs the fragments of Notari's career, but she situates them within the architecture of Naples, the city in which her films were made. The Neopolitan arcades, which housed large new stores as well as cafes, were the sites for exhibition of films of spectacle. Notari's cinema thus grew up along with modern urban culture, near the train station and among the arcades, where shoppers and *flaneurs* came and went. But as Bruno notes, Notari's cinema was a regional cinema, specific not only in location but in dialect as well. With the rise of fascism, a new ideology that emphasized unity and the grand heritage of Italian history, local and regional cultures were suppressed. Bruno thus connects Notari's demise as a filmmaker not merely to the industrial changes to cinema that were sweeping the world with the coming of sound, but to specific national, political, and social conditions as well.

Despite the differences in settings – city versus wilderness – between Notari's and Shipman's films, there are many commonalities between the careers and lives of these two women. Shipman also used real locations, non-professional actors, regional accents in intertitles, and melodramatic accounts of women's travails and triumphs, and she enlisted her son and her husband as cast and crew. Many of Shipman's productions have been lost, others were never completed, and evidence such as her memoir, letters, and novelizations will be used in this text to reconstruct her career.

Back to Nell Shipman

My research on Nell Shipman arises from a conviction that, whether she was a first or not, whether she was feminist or progressive or not, whether she was a superb or even competent filmmaker or not, whether she was as 'worthy' of a contemporary feminist scholarly treatment as – say – Germaine Dulac, we will nevertheless be richer for knowledge of women like her. Knowledge of these historical figures can assist not only in producing insight into the vast range of women's interests and activities, but can construct a new understanding of the film industry in its formative years.

chapter two

Women with Megaphones

Nell Shipman in Hollywood

Of course, it wasn't Hollywood then. The towns that are now simply areas of Los Angeles (Burbank, Pasadena, Glendale) were equally production centres, and independent regional companies were scattered over the nation. The Mandarin Film Company was located in San Francisco, Alice Guy Blaché's Solax Company in New Jersey, and Oscar Michaux and Selig in Chicago. The film industry was moving generally to California in the early teens, called by the wide variety of geographical terrains, cheap land, and the constant sunshine.

With her husband Ernest, Shipman moved to California in 1910. She tells the beginning of her career as a screenwriter this way: 'Ernest, scenting the golden future in store for even such shoddy entertainment, figured a day was coming when better-heeled motion picture makers would actually pay authors for the rights to their works. His actress wife, temporarily out of the Legit – besides being overweight and not healthy after her bout with maternity – was thrown into the maelstrom of film writing.'[1] She got her chance, apparently, by entering a contest 'in the art of writing for the screen.' She writes that she won first and second prize 'hands down. There were no other contestants!' (*Heart*, 49).

Tom Trusky notes that the first known scenario that Shipman wrote is the presumed lost *Outwitted by Billy*, produced by Selig in 1913 (169n). *Outwitted by Billy* (if that is the 1913 Selig release) must have been produced some time after it had won the contest, as Shipman's memoir includes details of a series of short mystery films credited to her as author and produced in 1912. She starred in *The Ball of Yarn* (1912, d. Norval MacGregor), one of a series of ten that she had written featuring a character known as 'the female Raffles' (168). In an undated advertisement headlined 'The Female Raffles Series of Photo Plays by Nell Shipman,' the serial scenario is described:

> The 'Female Raffles,' Jess Craydon by name, plots with 'Gentleman Jack,' her crook pal of 'the Underworld,' to steal a noted diamond necklace which is to be given as a wedding present at a forthcoming society wedding. Jess applies for, and secures, position as companion in the West Side mansion, and is assisting the hostess to unskein yarn and wind into a ball when diamonds are brought from bank by messenger. The necklace is first examined by those present, and while attention is occupied with other jewels, Jess contrives to palm the necklace and deftly winds it into the ball of yarn. Loss is discovered, Jess accused. She drops ball on floor and defies them. Detective Rance arrives and recognizes Jess as the 'Female Raffles' and orders her searched. Not finding the jewels, they cannot detain her, and she departs, deftly kicking the ball of yarn under settee, as she leaves.
>
> Gentleman Jack appears that night to get possession of ball, but is outwitted by Teddy, the six-year-old grandson; and here follows a series of tense situations, an abduction, a chase, further efforts on the part of the crooks to get the jewels, always being outwitted by 'Teddy,' who unconsciously manages to thwart their clever schemes, and finally receives the reward (168n).

Shipman's own version is typically more acerbic in her description of both the production and reception of the film. *Ball of Yarn* was so bad, she admits, 'that even Ernie couldn't book it' (40). 'In *Ball of Yarn*,' she writes, 'I, as a wicked female, wound the stolen gems into the yarn I seemed to be knitting. This opus was shot on an open stage, back at a cottage in Echo Park ... Norval [MacGregor], a stage director as well as a fine actor, carried his theatrical technique over into the flickers. We made long entrances and exits. We gathered as a group to spout intertitles. To make room for this staged play, the hand-cranked box camera was so far back it was practically in Echo Park Lake. *The Ball of Yarn* never felt the hot breath of a projector, so no man lives today to point the finger of scorn at its star and author' (44).

In her autobiography, she mentions a number of other titles, including some that Tom Trusky's notes say she did not write or were not produced. Another two-reeler, *The Wreckers*, was bought by Vitagraph for $25.00 per reel (40). *The Shepherd of the Southern Cross* was produced in Australia in 1914. *Under the Crescent* was a series of six two-reelers that 'through Ernie's wire-pulling and promotional perspicacity' had been sold to Universal in 1915 (41) and published in a novelized version the same year by Grosset and Dunlap, who paid Nell a fee of $1000 (42). Shipman describes *Under the Crescent* with her usual cavalier wit:

> The mainspring of this opus was an American actress named Ola Humphrey who, as a star touring the near-East, had met and married a real, live, regular and authentic Egyptian Prince. A ready-made set-up if ever! The marriage ended conventionally in divorce. Ola was still called Princess, but no longer resided in Cairo. No matter: I changed 'Hassan' to 'Toussan,' plunked the lady into a harem, veiled her, abused her, put her through a series of nerve-shattering adventures by stirring in parts of the British Army, added an American lover and spiced the potage with intrigue, poison, passion, dancing houris and most everything Universal's set department and wardrobe might devise (41).

Kalton C. Lahue wrote that *Under the Crescent* 'was not particularly dramatic, nor did it contain strong action or suspense; its strong point revolved around the well-maintained atmosphere it conveyed.'[2] It is conceivable that Lahue had seen *Under the Crescent* in the period of its original exhibition; we will have to trust his assessment, as the serial is now lost.

There is some historical uncertainty about Shipman's first film as director. In the memoir, she notes that a 'summertime location job at Tahoe was [her] first movie break' (*Heart*, 43). She was there with a 'two-reel opus she had written for Mr. [Jack] Kerrigan,' 'an outdoor yarn' in which the handsome young leading man wore a buckskin suit. Shipman came to direct when the leading lady ran off with the studio-appointed director, and Jack Kerrigan, the Universal star, insisted that she 'take up the megaphone' (44). Two-year-old Barry had a part in the film.[3] Shipman also mentions that she was out of work 'as a stage actress' at the time; the phrase indicates that she had not yet made the career move to motion picture acting that was to come as early as 1915. However, by

June 1916 she had already completed *God's Country and the Woman*, her first Curwood feature (six reels, copyright 15 April 1916) (170n).

Rollin Sturgeon, the director of *God's Country and the Woman*, hated stage actors. He often 'held forth on the evil of stagey mannerisms, startled reflexes, looks off-camera which made the actor register the thing he was supposed to see with craned neck, stiff jaw, popped eyes, even that gesture – worst of all on camera – an uplifted hand as if to ward off some baleful sight' (52). Shipman considered herself lucky to have landed the role:

> Rollin Sturgeon was the director who hired me, not because I could act, in fact he loathed all stage performers, but I was the type: athletic, a swimmer, someone who could get around the wilderness without stubbing her toe on a pinecone. My landing the lead in such a picture to co-star with two Vitagraph favorites, Bill Duncan who was leading man, and George Holt, the heavy, was my break; the happening for which actresses of today still pray. To me the lure was the fact that we'd spend three months of winter in this then unknown and almost uninhabited mountain resort, that I'd act for an important company and be paid for my fun. I was to drive a team of sleddogs, paddle a canoe, travel on snowshoes, undergo pages of Curwoodian drama in a setting which if not quite like my own Northwest was near it (50).

Shipman claims that Vitagraph was the first company 'to tackle a multi-reel feature shot in the mountain locale ... and the budget was staggering for 1915 – $90,000.' The film's generous budget was attributable to the popularity of writer James Oliver Curwood. *God's Country and the Woman* was shot in Big Bear Valley, a popular northwoods movie location due to its photogenic scenery, snow in winter, and proximity to Hollywood. During production, the director discovered that Shipman had a facility for dialogue and enlisted her in the script process – all 'for free, of course. No one then thought beyond the weekly stipend or asked payment for extras' (49–51).

Shipman had a terrific time on the shoot. The morning calls were for eight o'clock, made-up and ready for the hike to the mountain set-ups, where they would spend all day shooting 'hours of takes and re-takes as [they] stood in the snow and the bitter wind off the lake' (50). At night she danced marathons and in off moments skied and played in the snow. Although leading man William Duncan, an Essanay studio veteran who knew his way around studios, worried that she might break her 'silly neck,' he also mentored her in a 'stern semester' (51). Shipman was determined to do her best not to overact, to hit her mark, to 'be smooth, cool and flowing!' (52). And she evidently was. *Through the Wall* (lost; copyright 21 September 1916) and *The Fires of Conscience* (lost; copyright 24 September 1916) followed *God's Country and the Woman*.

Shipman was now ensconced as a Vitagraph contract actor. In her memoir she recalls a loan-out to Famous Players–Lasky for a Lou Tellegen vehicle, *The Black Wolf* (1917). Shipman notes with some glee the difference between 'plain old Vitagraph' (45) and Famous Players–Lasky:

> Even the lunch break was different. At Vitagraph, we ate 35 cents worth in the lunchroom across from the studio. On location we had box lunches with the inevitable hard cheese slice curling away from the two pieces of stale bread, one apple, one doughnut and a half pint of warmish milk.
>
> With these foreign imports [Europeans Lou Tellegen and director Frank Reichler], it was caviar and champagne, served by a liveried chauffeur. I tried not to wolf such unaccustomed fare while listening to Smart Set talk which sprayed names like confetti. Star and Director outdid one another in the compliments bestowed on the Leading Lady [Shipman], whose hat size grew out of all proportion to what was under the chapeau (46).

The Black Wolf included an exterior Spanish castle set, with Shipman standing on a balcony and leading man Tellegen perched on a ladder by which he entered and exited the putative bedroom beyond the balcony. They also shot scenes on horseback on location at the Baldwin Ranch in Santa Anita, where Shipman had to ride side saddle in full riding habit, complete with top hat, veil, and choker collar. She recalled having removed her boots because they pinched and she knew that 'if [her] feet hurt it would show in [her] face.' She also knew that as the shot was a 'medium-close' her bootless feet wouldn't show (47).

Soon after, Shipman was offered a seven-year contract with Goldwyn:

> It started at less than Vitagraph was paying and had built-in options guaranteed to blast one off the Lot. But it was for seven years, the legal limit, and promised eventual stardom. Cheekily, I turned down the offer. Probably as

Lou Tellegen and Nell Shipman in a publicity still for *The Black Wolf* (1917).

silly a move as a neophyte ever made. But I did not like the way they dressed their contract players. This was in the period of curly blondes with Cupid's-bow mouths; and Wardrobe's main idea was to bind down a bosom with a swatch of shiny material which met yards of floaty material at the waistline and looked like a flowery pen-wiper. This long-legged, lanky out-doors gal, who usually loped across the Silver Screen in fur parkas and mukluks, gagged at such costuming. And had the nerve to refuse it (46).

But Shipman did not dress herself only in parkas. She spent her 'skimpy savings' on a 'long-tailed, blue-sequined gown' that she was delighted to say caught the attention of Cecil B. De Mille (46). By this time, the industry was located in what we now know as Hollywood, in the centre of Los Angeles. The studios were becoming well established, and towns like South Pasadena and Glendale, where Shipman lived for some time, were on the outskirts beyond the orange groves.

Working on studio sets afforded Shipman many opportunities to see other Hollywood notables at work. In the memoir, she mentions watching a De Mille 'Bacchanalia' in process. 'Mr. De Mille, a stickler for realism, had ordered real brandy to top real wine. No cold tea. The orgy was for real and the scene so out of hand no actor, from stars to extras, could function. They say it took three days to sober them up. The sight was prodigious, if messy. I stood watching Mr. De Mille wade through the vineyard, shouting into his megaphone, trying to cover the bared breast or prone and sprawling undressed extras' (48). Another time, on another set, she watched Hobart Bosworth and Theodore Roberts steal a scene from Mary Pickford (49). After a particularly trying day on location, she spent the evening shooting craps with William S. Hart's cowboys, actors from a rival company also on location. She won forty dollars – a huge sum in a time when 'a glass of beer and a phone call still cost a nickel each ... There was nothing to do but spend my winnings on drinks for both outfits' (61–2).

From the moment of her first association with James Oliver Curwood in *God's Country and the Woman*, Nell had become typed as an outdoor heroine. By 1918 her name was featured 'in programs and marquees' (56), and she took 'the girl from God's country' as her own publicity sobriquet (50). It is probable that she featured in similar roles in *Cavanaugh of the Forest Rangers* (copyright 16 February 1918), *The Home*

There was more to Shipman's closet than parkas and mukluks.

Trail (copyright 18 March 1918), and *The Girl from Beyond* (copyright 8 April 1918), although these films have not survived. This tight production schedule indicates the demand for Shipman's services, but it was also the order of the day. Contract players were paid by the week, so had to be kept working, and a large budget film typically had a twenty-one-day shooting schedule.

Shipman starred in another Curwood feature, *Baree, Son of Kazan* (presumed lost; five reels; Vitagraph, copyright May 1918). In this one there was 'a dilly of a river scene,' dangerous enough that they had hired a stunt double for Shipman. It was a thirty-foot, feet-first free jump into the surf; if not timed perfectly, the jumper landed on the rocks instead. The stunt woman was pregnant and terrified by the assignment, so Shipman offered to do the jump, with the proviso that the stunt woman would be paid anyway. The water was so cold that Shipman passed out as she drifted with the current, and she had to be harpooned by a long stout pole plunged into her 'long soggy false hair' and hauled in 'like a hunk of spaghetti on a twisting fork' (61–2).

Baree, Son of Kazan was a typical Curwood wilderness and wild animals melodrama, featuring a wild wolf-dog as the eponymous character. Shipman hilariously recalls shooting one of the scenes, in which a pack of wolves was to attack a moose. The moose was played by a black pony equipped with a set of papier-mâché horns that wobbled pathetically as the 'moose' was 'wallowing hock-deep in drifted snow ... In hot pursuit yelped the dogs, malamutes doubling as wolves, which would have been good casting except that their bushy tails arched to their neck ruffs and wagged. Props had tried to overcome this by stringing the tails with ribbons of BB-shot but the dogs did not like this addition and were stopping to bite the shot. The moose was doing worse. He'd given up the chase and was lying down' (62). Whether *Baree, Son of Kazan* was as luxuriously budgeted as the $90,000 *God's Country and the Woman*, we do not know. Shipman's anecdote suggests the contrary.

In *A Gentleman's Agreement* (Vitagraph, copyright July 1918) Shipman narrowly escaped drowning in a scene that involved two men and an overturned canoe. She recounts the near-death experience in vivid detail and great length in the memoir, indicating the mark the incident left on her memory even fifty years later. In her novel *Abandoned Trails*, Shipman condenses the narrative to quotable length:

'The leading man wasn't a very good swimmer ... and when we got into that wild, white water he forgot what little he knew. I was lucky enough to reach him and we made that big rock out there in the middle. Then poor Jim let go of me – he was scared stiff, you know – and I was swept on downstream towards that place. Can you see it? Where the whole river seems to pour under the rocks? It was "bye-bye" if I hit that and there did not seem a chance I wouldn't, the current was too strong for me and the boulders too big and slippery. But, do you know, over by the bank I saw two little rocks, like this ...' she shaped her hands, finger-tips pressed. 'Like hands, praying,' said Dirk. 'Exactly! I was praying, so I guess I conjured those rock-fingers. I thought – "if the current will only carry me over there I can grab that tiny pinnacle!" And it did! I had just time to seize it as I was swept by. The others came running and pulled me out, but it was touch and go, I can tell you. And what do you think? It was Sunday and a lot of sightseers were about, watching us make Roman Holiday. When they saw Jim drowning and me being swept down to death, some dame remarked: "Oh, let's go home. It's just Movies!"'

'The risks taken making pictures aren't worth the candle,' said Dirk. 'Believe me, I'm glad I'll be with you on this location! There'll be no monkey-shines with the river then!'

'No?' she said, laughing. 'Well, I've never been doubled – yet! But, Gosh! It sure makes me sore to sit in a picture theater, watching myself pull some crazy stunt, and hear people say: "She didn't really do that! It's a trick! They do it with the camera!"'[4]

In another scene, Shipman was to attempt to rescue her mother (in the script), played by a character actor who was terrified of water. The director finally ordered the actors to simply push the older woman under. 'So, in rather rough and very cold water, the raft lashed to a dockside where the cameras were set up, the realistic scene was finally done. But my poor friend caused so much fuss and fury it took hours of pleading, reassurances, droughts of hot coffee and nips of whiskey to get our gal under water' (*Heart*, 57). The scene took so long to shoot and was so harrowing for all that Shipman ended up passing out and had to be taken to hospital.

Shooting on location was nerve-racking enough, but there were dangers in the studio as well. When Vitagraph moved to Prospect and Talmadge Streets in Hollywood, they built the 'first Dark Stage lighted with Kleigs and Cooper-Hewitts. The open-faced Kleigs were murder. The carbons sputtered as they burned and cast off dust for future smog. Kleig eyes were an occupational hazard. The only known remedy was a compress of cold tea-leaves. After a long stint under the Kleigs and the sickly violet-tinted Coops, a performer could only blink red-eyed and wish the old open sun-lighted stages back' (63–4).

In this new studio they shot *The Wild Strain* (five reels; Vitagraph, copyright 19 January 1918). As her Vitagraph contract progressed, only from time to time was she able to get out of moccasins and into gowns and high heels. *The Wild Strain* was one such occasion, when she starred as a society girl with 'a wild strain' that led her to doing high kick dances and riding bareback on a circus horse in a satin dress and wig. Gayne Whitman (originally named Al Vosberg) was her leading man; with him she had finally found a co-star who was tall enough that even in her high heels she could rest her 'overly coiffured head on [his] manly bosom.' Shipman mentions working with two other leading men who, at five feet ten inches, had to put lifts in their heels to equal her height (62).

Tom Trusky writes that 'steady employment, primarily at Vitagraph Studios, and better roles, which translated as high billing, characterize Nell Shipman's rise to stardom during 1915 to 1919.'[5] Shipman, on the contrary, writes that she was 'demoted to two-reelers, Westerns known as *The Wolfville Series*, it being taken for granted I'd break my contract before descending so low.' She seems to have taken the demotion as a creative opportunity instead, and 'had a ball' using 'every trick in the book to influence their director with gags, gimmicks, wild strains and catsup-blood stains so that the program fillers turned out winners ... Bookings soared.'

Meanwhile, *Baree, Son of Kazan* went into release and was successful, ensuring that her contract with Vitagraph ended on 'a high note' (*Heart*, 65). Trusky quotes a letter from Ernest Shipman that claims her salary as $300 per week by the end of her four-year Vitagraph contract (171–2).

Shipman was able to leave Vitagraph when her contract expired, informing them that she was not 'available for renewal' since she had struck an exclusive independent contract with James Oliver Curwood. She was committed to adapting and starring exclusively in features

Nell Shipman in costume, probably for *The Wild Strain* (1918).

Unidentified actors and Nell Shipman, possibly from *The Wolfville Series* (1916–17).

based on his stories. *Back to God's Country* (1919) followed almost immediately. An enormous critical and box-office success, the film established Shipman's reputation as a star. Immediately after *Back to God's Country*, Shipman took up the megaphone as director.

Women Filmmakers Shipman Might Have Known

Shipman's memoir claims for her the status as the first women to '[defy] the Establishment' by going independent. She notes that only a few male stars 'sought to wear two hats as Producers and Actors but, so far, women had not stepped beyond the boundary of being non-acting Directors' (66). However, women actors quickly followed her lead: most of the women directors in Hollywood in the period were also actors, and to some degree this has been the case throughout the ensuing years. Many women directors got their start as actors before film schools and training programs in film directing were widely institutionalized. Many women in Hollywood worked in powerful creative positions, and Shipman must have known of many of them, although she does not mention any in her memoir.

It would have been impossible for her not to know Lois Weber (1881–1939), at least by reputation as one of the highest paid directors in Hollywood in the period. 'In her own time,' writes Gwendolyn Foster, 'Weber was as well known as D.W. Griffith and Cecil B. DeMille.'[6] Furthermore, Dal Clauson, the second camera on *Back to God's Country*, had just finished shooting a picture for Weber when he travelled with Shipman's crew to Lesser Slave Lake.[7] It seems likely that in the close location quarters they would have traded a story or two.

Shipman also must have known of Frances Marion (1890-1973), the most powerful screenwriter in Hollywood, who made her early career in partnership with Mary Pickford, the most powerful woman star at the time. 'Since 1917, she had been the highest-paid writer in Hollywood – male or female – and was hailed as "the all-time best script and story writer the motion picture world has ever produced."' Marion became the first woman writer to win an Academy Award when she won Best Original Screenplay for *The Big House* (1930). At that time, Marion was credited with writing over one hundred produced films, including Pickford's most famous vehicles, *Rebecca of Sunnybrook Farm* (1917), *The Little Princess*

(1917), *Pollyanna* (1920), and a dozen more.[8] Marion also directed three features, *Just around the Corner* (1920), *The Love Light* (starring Pickford, 1921), and *The Song of Love* (starring Norma Talmadge, 1923), and continued her career as a screenwriter until 1940.[9] Like Shipman, Frances Marion worked in genre films and sequels, completing eleven six-to-eight-reel westerns starring her husband, Fred Thomson, and his magnificent horse Silver King, between 1925 and 1928. Marion wrote all of the Thomson films under the pseudonym Frank M. Clifton.[10]

Shipman also must have been familiar with the work of Grace Cunard (1893–1967), whose career in many ways paralleled Shipman's own. Like Shipman, Cunard joined a traveling theatre troupe at age thirteen and landed in Hollywood, where she made her first appearance as an actress in *The Duke's Plan* (1910). She appeared in many films before forming a successful partnership with Francis Ford, an actor and director who was the brother of John Ford. Best known for the highly successful action cliffhanger serial *The Broken Coin* (1915), Cunard's typical heroine – like Shipman's – was active, determined, resourceful, and physically capable of saving herself and others. Like Shipman, too, Cunard performed her own stunts and went on to write and direct a string of serials, historical films, westerns, and melodramas between 1913 and 1922.[11]

Cunard was among many women directors who worked in studios such as Universal in the teens and twenties. There were powerful women writers, as well, who wielded considerable creative control over the productions, especially if, like Gene Gauntier (1885–1966), they also starred in the films they wrote and sometimes directed. Gauntier received directorial credit for *Grandmother* (1910), which she also wrote. She was another 'serial queen,' who wrote hundreds of episodes in which she starred and performed daredevil stunts. Gauntier recalled:

My own work was not light, and only youth and a strong constitution could have stood up under it. I was playing in 2 pictures a week, working in almost every scene, and writing 2 or 3 scenarios a week, in the effort to keep up with our production. And my screen work was all strenuous, horseback riding for hours each day, water scenes in which I committed suicide or floated on spars in shark-infested waters, climbing trees, coming down on ropes from second-story windows, jumping from roofs or rolling down to be caught in blankets, overturning skiffs, paddling canoes, a hundred and one 'stunts' thought out to give the action the Kalem films demanded. I was terrified at each daring thing I had to do, but for some reason I continued to write them. They never seemed difficult when I was seated before the typewriter in the throes of creating them, but as the moment for performance drew near they assumed unwarranted aspects of terror. A 'double' was never even thought of in those days![12]

Like Cunard and Shipman, Gene Gauntier embodied the self-determined and adventurous New Woman of the early twentieth century. Others, such as Kathlyn Williams and Ruth Stonehouse, also worked in the Hollywood genre of the heroic woman serial, which was a staple of the industry for many years. Shipman had cut her movie teeth on serials, having sold her novel *Under the Crescent* in a serialized version for the screen, and she was never averse to formulaic repetition. She must have been aware of the women who were working alongside her (at least metaphorically) in the commercial industry.

It is unlikely, however, that she knew of the African-American women filmmakers who were making feature films at the time, for they worked in local eastern and southern centres outside of Hollywood. Henry T. Sampson notes the films of Tressie Souders and Maria P. Williams.[13] *A Woman's Error*, written, produced, and directed by Souders (1922) is considered the first film to be directed by a black woman in the United States. Although Sampson lists her as Tressie Sanders, Yvonne Lynn Welbon tells me that she has found press clippings from newspapers of the time that list her as Souders. *Flames of Wrath* (1922) was produced and directed by Maria P. Williams. Welbon has also amassed considerable research on Eloyce Gist, another African-American feature director.[14]

Shipman may have known of Musidora (1889–1957), for she was one of the greatest stars of the French silent cinema, owing her reputation to the part of Irma Vep in the popular adventure serial *Les vampires* (d. Louis Feuillade, 1915–16). Worshipped by the surrealists for her subversive eroticism, Musidora created a memorable vamp character, a sexy villainess in black leotards, a persona she replicated in *Judex* (d. Louis Feuillade, 1916). Although Shipman's brand of voluptuous natural womanhood was very different from Musidora's fashionable sexual allure, they shared many commonalities besides their serial queen fame. Musidora wrote a novel, and was a writer, director, and producer with her own company; like Shipman, the four feature films that she directed showed her taste for real locations and stylistic experimentation. Musidora was dubbed 'queen of the cinema' in 1926, but her film career ended with the coming of sound.[15]

In 1912 Shipman wrote *Shepherd of the Southern Cross* (originally titled *Shepherdess of the Southern Cross*), which was produced by Australasian films in 1914. Although Shipman does not appear to have travelled to Australia, it is conceivable that she had heard of Lotte Lyell (1890–1925), the woman who can be seen as Shipman's Australian counterpart. Lyell wrote, starred in, and – with Raymond Longford – directed twenty-eight films, entering the film industry in 1911 and continuing until her death from tuberculosis in 1925. A champion horseback rider, Lyell created and played the role of the strong-willed outdoor bush girl. Like her Hollywood counterparts, she performed her own stunts in a series of outdoor adventure films. She also played a working girl employed in an urban factory in *The Sentimental Bloke* (1919),[16] which Gwendolyn Foster attests was 'an international success'[17] Despite business trips to New York to sell her films, Shipman lived in the wilderness for most of the years between 1918 (when *Back to God's Country* went into production in the barren lands of northern Alberta) and 1924 (spanning the years in the backwoods of Priest Lake, Idaho). Thus, it is difficult to speculate whether she was familiar with Lyell's work, although she may have been aware of her existence.

Another actor/director of international reputation was Leni Riefenstahl (1902–). Although Riefenstahl's career as a director was concentrated in the sound era (1930s and after), she became famous initially in the twenties. Although she began her career as a balletically trained dancer, her lustrous beauty soon propelled her into movies as a star of the German equivalent of the serial queen shorts, the 'mountain' movies whose best-known director was Arnold Fanck. In *The Holy Mountain* (d. Arnold Fanck, 1926) she played a young dancer who becomes enthralled with mountain climbing. In the twenties she starred in a series of these genre films, which featured breathtaking feats of climbing skill against the backdrop of the magnificent landscapes.

Like many of the bright young women both then and now who learned the art of directing from their participation as actors, Riefenstahl soon moved into directing. *The Blue Light* (d. Riefenstahl, 1932), in which she also starred, is the culmination of the monumental and mystical elements of the mountain film genre. Although it is a sound-era film, it bears the stylistic marks of the silent era, as musical accompaniment provides most of the sound, and dialogue is sparse. In every way the work is reminiscent of silent-era genre films.

Riefenstahl plays Junta, a bare-foot goat herder who wears a strategically tattered dress and scampers across the daunting terrain with the sure-footedness of the goats she tends. On the nights of the full moon, she is drawn to the source of a mysterious blue light that emanates from the mountain, formed by the refraction of the moonlight from a cave of magnificent blue crystals high up on the peak. The tragedy of the nearby village is that, one by one, the local young men are also drawn to seek the source of the mystical light, but lacking her skills at climbing, each young man falls to his death on the mountain. Junta comes to be feared and reviled in the village, for only she is capable of surviving the climb (in the dark) to bring back a few crystals for sale to tourists. A well-meaning traveller, infatuated with Junta's beauty and seeking to benefit both her and the community, follows her to the crystalline cave. When he reveals the secret path to the villagers, they greedily mine the cave, so that on the next full moon, when Junta discovers that the mystical source of her strength and spiritual beneficence has been destroyed, she plunges off the mountain to her death.

Exploiting the genre elements of the mountain movies to their fullest, with its characteristic cast of lederhosen-clad villagers, semi-expressionistic village streetscapes, heroic feats of climbing, and the sublime moonlit mountain landscape, Riefenstahl imbues the genre with a mystical force that is matched only by her own star quality. Although very different from the bush-ranging films of Australia, the shark-infested waters of the Hollywood serial queen movies, or the snowbound wilderness films of Shipman's own practice, this genre is comparable in every way to the industrial models of other countries.

Lotte Reiniger (1899–1981) continued her career not only well into the sound era, but throughout her lifetime. Reiniger made her first film in 1919 and her last in 1979, and she worked steadily during all those sixty years. She began her career in Germany, but in 1935 she moved to Britain, where she worked at Crown International and the GPO film unit. After the war she and her husband made films for American television. She moved to Canada in 1963, where she spent the duration of her career, which lasted until two years before her death.

What makes Reiniger's story so unusual? She was an animator. Pioneering an animation technique that used cut-out silhouette figures that were elaborately moved frame by frame, she designed for the purpose a multi-plane camera that separated out foreground and background, thus expediting the painstaking animation process.

Reiniger directed a feature-length animated film, *The Adventures of Prince Achmed* (1926). An adaptation of the *Arabian Nights*, the film is absolutely enchanting. The silhouette figures are extremely elaborately cut. Prince Achmed has nifty turned-up shoulder pads, a jaunty topknot, and a lacy lower garment. He rides an ostrich, whose tail feathers are delicately individuated, through a landscape in which distant hillsides are suggested by sand against backlit glass and, in the foreground, wave stylized plants and flowers reminiscent of Aubrey Beardsley drawings. Although the film took three years to complete, it bears marks of nothing except the most blithe and fluid spirit. Jean Renoir described her as 'a visual expression of Mozart'[18] and an admiring animator said in 1980, 'the movement in her films is so superb that after the first few seconds you forget you are looking at flat paper. You see dancers whirling around as if they're three-dimensional.'[19]

Because Reiniger finished her career in Canada, we have access to her films, including *The Adventures of Prince Achmed*, short films such as *Papageno, Harlequin, Frog Prince*, and *Stolen Heart* from the 1930s, as well as the work she did for the National Film Board in the 1970s. Because the NFB fostered animation, Reiniger was extremely influential there, leaving a legacy that extended the already lengthy life of her films.

Although Shipman may not have known of Reiniger, she may have been aware of a few other European women filmmakers. Her contact with Mabel Dodge Luhan, a member of the Gertrude Stein circle of American expatriates in Paris, might well have apprised her of the work of Germaine Dulac (1882–1942). Dulac not only directed nearly two dozen films over fourteen years (1916–29), but also wrote for a feminist periodical (*La française*) and edited and published a journal of theory and criticism (*La fronde*).

Although Dulac worked predominantly in the avant-garde, she – like Shipman – made episodic serials. *Âmes de fous* (1917) is a six-episode serial that combines the structural elements of the cliffhanger with the surreal-istic and impressionistic techniques for which Dulac is best known. She repeated its success with *Gossette* (1923), again in six episodes, which Flitterman-Lewis describes as 'a conventional adventure story' with 'poetic evocation by technical means.'[20] Dulac's work is noted for its impressionistic deployment of technical devices such as double expo-sures, superimpositions, masks, and distorting lenses – a play with cine-matic language that has resulted in her being described as 'responsible for "writing" a new cinematic language that expressed transgressive female desires.'[21]

Sandy Flitterman-Lewis has done the most comprehensive study of Dulac's work to date. Unfortunately, *To Desire Differently* was published before Dulac's feature-length film *La belle dame sans merci* (1920) was dis-covered in the Netherlands Film Archive in 1997 and was restored, with a score of contemporary music arranged to accompany its exhibition. The transgressive force of *La belle dame sans merci* comes through the operations of the narrative. The story concerns a famous music-hall star who eats and spits out men as surely as they throw themselves at her feet. Complications ensue when she eschews her glamorous city life and moves to a small town, where she has to quell the suspicions of her neighbours and befriend the wife of the man whom she is rumoured to have seduced. Gwendolyn Foster argues that 'the knowledge of Dulac's lesbian sexuality allows for a new and more incisive reading of *The Smil-ing Madame Beudet*,'[22] and a similar argument can forcefully be made for *La belle dame sans merci*. The latter offers a critique of the emptiness of glamorous urban careerism, the claustrophobia of parochial village life, and the simplistic constructions of the vampish maneater; it also embraces a concept of community in which friendship between women is essential to social well-being. It is a significant and complex work in the dramatic mode, showing few traces of the cinematic pyrotechnics of Dulac's earlier and later films.

If Shipman may well have been acquainted with some of the women filmmakers who were her contemporaries, others were less well known in North America, and remain in relative obscurity to the present. Indeed, of the many European women filmmakers of the period, only two, Germaine Dulac and Elivra Notari, have received extensive scholarly treatment, as was discussed in chapter 1. Much less information is available on Soviet women filmmakers such as Olga Preobrazhenskaya, Esfir Shub, and Elizaveta Svilova. Marie-Louise Iribe, Rose Lacau-Pansini, and Renée Carl made features in France during the twenties, but are little known.[23] Adrienne Solser, from the Netherlands, is a name that is not mentioned in any of the current texts, but I believe that Annette Fuerster is working on a study of her.

Of the Russians, Esfir Shub (1894–1959) is the best known. She is widely credited with inventing the compilation film, a method of appropriational filmmaking that relies on the use of pre-existing footage. Early scholarship (frequently requoted) also assigns her the 'discovery' of 'some crucial principles of editing and intertitling.'[24] Notes also frequently underline her importance by asserting her influence on Eisenstein, Vertov, Pudovkin, and Kuleshov: 'Eisenstein learned from Esfir Shub by observing her editing techniques. ... Her relationship with Eisenstein was that of a collaborative friendship.'[25]

It does seem to be the case that a community of filmmakers creatively nurtured each other in the revolutionary Soviet period, but such a modest estimation is outweighed by the frequent use of words such as 'prefigure,' 'pioneer,' and 'influence' in the notes on Shub. Although I tend to be sceptical of making such claims, we can note confidently that Shub's first two compilation documentaries, *The Fall of the Romanov Dynasty* (1927) and *The Great Path* (1927), stand as substantial documents in international film history, as the regular inclusion of these films in histories of documentary continues to attest. Shub's career spanned the silent and the sound period, as she continued working until 1946. In the face of this recognition, it seems odd that research on her work is not more prolific. There is only one early article,[26] in addition to the chapters and notes in survey texts.

Elizaveta Svilova (1900–75) has been overshadowed consistently in the mainstream histories by her husband and partner Dziga Vertov. Many of the feminist texts lament her 'uncredited' invisibility, and Attwood's *Red Women on the Silver Screen* limits Svilova's role in the Dziga Vertov films to that of editor, mentioning her on only one page of the book.[27] On the contrary, not only is she credited as co-director with Vertov on *Kino Glaz* (1924) and many of the later short films, but she continued to earn a living for both of them after Vertov was denounced as a 'formalist' in the mid-thirties. As well as editing other people's films, she directed a series of documentaries in the thirties and forties.[28]

Olga Preobrazhenskaya's magnificent feature *Peasant Women of Ryazan* (1927) is available for contemporary study. After a career as a stage actress, Preobrazhenskaya (1881–1971) starred in *Keys to Happiness* (1913) and became an overnight success as a leading actor. She directed her first film in 1916 and made films for children in the 1920s: *Fedka's Truth* (1925), *Kashtanka* (1926), and *Anya* (1927). Maya Turovskaya notes that *Peasant Women of Ryazan* 'can be considered the first "woman's film" in both senses of the term – it was directed by a woman, and it addressed woman's *dolya* [destiny].'[29] Notes on Preobrazhenskaya repeat the now familiar refrains of 'firsts' and 'fews,' while also noting the presence of other women directors (Svilova, Iuliia Solntseva, Vera Stroeva, among unnamed others) in the Soviet cinema of the 1920s.[30]

Such claims aside, *Peasant Women of Ryazan* is a progressive and accomplished work that takes an 'unabashedly feminist approach' to its melodramatic tale of two village women.[31] One is a strong, independent, New Woman type, and the other a traditional wife who is raped by her father-in-law. The mise en scène emphasizes both the work and play of the women of the peasant village. Scenes of work in the fields and barns and of the melodramatic rape and subsequent suicide are countered by the wonderful sequence set in a spring celebration that features a giant swing. Perhaps eight women wearing their finest flowered and embroidered dresses sit on either side of the swing, deliriously soaring high in the air. By turns the camera replaces the women's point of view of the wildly alternating clouds and earth in a dizzying assault on the spectator's senses.

Gwendolyn Foster's account first cites *Peasant Women* as an 'uncompromising critique of patriarchal power structures in Russian peasant culture,' but ends with a judgment of the film as a 'highly schematic melodrama.'[32] Maya Turovskaya adds that 'despite her depiction of the new woman, Preobrazhenskaya still belonged to the old cinema, with its traditional narratives and styles.'[33] Lynn Attwood notes that the film 'was a great box office success ... commended for its technical accomplishments, its rural setting ... and its exposure of pre-revolutionary rural traditions.'[34] Nevertheless, there are as yet no individual studies of either this delightful film or its creator. Preobrazhenskaya continued to work until the 1940s, when her career was cut short by the Stalinist purges.[35]

Shipman spent some time in Europe after her bankruptcy in 1924. Broke and depressed, she and son Barry holed up in a Spanish beach town with a new partner, the American painter Charles Ayers. However, it is unlikely that she took in much cultural activity, or that she knew, for example, the work that Elvira Notari was doing in Italy at the time or of much other European film activity by women or men. At least we have no evidence of such knowledge, as the European period is dealt with very cursorily in the memoir, and in later documents (letters, articles, and novels) she remains massively consumed with her own life and career. Her cultural attention, if any, was directed to the popular genre cinema in which she made her own films.

I do not mean to argue in a utopian fashion that Shipman's films were generated from a cinema sisterhood. However, in setting out this international context, it is apparent that Nell Shipman was neither ahead of her time nor heroically alone. There were many women like her, working independently in the film industry in the early days of cinema, and some of them, especially in Europe, continued to work as directors well into the sound period.

⁜   ⁜   ⁜   ⁜   ⁜

chapter three

Back to God's Country

After Shipman's success as star of two James Oliver Curwood adapta-tions, *God's Country and the Woman* (d. Rollin S. Sturgeon; sc. Christine Johnston;[1] Vitagraph, 1916; lost)[2] and *Baree, Son of Kazan* (d. David Smith, 1918),[3] she was hired as both screenwriter and star of their next great project, *Back to God's Country* (d. David M. Hartford, Canadian Photoplays Production, 1919) which she adapted from Curwood's short story 'Wapi the Walrus.' Curwood offered an exclusive contract, binding Shipman to adapt and star in his vehicles, with husband Ernest Shipman as producer. Ernest raised the production financing for *Back to God's Country* in Calgary, under the Shipman-Curwood Motion Picture Pro-duction Company.

Back to God's Country reprised the Shipman character from the suc-cessful *God's Country and the Woman*. The earlier film had established Shipman as the 'girl from God's country,' usually clad in parkas and mukluks, snowshoeing and dogsledding across the frozen North. Ship-man knew that the original story 'was trash as a movie; a mere outline, a character-study of a Great Dane dog and how he reacted to the need of the woman he loved. That was all.'[4] Her script for *Back to God's Country* shifted the thrust of the plot to the woman protagonist and wove the dog into her melodramatic story of romance, villainous menace, heroic escape, and a treacherous journey across the barren snows.

As in Curwood's story, a prologue introduces a Chinese immigrant drawn to the North 'by the lure of gold.' When he arrives at a northern outpost, accompanied by his Great Dane, Tao, the Asian man is humili-ated and then murdered in a bar. Captured by white men, Tao is brutalized, as are his many descendants; 'forty dog-generations later,' Wapi, the vicious killer, is the result.

The film then introduces the heroine, Dolores (Shipman), in her forest home, frolicking with a large bear. She lives with her father in a log cabin, and the young male love interest, Peter, arrives in the course of doing his work as a government cartographer. Enter the villain. After killing Dolores's father, he is temporarily forced out of the picture as Dolores escapes his evil designs and reunites with the cartographer to live with him in the city. But she always dreams of going back to the wilderness, and they plan to return after Peter has taken care of an assignment in the North.

Here the meat of the story unfolds. As it turns out, the captain of the ship on which they are travelling is the villain from the earlier episode, and he is in league with Blake, the manager of the isolated trading post that is the ship's destination. Blake is also the owner of the dog Wapi. When Dolores's husband is seriously injured and the trading-post manager aligns himself with the villain to threaten her virtue, she is forced into intrepid heroine mode to rescue her husband and defeat the villains. She is assisted by Wapi, who has been miraculously gentled. After a 150-mile dogsled chase and narrow escape, they arrive at Fort Constance, where the husband returns to health. The denouement depicts Dolores's newfound bliss in a comfortable log cabin with her husband, Wapi, and a new baby, back in the edenic forest where they belong.

God's country films reappeared three times after Shipman's great 1919 version. *Back to God's Country* (d. Irvin Willat, 1927) followed quickly on Shipman's success, but it is presumably lost. *God's Country* (d. Robert Tansey, Action Pictures, 1946) is a remake in title only; it is set in the contemporary period (the heroine even stumping around the forest in 1940s high heels with little bows) in the northwestern forest rather than the Yukon tundra of the Klondike period, and it overlaps the other two versions in neither plot nor characters. Its title, however, links it to the other two and clearly capitalizes on the generic expectations of the wilderness adventure melodrama, and the film bears some significant marks of the generic concerns at the heart of this chapter. *Back to God's Country* (d. Joseph Pevney, Universal, 1953) is a remake of the Shipman film in every sense: based on the same Curwood story, it involves the same characters, topography, and narrative trajectory.

Curwood and Shipman

Wilderness and adventure stories had topped the American literary best-seller lists since the early 1910s, with Zane Grey and Jack London the leading exponents of the form. T.E. Harre's *The Eternal Maiden* (1913), a tale of feminine virtue in an 'Esquimaux' setting, was an early example of the trend towards settings in the Canadian North.[5]

Novels of the Canadian woods took off in popularity around 1914, with American authors such as Harold Bindloss, H. Footner, Virgie Roe, B.W. Sinclair, and Alice Jones among the top sellers,[6] although their fame did not rival the lasting prominence of Grey and London. Canadians Ralph Connor (a pseudonym for Charles Gordon),[7] Ernest Thompson Seton, and Charles G.D. Roberts, who was said to have invented the realistic animal story, were also well known in the United States, as was Margaret Marshall Saunders. As Marshall Saunders, she wrote *Beautiful Joe* (1893), one of the first best-sellers in North America. The continued popularity of this novel is phenomenal: as a child in the 1950s, I wept copiously into its pages and still remember the cover illustration of the large dog with a white bandage tied around its head to cover the ears that had been cruelly chopped off.[8]

By 1917, 'the novel of adventure or mystery, ... [and the] story of the great outdoors still made up a considerable part of the year's fiction,' but the genre was beginning to be nudged off the top of the best-seller lists by novels of contemporary everyday life or exotic romance.[9] Well into the twenties, however, the wilds of the Canadian Northwest were a commonplace setting for popular fiction,[10] and wilderness films remained a minor staple of the movie industry, continuing to be made well into the 1950s.

Before 1910, James Oliver Curwood had had modest success with wilderness and local colour adventure novels, but with the publication of *Kazan* (1914), a story of an escaped sled-dog who returns to his own wild wolf kind in the Canadian Far North, his fame had begun to equal that of Jack London's *White Fang* and *The Call of the Wild*. *Kazan* was followed in 1915 by the publication of *God's Country and the Woman*, a 'lively melodrama of the Canadian Northwest.'[11] A story of a 'love so deep and confident in the breast of the hero that it pierced the curtain of apparent unworthiness in which the heroine had felt it necessary to cloak her own actions,' *God's Country and the Woman* enjoyed great sales and was made into the film that began the partnership between Shipman and Curwood. Curwood returned to the animal kingdom with *The Grizzly King* (1917) and *Baree, Son of Kazan* (1918), the latter again starring Nell Shipman in the film version. By the end of the war, Curwood had achieved a short-lived position alongside Zane Grey and Jack London as the best-selling authors of wilderness adventure.

Many of Curwood's novels were made into films. In addition to the Shipman vehicles and their remakes, the list continued well into the 1950s.[12] Although westerns were always the most popular genre in North American cinema, both dog stories, dating from *Rescued by Rover* (d. Cecil M. Hepworth; 1903), and adventure films were staples of the distribution syndicates. With Curwood, Nell Shipman had come to a productive partnership.

One of the most startling episodes in *Abandoned Trails*, the fictionalized autobiography that Shipman wrote many years later, is Shipman's first meeting with James Oliver Curwood. Their three-year professional relationship makes it difficult to believe that Nell and Curwood had not yet met, but that is what she recounts in both the memoir and the novel. Shipman and Curwood encountered each other for the first time in Calgary, where the crew gathered to begin the trek to the northern production location of *Back to God's Country*. Curwood, it seems, was furious about her adaptation of his short story. That Shipman had shifted the centre of the plot from the dog to the heroine was not the least of his concerns. He also challenged her on technical details, she writes.

'Scene one. Iris in ...' he checked her. 'Who is this "Iris"?' he demanded. 'There is no character in my story called Iris. Why did you add such a person? Practically every scene starts with her, or mention of her.' Joyce [the name Shipman gives herself in the novel] stared at him blankly. It did not seem possible that he was ignorant of that common, technical term – 'iris.' She wanted to laugh because, now, she knew she held the cards. But she kept a straight face and gravely described the workings of an iris, demonstrating with her fingers how the aperture of the camera opened on a small circle and grew bigger until the whole set-up was in. 'Set-up' had to be explained.[13]

In his notes to the second edition of Shipman's autobiography, editor

Tom Trusky implies that Shipman may have embellished the incident too extravagantly, even in the much briefer version of it in the memoir. Trusky notes that Curwood had authored over twenty-five screenplays for one film company alone (Vitagraph) during the period 1913–15, and suggests that Curwood 'may have been familiar with the term.'[14] On the other hand, screenplays in that period were not the detailed scenarios of today. More often they were brief plot outlines, written extremely quickly, sometimes during the process of production. In this historical context, it is not inconceivable that Curwood may have been ignorant of the technical terminology of detailed shot lists.

And Shipman decidedly was not. By this time she was a prominent enough figure that she was in a position to call the shots, both figuratively and literally. She had been instrumental in hiring Joseph Walker as cinematographer, for example, when he was a young man getting his start in the business. She had seen a film that he had shot and asked to meet him, requesting an unusual test. Walker recalls that 'she knew exactly what she wanted' – to be made to look good outdoors in natural sunlight, rather than the conventional studio set-up. Walker used a technique he had learned from Billy Bitzer (D.W. Griffith's cinematographer): he opened the lens as wide as it could go without over-exposing, so that the background became soft and unobtrusive while the figure in the foreground took dominance with stereoscopic roundness.[15] Shipman was pleased with the effect and was instrumental in getting Walker hired to shoot *Back to God's Country*. 'It was my first motion picture of importance,' writes Walker.[16] In contrast to her relationship with Curwood, Walker and Shipman developed strong professional ties, working together on many more films.

In addition to the disparities in technical comprehension between novelist Curwood and scenarist Shipman, other tensions were developing as well. Shipman had had a serious flu the season before, and lost a lot of her hair as a result of high fever. With Curwood's wife waiting for him, as the train was about to pull out, Shipman tells of the author 'tackling' her: 'He said he but wanted to touch my hair, to remember its shining ripples. So please remove the fur cap pulled down over my worried brow so he might gaze upon the luxury! Wig, braids, all the appurtenances of his heroine's head were safe in a box. Under the sealskin cap were the meager leavings of double pneumonia and near fatal fever. I fought for my balding head. Not for my virtue, for I am certain J.O.C. had no such intentions. How could he with the train already whistling round the bend?'[17]

Abandoned Trails offers even more vivid background. Shipman's romance with Bert Van Tuyle, according to the novel, started to develop during the course of the train ride to the location. A few pages on, Shipman describes a breakfast meeting with Van Tuyle: 'He looked extravagantly handsome in a short, black fur coat, riding breeches and a fur cap. It was the Winter uniform of the Provincial Police, borrowed for use in the picture. Dirk [the fictional name for Van Tuyle] was to "double" as a Policeman so he had donned the costume. It became his well-knit, broad-shouldered figure and Joyce [Nell] looked at him, admiringly. "You sure look the part," she said. "And so do you!" he returned the compliment.'[18] Van Tuyle continued to woo Nell on location, stocking her cabin with firewood, extra lamps, a curtain for the window, and a bearskin rug for the floor.[19] The couple soon fell in love. Shipman's growing infatuation with Van Tuyle was counterpointed by her immense disappointment in Curwood.

In Shipman's novel, the Curwood figure and his wife arrive at the production location, where Shipman sets both the script meeting and the hair-tackling scene. Shipman describes their demeanour:

> The [wife] wore a neat cloth skirt, a short fur coat, overshoes and kid gloves. Her husband followed her ... He was busy picking his way along the slippery trail and Joyce [Nell] had time to note that he wore low shoes and rubbers and that his overcoat, turned up at the collar, was a fashionable grey ... The little man in the grey overcoat barely reached above her shoulder. He looked strong, lean and lithe enough and his features, so much as could be seen in the shadow of his tall sealskin cap with the tied-down earflaps, were aquiline and of a New England cast. He spoke through thin lips and did not smile.
>
> 'Are you coming, Richard [the fictional name for Curwood]?' the pretty little wife, with the wide, serious dark eyes, called from the sled where she was already sitting, adjusting a fur robe about her knees.[20]

This is Shipman's fictional introduction of the author whom she had admired so greatly until their meeting. She had expected him to be intelligent, literate, and manly. 'Instead he was an egoist, a hen-pecked little husband – in rubbers!' She came to re-evaluate Curwood's work 'to see the stereotyped hand of the cheap and popular hack behind the wordy pages.'[21]

Genre

As an independent producer, director, writer, and star of her own films, as well as a writer of articles and autobiographical novels, Shipman worked consistently in the realm of genre and formulaic sequels. One of her earliest projects in her film career, for example, was a series of two-reelers that she wrote for Universal called *Under the Crescent* (1915), which put actress Ola Humphrey 'through a series of nerve-shattering adventures.'[22] She adds that the scripts for *Crescent* 'were used as patterns for some time to come.'[23] From *God's Country and the Woman* (1916), she went on to *Back to God's Country* (1919), the earliest extant document of her work, and then to *The Girl from God's Country* (1921). Had she not gone bankrupt, my guess is that she would have made as many of these sequels as the market would bear.

In her encyclopedic study of an Italian woman director of the silent era, Giuliana Bruno charts a remarkably similar history to that of Nell Shipman in her examination of the career of Elvira Notari (1875–1946).[24] Like Shipman, Notari was eclipsed in the pages of history by her husband, whose name remains as the owner of their company; like Shipman, she churned out commercial genre films in many modes, which were self-distributed; she repeated her efforts with sequels and remakes to the limit of the market; her films were censored and she was bankrupted by the shift to sound and the formation of the large centrally based studios; and her cinema was derided as artisanal, inferior in production values, and melodramatically old-fashioned.

There is one interesting and formative difference, however, between the work of Shipman and Notari: the differing formations of regionality in their work. One of the factors in the impulse towards centralization and the standardization process that Bruno cites as instrumental in Notari's eclipse was an act of subjugation vis-à-vis the hegemonic culture. In filmic terms, this took shape as an opposition to regional film-making in favour of the cinema of 'super-spectacle,' which emphasized historical and literary epics as a founding myth for the establishment of Italy as a nation, tracing a 'spectacular' history of unity back to the Roman Empire. The 'birth of a nation' – for Italy was configured as such only in 1861 – and of a national cinema continued into the fascist era, wherein the images of force, the mythology of heroism, petit-bourgeois ideals of unity, projections of national stability, and an interclass cohesion and harmony were geared to manufacture national consent. 'There was little room in such a world view for regional, differential, and artisanal cinematic modes,' writes Bruno.[25]

Many features of such a topography were common to the American cinematic milieu in which Shipman worked. The founding myths of a nation were also a staple of the Hollywood hegemony, from Griffith to Ford, Capra, and Hawks, and included the heroic biopics of the forties, such as the many remakes of the Abraham Lincoln story, the co-optation by the United States of Alexander Graham Bell (whose Canadian context was excised from the 1939 film starring Don Ameche), and even the cleansing of Cole Porter, whose homosexuality was ellided in the biopic that presented him as a founder of an indigenous American culture.[26]

However, rather than the suppression of regionalism that Bruno notes in Italy, the American cinema celebrated the enormous geographical differences that the United States encompassed. Genres took shape around geographical areas that gave rise to specific characters, types of events, and historical references: gangster films differentiated between Chicago and New York; westerns set in Montana or Texas featured not only different landscapes but different characters and social issues; and the Midwest became the twilight zone of more domestic moral dilemmas featuring invasions from the big city or from outer space. Regionality then functioned as an adjunct to the founding mythology of a hegemonic nation, celebrating the commonalities among regions in constructing individual heroism, frontiersmanship, and the vast melting pot carved out of the varieties of rugged terrains to be conquered and civilized.

In contrast to the geo-political imaginary community of the United States, indeed participating in its creation from the margins, Canada came to function in the narration of America as its outside or beyond. From the earliest days of cinema and throughout the thirties, forties, and fifties, the far-flung wilderness of Canada remained in the popular

American imaginary as an exotic other, a kind of wilderness paradise. As opposed to the lawless western frontier or the sun-baked California desert, Canada was consistently represented as the land of forests and lakes, ice and snow. Animals and humankind co-existed there in bucolic harmony, and villainy was always quelled either by the red-coated Mounties, who always got their man, or by the solitary hero enlisting the local animals for his or her assistance.

In his filmography of Canada and Canadians in feature films, Ian K. Easterbrook lists over thirty feature films after 1930 that were set in the Canadian Northwest;[27] the literary popularity of Jack London, Zane Grey, and James Oliver Curwood ensured about the same number before that time. Although these numbers are not great, given that Hollywood produced up to five hundred features per year in this period, nevertheless the longevity of the genre indicates its continuing hold on the popular imaginary. This is the terrain that Shipman's productions occupied throughout her producing career and that later productions by others continued, including many films based on Curwood's wilderness novels, the hypotexts of Shipman's 'God's country' films.

Consistently occupying precisely the generic terrain of melodramatic adventure films, Shipman's films were always set in Canada – 'God's Country' – in a northern wilderness landscape. As in other genres that use spatial metaphors to exhibit their trajectories of meaning, such as road movies or city films, the film titles include spatial references to indicate the location or origin of events.[28] The seasonal atmosphere – rarely specified in the titles – is more or less constant: winter. The phrase 'the great white north' was used in an intertitle in Shipman's *Back to God's Country*, and the phrase has remained a popular signifier of the Canadian landscape to this day. The historical period evoked is usually that of the gold rush or fur trade, with an occasional evocation of the building of the railroad.

The population that inhabits this historical landscape is marked by predictable generic characters: the Mounties, of course, along with the villains who sometimes masquerade as Mounties; the Inuit, Indians, and Metis; the usually villainous French Canadians; various minor characters who work in the trading posts or on the ships and railroads; and the occasional foreign immigrant. The social anatomy of the films is thus also territorial: the sparsely populated and geophysically hostile wilderness produces a marked fissure between inside, the melodramatic milieu of women, and outside, the terrain of adventure for men, heroes, and outlaws. We can see a socio-sexual parallel between the geography of the wilderness and the topographies of narrative in this genre, which organizes a particular spatial itinerary and social anatomy.

Ian K. Easterbrook's valuable filmography lists keywords under which these films can be categorized, and those keywords provide a topo-analysis of the generic features of the wilderness and Northwest films: Alaska Highway, Arctic, bank robbers, Canadian Pacific Railway, criminals, dancehalls, doctors, dogs, escape, French-Canadians, fur trade, gold, horses, Indians, Inuit, Klondike, lumber trade, miners, mounted police, murder, Northwest, outlaws, pioneers, prospectors, Rocky Mountains, ships, smuggling, thieves, trading posts, trappers, Yukon. In terms of narrative conventions, salient features are the scenes of bucolic bliss featuring harmony between humans and wild animals, an initial crisis often precipitated by a villain disguised as a Mountie, cruel treatment by the villain of an animal who will become a hero of the film, and the climactic chase by dogsled over the frozen tundra. These are melodramatic adventure films in which characters are generically constituted: villainy is spontaneous and unmotivated; minor characters can be co-opted or incapacitated without a flicker of resistance; femininity is virtuous and displays essentialist connections to nature; and heroism is untainted by anxiety, self-reflection, physical weakness, or fatigue.

Historiography

Even in a period of transition and transformation, doxas rise up fast and sharp. It is already apparent in academic film scholarship that there are limited reasons for approaching an historical text. Tom Gunning allows that 'analysis of the individual film provides a sort of laboratory for testing the relation between history and theory. It is at the level of the specific film that theory and history converge, setting up the terms of analysis. We could even say that the individual text stands as a challenge to both theoretical and historical discourse, revealing the stress points in each as they attempt to deal with the scandal of the actuality of a single work as opposed to the rationality of a system.'[29] He suggests further that we should be looking for specific nodal issues – 'the way individual works can transform aesthetic norms, not simply actualize them.' Another possible scholarly motive is to 'reveal the individual texts as contradictory and dynamic.'[30] He goes on to say:

> An historical textual reading uncovers the conflict still alive and wriggling throughout the film itself, as modes of discourse continue to struggle for dominance in our reception of the film. [Thus] an historical analysis of a text does not simply dissolve it into its positivistically discernable elements ... but into its processes of production and reception ... What [historical readings] undertake is more than a placing of a text into an historical context. The context itself is seen as a field of conflicting discourses and the dynamic of the text derives from this complex genesis. Therefore historical textual analysis demands more than micro-analyses. The analyst must establish the clash of discourses that surround the text.[31]

Sandy Flitterman-Lewis is equally firm in her notions of what feminist film historiography and a history of feminist filmmaking would entail. 'A feminist cinema must necessarily conceive its challenge textually,' she declares. A feminist filmmaker, she goes on, must understand the entire cinematic apparatus, including the fact that the apparatus is designed to produce and maintain its hold on the spectator by mobilizing pleasure through the interlocking systems of narrative, continuity, point of view, and identification.[32] A history of feminist cinema, therefore, will construct that history in terms of textual resistance to the dominant mode.[33]

Flitterman-Lewis has chosen her exemplary filmmakers wisely: Germaine Dulac, for example, who worked in France during the same period as Shipman was working in America, operated within an intellectual, political, and aesthetic milieu in which she was able to work consciously as a feminist. A writer as well, Dulac theorized in her own terms the necessity to deconstruct the dominant model, emphasizing the materiality of the cinematic signifier versus the conventions of narrative causality and visual continuity of the traditional cinema. In short, Dulac precisely suits Flitterman-Lewis's historiographical prescription.[34] No 'negotiated' reading is required here, for we have 'the clash of discourses' in full battle mode in these consciously 'oppositional' texts.

The case of Nell Shipman is not so amenable to such readings. Far from oppositional to the dominant mode, Shipman was scratching her career out of the wilderness, trying her best to compete in that dominant commercial cinema. In the barren lands of northern Alberta, she was well out of earshot of 'the clash of discourses.' The attempts of Shipman, the controller of the cinematic discourse, 'to originate the representation of her own desire'[35] map almost exactly onto patriarchal configurations of femininity – Freud's 'normal' woman, and loving it. Shipman's is not a cinema that poses 'the difference of women's filmmaking'[36] but one that plunks its ample derriere firmly on its generic base.

In Shipman's films we find, a fortiori, a patriarchal, non-oppositional construction of femininity. Shipman's character includes an intuitive rapport with animals and nature that functions as constitutive of feminine subjectivity and emphasizes an unproblematized heterosexuality. This sexuality features a closeness to and unclaustrophobic comfort in her own body that is displayed with at least moderately exhibitionist gusto. The heterosexual feminine body on display is accompanied perforce with an acknowledgment of its potential victimization due to the spontaneous lust that in such melodramas is constitutive of villainous subjectivity. We find something approaching hysteria, madness, even stupidity, in the almost pathological femininity of the Shipman character. For my contemporary students, Shipman/Dolores in *Back to God's Country* represents everything that as feminists they deplore in a woman.

Furthermore, she makes absolutely no attempt to 'restore the marks of cinematic enunciation so carefully elided by patriarchal cinema.'[37] It's a bit embarrassing, really. Here I find myself identifying with Irit Rogoff's 'scholastic mortification' upon finding that her subject, 'a woman whom [she] had constructed in [her] mind as an autonomous female artist, a feminized version of the masculine participant in the heroic avant-garde project of the pre-war years' was in fact replete with 'thoroughly conventional bourgeois anguish.'[38] Putting aside any shadow of 'scholastic mortification,' I intend to argue here that it is within the terms not only of conventional narrative cinema but also of conventional patriarchal definitions of gender that Nell Shipman's work defines heroic femininity.

Femininity and Nature

In her autobiography, Shipman offers her down-to-earth, pragmatic analysis of her first encounter with Brownie the bear:

> Big Brownie was my first wild animal encounter on camera unattended by keepers, guns, wire, whips or cages. At Vitagraph I'd handled sled-dogs but now I was acting with a free, large bear who might bite, hug or merely swat. She reared, put an arm about my waist, drew me close, gave me a tentative sniff, then licked my cheek, pushed me gently aside and dropped to the ground at my feet. While I relaxed in her embrace I knew my theory was okay, and that it was a fifty-fifty deal between human and animals. Had there been a seedling of fear in me I would have felt it sprout, recognized alarm or a least a faint quiver of concern. It could lie in the deepest, darkest thought-cell but would communicate. It simply was not there. All about us and within us was serene, untroubled, unquestioned. No personal bravery in this, just a fact of communication.[39]

Shipman's femininity is in part defined by and through such intuitive connections with animals and nature. This was a feature of the Shipman character not only in the Curwood adaptations, but in her own independent productions as well. In *Trail of the North Wind* (1923), for example, the construction of feminine subjectivity hinges on communication with animals of all kinds. Montages and tableaux exhibiting the wild animals and Shipman's communication with them are trademarks of her films, and her work with animals and the natural settings of her films were among their chief commercial features. In *Abandoned Trails* she notes that 'a picture lacking Brownie in a leading part would invite failure.'[40]

Back to God's Country, for many years the only feature film of Shipman's that was known, includes the most excessive of all the displays of human–animal communication. In an early scene, Dolores (played by Shipman) lolls about in erotic play with Brownie the bear, nuzzling her snout and tweaking her ears, as skunks, squirrels, raccoons, and baby foxes cavort about her. This is the epitome of life in God's country, representing a paradisiacal vision of interspecies love and harmony.

Although William K. Everson complains of *The Grub-Stake* (1923) that 'Midway through the film, its narrative comes to a virtual halt when

Nell Shipman and Brownie the bear in the backyard, Highland Park (1920).

Shipman's character discovers a Disneyesque hidden valley, shares a cave with a bear, and communes with nature and wild animals for a reel or two,'[41] I would argue that such moments of intransitive display are central to the Shipman oeuvre. They become generic elements equivalent to the star turns in Fred Astaire or Gene Kelly musicals, functioning pivotally in the construction of the central persona as ego ideal. And just as in Astaire or Kelly films, the casual and effortless grace that marks the exhibition of the star's extraordinary capabilities indicates that such achievements are not the result of practice, effort, training, or the like, but rather innate, natural, endemic. Shipman's casual, playful relations with animals are based on an intuitive rapport that attests simultaneously to her almost superhuman heroism and to her essentialist femininity. Indeed it is such superhuman qualities – displayed with such 'natural' insouciance – that justify stardom.

In *Back to God's Country*, those two functions are aligned in the subjective split-screen shots in which Dolores longs for her forest home. The difficult technical effect seems to have been Shipman's idea:

In *Back to God's Country* we pulled a psychedelic montage out of our hats ... I was to dream of my Northwoods home and my wild animal friends. The lenseman genius, Joe Walker, went along with my notion. I claimed that people did not dream clean-cut single visions but mixtures. I wanted the wilderness inhabitants to blend in and out: here a wolf, there a bear, over in a tree a cougar, a raccoon washing his dinner in a stream, squirrels popping in and out, bobcats peering, porcupines bristling, all of them dissolving in montage against the dark background while I, at the bottom of the frame, dreamed it. It was the most difficult double-exposure ever attempted ...

There were numbers of takes, covering shots where one or no more than three animals would dissolve above my dreaming head but the topper was to have a total of twenty-eight animal characters. Starting that strip of negative it meant that at a future date, when we were on the Kern River location along with the zoo, the film would pass the aperture twenty-eight times. If you'll consider the gross area of 35 mm film mentally and cover it section by section with pin-point spaces upon which each image was to show, you've a notion of what Joe Walker was attempting. I doubt that a computer could master it today [1968]. The tiny scenes had to come in and out, not over-lapping each other but in a patchwork pattern. Anything could go wrong, a buckle, tear or miscount, Lab trouble in developing, a bad animal actor in a take – and no retakes! – Light which did not match the over-all scene, a thousand to one chances for success. But a Dream![42]

Spectacles of human–animal contact are common also to the 1946 remake, *God's Country*, and here the specifically gendered nature of the connections between humans and wild animals is comically underlined. As in Shipman's *Back to God's Country*, the love interest in Tansey's *God's Country* comes from foreign parts, perhaps even the city. He is alarmed, understandably enough, by the sight of a bear ambling casually towards him. However, less credibly and therefore comically, he's also alarmed by the little squirrel who runs up his arm. The woman protagonist laughingly introduces him to her forest friends through the cinematic device of creative geography.[43] In the parallel comic plot, Buster Keaton is harassed by a raven and a squirrel, both of whom 'help him' to cook dinner, and by a mountain lion (through creative geography) who incites the comic scene of Keaton frantically paddling the tethered canoe in an attempt to escape. In both films, it is the woman who exhibits her essentialist relations with nature through the display of intuitive connections with the animal world. In terms of genre, the narrative topography of the wilderness adventure is transformed into the domestic space of melodrama – their 'forest home' – through the woman's natural connections.

Such features are markedly absent from the 1953 *Back to God's Country*, in which the wilderness has been thoroughly masculinized and urbanized. Wild animals do not figure in the scenario at all. This is no 'forest home,' and, significantly, it is the woman who is the stranger from the city.

In addition to Shipman's technical virtuousity at the textual level of *Back to God's Country*, her extraordinary communication with the world of nature is an essential element in the constitution of heroic hyper-femininity within the narrative. Rather than the narrative coming to a virtual halt, as Everson complains, I would argue, on the contrary, that the plots of Shipman's films are very often devices constructed precisely to afford such moments of intransitive heroic display.

Femininity, Interspecies Communication, and Feminine Desire

It is in Dolores's relation with the dog that conventional definitions of femininity, here heavily inflected with an intuitive rapport with the animal/natural world, are aligned most transparently with courage and heroism. A variation on the bad dog story, *Back to God's Country* features Wapi, a fierce Great Dane who responds to the gentle touch of a woman's hand. In contrast to the relatively domestic achievements of the dogs in the later Shipman films such as *A Bear, a Boy, and a Dog* and *Trail of the North Wind*, *Back to God's Country* presents the dog Wapi (played by matching Great Danes Tresore and brother Rex) in a much more heroic mode. When the time comes for the inevitable chase and rescue, Wapi is at the woman's side. Paradoxically, such scenes define Dolores's helpless femininity, her fearless heroism, and her control of the discourse. And they define them as intertwined.

From the outset of the film, Wapi is a featured player in the events. In the heroic genealogy of the prologue, Wapi's ancestor, the Great Dane Tao, is introduced sitting quietly, gently blinking his eyes, in the first medium close-up of the film. When his master, 'the yellow man,' is killed, the huge dog is taken. The extreme close-up that introduces Wapi the Killer, the result of the cruel mistreatment of the line of Tao's descendants, contrasts tellingly with the earlier introduction of gentle Tao: in a very dynamic series of shots, Wapi foams at the mouth as he snarls and hurls himself at the camera.

Wapi's presence and consciousness are interlaced particularly throughout the intricately intercut dramatic scenes leading up to the climax, in which Wapi is instrumental. An uncanny extrasensory communication materializes between Wapi and Dolores. Before they ever meet, there is a cut from Dolores on ship to Wapi at the trading post, followed by the title, 'Like a great winged-bird the Flying Moon [the ship] brings to Wapi a strange and thrilling message from the white man's world of his forefathers.' A close-up of Wapi in vicious killer mode follows this intertitle. Again in the scene where the villain is trying to have his way with Dolores on ship, her plight is intercut equally with shots of Wapi far away across the ice and Dolores's helpless husband lying injured in his bed in the next cabin. Wapi, like her husband, senses Dolores's plight. And this is all before they meet!

The first meeting between woman and dog is instrumental in the construction of canine subjectivity and the delineation of interspecies intersubjectivity. In one of the most affecting scenes in the film,

Dolores's fearlessness and her femininity are marked by her actions and underscored by the intertitles. Dolores has decided to take matters into her own hands, and strikes out across the ice and snow to seek help at the trading post, not suspecting that it is run by a man in cahoots with the villainous ship captain who is plotting Dolores's seduction and her husband's death. Cut to Wapi snarling viciously in close-up, fighting with the other dogs. Blake, his owner, takes a whip to Wapi just as Dolores approaches. Without hesitation, she flings herself between the whip and the dog. Dolores's fearlessness and her courageous attempt to rescue the abused dog are underlined by Blake's warning: 'Look out! That dog is a devil ...' (intertitle). But as he speaks, the killer dog miraculously becomes quiet, as the intertitle – by this point in the film virtually synonymous with Shipman's discourse as enunciator – comments 'A new miracle of understanding, roused by the touch of a woman's hand.'

Joseph Walker adds an interesting footnote to this scene. The two Great Danes, Tresore and Rex, who doubled as Wapi, looked identical but had opposite temperaments. One was gentle, but the other was so savage that he had to be muzzled when not 'acting.' In the scene in which Dolores and Wapi first meet, the vicious dog was to be replaced by the gentle dog on a fast cut. Walker recounts:

> We were ready to film. The trainer led the muzzled dog into position.
>
> We started the scene. [The villain] started his beating attempt and the dog responded ferociously to this aggressive action. It became frightening to watch.
>
> We were about to cut the cameras and make the switch to the gentle dog, when Nell cried out suddenly, 'Keep the cameras going, boys! Do you hear? No matter what happens – *don't cut!*'
>
> Not knowing what to expect, Dal [Clauson, the second camera] and I kept at our steady cranking. What we saw, all but threw us off tempo.
>
> Nell rushed into the scene, protesting the driver's brutality, then threw her arms around the ferocious dog. We stared horrified; no one dared to speak. Even the trainer stood motionless, afraid to intercede. With the dog's face close to hers, Nell's lips moved as though murmuring friendly and comforting words. The dog looked her in the eye. Then slowly he lowered his head, allowing her to stroke him.[44]

Walker's anecdote extends the heroinism of Dolores's character to Shipman's real life. Tom Trusky, however, notes that Walker may not have been aware that Shipman began to befriend the dogs from the time they arrived in Calgary.[45] Nevertheless, Walker's admiration for Shipman both on and off screen is clear here.

In Shipman's *Back to God's Country*, the mutuality of the connection between the dog and the woman is underlined by a scene depicting the dog remembering or desiring: a shot of Wapi chained to a stake dissolves – signifying his thoughts – to a matching shot of Dolores at the dog's side, embracing him. That memory or wish triggers the dog's action, for he breaks his chains and follows Dolores's scent to the ship. The scene closes with an iris-in on the woman embracing the dog and kissing him on the face. This kiss signals the transformation of Wapi's status in the film. From this point in the tale, Wapi takes the position of heroic lover, the traditional function of the human male protagonist.

The central relationship of the woman protagonist with the dog is shared by the two later remakes as well, but there are telling differences in the representation of the relationship and its ramifications for the construction of the heroine. In *God's Country*, the 1946 remake, a feel-good comedy that centres on the blossoming love-interest between the woman protagonist and the attractive stranger, displacement of the bad male master by the good woman is no longer a feature, as both main characters are dog owners. Anticipating the slower development in the overarching human plot, Lynn O'Mally and Lee Preston's German shepherds come together in a parallel canine love-plot, rapidly producing a litter of cute little pups that become the subjects of a succession of intransitive scenes of sentimental spectacle. There are no killer dogs to tame in this film – indeed both shepherds epitomize harmless canine domesticity – and in contrast to the miraculous intuitive connection between the heroine and the dog in the other two films, in *God's Country* it is Preston's dog who senses – apparently from miles away – his owner's dangerous situation, running to intervene in the fight and killing the villain just in the nick of time.

The instinctive rapport between the woman and the killer dog reappears in the 1953 remake. In both Shipman's version and the 1953 Rock Hudson vehicle, virtually identical scenes depict Blake cruelly whipping the viciously lunging and snarling Wapi, followed by the intervention of the woman who heedlessly approaches the dog despite warnings that the animal is a killer. In Shipman's version, the feminine–canine connection is underlined by an intertitle, 'roused by the touch of a woman's hand,' while the 1953 film makes do with a simple close-up of the miraculously gentled beast.

Whereas human–animal communication in the 1953 version also aligns itself with essentialist femininity, Shipman's *Back to God's Country* demonstrates the connection not only between interspecies understanding and gender, but also with courageous feminine heroism. While the display of that remarkable understanding is intertextually symptomatic of Shipman as persona and star, in her *Back to God's Country*, as in most of her work, she stands for Everywoman, for she is virtually the only female character in an all-male world. The intertitle asserts that it is 'a woman's hand' – not necessarily *this* woman's hand – that promotes the animal's peace; the 'miracle of understanding' is explicitly connected to womanhood, which is by nature heroic.

The Female Protagonist as Heroic Rescuer

There are substantial similarities between the women characters that Nell Shipman created for herself and the melodramatic serial-queens of Hollywood. In the more than sixty such serials produced between 1912 and 1920, as Ben Singer points out, the singular feature of these melodramas is the emphasis on the active female heroine 'who exhibits a variety of traditionally "masculine" qualities: physical strength and endurance, self-reliance, courage, social authority, and freedom to explore novel experiences outside the domestic sphere.'[46] Like the serial queens, the character of Dolores in *Back to God's Country* is an extremely active heroine who pilots a dogsled 150 miles across the icy tundra to get her wounded husband to a doctor, physically battling the villain in the process and emerging victorious. When she is threatened with rape by the villain, an intertitle attests to her bravery and self-reliance: 'Dolores determines not to tell [her husband] but to fight out her own salvation.' An accurate markswoman with no fear of weapons, she holds the villain's accomplice at gunpoint, then shoots him in the shoulder to force him to assist her. Later she commands the sled-guide also at gunpoint. Eventually disempowered by the loss of the gun, she activates the dog as her agent, and thus effects the triumphant escape and rescue.

The woman as active, competent, courageous, and self-reliant may be found in other genres such as the western as well, but rarely is the woman the rescuer. This is the position that Shipman charts for herself (as both writer and star) in her first great vehicle, *Back to God's Country*; similar action-rescue scenarios form the plots of *Trail of the North Wind* (1923), *The Grub-Stake* (1923), and *The Light on Lookout* (1923). The construction of heroine as rescuer in these films can be seen more pointedly, in *bas relief* as it were, in comparison with a film that Shipman wrote, directed, and starred in immediately following the completion of *Back to God's Country*. In *Something New* (1920),[47] there is a sense of conscious play with the concept of heroine as rescuer as the formative narrative device of the film. The beauteous heroine (played by Shipman) is captured by banditti and spirited away to their mountain lair in Hell's Kitchen, where the outlaw leader threatens her virtue and her life. The hero, Bill (played by Shipman's lover Bert Van Tuyle), comes to rescue her – an unusual scenario for a Shipman script. The deliverance of the 'Girl' from the 'Bad Hats' is carried out with ludicrous ease. The tables are turned, however, when Bill is gratuitously wounded in the head, and the heroine must navigate them both to safety through the performance of feats of ingenuity, bravery, and skill that equal in every way those of the hero.

That this scenario is constructed around consciously ironic variations on genre conventions of the heroine is indicated by Shipman's foregrounding herself as enunciator of *Something New*: the film opens and closes with scenes of Shipman as the 'Writing Woman,' typing out her story on her Underwood machine. The last shot of the film is a close-up of Shipman laughing in delight, having pushed the typewriter off the table to end the story, and presumably to break the mould along with the machine. Ironically, Shipman brought an end neither to her own revisiting of the successful formula (for she continued the pattern in all her films after *Something New*) nor to remakes by other producers working either from Curwood's hypotext or with the generic elements that Shipman had established.

In the remakes of the God's country narratives by other producers, however, the women protagonists show little of the heroic characteristics of the Shipman model. In the later films, women are reduced to a one-dimensional functionality based solely on their feminine sexuality, operating as mere love-interest. In *God's Country* (1946), the heroine Lynn O'Mally is the niece of the trading-post operator, and she effects no functional instrumentality in the plot. Although she performs generically in relation to wilderness films, her character bears none of the marks of heroism with which Shipman's character is always inscribed.

In the 1953 remake of *Back to God's Country*, on the other hand, the woman protagonist is somewhat more functionally complex, for she is not only the potential victim of the villain's lustful designs, but she also eventually rises to the challenge of quasi-heroism to accompany her wounded husband – against his wishes – on the trek by dogsled to the next outpost. Her heroism is severely limited, however. She makes the odd decision on her own, such as to accompany her husband and to camp in a certain spot for the night, but, as in the original James Oliver Curwood story on which the screenplay is based, the real hero of the story is the dog. In both of these remakes, therefore, feminine subjectivity is constructed on the basis of generic characterology and substantially reduced in heroism from the Shipman mould.

The divergent constructions of the woman protagonist are illustrated aptly by the comparative functions of the avalanches that occur in both *Something New* and the 1953 *Back to God's Country*. In the 1953 production, the woman causes an avalanche of snow by shooting off a gun at an inappropriate moment, despite her husband's attempts to warn her. The avalanche thus functions not only as a tension-producing plot device, but also as an indication of her ignorance of the wilderness terrain. She is literally out of her element, having vacated the domestic space that is the proper sphere of the melodramatic heroine. It is only through the miracle of genre conventions that the couple is able to emerge unscathed from the mountain of snow that has descended upon them. Needless to say, no similar episode appears in Shipman's *Back to God's Country*. It would be unthinkable for a Shipman heroine to indicate such naivety about the dangers of the wilderness. Heedlessly shoot off a rifle with a huge bank of snow hanging just overhead? Never.

In *Something New*, on the other hand, the avalanche of enormous rocks is deliberately brought on by Shipman, who manages to shove a huge boulder off the cliff on which she and her lover are trapped and wipe out her villainous pursuers in a tremendously graphic climax. All of this occurs as the male protagonist stands helplessly aside. This avalanche, therefore, functions instrumentally in the construction of the woman protagonist as the rescuer and hero, underlining her understanding of the wilderness terrain ('the Land that God forgot' [intertitle]), her clear-headed ingenuity under pressure, and her capability in handling the new technology at her command – the Maxwell auto, which, incidentally, is anthropomorphized as feminine in the promotional intertitles.

In the serial-queen melodramas, in addition to the exposition of Amazonian prowess, Ben Singer notes another representational strain involving the lurid victimization of the heroine by the male villains. In 'perhaps a third of the genre,' the serial-queen films 'amplify an extremely graphic spectacle of female distress, helplessness and abject terror ... The heroine is systematically assaulted, bound and gagged, hurled out windows or off bridges, terrorized by instruments of torture and dismemberment, and threatened with innumerable means of assassination.'[48]

Singer emphasizes two distinct conventions within the genre: woman as powerful in some examples and as defenceless victims in others. The construction of feminine subjectivity in Shipman's scenarios is complex rather than generically one-dimensional, however, for it is inscribed not only with her customary Amazonian heroism, but cross-hatched with melodramatic feminine helplessness as well. Moments of vulnerability may ramp up the tension for a moment or two, but heroic capability always prevails in the end. Nor is heroism achieved at the expense of conventional normative femininity, for Shipman's character always gets everything she wants: heroic achievement, love with a suitable partner, and a sweet little baby – with mood-enhancing log cabin.

Is the Nude Rude?

In Shipman's *Back to God's Country*, the construction of feminine subjectivity not only operates upon Shipman's intuitive communication with animals and nature, but this natural connection is also relayed to a level of unaffected heroic corporeality. As a character and as a star, Shipman doffs the fetters of ladylike decorum, to cavort not only in nature, but *au naturel*.

The famous nude scene, which was fully capitalized upon in advertisements for *Back to God's Country*, cannot be explained away by the usual relations of economic and sexual exploitation that are rebuked by contemporary 'no nudity' clauses in the more powerful female stars' contracts. Diegetically and extra-textually, this is one of the scenes that again defines Dolores/Shipman's femininity through a closeness to her body, and through essentialist connections to nature. Those elements are also inextricably linked to a fearless rejection of social hypocrisy that brooks no moral outrage and to Shipman's own control of the cinematic discourse as enunciator.

As Dolores is bathing in a glorious mountain pool, the villains leer at her through the bushes and hatch their dastardly plan. The scene originally functioned, in Shipman's script, to convey a simple definition of the elements of femininity, situating Dolores firmly within nature as the essentialist landscape of feminine subjectivity and constructing the conditions of generic craven villainy. The scene was first shot with Shipman wearing a modest flesh-coloured wool bathing costume. After the first take, however, when she saw the wet thick wool bunch and wrinkle about her body, Shipman firmly stepped in, shedding the costume and directing the cinematographer so that the mise en scène would invite no prurience while still making her unadorned flesh amply evident. For the period, the gesture indicated a sense of easeful corporeal display at a time when melodramatic heroines were marked by Gish-like modesty and nudity appeared in films only in scenes of epic debauchery. Shipman seems to have been proud of the scene. In her autobiography she suggests that they were conscious of their daring in constructing the scene 'which might not be used since we now lived under the firm thumb of the Will Hays office and didn't crack blue jokes.'[49] Her characteristic sense of humour prevails as she notes that, because Brownie is with her by the pool, she privately captioned the scene 'In a Dark Pool with a Bear Behind.' She adds proudly, 'I know that a beautiful foreign import [Hedy Lamarr] was photographed in the nude in a feature called *Ecstasy* but I really was "first."'[50]

The historical spectator's readings of the scene, like our own, would be guided by inscriptions of Dolores's virtue, her 'naturalness,' and her femininity, sustained diegetically and semiotically from the early scenes of the film. In addition, the movie was advertised with posters featuring a drawing of Shipman pulling a shawl across her evidently naked body as she stood knee-deep in water. In the trade papers, the promotion was even more explicit, featuring a sketch of a naked female body arching lyrically on tip-toe, with this advice to exhibitors: 'Don't Book "Back to God's Country" unless You want to prove that the Nude is NOT Rude.'[51] Thus the historical spectators' readings would be affected by the inter-penetration of the textual with the extra-textual (the promotion and advertising strategies). Such intertextuality invites a reading that invokes a provocative challenge to the constraints of contemporary mores about the display of women's bodies. It also ascribes a forthrightness, fearless-ness, and control of the discourse to Shipman herself as enunciator and star.

Although it is not uncommon today to think of women who lived a century ago as hopelessly encrusted in outmoded attitudes – they must have been straight-laced, prudish, and sexually repressed – Shipman's autobiography and her autobiographical novel paint a very different picture. She represents herself as sexually experienced without any recriminations or slurs of being a 'loose woman.' In *Abandoned Trails*, for example, she presents her extramarital relationship with Bert Van Tuyle as belonging to the world of nature, as natural as the flowers in May. The novel segues dramatically from a scene with her husband to a new chapter in which a lyrical description of poppies, lupins, willows and 'fire-tipped' pines introduces the illicit lovers 'Dirk and Joyce' in a prone embrace among the wildflowers. In a later chapter, which returns to the same scene, the whole world of nature seems to celebrate their love affair. As they lie in the poppies and lupins, the river seems to sing to them: 'Life is a river! Love is a river! Follow both, fast and faster! Man and Woman, never alone! Hand in hand, like the river running with the sky in its breast, like the white clouds floating in the blue water!'[52] As the river sings to them, Shipman asserts her own sexuality and sexual desire: 'She felt the warm, deep throb of his being as surely as she knew the pulsing of the earth whereon they rested, and she was aware that her own desire beat in rhythm with both.'[53]

In the same scene, the lovers discuss marital arrangements. Joyce (Nell) confesses that her marriage (to Ernest Shipman) was 'nothing but a ladder' designed to put her 'over the top' in show business, and that her husband had not only been well aware of the basis for their partnership, but also had given her '"moral" freedom.' She recalls 'the affairs that had sweetened the years since she first found out that marrying [Ernest] meant playing a concubine in a glorified, if geographically scattered, harem.' She describes her own extramarital sexual liaisons with another 'natural' metaphor: 'Swiftly passing "affairs" these had been. Light love, easily given, easily retracted. Carving no groove they fled like the river over its shallows; riffling the pebbles but lacking strength or will to move them from its course.'[54]

Joyce agrees to divorce her husband, now that her parents are gone. Dirk, however, is encumbered with a wife 'back East' who is content with their separation but would not grant a divorce. To this news Joyce's response rings with the free thought of modernity: 'I am so damn sick of the words "marriage" and "divorce." They are so empty. What have words to do with love like ours?'[55] Later in the novel, despite her legal husband's assertion that 'he did not give a damn about staying married to her, he only resented the loss of the business he had built up about her,' for some reason he gives her a hard time about the divorce, suddenly turning 'prudish and pretend[ing] the role of an outraged husband.' Warned by her lawyer that she must wait a year before another marriage, Joyce responds, 'I don't believe in marriage.' Reflecting on 'the easy grinding of the Los Angeles divorce mill,' she asserts to Dirk that 'Every moment we are together marries us that much more and it would take more than the snappy decision of a bored Judge to divorce us!'[56]

To some degree Shipman ascribes her modernist comfort with sexuality and casual sexual relations to her experience in theatre and show business, where an 'unstarched laxity existed. Joyce thought how many boys there were ... who could say they had seen her in bed, held her hand, kissed her, buttoned her dress, tied her shoes.'[57] In vaudeville and the movie industry, it seems that sexual libertarianism was an everyday feature. Extramarital affairs, sexual promiscuity among both men and women, homosexuality and lesbianism were routinely laundered in studio publicity,[58] and the instauration of the Hays office in 1922 indicates the lengths to which the major studios had to go to revive conformative morality, at least at a public level. Like Frances Marion, who enjoyed heterosexual relations with many partners and scoffed at the stuffiness of her best friend, Mary Pickford (even though Pickford had begun her affair with Douglas Fairbanks while they were both married to other people),[59] Shipman equates prudery with philistinism, admits she likes 'good, clean dirt; yarns as homely and natural as the sod,' and laments 'How long it had been since she'd heard a smutty story!'[60]

An example both of Shipman's lack of prudery and of her control of the cinematic discourse is recounted fictionally in *Abandoned Trails*, in which it becomes apparent that Bert Van Tuyle was not such a free-thinker. At the premiere of their latest film, Dirk reacts with jealousy to an old friend's congratulatory pat on Joyce's knee. Dirk's jealousy quickly escalates into a quarrel, in which Dirk, watching the scene in which Joyce kisses the leading man in close-up, remembers the circum-stances of shooting the scene: 'Dirk remembered his own curt com-mand to "cut!" when this scene was being made. There was a fade-out on the end of it and the make-believe lovers kept on kissing right to the last camera click. "Why?" he had demanded angrily, later, in Joyce's dressing room. "Didn't I yell 'cut'?" "Yes," she said, brazenly, as open-eyed and innocent as an angel, "sure you did, but I hate to see the slight-est movement from the actors during a fade-out. It spoils the feeling of the scene."'[61]

Van Tuyle was an outsider to show business, Shipman explains: 'Poor Dirk could not understand the quick, meaningless kisses of fellow actors, no warmer than laymen's handshakes, sprayed on the sudden breeze of convivial re-union and forgotten the next instant.'[62] Van Tuyle's jealousy and sexual prudery remained grievous problems for Shipman, and the seeds of the demise of their relationship are sown in the first third of the novel. She sees his 'crude narrowness' as 'tiresome and stupid,' and tells him so.[63]

Shipman's modernist defiance of social convention carries over into the sexual spontaneity of Dolores's character in *Back to God's Country* and is underscored by her robust and artless physical informality.

Natives and Others

In all three God's country films, the narrative topography is intertwined with the landscape not only as the locus of the action but also through relations with its indigenous inhabitants, who function in the construc-tion of generic feminine or masculine heroism and/or villainy. As the decades progress, we can trace an increasing objectification and vilification of the indigenous characters in the three extant paratexts.

From a contemporary perspective, Shipman's *Back to God's Country* is marred by the quotidian racism of her era. Terms such as 'esquimaux,' 'half-breed,' and 'Yellow Man' (for a Chinese immigrant) are applied in intertitles apparently without conscious reflection. This was the common parlance of the period, as can also be seen in D.W. Griffith's *Broken Blossoms* (1919), in which, despite Griffith's avowed intentions of presenting the Asian protagonist sympathetically, Cheng Huan is referred to in the same way and called 'Chinkie' by other characters. Gina Marchetti points out that a 'deep-rooted hatred of the Chinese [was] prevalent in the American popular media since the mid-nineteenth century.'[64] However, Shipman aligns herself as enunciator (through the verbal textual elements, the intertitles) and as character (through the actions of the heroine Dolores) with a progressive anti-racism that sets her apart from the brutish attitudes of the white male villains.

In all three versions of the film the function of relations with the indigenous inhabitants of the wilderness landscape, the Inuit and other Native characters, is equally instrumental. In *Back to God's Country*, Shipman introduces a scene of her own invention – the episode does not appear in Curwood's hypotext – the only scene in the film in which Dolores connects with another woman. The sailors on the *Flying Moon* have brought some 'eskimo guests' on board, and the quotation marks of the intertitle ironically underscore the racism and sexism of the rapacious designs of the white men. The enunciative apparatus of the intertitles – equivalent to Shipman's authorial voice – decries such exploitation through the use of sarcastic comments aimed at the exploitative ruffians. Nevertheless, ideological discrepancies abound in this scene. For one thing, the Inuit women are played for comedy in scenes of them marvelling at a modern invention, the phonograph, and chomping into bars of Fels Naptha soap with great appetite. However, in an escalating imbrication of contradictions and an abrupt shift of tone from comedy to melodramatic virtue in peril, the heroine Dolores lashes out in protest and attempts to rescue an Inuit woman from the unwanted sexual advances of one of the sailors. The staging, action, and mise en scène of this episode mark it as a melodramatic statement of

Dolores's character: her high moral intentions and her anti-racist and proto-feminist impulses, along with women's generic vulnerability.

Neither of the later versions evince such 'progressive' – albeit mitigated – attitudes towards the indigenous population. The 1946 remake of *God's Country* stands as a transitional marker between the 1919 and 1953 versions of *Back to God's Country* in the representation of the Native inhabitants of the narrative topography and their relations with the central characters. Here we have *a fortiori* the stereotypical 'good Indians,' speaking painfully comic pidgin English, dressed in buckskin suits with feathers in their hair, and accompanied by devoted silent wives and dusky little children with stereotypical 'Indian' names such as Little Eagle and White Cloud. The 1946 'good Indians' dwell in the forest surrounding the trading post run by the heroine Lynn O'Mally and her good-hearted elderly uncle. Although, historically, the trading posts that were established by the Hudson's Bay Company throughout the Canadian Northwest exploited, corrupted, and infected the indigenous population, in *God's Country* the individualist entrepreneurs are the 'friends' of the Natives, and it is this historical inaccuracy that the male love-interest from the city must learn, with all attendant sentimental comedy. As the ecological subplot spins out, all four sets of characters – the Native families, the animals, the trading-post operators, and the urban stranger with his comic guides – must come together (to the swelling strains of 'Only God Can Make a Tree' on the soundtrack) to preserve their Canadian forest paradise from avaricious loggers.

The 1953 version reverses both the relations with the Inuit characters and the racism/anti-racism of the subtext of Shipman's 1919 original. In the later film, the Inuit characters, both men and women, are in league with the villain Blake, and conspire at his bidding to sabotage the heroic couple. They are clearly not only at Blake's command, but they have been co-opted to his villainous position. Blake's woman servant, for example (who looks more Mexican than Inuit or Native, in an off-the-shoulder peasant blouse, smouldering eyes, and long black curly hair), offers sexual favours along with a tray of canapes. The other Inuit characters, who lie, give false directions, and misuse their superior knowledge of the landscape and technology (placing magnets in the sled to impede the hero's compass), are simply Blake's abject lackeys, and, as such, neither have connection to the heroic couple nor call on the spectator's sympathies. Like the 'good Indians' of the 1946 paratext, the 1953 indigenous characters are represented as more or less simple-minded and specifically morally inferior not only to the stalwart protagonist couple but also to their employer, Blake, whose villainous designs are consciously acknowledged as the articulation of his own individual will.

While Dolores struggles valiantly in Shipman's version, sisterhood is not powerful enough, and both women are overcome. Dolores will live to save her own virtue and her husband's life, but she cannot change the Inuit woman's destiny. Although she is ineffectual in her attempt to save the Inuit women, who are ridiculed and raped by the men on ship, it is in these moments that Shipman's patriarchally defined femininity slips from the bonds of mere historical curiousity, and bespeaks an anti-racist and proto-feminist heroism that reaches out of the past directly into current feminist debates. It is Dolores's progressive femininity, marked here as a doubled difference of gender and ideology, with which we can finally identify.

Hysteria at the Climax

The climax of Shipman's film depends upon a two-step relay of negative and positive elements, hysterical and heroic forms of femininity. Dolores is mushing across the arctic landscape, her injured husband laid out in the sled, while the villain is in hot pursuit with his dog team. At one moment, for no earthly reason, Dolores drops the revolver and leaves it behind. The text jeers with an insert: MCU (medium close-up) gun up to its handle in snow.

Here we have a moment of the type we used to find with such glee in the classic realist text, that instance of overdetermination, when the ideological imperative overcomes narrative plausibility, the text is fissured, and a moment of spectator alienation breaks the hold of narrative continuity. It is the moment when everyone groans. That groan signals a recognition of the discursive pressures upon the woman protagonist to be scatterbrained, incompetent, and stupid, conforming to a patriarchal stereotype of hysterical femininity. And they groan again only a few seconds later when, as if to underline the patriarchal operations of the text, the invalid husband briefly rouses himself to say

'Dolores, give me the gun' (intertitle). In close-up, Dolores responds by hanging her head in shame. Here we have the quintessentially feminine moment, the moment beyond language, when words have left her, and her only response is the purely affective language of emotion. It is, as Catherine Clement writes, a 'losing song; it is femininity's song.'[65] In Irit Rogoff's terms, Dolores is here 'the site of uncertainty, ambiguity, and disorientation.'[66]

In Shipman's text, however, that moment beyond language is simultaneously the woman's moment of shame and the instance of the spectator's recognition of the overdetermining operations of the narrative in the construction of femininity. 'Here we can perceive the need for negotiations between contradictory forces,' writes Rogoff,[67] and for Tom Gunning, we find that de rigueur clash of discourses, alive and wriggling across the text. It is at this moment, and out of the very depths of the damages that such an overdetermined femininity has produced, not only upon the character of Dolores but also upon narrative plausibility, that the climax of the film is constructed.

Wapi, taking up the traditional melodramatic function of the human male protagonist as heroic lover, must rescue the imperilled heroine. As the chase begins, a title indicates that Wapi's 'hour of destiny is at hand.' Close-ups of Wapi are intercut with shots of Dolores worrying and the villain approaching in this high-speed chase by dogsled, a scene rivaled in its quintessential Canadianness only by the canoe chase in Joyce Wieland's *The Far Shore* (1975). A title pierces the dog's consciousness: 'Sensing the swift approaching menace of the men and beasts he hates.' Cut to a close-up of Wapi and Dolores. A few minutes after Dolores's moment of shame, a still photo of Wapi in close-up forms the uncharacteristic figurative background to the generic title 'Her Last Hope,' dramatically marrying signifier and signified in one image underlining the relation of feminine desire to the animal subject.

This rather complex relay of interspecies desire, it must be recalled, is the creation of the woman screenwriter and star. The dog, then, in the expression of its desire, must be seen as the representation of the excessive desire of femininity, a transgressive desire that exceeds the capacity for satisfaction through relations with the woman's human lover/husband.

As Wapi runs off to attack the dogs pulling the villain's sled, an intertitle intones: 'Fighting at last the greatest of all his fights – for a Woman.' Once again, the enunciative apparatus draws the connection between the feminine and the heroic action; the dog at its most heroic functions merely as the agent of the woman's desire. And once again – thank goodness – we have that welcome clash of discourses. On the one hand, the narrative and specifically generic demands for an action climax overdetermine the woman's helplessness in the scenario; on the other, the discursive connections that previously have been established between the woman, the animal, and essential femininity produce her as the controlling agent in the action. It is due to her intrinsic qualities as a woman – including her hysteria and helplessness – that she can command the obedience of this heretofore untamable beast.

The dog's attack on the villain's sled features in the 1953 remake as well, with equally telling ramifications for the construction of feminine heroism. Through the divergent representations of the dog's climactic attack on the villain, the differences between Shipman's heroine and the 1953 female protagonist are diegetically marked.

The long prologue to Shipman's text, setting out the genealogy of the canine protagonist, is crucial in this regard. In *Back to God's Country* (1919), as in Curwood's short story, a Chinese immigrant wanders into a frontier bar with his companion, the magnificent Great Dane Tao. In a scene of callous and gratuitous racism, the 'Yellow Man' is murdered. Wapi the killer dog is the psychically deformed descendant of the captured and abused Tao.

The rhetorical flourishes of the prologue establish the intertitles as central to the enunciative apparatus of the film, which stand for Shipman's authorial voice. These titles shirk neither moral attitude nor affective sympathy as they tell this tale. At the outset of the film, then, Shipman as enunciator distances herself firmly from those white men, and the marks of that difference are found not only in gender but also in attitudes of racism or anti-racism. Though we may criticize the Orientalism of the treatment of the Chinese man – Shipman's feminization of him as ultra-sensitive and vulnerable, spiritually and socially superior, as well as more aesthetically pleasing – nevertheless the high moral tone of the prologue and intertitles indicates a consciously progressive anti-racist platform.

In contrast, the 1953 remake retains only a trace of this raced genealogy, and that trace marks only one brief – though crucially functional –

narrative moment, the dog's climactic attack on the villain. Whereas in Shipman's version, Dolores commands the dog to attack the villain, thus transforming him into the instrumental agent of her heroic determination, the 1953 version faithfully follows Curwood's hypotext, in which Wapi 'thinks' and somehow remembers the cruel treatment of his ancestor Tao. In the 1953 film, Wapi's memory is jogged by the sight of a small Chinese shrine in the middle of nowhere, and this trace of his atavistic past charges him to seek his own revenge on the murderous Blake, allowing the fleeing couple to achieve the happy ending of the film. No explanation of the significance of the shrine is offered in the 1953 film, for the prologue has been excised; only the deployment of cinematic language (point-of-view shots and montage) links the dog's encounter with the shrine in a causative relation with his attack on Blake. With the male protagonist rendered helpless by his injury and the female protagonist helpless simply by nature of her femininity, the dog emerges as hero of his own volition rather than as the agent of the female protagonist's heroic attributes. Thus, the narrative topos of the later film can be variously read in its traces of intertextuality. While motivating Wapi's attack on Blake with greater complexity than mere revenge for past physical abuse, at the same time the narrative twist also strips the 1953 version of the progressive anti-racist textual elements that the 1919 original foregrounded.

In the reworkings of the God's country scenario, we can see a progressive paratextual depletion of the female protagonist's heroic attributes in relation to the climactic narrative moments involving the instrumental agency of the dog. In *God's Country*, the dog responds to his master's plight, situating the male protagonist as central and evacuating the female protagonist from the heroic equation altogether. In the 1953 remake, the dog acts as the agent of his own psychic agenda, effectively reactivating Curwood's hypotext of the generic heroic dog story, with similar results for the construction of the woman. In Shipman's original, in contrast, the dog attacks at Dolores's bidding, substantiating her claim to central heroic status.

God's Country

Shipman's heroism is intricately bound to the landscape on which the narrative is played out. Her wilderness skills – driving the dog team, shooting a gun, navigating the route – are matched by her strength and endurance, necessary qualities for heroism in the fierce conditions of the Canadian north.

Shipman's *Back to God's Country* was shot almost entirely on location in northern Alberta. Although *The Silent Screen and My Talking Heart* recounts the bare bones of the production adventures,[68] *Abandoned Trails* fleshes out the details considerably. They travelled by train to Lesser Slave Lake – the middle of nowhere, about 150 miles north of Edmonton. There was no train station, no hotel, just a 'snow-drift.'[69] The village was 'nothing but a collection of fishermen's shacks on the shore of an ice-bound lake.' The cabins had stoves and blankets, but you could 'chuck a cat through the cracks' and the snow came drifting in.[70] The dining hall was 'an unpainted board shack with a long table running its length. The table was made of three planks and the benches were single boards. At the opposite end from the door a cook stove was presided over by a fat-faced Chinaman, clad in a black overcoat. His mattress was unfolded near the stove and the bedding showed signs of recent occupancy ... A lamp with a sooty chimney hung near him and a larger one was suspended over the table. Boxes of supplies lined the walls but, in the dreary half-light, even these signs of grub-to-be failed to lift the gloom.'[71] To this desolate and numbingly cold location the Hollywood director's wife had packed formal evening clothes!

Shipman's autobiography reports that they shot one scene, in which Dolores 'mushed endless camera miles across the frozen waste,' in temperatures of sixty below. They 'had to keep the camera outdoors at night or static developed because of temperature changes. They loaded film in black changing bags on dirt floors of our chilly cabins. The men's whiskers grew and ice rimmed the bristles. Our company manager, Bert Van Tuyle, suffered a frozen foot. Leading man Ronald Byram contracted pneumonia' – from which he eventually died.[72]

The deprivations of the North lasted only two weeks, but they were two weeks 'of ice and snow, of trying runs behind the dog-teams, of scenes played at night, lighted by flares, when the thermometer registered fifty below.'[73] Van Tuyle's frostbite episode is recounted in Shipman's novel:

Dirk got the frosting one night when they worked, with flares, in a still, deadly cold that hovered at fifty below. He was playing a dog-musher, standing in the snow outside a cabin while the Heavy entered, waved in the direction of a supposedly running away heroine, jumped into a sled and said: 'We must overtake that team, Archibald!' or words to that effect. Then the dogs were expected to swing out into the 'Barrens' at top speed.

The villain went through his action over and over and Dirk 'mushed' the inert dogs, only to hear [the director] yell – 'cut!' The get-away was too sluggish. Dirk felt his foot growing numb and wondered but, keen to get the scene at any cost, he did not complain. Hours after, taking off his boots in the warm bunkhouse, he saw the puffy, white-fleshed toes and almost yelled with pain when he touched them. The native warned him away from the stove and rubbed snow and kerosene into the frosted places. The pain, Dirk admitted, was excruciating but his thoughts – all their thoughts, in fact – were on [the leading man], tossing in his bunk and feverishly asking to be taken home.[74]

Tom Trusky's note on the episode offers an amusing addition to the frostbite story: 'Bert Van Tuyle repaired to a hotel in San Francisco to cure his Lesser Slave Lake frostbite. Van Tuyle's questionable and highly flammable medical regimen is recorded by [cinematographer] Joseph Walker in an unpublished chapter from his autobiography ... According to Walker, Van Tuyle, heeding advice of an Alaskan sour-dough he had met on the train heading south from Canada to California, ordered St. Francis bellhops to bring him a washtub, kerosene, cigarettes and liquor, and proceeded to soak, smoke, and get soaked.'[75] Later, after gangrene had set in, toes on Van Tuyle's right foot were amputated.[76]

Shipman came through the material discomfort, extraordinarily hard work, and ferocious temperatures not only unscathed but, in her stylish chinoiserie coat with the lynx-trimmed hood, looking extremely smart as well. And this is no frivolous detail (although I admit that I have dreamed for many years of having a similar one made for myself): even her coat signifies her wilderness acumen, as she is not only dressed suit-ably, but the provenance of the material, a four-point Hudson's Bay Company blanket, inscribes the garment with Canadian-ness.

Contemplating the landscape, it is tempting for Canadians to com-pare ourselves with Australia. We have a similar history of British colo-

Nell Shipman in familiar costume.

nialism (also inscribed in Shipman's trade-marked garment) and a sense of ourselves as 'extra-cultural' in relation to Europe; we have seen the landscape, particularly the vast expanses of the prairies and the northern tundra, as a wilderness or wasteland organizing or mirroring Canadian culture. As Ross Gibson says of the Australian landscape, to white colonial sensibilities, most of Australia has traditionally been construed as empty space devoid of inhabitants, architecture, agriculture, and artefacts.[77] Gibson contrasts Australia with England, in which every region, indeed every acre, evokes myth and history; in a virtually unlimited national semiosis, English people inhabit a culture that covers the countryside.[78] Australia, says Gibson, unlike England, is neither here nor there. Or he might have said, as Gertrude Stein said of Oakland, 'there is no there there.'

Gibson asserts that in Australian cinema, the indigenous landscape becomes a projective screen for the persistent national neurosis deriving from the fear of and fascination with the preternatural continent. He argues that Australian art is thus premodern, concerned with the primary process of turning nature into culture, as opposed to the cultural self-referentiality of modernism, which creates itself from the raw materials of extant culture.[79]

In that paradox of neither here nor there, Gibson lays out a strategy for analysis that plays dialogically across both the uncharted and the symbolic. While extensive stretches remain unsurveyed, other areas bear up under mythic connotations; in some ways the continent is a symbolic terrain, but in others it is comprehensible only as 'extra-systemic' or uncultural.[80] The net effect of the hermeneutic is that Australia is figured as a paradox – half tamed, yet essentially untameable; conceding social subsistence, yet not allowing human dominance. The trope of this paradoxical region as the structural centre of national mythologies is used to explain the inconsistencies of a colonial society: just as the land is grand yet unreasonable, so also colonial society is accepted as both marvellous and flawed.

In Nell Shipman's films and James Oliver Curwood's novels, God's country is always Canada, usually in its most far-flung reaches. The Canadian Northwest – God's country – is contrasted in Shipman's work with the setting of *Something New*, the Mojave Desert, which is described in an intertitle as 'the land that God forgot.' Here, the conceptualization of Canadian nation-ness seems to partake of a mythical premodernity akin to what Benedict Anderson describes as the cultural roots of contemporary notions of nationalism. The locality referred to as 'God's country' is precisely that continuous, horizontal landscape characterized by a conception of temporality uniting cosmology and history.[81] The origins of the world and of its human inhabitants are identical here. Although the frozen tundra of northern Alberta may seem to us to have even less there than Gertrude Stein's Oakland (there is no there there) or Ross Gibson's Australia (neither here nor there), for Nell Shipman, there is where here both begins and ends.

Like Australian cinema, the Canadian cinema also presents Canada's uncharted frozen wilderness as an awesome opponent, rather than as pastoral locus for the organization of social life. And like Gibson's Australia, the desolate Canadian landscape projects the trope of the extra-cultural, existing well beyond the boundaries of the European symbolic order as a sublime structuring void.[82] Shipman's heroines inhabit primitive dwellings isolated from any form of community. The log cabins, abandoned mining camps, lean-tos, and woodsheds that shelter her from the elements are minor players in the dramas, which tend to fling themselves across the landscape. Treks or chases by canoe or dogsled, on snowshoes or by foot, provide the only movement in the panoramic wide-shots that dominate her cinematic lexicon. Low-lying tundra, snow-covered mountains, frozen lakes, and the odd rocky outcrop lay themselves haptically across the screen, often obscuring the distinction between land and sky, or allowing the bleak white polar sky to force the horizon to the lowest quadrant of the screen.

In this harsh landscape (both actual and textual) the narrative is dealt with expeditiously, making the most of the terrain and expending as little human power as possible: rarely has a scene more than four characters; more often there are only two, plus a dog. The chase by dogsled, which forms the climax of the film, is a series of very wide shots usually with the two sleds and dog-teams broadly separated but still in the same shot. Wide shot piles upon wide shot, as the panoramic gaze is interrupted only for expedient close-up inserts that crank up the tension a notch or two. Shipman drives the sled, cracks her whip, runs behind the sled, and so on. The climactic point of the narrative is as unadorned as the landscape itself.[83]

The 1953 version of the film is virtually baroque in comparison. Unlike Shipman's text, in which the trading post was a lone frame building not far from the seashore, the place inhabited by the villain Blake in the latter film has become a bustling port town, and Blake's dwelling sports a sophisticated interior complete with luxurious furnishings, ornate lamps, and a piano that Hugh O'Brien (playing Blake's oily henchman) tinkles to accompany his own lounge-lizard crooning. Even the Inuit live in settlements – each with its own little signpost or trail-marker stuck in the snow in the middle of nowhere.

The terrain outside the town bristles with dangers around every twist and turn, hill and dale. Marauding wolves menace the cosy little campsite where Dolores and her husband take shelter for the night, an avalanche raises its voice from a mountain of snow, and tall snowdrifts provide hiding places for approaching enemies or heights from which to jump in an ambush. In this fear-laden landscape, the Inuit use their superior wilderness knowledge to confound the wounded hero and his helpless wife, attaching magnets to their sled so that their compass sends them around and around in circles in the suddenly featureless terrain.

This is a landscape that is deeply encoded, far from the sublime 'extra-systemic' void of Gibson's Australian outback.[84] In this generic landscape of terror, every close-up signifies a danger lurking just outside the frame, every looming foreground visual invites an ambush, and even the unmarked infinity stretching ahead promises a dizzying confusion. This is a landscape that produces its own narrative, that narrativizes itself. Needless to say, it is a studio landscape: an imaginary geography, literally constructed, produced, always already narrative. As a studio landscape, it is articulated in close-ups and medium shots rather than the haptic panoramas of Shipman's earlier location text, and it is thus a significantly humanized landscape, in which the budding star Rock Hudson is luminously backlit against the bright white snow, his fur-trimmed parka outlining a soft aura around his cheekbones.[85] Medium shots frame the approach of the villain, Wapi snarling as he tackles the menacing wolves, and the Inuit guide brandishing a torch. The wide shot is reserved for the climactic moment in which Wapi tears the villain to shreds behind a foreground snowdrift that obscures the back-lot horizon.

From the premodern ontology of the earlier text, the metonymic system of articulation of the later film suggests a movement towards modernism. As opposed to the primary process of turning nature into culture, as Shipman's 1919 film does with its use of location settings and the panoramic gaze, the 1953 text creates itself not only from the raw material of extant culture, but specifically from the papier-mâché snow-drifts, painted backdrops, and all-purpose simulacra of the Hollywood studio. Rising in the full splendour of generic self-referentiality, the northern wilderness landscape of the Hollywood studio narrativizes itself as a symbolic terrain, a simulacrum, a sign ingesting its referent. Even the signification of the territorial title has been overturned, for 'God's country' denotes the American home to which star Rock Hudson and the little lady (played by Marcia Henderson) intend to return, rather than the sublime wilderness terrain of Canada to which the title referred in Shipman's work. If the landscape, imagined or real, has always been one of the principal contours through which identity is fig-ured, what has become of God's country? And what has become of the girl from God's country?

Certain conclusions are unavoidable. The heroic construction of the female protagonist has been cumulatively evacuated not only as the decades proceed but as the enunciation of the text shifts from that of the independent woman creator/writer to male-dominated studio vehi-cles. The multidimensional intertextuality of the heroic female protago-nist in Shipman's original has also given way to a one-dimensional generic figuration in the later two versions. Along with the depletion of the complexity and status of the heroine has come the transformation of specific generic conventions, notably the social-moral anatomy of the generic landscape and its inhabitants, both human and animal. More-over, the referent of the territorial indicator – God's country – has been transposed chauvinistically from the sublime northern Canadian land-scape to the return destination, the United States.

Pevney's *Back to God's Country* (1953) is the product of the bleak moment just after the Second World War, the postwar/Cold War era in which materialism, misogyny, racial disharmony, and social paranoia flourished and were repeatedly mirrored in the popular artefacts of the period, from film noir to crime novels and alienated delinquent teen movies. The Hollywood studios were scrambling to retain their hege-mony in the face of the end of monopoly practices as well as the onslaught of television. That Hollywood at this moment returns to a successful formula from nearly four decades past and casts Rock Hudson in the lead – an early role in his grooming for superstardom – attests to a cynical desperation that is mirrored in the thoroughgoing conservatism of the text: its American and urban chauvinism, its transparent racism and misogyny, and its vigorous displacement of the woman as heroine.

Appearing just at the end of the great Hollywood studio period, a moment before the destruction of the system of vertical monopolies that had been the studio system's golden egg, Tansey's *God's Country* (1946) seems to speak from a rosy and complacent sentimental liberalism. As Nick Roddick writes of the Warner Brothers films from the same era, 'they stress specific values such as truth and tolerance' but achieve 'little more than reaffirmations of the American way of life.'[86] American values of human decency walk the talk in *God's Country*, with the transformation of the heroic woman into domestic love-interest while retaining her essentialist connections to the natural world. The male protagonist is reaffirmed as active agent of the narrative, and members of the indigenous culture are paternalistically stereotyped as 'good Indians' and friends to their entrepreneurial exploiters.

Nell Shipman's *Back to God's Country*, in contrast, emerges from a moment in cinema history that was dominated by independent and artisanal innovation, the germination of genres, and maverick individualist entrepreneurship. It comes also from the period of liberal optimism just after the First World War, in which America's shift to industrial capitalism and an urban consumer economy brought jobs and the vote for women, the dawn of a cultural renaissance for African Americans, and new respectability for progressive humanist and socialist values. Shipman's proto-feminism, consciously articulated anti-racism, animal-rights activism, and rural Canadian chauvinism are complex and contradictory, bespeaking a struggle to come to terms with the new values of this new world.

Leaving God's Country

By the end of the production, all partnerships were off. Nell's marriage to Ernest Shipman had ended and her ties with Curwood, begun with such high hopes and mutually exclusive contracts, were immediately dissolved. Shipman emphasizes Curwood's anger over the heroic role given to the woman protagonist, for in his short story the dog was unrivalled as heroic protagonist. Later she recalled Curwood's displeasure when she refused to allow her magnificent mane of dark curly hair to be let loose in the film. One could easily speculate that both husband Shipman and partner Curwood (both of them just over forty years old, to Nell's luscious twenty-seven years) were both consumed with jealousy during the shoot over the affair with Bert Van Tuyle, the dashing young production manager.

Almost immediately, in an article in the *Moving Picture World*, Curwood announced the formation of James Oliver Curwood Productions 'under which corporation his future personally produced super-features taken from his successful novels of the great out-doors will be filmed. Mr. Curwood has associated with him David M. Hartford, as director, and Ernest Shipman, who will be in charge of the publicity and sales departments, with headquarters in New York.' The article goes on to claim, undoubtedly on the basis of Curwood's press release, full credit to Curwood for the success of *Back to God's Country*:

> Mr. Curwood was one of the first of America's prominent authors to realize the absolute necessity of an intimate co-operation between author and director in order to achieve the greatest results; and when 'Back to God's Country' – a First National Special that has created a sensation – was filmed on the edge of the Barren Lands of the far north, it was Mr. Curwood, with a record of fifteen years of exploratory work and adventure behind him, who went ahead with Mr. Hartford and worked hand in hand with the director for the biggest possible results. In filming Curwood's big stories of nature Mr. Hartford and the author 'sit in' together at every stage of the game.[87]

As we know, Curwood's claims are completely out of line with Nell Shipman's account.

Back to God's Country enjoyed profits of 300 per cent over production costs, although Nell saw precious little of that money. Curwood immediately capitalized on the success of the film with a republication of his short story 'Wapi the Walrus,' now retitled after the film, in a collection of short stories illustrated with stills from the production.[88] The association between Curwood and Ernest Shipman apparently did not last very long. Two Ernest Shipman productions, both directed by Henry Mac-Rae, appeared in 1921: an RCMP story, *Cameron of the Royal Mounted*, was produced in Alberta partly as a result, Ernest Shipman claims, of 'the hearty support and encouragement of the Canadian Government'; *God's Crucible* was produced in Winnipeg.[89] Curwood was not associated with either film.

Nell Shipman retained control of the zoo of wild animals, including the dogs Tresore and Rex, and – of course – Brownie the bear. Her new life as an independent producer and her partnership with Bert Van Tuyle were about to begin.

⠒   ⠒   ⠒   ⠒   ⠒

chapter four

Something New

Although *Back to God's Country* was reaping enormous box office returns, somehow Shipman's share of the profits was slow to arrive. 'My whack was a delayed take while everyone else connected with the picture was getting theirs. I had annoyed Mr. Curwood and part of the management so I got it last.'[1] Tom Trusky adds that Shipman's 'relationship with Bert Van Tuyle began on the Canadian-American production; it could be that Ernest Shipman knew of their relationship and saw to it that his soon-to-be-ex fourth wife was paid last.'[2] On the other hand, Joseph Walker attests that both Shipman and Van Tuyle 'were discreet; carefully concealing their feelings ... These were not days of open permissiveness and a scandal would not be tolerated. After all, Nell was a married woman with much at stake, and Ernest Shipman was a man not to be taken lightly.'[3] Nevertheless, when Shipman and Van Tuyle clasped each other in 'a tight embrace' at the end of the shoot, Walker wondered if the romance had come as a surprise to the crew.[4]

Leaving her husband and her partnership with James Oliver Curwood behind, Shipman returned to southern California to make movies independently. She bought a house in Highland Park, where she lived with her son, Barry, a housekeeper, the collie Laddie, and Brownie the bear. Bert Van Tuyle built a structure on the next-door lot, where Shipman did the editing of the movies. Shipman referred to the building as a 'bungalow,'[5] but Barry Shipman later described it rather differently: 'Bert had also built a one-room shack used for film-editing. It [had] a small cot in it, ostensibly where Bert [slept] at night.'[6]

'To pay the room rent and keep eating' while they were waiting for the proceeds from *Back to God's Country*, Shipman took on two industrial commissions financed by automobile companies, *Trail of the Arrow* (presumed lost; two reels; copyright 24 February 1920) and *Something New* (four reels, copyright 13 September 1920). Cinematographer Joseph Walker was the connection for both projects. He was a friend of O.K. Parker, the advertising manager for the Hudson-Essex Automobile Agency, whom he had known from the days when Walker made promotional shorts.[7] Although Walker rapidly established himself as one of the top feature cinematographers after Shipman hired him to shoot *Back to God's Country*, he had only recently shot and directed a similar promotional project, entitled simply *The 1918 Maxwell*.

The 1918 Maxwell is a simple sequence without any pretensions to narrative. There is a brief display of the automobile outside the showroom: the paint shines, the leather upholstery gleams. An intertitle notes that loading of supplies and camera comes next, and that is just what we see. Two men leave Los Angeles in the Maxwell. An intertitle points out that where they are going, no car has gone before, as there are no roads. Until the return to the city, the rest of the film features the car driving through desert, over large boulders, through sagebrush, across salt flats, through shallow ponds, and up and down rocky hills. Halfway through the drive, the film is interrupted by an insert of an affidavit attesting to the lack of damages or repairs.

Cinematic continuity is non-existent. Sometimes the car drives out of the frame with one man in the car, and sometimes with two, apparently according to the demands of the shooting set-up. There is no suggestion of a time frame or a destination: at one point the car simply drives around in a circle. Eventually the car returns to Los Angeles, and a brief tour of the large building site of the new Maxwell showroom at Figaroa and Seventh ends the exposition. This is a simple documentary-style industrial promotion that makes no other claims for itself.[8]

When Walker tossed Shipman the Hudson-Essex contract, a 'commercial' for an Essex automobile called the Grey Ghost, she took a very different approach.

Trail of the Arrow

Unlike Walker's documentary, Shipman's *Trail of the Arrow* embeds the exposition within a narrative. Although the film is no longer extant, there is some evidence of its approach. *Trail of the Arrow* weaves its story around a man by the name of Bob Battle who develops an aversion to women drivers when a woman motorist damages his fender. As a result of the accident, he challenges Shipman and her friend Marjorie Cole to a race. He makes a $1000 bet that the two women could not drive the Essex over a dangerous route in the Mojave Desert, the 'Trail of the Arrow' that led to a desolate desert punchbowl location. They immediately take him up on the wager.

Shooting the film in the torturous conditions of the Mojave Desert 'in the deep of a 120 degree summer' in August 1919, 'the Essex Arrow was driven over rocks, through sage brush, up and down timbered slopes and over declivities until it seemed as though everything in the car would be smashed to atoms. The car was tilted at such angles that the daring girl drivers had to be lashed to the seats to prevent them being thrown from the car.'[9] Undoubtedly the driving sequences were similar to those in Walker's *The 1918 Maxwell*, for we find like sequences in *Something New*, which Shipman made with Walker as cinematographer just over six months later. Shipman writes in her memoir, 'The only highlight I can recall on [*Trail of the Arrow*] was driving through a brush fire and finding out later that the gas tank cap was missing.'[10]

Two women buddies in a car running a race against time and an angry man: is this *Thelma and Louise*? No, it's *Trail of the Arrow*. But the situation clearly anticipates the variations on the road movie that in the late twentieth century came to be known as the female buddy movie. Road movies are by definition movies about cars, trucks, motorcycles, or some other individually powered mode of modern transportation, and for many critics, it is a masculine genre. The car as a mode of transportation, like many of the new technologies of modernity, seems to have been coded as masculine from the get-go, and women have been characterized, consequently, as intermittent, unusual, and stereotypically incompetent interlopers in this man's world. Thus, in Timothy Corrigan's view, the road movie is almost exclusively concerned with male subjectivity and masculine empowerment in a world that is virtually absent of women – a male escapist fantasy in which masculinity is identified with the machines (cars or motorcycles) and the road is a space apart from home life, marriage, and employment.[11] Noting 'the insis-

tence on the extremely linear narrative structure of the road movie,'
Shari Roberts sees the characteristics of the generic structure itself as
masculine: directness, aggression, independence, control, and individual choice.[12]

Roberts underlines the gendered construction of the genre by examining recent road movies with women as protagonists, such as *Thelma
and Louise* (d. Ridley Scott, 1991) and *Boys on the Side* (d. Herbert Ross,
1995). Fleeing patriarchy and its effects on their lives, in these films the
protagonists take to the road and, in doing so, they disrupt formal genre
norms by introducing concerns associated with women and feminism to
produce a critique of patriarchal culture and of the masculinist genre
itself.[13] Roberts concludes that, 'because they attempt to escape patriarchy within a masculinist genre, these female protagonists are unable to
avoid cultural constructions of femininity ... In the end, Thelma and
Louise refuse the Western trope of the final shoot-out, choosing instead
a bittersweet freedom from patriarchy through their suicidal accelera-
tion into the Grand Canyon. In sum, although the feminine road films
critique dominant ideology, because of their attempted escape specifically into a masculinist genre, these films tend metaphorically to raise
their hands in "feminine" despair.'[14]

These despairing films, made in the last decade of the twentieth century with its understanding of the disappointments of modernity, contrast markedly with the exuberant optimism of Shipman's *Trail of the
Arrow*, produced in the first decades of modernity, not coincidentally
the heyday of the serial-queen adventure genre. Celebrating the new
technologies of modernity, the serial-queen movies also produced the
confusions or perversions of gender roles as comedy.

In *Trail of the Arrow*, Shipman undoubtedly takes full advantage of the
genre conventions of her day. We can only speculate on the representation of the two women 'buddies' in *Trail of the Arrow*, for the film is no
longer extant. However, we know from Shipman's memoir that Marjorie
Cole, Shipman's co-driver in the Essex adventure, was a close friend and
constant companion. 'My pal, Marjorie Cole and I,' she writes, 'used to
make a left-hand turn around the officer who stood on a wooden platform in the middle of the Seventh and Broadway intersection and hand
him a big red apple as we blasted past with the Dodge cut-out wide
open. This marvelous girl was my partner in the ownership of a racing

car with bucket seats but no windshield. It got stuck in reverse one day, on Broadway, and we backed the full length of the thoroughfare, to mixed emotions from the traffic officers and general applause from other drivers.'[15] It would be surprising if the fun-loving, joy-riding spirit of these two incidents were not represented in some way in *Trail of the Arrow*, or if the affection expressed in the phrases 'my pal' and 'this marvelous girl' was not evident in the representation of female companionship in the film.

And who can imagine that the male protagonist would not have been played for comedy? In *Trail of the Arrow*, Battle's motive clearly involves not only demonstrating the insufficiencies of women in automobility but also underscoring the appropriateness of patriarchal culture's efforts to curtail women's activity in the public and political spheres. Through the character of Bob Battle, Shipman's scenario implicitly argues that the gender codes of patriarchal culture are not natural or inherent, but actively and intentionally enforced. Unwilling to run a fair race, Battle devises all kinds of hazards to cause the women to lose and thus accept their proper sphere, which for him and for patriarchy is clearly not on the road or at the wheel. But the women still defeat him in the end.

The plot of the film indicates that Shipman uses and abuses the adventure comedy elements precisely 'for a sneak cultural attack' on patriarchal structures. Like Roberts's characterization of the recent female buddy road movies, *Trail of the Arrow* explicitly poses a challenge to patriarchal culture and its attempts to limit women's mobility. Or, as Katie Mills puts it,

> The road story wields a big jackpot in identity re-vision, because it narrates resistance to the status quo ... As a site of deviant discourse, the road offers a territory of enunciation that can be appropriated by cultural rebels who use film genre as a shared public 'forum,' a metaphoric commons or *polis* from which to launch a critique of society. But the road story does not merely entertain with tension-releasing fantasies of rebellion. Its very familiarity can be the basis for a sneak cultural attack on the narrative and identificatory structures which shape one's private self-identity and one's willingness to protest publicly against structures which are [misogynist].[16]

In this 'shared public "forum"' of genre, Shipman's optimism about the future for women in modernity is explicit, as the intertitles of the film directly comment on the aspirations of the suffragist movement. The representative of patriarchy is not only defeated by the women's abilities, but gracefully concedes the error of his ways. He expresses his new conviction that women should have 'the right to vote and drive automobiles and do anything else they desire!' (intertitle).[17]

Nearly eighty years later, Katie Mills still sees the need to 'demand the postmodern road movie to refuse to fall subservient to an antinomy in which models of resistance, spontaneity, truth, independence and mobility are masculinized, and passivity, acquiescence, fixity and fatalism are feminized.'[18] In *Trail of the Arrow*, Shipman explicitly refuses such constructions. Moreover, Shipman's scenario is not just a simple case of role reversal. The women drivers do not take on the disguise of masculinism and its connotations, nor is their womanhood a masquerade of femininity. Neither is gender subverted by their activity. On the contrary, the scenario pits the man against women *qua* women and effectively demonstrates that 'resistance, spontaneity, truth, independence and mobility' are shared human, rather than gendered, characteristics. If, as Roberts points out, the protagonist of the road movie 'begins a quest ... for a better life, a new social order, or fulfillment,'[19] these women at the very least make it to the finish line with their friendship and their femininity intact and the man appropriately cowed. From the evidence of the other extant Shipman films, in which her character tends to be expressive, youthful, and enthusiastically affectionate, my guess is that some gesture of affection in triumph would have marked the victory of the two women in *Trail of the Arrow*.

Shipman said at the time: 'I have proven that woman is on a par with man in driving a motor car, as she is in every other walk of life. The ability is there. All she needs is the experience – the physical training — the freedom from restraint.'[20] Seizing the challenge of competition, speed, dynamism, and aggression, Shipman constructs a narrative that emphasizes female friendship, equality between men and women, and a geographical, political, and personal freedom for women. She is not fleeing from patriarchy, but accepting its challenge and defeating it. Equally at home on the streets of Los Angeles or the roadless tracts of the wilderness, she embodies and embraces technological and spiritual modernity and declares it a new world for women.

Women and Cars

Although women were a small minority of drivers well into the twentieth century, Shipman was by no means alone in either her assertion of women's capabilities at the wheel or her embrace of the potential of modern technology for the construction of gender equality or freedom for women from conventional gender roles. In a well researched and tremendously engaging book, *Taking the Wheel: Women and the Coming of the Motor Age*, Virginia Scharff has written a multidisciplinary cultural history of women's relation to the automobile in the first decades of the twentieth century.[21] I will cull from it extensively here to outline the context in which Nell Shipman appears as a heroic woman driver.

Novelist Edith Wharton saw immediately that motoring would be an 'immense enlargement of life.' She first rode in an automobile in Italy in 1903; after an exhilarating fifty-mile ride, Wharton 'swore then and there that as soon as [she] could make money enough [she] would buy a motor.'[22] On the earnings from her novel *The Valley of Decision* Wharton purchased a Panhard-Levassor, a French car, in spring 1904.

Gloria Swanson's response to her first drive echoes Wharton's excitement. Recollecting that exciting day in Griffith Park in 1916 when her fiancé, Wallace Beery, taught her to drive a car, Swanson enthused, 'The car moved, and I started steering it down the long dirt road. I'd never had such a thrill. Nothing existed in the whole world but the power of that car. The tiniest turn of the wheel and the whole thing responded. I had the feeling I could go anywhere and nothing could stop me.'[23] 'The Wonderful Monster,' a serial published in *Motor* magazine, fictionalized the same experience, thus suggesting its widespread cultural currency. In the story, the woman driver 'wanted to feel the throb of [the car's] quickening pulses; to lay her hand on lever and handle and thrill with a sense of mastery; to claim its power as her own – and feel its sullen-yielded obedience answer to her will.'[24]

Such connections between female desire, velocity, power, and sexuality were alarming to moralists, provoking many types of warnings about the incendiary desires awakened in women by the power of the automobile and the thrill of speed. Although many women shared Shipman's enthusiasm for the technologies of modernity, other political, social, economic, and cultural segments were conflicted about modernity in general and women's place within it. Virginia Scharff notes that 'the open vehicles of the day, built chiefly by carriage-makers, were high-riding, sometimes doorless affairs that exposed all passengers to public scrutiny, and women seemed to be particularly on display.' They had been equally on display in horse-drawn carriages, but the novelty and rarity of the automobile captured much more attention: 'Autos were novelties that brought people out to gawk by the roadside.'[25] In addition, such 'modern females terrified traditionalists ... with their public exhibition of spending power, and with their refusal to see constraint as protection ... Climbing into an automobile, a woman rejected the cloister, certainly, and potentially also the female sphere of hearth and home.'[26]

The sense that the automobile opened a new world for women was shared by many of the early women drivers. With women taking to the road as motorists in escalating numbers, the social challenge to women's traditional sphere became increasingly marked. Not only did women have earning capacity and property rights that enabled them to own cars, but the independent mobility of the 'chauffeuse' afforded opportunity for learning new skills, for personal and political freedom, and for travel, sport, and business. 'Extending that potential to women meant both expanding the private sphere into the realm of transportation and, paradoxically, puncturing women's "sphere" by undermining the already strained notion that women's place was in the home ... The auto represented a new, movable field upon which women's struggle for power and autonomy would be played.'[27]

Appropriately for its status as another of the major technologies of modernity, the film industry was quick to see the thrilling potential of women at the wheel. The first film to feature a woman driving a car was *An Auto Heroine* (one reel, Vitagraph, 1908), starring an unnamed but daring actress. The film was hailed as one of the more notable productions of the day by the reviewer for *New York Dramatic Mirror*: 'There is a thrilling automobile race in this picture with accidents, smash-ups, and fast running, to all appearances the real thing. The inventor of a new type of racing machine is kidnapped by rivals, who in this way seek to prevent him from winning the race, after first trying to tamper with the mechanism. But his daughter takes his place and drives the machine to victory, winning the cup to the joy of her father, who in the meantime has been released. The film is one that will bear seeing more than once, and should prove a very popular production.'[28]

Hollywood's first great car chase also featured a woman at the wheel. In *A Beast at Bay* (d. D.W. Griffith, Biograph, 1912) Mary Pickford plays a young motorist who picks up her boyfriend in her car for a day's outing. When he refuses to become involved in a quarrel with a tramp who insults him, Pickford accuses him of cowardice and drives off alone. Her courage is tested when an escaped convict highjacks her car and forces her to drive him through the countryside at top speed. Eventually, the convict forces Pickford to go with him to a barn, where she is finally saved from her nemesis by the timely arrival of her boyfriend.[29]

After Gloria Swanson made a high-speed automobile entrance into the Keystone lot, a scenario was immediately concocted that featured Swanson at the wheel. In *The Danger Girl* (d. Clarence Badger, Keystone, 1916) Swanson wears a dress as she races her car and switches to overalls when she changes a tire.

Because motoring in the open, high-riding, smoke-belching automobile was a dirty business in its early days, both driver and passengers required protective clothing. The duster or motoring coat was usually made of leather, rubber, or fur; goggles were necessary, as was protective covering for hair and hat. One of the items featured in a magazine article 'What the Motor Girl Is Wearing' was an all-weather women's motoring mask made of mica with a translucent veil; it approximated a large bucket inverted over the head.[30]

By the time Gloria Swanson wheeled into the Keystone lot, however, automobiles, roads, and personal driving equipment had changed considerably, and the modern woman made her appearance on the American road:

Sleek and streamlined, she had slipped the ponderous drapery of Victorian clothing. The hem of her dress no longer trailed on the ground. Often enough, now, it swung free at knee level. Some youthful female motorists, sporting the bobbed hair and daring demeanor of the flapper, even abandoned dresses altogether in favor of suits with knickers. The cumbersome picture hats and veils of the early motoring period had given way to snug-fitting cloches, and tailored motoring coats replaced heavy dusters. Whether a sedate housewife or a high-spirited jazz baby, the woman motorist of the twenties announced with her very clothing that she took mobility for granted.[31]

We do not know what Shipman and Cole wore in *The Trail of the Arrow*, but we can bet that the modernist optimism of the scenario regarding the liberating possibilities of women's automobility, combined with the exhilaration of the sense of power and speed and the trying conditions of the desert location, would have been appropriately reflected in their outfits.[32]

The Speeding Sweethearts of the Silent Screen, 1908–1921

Economic forces were not immediately supportive of women as drivers or car owners. The automobile industry sought to capitalize on women's spending power while at the same time limiting the sphere of women's mobility by attempting to market the electric, rather than gasoline-powered, car as the appropriate vehicle for women. Less dirty and easier to drive than the gas-powered vehicle, it was also severely limited in its capacity for velocity and in the range of mileage.[33]

A major change for the woman driver was the self-starter, available as early as 1906, making cranking unnecessary. In the next few years, in an effort to market gas-powered cars to women, the Maxwell-Briscoe company sent an all-woman crew on a highly publicized cross-country drive. Meanwhile the White Motor Company promoted its coupe – a closed car with doors on both sides wide enough to accommodate cumbersome skirts – as 'a woman's town car.' Calling attention to the many little accessories, the company boasted that 'nothing has been overlooked that could contribute to a woman's satisfaction in a car which is so particularly designed for her personal use.'[34]

Popular culture rather more quickly took to the bold new women at the wheel. In the first decade of the new century, women motorists were celebrated in popular songs ('The Lady Chauffeur'), stage shows (*The Motor Girl*), and several series of adventure novels for girls such as *The Motor Maids*.[35] Publicity about Hollywood's emerging film stars also drew attention to women as drivers. Fan magazines regularly highlighted the stars' love of driving and reported on their fabulous cars. Mabel Normand had a custom-built Mercer Runabout with a 'dressing table and

makeup mirror that folded into her car door.'[36] Other actresses rede-
signed their cars for their specific professional and personal needs.
Bessie Eyton converted the little Maxwell that succeeded her big Paige
into a dressing room on wheels, an innovation that attracted the attention of Mary Pickford, who drove a similar Maxwell at the time. Pathé
serial queen Ruth Roland drove a foreign coupe that she had designed
herself, a robin's-egg blue sedan upholstered in cream-colored cretonne
with a pattern of red parrots on green fronds.[37]

The plot of one silent film was derived from a well-publicized incident
involving a star, Bebe Daniels, whose love of fast driving had landed her
in the headlines. When Daniels was caught for speeding at over seventy
miles per hour in Orange County, the judge chose to make an example
of her and gain publicity for himself by sentencing her to ten days in
jail. The star's much-publicized jail sentence became the subject of *The
Speed Girl*, released by Realart in the fall of 1921. The comedy cast
Daniels as a movie star famous for doing stunts in cars. She becomes
romantically involved with a naval ensign and drives him to San Diego to
join his ship. Thanks to her fast driving, he reaches the ship before it
sails. However, as a result of the schemes of a jealous boyfriend, she is
arrested by the police for speeding and serves a term in jail. Accompanied by an illustration of Daniels in a sports car 'going at the speed of a
rocket,' *The Speed Girl* was advertised as 'a six cylinder hundred and
twenty fun powered record-breaking comedy with Bebe at the wheel.
The brakes are off. Slip her into high. Now step on it!'[38]

Some stars not only owned and drove cars, but also prided themselves
on their mechanical skills with repairs. Lubin star Ormi Hawley was a
skilled auto mechanic,[39] and Vitagraph principal Mary Anderson told a
magazine interviewer in 1916, 'As much as I like to drive ... I believe it is
just as much fun doing my repairs.'[40] One silent film actress was an
inventor of mechanical improvements for cars. Florence Lawrence, the
Biograph Girl who emerged in 1910 as America's first real movie star
under Carl Laemmle's banner at IMP, was an automotive pioneer as
well as a major early force in cinema and a committed suffragist. She
invented an '"auto signaling arm," which, when placed on the back of
the fender, can be raised or lowered by electric push buttons, thus
indicating the intention of the driver. The one indicating "stop" works
automatically when the footbrake is pressed.'[41] Lawrence's mother,

Charlotte Bridgwood, was also an inventor and is credited with inventing the automatic windshield wiper, perhaps in collaboration with her daughter.[42]

A 1915 yellow Stutz Bearcat was publicized in studio-generated material supporting Pearl White (star of *The Perils of Pauline, The Exploits of Elaine, The New Exploits of Elaine,* and *The Romance of Elaine*). One publicity anecdote related her exploits zooming around the countryside in her Stutz: when she drove into a small town, she was fined five dollars for speeding. Instead, she paid ten dollars because, as she told the village justice, 'I'm leaving your goddamned town as fast as I came in!'[43]

The 1915 cream-colored Maxwell cabriolet that belonged to Mary Pickford, 'the queen of Hollywood,' was particularly famous. Although she often rode in her own chauffeured limousines, Pickford also had smaller cars that she drove herself, especially her beloved Maxwell, which she called 'Fifi.'[44] In 1915, in collaboration with screenwriter Frances Marion, Pickford began writing a nationally syndicated newspaper column, 'Daily Talks.' In one column, Pickford wrote: 'Virginia D., Portland, Ore., wishes to know what I think about women driving automobiles. I see no reason why a woman shouldn't drive her own car. I drive mine, and I drive it through the crowded streets of New York. You know the men say that women shouldn't drive cars because they can't keep their heads in time of accident. I don't believe that. If a woman has poise and is not nervous she is ready for any emergency.'[45]

Poise was the least of the requirements for the driving actresses of the silent cinema. When featured players performed their own stunts and rear-projection was unknown, skill behind the wheel became a prerequisite for actresses in action films that increasingly featured car chases and whose titles often indicated the centrality of the driving heroine (e.g., *An Auto Heroine, The Speed Queen, Mabel at the Wheel,* and *The Speed Girl*).

'Automania' became endemic to Hollywood films. The women who drove cars in the movies also helped to shape the new attitudes towards women and mobility that were quickly taking shape in the early decades of the twentieth century. *Mabel at the Wheel* (d. Mabel Normand, starring Normand and Charlie Chaplin, two reels, Keystone, 1914) indicates something of these new attitudes. The plot involves a love triangle between Normand, her race-driver boyfriend, and the villain, a jealous rival played by Charlie Chaplin with top hat and long frock coat. On the day he is scheduled to race, the boyfriend is kidnapped by Chaplin and his henchmen. Normand takes her boyfriend's place at the wheel and, surviving attempts by the villain to sabotage her, drives the racing car to victory.

Normand not only wins the race and undermines her antagonist's attempts at sabotage, as Shipman does also in *Trail of the Arrow*, but here we can see the outlines of a heroine who does not need to be rescued by her boyfriend. William H. Drew comments: '*Mabel at the Wheel* created a new form of heroic comedy in which the comic woman protagonist's actions reveal qualities of courage and resourcefulness ... Nothing can alter the triumphant images of the young, beautiful, confident [Normand], the comedic goddess who drives the racing car to victory in *Mabel at the Wheel* and, in the final shot, is hoisted on the shoulders of a crowd cheering the heroic woman who had invaded male territory – and won.'[46]

In *The President's Special* (d. Charles Brabin, two reels, Edison, 1914) an overworked telegrapher falls asleep before he can flag an excursion train filled with children and prevent it from colliding with the President's Special, which has the right of way. When he awakes, he agonizes over the fearful expectation that his negligence will lead to tragedy. Meanwhile, his wife, realizing the imminent danger, has cranked up her Model T Ford touring car and sped after the train in an effort to stop it. The film intercuts shots of the train with the heroine roaring down the road at full speed, clouds of dust trailing behind her car. In the nick of time, the resourceful woman catches up with the excursion train and stops it before the President's Special whizzes through.

It would be pointless to argue that in two years Hollywood or any other part of the world reversed its attitudes towards gender roles. On the other hand, Hollywood produced a generation of serial queens who performed daredevil stunts in cars, motorcycles, and trains, defeated the villains, and, from time to time (and always, in Shipman vehicles), rescued the hero. Drew notes that 'This type of action melodrama soon became a regular feature of the serials,' particularly citing the Kalem railroad series *The Hazards of Helen* (d. J.P. McGowan, 1914–17). The star, Helen Holmes, 'was an avid race-car fanatic, and very often barred from participating in contests because women were not allowed to compete.'[47] In both the immensely popular serial *The Hazards of Helen* and *The Girl and the Game*, the 1915 Mutual serial Holmes co-authored, Holmes's driving skills were featured in scenes in which she 'drives a car at high speed around mountain curves, outraces a speeding train, leaps from her moving car to the locomotive and brakes it to a halt.'[48] For a 1917 serial, Holmes set a new record in thrills, as the *New York Dramatic Mirror* noted: 'Helen Holmes, daring motion picture actress, drove an automobile at top speed off the dock at San Pedro, Cal., four times in an attempt to make a thirty-foot leap onto a barge and the fourth time she did it. The "stunt" was staged for the ninth chapter of *The Railroad Raiders*, Mutual-Signal photonovel. Her hair-raising ride is easily the most sensational performance of the year in motion picture adventure drama.'[49]

Helen Gibson, who took over the title role after Helen Holmes left *The Hazards of Helen* in 1915, continued to star in the 119–chapter serial until the series came to an end in 1917. Like Holmes, Gibson was an expert driver who performed daredevil stunts in cars. In one scene, for example, in pursuit of the villains, Gibson jumps from her galloping horse to a car, taking over the driving from the startled owner. In the chapter 'The Open Track' (*The Hazards of Helen*) she is driving one of the heavies in her touring car when he tries to molest her. She puts up a fight and is able to push him out of the car before it goes out of control. Racing first in her car and then on a motorcycle, she once again saves the day and prevents sabotage of the railroad by a gang of counterfeiters. Drew comments: 'The electrifying stunts performed by the attractive stars of these action-adventure films was the most striking challenge to the traditional mythology that women were "the weaker sex," unable to respond rationally to dangerous or frightening situations. The cool, determined resolve of the serial queens ... provided women (and men) week after week with overwhelming images of powerful women, females who often demonstrated their bravery through their skill at handling motorcars under the most hazardous of circumstances.'[50]

From this collection of anecdotes and commentary, it becomes evident that Shipman was certainly not alone in her enthusiasm for or her adeptness at handling the new technologies of modernity. Although she had become isolated from the Hollywood studio industry as an independent, nevertheless she was working within a popular mainstream medium that showcased skilled adventurous women at the wheel. In this, Shipman was among her peers.

Automobility and Women's Emancipation

Just as Shipman's *Trail of the Arrow* ended with the assertion that women should have 'the right to vote and drive automobiles and do anything else they desire!' campaigners for women's rights saw the radical political potential of women's driving. 'Some women suffrage activists,' Virginia Scharff writes, 'aware that the motorcar provided a symbolic vehicle of women's autonomy and an important means of transportation for the women's rights crusade, attempted to make an explicit connection between female automobility and feminist politics.' In 1910, the Illinois Equal Suffrage Association sponsored the first major effort to use the automobile on behalf of women suffrage, a series of automobile tours of the state. From that time forward, the suffrage movement used the auto not only as a mode of transportation, but as public platform, object for ritual decoration, and emblem of the cause of women's emancipation. In the summer of 1910, fifteen auto parties toured Illinois, bringing movement veterans to outlying areas for public open-air meetings. Similar tours were organized in California in 1911 and Wisconsin in 1912. The women spoke from the cars and advertised their presence with brass bands. These auto tours attracted far more attention and many more people than the traditional 'parlour meetings' that primarily reached the already converted.[51] As Scharff points out, 'In making such excursions, suffragists not only carried the message to new listeners, they also demonstrated women's equality at the wheel.'[52] Women racing and touring in cars also promoted the notion that motorcars were a safe and reliable form of transportation, and focused attention on the auto as both a symbol and vehicle of women's emancipation.

The First World War brought the value of such mobility into sharp relief as, for thousands of women in Canada, the United States, and Europe, the coming of war meant putting their driving skills at the service of their nations. Driving ambulances and transporting goods and services to the battlefield demonstrated women's strength, resourcefulness, mechanical skill, and grace under pressure. Women even worked as mechanics during the war.

Gertrude Stein was one of the women who offered their services and their vehicles free of charge. Already living in Paris when the war broke out, Stein contacted a cousin in New York and had a Model T Ford shipped over to her in France. She named the car after her Aunt Pauline, a person 'who always behaved admirably in emergencies and behaved fairly well most of the time if she was properly flattered.' When they first got the car, her partner, Alice B. Toklas, suggested that Stein should take it completely apart and put it back together again so that she would know how it worked. Although she declined to dismantle the car, Stein could change a spark plug herself; still, she relied on her personal charm and her eccentric appearance to enlist passers-by when the car needed extra-hard cranking or a flat needed fixing. With Toklas as the navigator, Stein drove as eccentrically as she wrote, at top speed and always 'against the lines.' Often they got hopelessly lost because Stein was carried away by conversation – usually her own monologues; Stein said that she talked all the time and listened all the time as well, but in the car, she did not seem to have the same facility for listening. Nevertheless, they managed to bring supplies to hospitals, to distribute 'comfort kits' to soldiers, and to evacuate the wounded when necessary.[53] Stein and Toklas became such fixtures on the roads of France that a photograph of the two of them and the Ford was made into a postcard and sold in the United States to raise money for the American Fund for French Wounded.

Driving, touring, campaigning, serving, repairing: these activities helped to redefine the parameters of femininity and the image of ideal womanhood.[54] Robust athleticism, competence and efficiency, courage and independence became the marks of the new woman, just as they were configured in the robust characters that Shipman constructed for herself in her independent scenarios.

Making *Something New*

In 1914, the Maxwell Motor Company explicitly aligned its marketing goals with women's political and professional emancipation. It announced a plan to hire automobile saleswomen on an equal basis with men and held a reception at a Manhattan dealership featuring not only speeches by prominent suffragists such as Crystal Eastman but a woman dressed in a leather apron and blue jeans assembling and disassembling an engine in the showroom window.[55] The progressive attitudes of the Maxwell Company towards women drivers may be seen to culminate for

Shipman when they hired her as director and producer of a promotional film in 1920 – the film that Shipman turned into a short dramatic feature, *Something New*.

Something New (four reels, copyright 13 September 1920) is a fifty-minute feature that Shipman made on the budget allotted for a commercial for the new Maxwell. The plot is flimsy at best. Our heroine arrives in Mexico for a visit with an old uncle, the custodian of a mine. Almost immediately, the mine is attacked by banditti, the 'Bad Hats,' who capture the woman and spirit her away to 'Hell's Kitchen,' their mountain lair. She has had the wit to tie a note to the collar of the faithful pooch, who runs off to find Bill (Bert Van Tuyle). Love-interest and driver of the Maxwell auto for the first half of *Something New*, Bill arrives in the open car and the chase begins.

Shipman writes that Van Tuyle was 'once a star driver in the days when thundering motorcars went out for Century [turn-of-the-century open road] Runs over roads which were practically nonexistent.'[56] Trusky adds a note from a newspaper story: '"Van Tuyle was 24 when he organized what is believed to be the first automobile club in the United States. The year was 1901 and the place, Rochester, New York." In 1910, "Van Tuyle became one of the first 12 men to cross the United States by automobile."'[57] Although Trusky cautions that this story is 'rife with misinformation,' Joseph Walker relates that when he first met Van Tuyle, he 'was newly arrived in California from Pennsylvania, where he'd been an executive with an automobile club.'[58] Van Tuyle's past may be somewhat hazy, but, from the evidence of *Something New*, he certainly knew his way around cars.

The idea of *Something New*, writes Shipman, 'was that the Maxwell went places no horse, or even men on foot, could traverse! We drove it over rocks bigger than itself, up canyons hub-deep in sand.'[59] When the heroine is captured by banditti, Bill drives the car, his only means of locomotion, to rescue her. Feats of driving skill and the prodigious capabilities of the car form the bulk of the film. The car is manoeuvred down steep rocky inclines, bounces across boulders, mows down cacti, and negotiates unbelievably tight turns – all in cinematic real time (i.e., without cuts). When Bill finally reaches the outlaw hide-out, the rescue is effected with ludicrous ease and the couple takes off in the Maxwell again. As usual in a Nell Shipman film, however, the hero is gratuitously

Alone at dawn, in a melodramatic posture, *The Grub-Stake* (1923).

injured. Although he keeps driving for a while, eventually human frailty prevails and he passes out at the wheel. Busy pointing a gun back towards the pursuing Bad Hats, the heroine does not notice that Bill has fainted until the very last moment, when the car is about to plunge over a cliff. As luck would have it, the car stops just in time – in a wide shot that shows the car coming to a halt only inches from the cliff's edge.

From this point on, the heroine must pilot the Maxwell. And Shipman does not fail us, as her driving skills are a match for Van Tuyle's. She essays countless incredible feats of automobile manoeuvring, until they reach a precipice where they are trapped with the banditti climbing by foot up the mountainside towards them. As the male protagonist stands weakly to one side, she backs the car again and again into a huge boulder, which she eventually dislodges to send it smashing down the mountainside in an avalanche that annihilates the Bad Hats. A ghastly close-up of an anguished death mask closes the sequence.

The production was not without its mishaps. Shipman writes of a near-death episode when

> 'The Girl,' now a captive of the Bad Hats and on horseback, her wrists tied behind her, pitched from her mount and banged her head on a rock. The assistant director had offered to untie the wrist bonds but she said, 'Oh, no. Next shot a close-up, leave 'em be,' or some such silly words. So, jogging through a narrow defile, twenty mounted Bad Hats as her escort, this boastful horsewoman did a dive for a waiting rock. Again, this footage must carpet the cutting-room floor, since 'She' must, of course, conclude her movie adventure right-side-up in her sweetie's arms. But we saw the rushes and it was a beautiful thing to watch those following Cayuses part like hair under a comb and, for all the narrow trail, fail to even brush the recumbent, out-cold form of the Leading Lady.[60]

On another occasion, the Maxwell rolled three times. 'By a miracle which seemingly insured Girl and Man from destruction, [they] survived' and the Maxwell company's mechanic repaired the damage. They had at least three bouts with repairs to the car. It ended up without fenders, without paint, and thoroughly pounded. The 'bashed-in rear-end,' the result of pushing the boulder over the cliff, was not fixed. At all the screenings, 'that self-same Maxwell stood fenderless, paintless, battered, in the theater lobby. An immodestly lettered sign claimed she'd come through the Hell of the Desert and a thousand Gun Shots exactly as she came spanking-new from the Factory! It was almost true.'[61]

William M. Drew's summation of the film's achievement is superlative; it is worth quoting in full:

[Shipman's] comic epic narrative in *Something New* combines a light-hearted, tongue-in-cheek approach to melodramatic situations with breath-taking action scenes of genuine heroism. But underscoring this blend of humor and excitement are deeper, harmonizing motifs that unite the masculine and the feminine, industrialism and environmentalism. The relationship that develops between Bert Van Tuyle and [Shipman] in the film is one of true comradeship between a man and a woman facing and overcoming perils together in the wilderness. And the Maxwell car racing through the desert manages to adapt to the rugged landscape without the existence of highways disrupting the natural order.

Employing her talents for acting, writing, directing and stunt driving, the comely Nell Shipman mastered the action-adventure genre to an extent unmatched in cinema history by any other woman director. And her expertise behind the wheel in scenes of thrill-packed action that continue to amaze the viewer gave women a heroic vision of femininity capable of measuring up to any situation. Appearing at a time when the enactment of woman suffrage seemed to foretell a miraculous transformation of gender roles by opening up opportunities for women, *Something New* is suffused with the optimism of the new era, eloquently expressed in the final title: 'Be it motor or maid – there is always something new!'[62]

Mass Culture and the Contradictions of Modernity

Although William M. Drew's praise for Shipman's achievement in *Something New* is enthusiastic, he has placed Shipman's feats in a context of women screen stars of the silent era driving both in films and in their private (public) lives. His monograph is premised on the argument that 'the actresses of [the silent era] have too often been stereotyped as either frail, frightened creatures tied to railroad tracks by the villain or pretentious Norma Desmonds waited on by men hand and foot. In reality, most silent film actresses were strong, resourceful women both on and off screen whose careers reflected even as they encouraged the emancipation of women in the early decades of the twentieth century.' He writes that 'Nothing is more illustrative of silent film actresses' assertiveness than their adoption of the automobile during the 1910s when the new invention in transportation, like that other new invention, the cinema, was transforming and reshaping the very fabric of society.'[63] He concludes his monograph with a stirring statement:

> A decade of numerous films and the attendant publicity stressing the driving skills of the screen actresses who were the best-known, most beloved women in the world must surely have played a significant role in gaining acceptance for women motorists ... But the motoring experiences of the silent film actresses had deeper implications that went beyond their contribution to the revolution in transportation ... Through their skill at the wheel, the silent film actresses demonstrated that gender distinctions are much subtler than a simple and fallacious attempt to define particular activities, interests or aptitudes as either masculine or feminine. By rivaling their male counterparts in bravery, endurance and ability in driving cars, the silent film actresses of the teens had projected onto the screens of the world a sexual egalitarianism that was indeed 'something new.'[64]

We may long for such conclusions and the hope they hold out for a more sexually egalitarian future for women. In the nineties, many feminist scholars also took this optimistic tack, preferring to read films as figuring women as 'empowered' rather than as the exploited, objectified, specularized victims of film criticism of the seventies and eighties. However, at this juncture, despite more than a century of cinematic representation of powerful women and the oscillations in sexual egalitarianism in the social sphere, now when, for example, the wage differential between men's and women's salaries is far from equal, we clearly need a more nuanced reading.

Significant to Drew's analysis is the fact that the films he discusses are predominantly comedies, the most common fictional form in the early stages of the development of narrative.[65] Many of them are also chapters of serials, considered transitional forms pointing towards the development of the feature-length narrative film. The serials were the first attempts to develop very long and complex screen narratives, and they served formally to bridge the short film and the feature, which came to dominate film production and exhibition after 1915.[66] As such these auto films, with their intrepid heroines, present interesting reading challenges involving issues of gender, genre, and modes of representation.

Miriam Hansen's work on forms of exhibition in relation to shifts in film form situates the increasing narrative channelling of gazes and themes and the move from the nickelodeon to the movie palace in relation to the effort to appeal to white middle-class women spectators. The incorporation of white middle-class women was a move towards establishing greater moral control of the cinema than had been exercised in the early exhibition venues, where the representation of transgressive subjects was the principal attraction in predominantly working-class spaces like the nickelodeon. The regulation of gender was part of the reformist project, as was the shift towards moral themes embedded in longer and more legitimate narrative forms that produced coherent systems of vision.[67] It is now a commonplace in film theory that continuity editing (parallel editing, match-on-action, alternation, narratively motivated cut-ins, etc.) was the discursive development that preserved and unified this coherence.

As Jane Gaines points out, Sergei Eisenstein saw Griffith's cross-cutting as a sentimental liberal humanism that imagined socially disparate groups as moving towards reconciliation. As inaccessible as the point of infinity where parallel lines crossed, this visualized reconciliation was considered impossible by Eisenstein, who preferred a Marxist dialectic of the symmetry of contradiction. The incongruence of race, class, and gender relations could not be represented by Griffith's 'mechanical parallelism,' with its false reconciliation of the irreconcilable. Eisenstein saw Griffith's cinema as bourgeois and patriarchal because it tied traditional sentiment to the mechanics of shot alternation, epitomized by parallel montage.[68]

Since Laura Mulvey's watershed article, 'Visual Pleasure and Narrative Cinema,'[69] the connections between the cinematic narrative devices of continuity/coherence and the coding of gender have been endlessly analysed. In the new work on cinema history, we find Mulvey's arguments linked to the development of alternation or parallel editing – cutting back and forth between two shots or sequences – as a first step towards classical American narrative form and the systematic structuring of sexual difference: 'For my purposes,' Lynne Kirby writes, 'what is important is that sexual difference, and the regulation of both point of view and the representation of women, became constitutive features of narrative cinema around 1908–9, and that alternation developed in Griffith as the chief vehicle and formal principle for articulating the narrative system.'[70] Gaines adds that, in Eisenstein's analysis, Griffithian parallel editing was 'patriarchal, but not in any of the ways patriarchal form has been identified by early feminist theory, for Griffith's patriarchal provincialism was inherited from nineteenth-century melodrama and from Dickens in particular.'[71] Gaines thus provides something of a counterpoint to Kirby's technical binarism.

With the gentrification of exhibition spaces, the development of the cinematic narrative system, and the regulation of sexual difference came – 'not coincidentally,' as Kirby points out – an attempt to suppress comedy as a genre.[72] Comedy was the most popular form in the days of the nickelodeon. It was by nature anarchic in terms of the abrupt clashes of the visual field ('the cinema of attractions'). Further, its 'unruly' visual abandon, mirrored by its unregulated working-class exhibition venue, also supported a perverse, subversive, and heterotopic arena of human behaviour in which the transgression of gender codes was a constant feature.

The attempt to evacuate comedy from the new moral order of gender-coded middle-class narrative was not successful. 'The idea that slapstick comedies were to be deplored as vulgar, tasteless, and not for refined audiences persisted as a legacy of the reform period, but the spirit of joy in pre-1909 slapstick cinema was too strong to be held down for long. Audiences loved it.'[73] In the 1910s, film comedy joined the anarchy and nonsense of the earlier mode with the narrative techniques of continuity editing.[74] Inversions and perversions of gender, class, and age, as well as parodies of moral and narrative clichés, continued to mark the genre as it developed in the serials – thus confounding Kirby's technical history.

It is at this intersection of comedy, seriality, and narrative that we find the daring and accomplished serial queens celebrated in Drew's monograph, thus requiring a more complicated reading than his notion that we can take their exploits as direct equivalents to social vectors. Ben Singer reads the heroines' display of intelligence, courage, resourcefulness, physical agility, and strength in the woman-centred serial queen adventure melodramas as addressing female spectators through fantasies of female mastery and empowerment.[75] Singer rather balefully argues that such characteristics 'may have less to do with an earnest stake in a progressive ideology of female emancipation than with the utter novelty and curiosity-value of a spectacle based on the "category mistake" of a woman taking death-defying physical risks, getting filthy, brawling with crooks in muddy riverbanks – in short, of a woman acting like a man.'[76] Lynne Kirby tends to agree with Singer, describing serials like *The Hazards of Helen* as allowing the woman protagonist only 'occasional opportunities' to display heroism.[77]

Kirby argues that to allow such occasional opportunities for heroism 'is simultaneously to gesture toward a more "modern" woman and to underscore the unusualness of the gestures.' Kirby does concede that the serials speak 'volumes about both the kind of spectator the American cinema was appealing to and the kind of viewer it was cultivating: an active female.'[78] Likewise Singer emphasizes the feminine costumes and sometimes delicate beauty of the serial queens: 'The female spectator was thus offered the best of both worlds: a representational structure that indulged conventionally "feminine" forms of vanity and exhibitionism while it refused the constraints of decorative femininity through an action-packed depiction of female prowess.'[79] However, Kirby asserts in a footnote that there were 'compensatory mechanisms: Helen must be rescued from time to time, be interested in marriage, and never desire to be a [train] engineer or manager, i.e., a man with power. Her expressions of power are bracketed as such, and there is no expectation of movement beyond the specified bounds.'[80]

Let me counter Kirby's analysis with a plot summary for one 1916 episode of *The Hazards of Helen*:

Story to date: Helen Holmes prevents collision of train carrying her father and Storm; saves Storm from death on burning train; recovers accidental duplicate map of railroad cut-off, averting withdrawal of financial support; recovers payroll from thieves by desperate leap. Kidnapped by Seagrue; is rescued by Storm [and] Spike. Saves Storm, Rhinelander and Spike from death in runaway freight car; rescues Spike from lynching; captures ore thieves. Saves lives of Rhinelander and Storm trapped by mine cave-in, regains money stolen by Seagrue's agents. Helen accepts Storm's proposal of marriage. After daring ride, Helen uncouples freight and prevents terrible wreck.[81]

I find it remarkable that anyone could characterize such plots as allowing only occasional opportunities for female heroism or, as Kirby does, to emphasize the marriage proposal over the many other incidents of the adventure. While I would agree that we should not become too giddy with our hopes of empowerment, I wonder how long 'utter novelty and curiosity-value' (Singer) or 'unusualness' (Kirby) can persist. *The Hazards of Helen* alone was produced in 119 episodes, in the longest run of any of the many adventure serials featuring male as well as female protagonists, and the serial form remained a popular staple of the industry well into the twenties. At the same time serial queens like Gene Gauntier, Grace Cunard, Pearl White, and many others (as Drew points out) performed a plethora of death-defying and intelligence-demanding feats. Furthermore, in an age when doubles were unknown and rear projection was not yet available, the fact that these feats were shown in actuality and in cinematic real time casts them out of the realm of fantasies into that of *demonstrations* 'of female mastery and empowerment.'

Serials like *The Hazards of Helen,* whose heroine was a telegrapher, were also consistent with the emergence of white middle-class women into the labour force in the first two decades of the twentieth century. Virginia Scharff has demonstrated that the earning and spending power of working women had significant effects on the automobile industry, and Kirby indicates that the film industry felt similar influences: 'If American cinema could be said to be courting the middle class at this time, it was a new middle class that was being addressed, one in which many women now worked and hence had money to spend on entertainment.'[82] Underlining the industrial efforts to capitalize on women's economic independence, Eileen Bowser has noted the importance of the cross-promotional strategy of releasing a serial film simultaneously with the publication of its story in newspapers and magazines, particularly women's magazines.[83] The construction of women as consumers thus becomes confounded with their recognition as historical agents, for this is also the period of women's efforts in the First World War and the newly energized campaign for woman suffrage.

If the feminist movement adopted automobility in its campaign for woman suffrage, and cinema images of the 'new woman' such as Shipman's in *Trail of the Arrow* and *Something New* offered both automobility and active heroinism as arguments for suffrage, the advertising industry also targeted women as consumers. Thus, Kirby argues, even if the serial queens' adventures were not about consumption per se; they are 'very much about a "new woman" being formed in relation to a modern, urban-based, and increasingly advertising-directed mass culture and economy.'[84] Apparently approvingly, she cites T.J. Jackson Lears's analysis of mass culture as a move aimed at domesticating women's demands for equality and deflecting them into 'quests for psychic satisfaction through high-style consumption.'[85]

Sarah Berry takes quite a different view of advertising and the cross-promotional strategies of the Hollywood film industry.[86] While confining her text to the ties between the film industry and mass-market fashion in the 1930s, Berry argues that the popular fashion system offered women an opportunity to challenge and shape their social roles. In contrast to male identity and status, which have historically been defined in relation to work, women's social status has been associated with 'physical capital,' their beauty and style operating as factors in their exchange value for men. Berry follows Elizabeth Wilson's argument that, on an 'abstract level,' post-Victorian fashion suggested both modernity and the democracy of urban society and thus contributed to a subjective feeling of emancipation for women.

Conceding the promotion of specific gender, racial, and class stereotypes, Berry argues that Hollywood cinema was concerned from its inception with issues of social mobility, acculturation, and fantasies of self-transformation. At least through the thirties, she argues, Hollywood films are marked by a fascination with female power. In addition to advertising clothes, cosmetics, and accessories, powerful women stars appeared in costumes that could be purchased in department stores through studio tie-in lines. Rather than a mass dictatorship of style to the public, in Berry's view, the cross-promotional relationship between the film and fashion industries marks a point of diversification. Unlike European couture, which is predicated on exclusivity, consumer fashion is about popularity, dissemination, accessibility, and eventually the proliferation of consumer subcultures, which render it increasingly difficult for taste to be determined by an hereditary elite. Berry thus valorizes, in contrast to Kirby and Bowser, the links between fan magazines, star endorsements, studio merchandising of clothes, cosmetics, and accessories, and the newly discovered buying power of employed women who had their own money to spend.

By foregrounding the performative aspect of social status and promoting fashion as a means to upward mobility, the use of stars as fashion types demystified social class: as costume becomes cinematic spectacle, connections between performance, gender, and discourses of consumer fashion are underscored. Thus Hollywood bridged the gulf between urban and rural, representing mass-market fashion as a democratic levelling of social distinctions and contributing to the erosion of traditional social categories for women.

Berry's argument here adds contemporary nuance to William M. Drew's straight-forward celebration of the serial queens as representations of triumphant female empowerment, although her argument is more convincing to me than Kirby's negativity. Singer offers a rather more balanced view. Citing the specific connection between the serial queen genre and social issues of women's emancipation and independence, he concludes by emphasizing 'the paradoxes and ambiguities of women's situation within the advent of urban modernity.'[87]

Automobility, Visuality, and Femininity

Developing simultaneously, the cinema and the automobile must be seen as potent modern cultural forces – 'social, perceptual and ideological paradigm[s].'[88] The automobile in particular has been a highly charged cultural image, significantly at play in the development of narrative cinema, and a destabilizing force within a historical field that was – technologically, geographically, and socially – ineluctably altered. Yet, in an essay that deals primarily with classical and contemporary films, Kathleen McHugh argues that the cinema has conventionally placed women at odds with automobility.[89] 'The spectacle of the automobile,' she writes, 'the moving vehicle within moving pictures, has had one truly outstanding and apposite competitor: the woman, placed before the camera for display. As a spectacle, she is said to arrest narrative momentum, bringing it to a temporary, erotically contemplative halt.

Women in traffic, then, represent a contradiction in terms, a challenge to the visual and narrative coherence of the cinema itself. In classical cinema, women who took the wheel and drove were depicted as "bad" women in traffic.'[90]

Citing *Psycho* (d. Alfred Hitchcock, 1960), in which Marion Crane is murdered after a long tense sequence driving the car, and *Written on the Wind* (d. Douglas Sirk, 1956) in which Marilee Hadley recklessly careens to inappropriate sexual liaisons in her sportscar, McHugh argues that 'the hallowed domesticity of Hollywood's good domestically-oriented girls is frequently secured by way of comparison with bad girls who take the wheel into their own hands.' Further, 'the automobile frequently is represented as a significant threat to women who are struck down, blinded or blown up by or in automobiles as in *Suspicion* (1941), *The Postman Always Rings Twice* (1946, 1981), *The Big Heat* (1953), *Magnificent Obsession* (1954), and *The Godfather* (1972). In each of these ... narratives the car is used to threaten or destroy romance, domesticity or reproduction. Thus women's positioning as spectacle and their domestic and romantic narrative roles exist in conflict with their automobility. Many films use the automobile to literalize the threat of women's economic and sexual autonomy.'[91] McHugh is optimistic, however, about new trends in the cinematic representation of women and automobility: 'An array of recent films present "brave new girls" precisely in narratives where concerns with appearances and the gaze coincide with and are sometimes overridden by women, automobiles and agency.' The question of the cinematic gaze in the form of matching point of view shots, the nodal methodological issue that has given rise to the many studies of women as spectacle, is provocative in regards to women and automobility.

Psycho, one of McHugh's test cases, is exemplary for her argument. Marion Crane (Janet Leigh) steals $40,000 and drives away. Her transgressive criminality coincides textually with her transgressive visuality. Whereas in classical cinema, as many feminists would still argue, control of the gaze has been the province of the male protagonist and the woman is the object of his look, Marion Crane shares, with the 'subjective' camera, control of the gaze. From the moment she leaves the office with the money, every shot in the long ensuing sequences (first in the room, then in city traffic, and finally on the highway) is either of Marion (third-person camera) or from her point of view. This pattern is rigorously pursued with the exception of a couple of shots from the highway patrolman's point of view – at the car's licence plate, at Marion sleeping in the front seat, at her waking up to his tap on the window. From that interruption onward until she arrives at the Bates Motel, the third-person camera view of Marion or shots of her subjective point of view (complete with representations of obstructed vision as it begins to rain heavily) control the visual field. The result, as Pudovkin knew so well, is 'psychological linkage' between the spectator and the protagonist. We share her point of view, her difficulties with vision, her fatigue and anxiety, and her guilt over the theft. In representing the visual field as identical to Marion's gaze, Hitchcock, as it turns out, is playing a mean trick on the spectator. The reversal of the conventions of gendered visuality and the suturing processes of identification it sets in place position the spectator for a nasty surprise, and, as McHugh writes, sets Marion Crane up for 'a very bad end.'

That the identification of the female protagonist with control of the visual field occurs while she is driving a car is central to McHugh's argument. As spectacle, bringing narrative momentum to an erotically contemplative halt, woman 'stops traffic' rather than propels the narrative. Therefore women who drive, who propel the narrative through time and space not only through controlling automobility but also through controlling visuality, must be seen as transgressive, as bad women to be punished or domesticated.

Such an argument is clearly at odds with William M. Drew's optimistic view of women drivers in the silent cinema. He is, however, dealing with films from a period that preceded the thorough-going inflection of the classic cinema with the suturing process of the point-of-view shot–counter-shot pattern. D.W. Griffith's use of tracking shots to record 'the most thrilling pursuit ever witnessed,'[92] – the race between the locomotive and the touring car running parallel to the railroad tracks in *A Beast at Bay* (1912) – was considered technically innovative at the time, as was his use of closer reverse shots of Pickford driving the car, taken from a camera car driving ahead of her. Two years later, as both a director and an accomplished driver, Mabel Normand exceeded Griffith's innovative reverse-angle tracking shot in *Mabel at the Wheel* by mounting the camera on a platform attached to the front of the racing car itself for reverse-angle close-ups. This comparatively new technique in 1914 became standard practice for filming close-ups of drivers in the silent era.

Although off-eye-line angle–reverse-angle cutting combinations at climax points were well-established usage by 1915,[93] it was not until the dialogue-driven scenarios of the sound era that the combination of the protagonist's look with the shot–counter-shot pattern became the principal modus operandi of the cinema. Thus, we must not rigidly read backwards into the silent era the specularization of women that is said to have developed within the later period.

In *Something New*, although rigorously matched eye-line shots do not occur, there is a conscious play with Shipman's gaze both in the prologue featuring the Writing Woman and, to a small extent, in the narrative itself. In the prologue, as Shipman sits at her typewriter anxiously awaiting inspiration, she casts her eyes to the distance and visualizes an imagined sequence in which the hero, in advance of their meeting in the narrative, accepts a bet with a horseback-rider that his car can win a race on the roadless terrain. As the sequence ensues, the film cuts back and forth between Shipman at her typewriter gazing into the distance and the race, which Bill of course wins. At that point, her inspired typing begins. These point-of-view shots constitute the chief device that establishes Shipman as author and enunciator of the piece.

As the narrative opens, we find Bill and an older man chatting in town awaiting the arrival of the 'stagecoach' – a motor vehicle. The older man tells Bill that he is waiting for his niece, a Writing Woman, and the two of them watch the passengers descend from the coach. There is a conscious play with the gaze in this sequence, as the two men observe the arrival of a professional-looking woman wearing glasses and a severe high-buttoned coat (the epitome of the New Woman); they assume that she must be the Writing Woman. Cut to Shipman inside the coach observing, unbeknownst to the two men, the comic embarrassment of the men as the woman in glasses rebuffs their greeting. Shipman then approaches them from behind and surprises her uncle by flinging her arms around him.

As the sequence continues, close-ups of Bill and off-angles of Shipman identify the two principals as mutual objects of desire. As the Writing Woman drives away with her uncle in the horse-drawn buckboard, the sequence ends with reverse angles of Shipman turning backwards to wave to Bill and close-ups of Bill as he watches them going off down the trail. Although Bill gets the 'last look' in the sequence before he turns away to enter a building, his gaze is not privileged by close-ups of the heroine as Shipman's is of her specular object. While Bill looks fondly off, the heroine recedes into the three-dimensional distance in a wide shot. Shipman's angle of vision, however, includes an iconicized close-up and loving iris-in on Bill as she gazes at her attractive new erotic interest. We might be persuaded to read this construction as an instance of reversal of the specularization process so endlessly detailed in feminist theory of the seventies and an indication of the variance in cinematic language produced when the woman director controls the gaze.

It might be tempting also to figure the windshield of the automobile as analogous to the cinema screen, as Lynne Kirby does in her book on the railroad in silent cinema. Kirby sees the train window as the cinema's 'double' in its framed, moving image, its construction of a journey as an optical experience, its radical juxtaposition of different places, and spatial and temporal rupture. Because passengers sit still as they rush through space and time, Kirby argues, the experience of train travel, like the cinematic illusion of movement, is based on a fundamental paradox: simultaneous movement and stillness. The sequential unfolding of a chain of essentially still images and rapid shifts in point of view are shared in both experiences.[94]

Kirby characterizes the railroad experience as 'panoramic perception,' annihilating space and time. The experience of cinema spectatorship also includes a new temporal consciousness and orientation to synchronicity and simultaneity, she argues, institutionalized in the classical system of alternation or parallel editing. Both panoramic perception and the new cinematic temporal consciousness were premised on discontinuity and instability; thus the construction of the unstable modern subject as destabilized, de-individualized, and urban.[95] As has been argued in twenty-five years of studies of cinematic narrative, this discontinuous, destabilized subject is kept in play not only by the classical system of alternation (already in well-established usage in the teens) but by the suturing mechanisms of all the devices of classical continuity editing.

Kirby argues that the cinema worked, in terms of filmic representation and modes of spectatorial address, on 'the thrill of instability, which addressed a new subject cut loose from its moorings in traditional culture and thus potentially open to anything.'[96] She therefore emphasizes the relations between the cinema, the unstable urban subject of modernity, and the relatively new forces of advertising, marketing, and consumption especially targeting the white middle-class woman. *Something New* could be seen precisely as addressing this new subject, the destabilized modern urban woman, 'cut loose from [her gender] moorings' and susceptible to the exhortations of the forces of consumption. The remanence of the film is, after all, industrial marketing.[97]

Also a machine of vision and an instrument for conquering space and time, the automobile likewise transports the spectator into fiction, fantasy, and dream. A significant difference between the railroad and the automobile, however, colours this argument. As Kirby points out, women's involvement with the train was as passengers. Because, like the automobile, the railroad was coded as masculine in the popular imaginary, the woman's position within it was potentially liable to gender and identity disruptions or reinscriptions. Although the railroad, like the car, brought opportunities for tourism, mobility, new social and geographical spaces, and altered temporal consciousness, the woman's experience as a passenger on a train had neither the psychological nor the social advantages of driving an automobile. In the train, enclosed in a heterotopic space wherein the sexes and classes jostled and mingled, the woman controlled neither the space within nor the movement of the train through space.[98]

In a car, on the other hand, the thrill of velocity, panoramic perception, temporal discontinuity, and simultaneity were combined for the woman motorist with feelings of independent mobility, power, and control. Perhaps even more dramatically, the possibilities of exploring unknown territories and traversing the boundaries between wilderness and civilization were available through this early sports utility vehicle, the car. In contrast to the train, which could go only where the tracks had already been laid, in the automobile, as *The Trail of the Arrow* and *Something New* indicate, the woman driver could penetrate geographies where no roads existed, and where possibly no person, male or female, had ever been.

We might hope that the experience of motoring might be mirrored in cinematic representation by a shifting of the visual field such that the windshield becomes more than merely a metaphorical mirror of the cinema screen. Especially for the woman driver, the notion of the panoramic gaze in control of the visual field might shift our reading of the represented subject as well as of the spectatorial subject addressed. With *Something New*, however, we have no such luck. As the capture, chase, and rescue proceed, the filmic discourse adheres firmly to earlier paradigms, as alternation or parallel cutting between the pursuing bandits and the fleeing couple dominates the film. The principal device is the wide shot, deployed for its expository utility in showcasing the automobile and the heroic feats of driving. There are occasional medium shots, usually cut-ins indicating the hero's passing out, the heroine's determination at the wheel, and the like. But there is nothing approaching the approximate eye-line matches of the sequence that opens the narrative, no reverse-angle close-ups of the driver through the windshield à la Mabel Normand, and no panoramas through the windshield/screen illustrating the heroine's experience at the wheel.

Undoubtedly geographical, technical, budgetary, and industrial conditions can be called to account here. In order to mount a platform holding the camera and cinematographer on the front of the car, Mabel Normand had to be travelling on roads. Hence the emphasis on the thrill of velocity in *Mabel at the Wheel*. In *Something New*, although Shipman's Maxwell moves at a pretty good clip across the plateau upon which it is speeding towards the cliff, the emphasis is on manoeuvrability across impossible terrain, and the car generally proceeds pretty slowly as a result. It might have been impossible to get a legible shot if the camera were mounted on the car as it bucked and tilted over boulders and down arroyos. Second, with few exceptions, such as *Back to God's Country* and *The Girl from God's Country*, both of which had substantial budgets, Shipman's films were produced with minimal financing. The exigencies of shoe-string economics obviated expensive effects or elaborate editing. *Something New*, in which she stretched the budget for a commercial into a feature-length narrative, is an extreme example of low-budget production. The cinematic connections between feminine agency and panoramic mobile visuality are therefore reduced to third-person camera angles of a monstrative nature.

Modernity and Femininity

We can account for the differences between early- and late-twentieth-century road movies to some extent through differing attitudes both to modernity and to geography. In the early part of the century, modernity was identified with femininity in vexed and complex ways. Anti-modernists recoiled from the insubstantiality, fragmentation, and meaninglessness of modern urban life, as Roderick Nash and many others have commented.[99] For many social commentators of the period, the coming of modernity and urbanization resulted in de-individualization and emasculation. Not least among the dangers of modernity was the increasing number of young single women in the workforce. Modern life in general and urban life in particular were understood by anti-modernist men as a brutal force stripping society of its potency and masculinity, as President Theodore Roosevelt kept pointing out. Kirby cautions that 'to be for or against the city or modernity as such was no black-and-white matter; one could despise modernity, and be either reactionary or progressive, while enthusiasm for the city could align the progress it represented with either capitalism or socialism. The feminine connotations of urban-based culture could also be received very differently.' The unhealthy, neurasthenia-producing city combined with the technologies of mobility and the cinema could be seen as producing a 'suggestive subject,' which for advertisers was the (predominantly female) consumer.[100]

At the same time, champions of modernity and 'machine aesthetics,' especially within the avant-garde, used the female figure for widely divergent purposes: 'In both avant-garde discourse on the machine and mainstream concepts of "progress" and "modernity," woman has appeared as a figure for reflection, a topos of inscription of the conflicts and contradictions surrounding the modernization of late nineteenth- and early twentieth-century European culture and society. In addition to the association of woman with mass culture, the hated Other of both traditional and modernist male culture, women and machines were often seen as belonging to two different paradigms: women to nature and the past, machines to technological progress.'[101]

Gertrude Stein's view was just the opposite of Kirby's. As a practitioner of the avant-garde in literature, Stein was convinced that modernity, characterized by 'novelty,' belonged to women. She argued that men belonged to nominality, the historical past, and stasis, whereas women had the authentic capacity for creativity. In her writing she cultivated simultaneity, spontaneity, free association or automatism, and the melding of the unconscious and conscious minds. Although Stein had little use for the cinema, in her writing she constructed a new temporal consciousness in the form of the continuous present tense, metaphorically mirroring the simultaneity and sequentiality that mark the cinema. In her great epic novel, *The Making of Americans*, she blasted space and time into continuous overlapping circulation, and in the lyrical prose poem *Lucy Church Amiably*, she represented women in loving friendship as simultaneously at the centre of and on top of the world. Moving freely between the city and the country in her Model T Ford, which she designated as feminine, Stein celebrated woman's mobility, independence, and joy in the modern world. Stein's optimism may seem, from Kirby's standpoint, to be a delusion of modernism. However, as an expression of a woman's experience of the time, Stein's view appears to have been widely shared by other women.

In *The Trail of the Arrow* Shipman, like Stein, saw her automobile as feminine and as a site of female friendship. In *Something New*, however, a sexually egalitarian and heterosexual world is negotiated with more difficulty. Here the geography of the wilderness, rather than being sentimentally aligned with the safety and propriety of traditional values, is dangerous for the woman due to its reactionary hold on historical gender, ethnic, and racial coding. The criminality of the villains on horseback – the antiquated technology of the western, which, in Shipman's scenario, links men with nature – is located not only in their attack on the mine, but also in their inveterate rapacity. Traditional patriarchal attitudes towards women are also inflected with issues of racial alterity, for the villains are Mexicans, complete with sombreros, serapes, and guitars (to which an intertitle refers scornfully as ukuleles; another intertitle derisively refers to the bandit chief as 'Chile Con Carne').

The American men in the film oscillate between traditional and modern attitudes towards woman. Both the old uncle and love-interest Bill accept the heroine as a Writing Woman, exhibiting a modernist attitude towards urban working women who are adept at handling another new machine, the typewriter. The old uncle, however, exhibits traditional masculinist attitudes, protecting his niece when the bandits attack, cautioning her to hide, and attempting to dupe her into believing that he does not feel the pain that they inflict on him. Although she hides in a space upstairs, she is discovered when she repudiates her uncle's protection and seeks to defend him. At this point she is captured and dragged to the bandits' lair, where a stereotypical melodramatic attempt at rape is the bandit chief's plan. In this hostile and apparently primitive environment, wherein traditional conceptualizations of gender roles prevail, she cannot defend herself against the destiny of victimized femininity. She needs to be rescued.

However, when Bill arrives in his automobile, the modern machine that is demonstrated as fully capable of negotiating the uncharted wilderness, a new sexually egalitarian partnership becomes possible. While the heroine shoots at the pursuing bandits, Bill drives the car to the limit of his capacity, at which time the heroine takes over with full competency. While no intertitles reveal their conversation, they are shown to discuss strategy and route, as well as the technological solution to their dilemma (pushing the boulder off the cliff with the car). In a tight medium-shot the heroine implores the machine, characterized in the intertitles as feminine, to see them through. The villains defeated, the narrative ends with a close-up of the partners, their heads together, both smiling lovingly in a direct return of the camera's gaze.

For this narrative, the promise of modernity is a salutary combination of mechanical reliability, geographical mobility, creativity, and gender equality. However, Shipman tempers this promise with ambiguity in the construction of the framing device that opens and closes the film.

Enunciation

Something New is charming as a comic melodrama and interesting as an industrial project. Its interest exceeds these rubrics, however, for Shipman here foregrounds her authorial voice. A little background may be helpful. Shipman's personal partnership with Bert Van Tuyle extended to giving him co-directing credit, although this relationship became increasingly fraught with each project. Joseph Walker, who taught Van Tuyle how to operate a camera, saw immediately that Van Tuyle was an 'amateur ... [with] little artistic ability ... He learned the few basic rules of directing in short order. I noted, however, that like his camera work, he lacked a certain artistry he would need to ever be big time.'[102] In an anecdote, Walker also reveals that Van Tuyle was egotistical, quick-tempered, sulky, and a poor judge of cinematic effect, 'but what he lacked in artistry he made up for in drive and enthusiasm.'[103]

With Shipman, however, Van Tuyle's drive and enthusiasm seemed to be transmuted into rigidity, mechanistic efficiency, and egotism. *Abandoned Trails* dramatizes the increasing quarrels between Shipman and Van Tuyle over artistic direction and control: 'It was not their first clash. Later, talking over their prospects alone, Dirk put it up to her, frankly: "Before we start shooting, we've got to settle, once and for all, who is who. There was trouble all through the last picture. A scene is all set, the 'script – your own, which you've written, so you ought to know what you want! – calls for such and such action. I have the actors lined up, rehearsed, everything ready. Then you open up; want this changed, something else done differently. It makes me look – well, like a heel. I want to know, right now ... do I direct or do I not?"'[104] Joyce placates him, but stands her ground. She insists on her love of producing, the fluidity of the production process, and the primacy of the final product. He continues to insist on 'discipline,' to which she replies, 'What does discipline count in making beautiful pictures? Does a writer never re-vamp his work or an artist follow a thumb-line? What difference if everything smashes so long as you finally build – beautifully!'[105] Despite their differences over control of the discourse, they continued to work together.

Nevertheless, in *Something New* Shipman contrives a framing device that situates her firmly as enunciator of the piece, as the film begins and ends with scenes of the Writing Woman at her typewriter. In the opening scene, typically set in a natural surround, with evergreen trees framing her, she is seated outdoors, in natural light, at a small rough-hewn table. Her typewriter sits before her, with a sheet of paper at the ready. She frowns, fidgets, and gestures in the time-honoured tradition of representing the author at work. Impatiently she tears the paper to shreds. Finally, she smiles and begins typing away at breathtaking speed. The film segues into the narrative until the end, when the framing device returns, with a shot of the Writing Woman typing now so furiously, evidently in such throes of inspiration, that she tips the typewriter off the table.

Shipman's later reflections on film are immensely interesting. *Back to God's Country* had been popular and Shipman's stardom was at its crest, but she was not prepared for the reception of *Something New*. 'When *Something New* was exhibited at the Los Angeles Auditorium under Maxwell auspices, the critic on the [Los Angeles] *Herald* complained: "When our leading stars stoop to advertise a commercial object like a Maxwell automobile, the Motion Picture business reaches a new low."'[106] Fifty years later, her comment on such derogation was simply, 'I think of the comment today when I look upon the really great of our profession as they sell most anything from soup to nuts. But I also think of the residuals they get for crunching crunchies or spraying deodorants.'[107] As is clear from her memoir, in which Shipman recounts experiences that situate her firmly in a commercial, industrial context, residuals would have delighted rather than shamed her. She was making her way in an industry that was proudly popular, commercial, and profit-oriented.

What she is ashamed of, later in life, are her pretensions to Art. She writes of the framing device of *Something New*: 'She, as Producer-Scenarist, not to mention Star, fixed herself a tricky conclusion I blush to recall. Damned if she wasn't shown at the typewriter, outside a tent, in a beautiful Borrego Valley locale, writing like mad and so carried away with her own out-pourings she tipped the typewriter off the table and so, the end. All fantasy, see? *None of it ever really happened!* Like a dream sequence. Seemed to this viewer they still stoop to this gambit, but with English Titles. We did it silent. This, in the name of Art, far more damning than going commercial!'[108]

What are we to make of such a view? Not only does this disclaimer contradict the passionate paean to artistry dramatized in the scene from *Abandoned Trails* quoted above, but it can also be seen to undercut the project that Shipman's memoir undertook fifty years later, that of constructing herself as a notable figure in the history of the popular cinema.

The history of the cinema has predominantly been conceived in two ways, as a narrative of invention (of the cinematic apparatus itself, or of its modes of discourse) and as a narrative of authorship (the heroic figures who produced the art of cinema). Authorship itself has been imbricated with the history of invention, particularly of cinematic modes of discourse, as in questions of which individual genius brought the first close-up to the screen, who first theorized montage, or who specialized in overlapping dialogue or deep focus or subjective point of view shots.

As a method of study, authorship has also been an approach that favours particular notions of the artist, both as a point of origin and as a unified artistic sensibility. Michel Foucault lists the criteria for the scholarly elimination of texts attributed to an 'author.' First, those works that are judged inferior are ignored, thus effectively defining author as having a standard level of quality. Second, works whose ideas conflict with those expressed in the author's other works are suppressed, with the objective of defining authorship as a coherent conceptual and theoretical sensibility. Third, works that exhibit stylistic traits not ordinarily found in the author's other works are also suppressed, thus producing stylistic uniformity as a characteristic of authorship.[109]

Shipman's comments on *Something New* could well be seen as precisely the sort of excision that Foucault describes. Constructing her own narrative of her body of work as an author, Shipman's memoir tends to concentrate on the works that she was particularly proud of and disparages those that she considers inferior (authorship as a standard level of quality): she attends at great length to *Back to God's Country* and *The Girl from God's Country* and dismisses those 'bits and pieces, "fillers"' circulated by 'Poverty Row' distributors.[110] The memoir also emphasizes particular commonalities within her work (the author as having a coherent conceptual and theoretical sensibility): her work with animals, the wilderness, her own heroic characterology (the many dangerous stunts, the communication with wild animals, and her professionalism as a writer and actor). The memoir proudly details the difficult technical achievements of the films, underlining not only her industrial expertise but also particular characteristics of style (the double exposures and split-screen effects). Shipman's comment on *Something New* amounts to a disavowal not only of her interest in 'Art,' but also of stylistic devices that are inconsistent with the textual markings of her other works (stylistic uniformity as a characteristic of authorship).

Paradoxically, Shipman's remark on the claim to authorial enunciation of *Something New* also decries precisely the sort of textual marking that studies of authorship would valorize. Claims to enunciation, intertextuality, and even the disavowal in the framing device ('All fantasy, see? *None of it ever really happened!*') usually provide valuable material for authorial analysis.[111]

A related conundrum attends the contradictions inherent in the cinematic modes of discourse of this text, for *Something New* insists on the actuality of the feats of driving skill by filming them as sequence-shots in real time. Long pauses frequently occupy the centre of the sequence-shots, in which minute shifts in the car's wheel-base or failed attempts to back up or go forward are shown without cuts until the desired manoeuver is successfully achieved. These monstrative episodes are, of course, requirements of the work of the text as a promotional vehicle for the Maxwell auto. Nevertheless, although the narrative of the chase and rescue may be transparent fantasy, in the core of the film, the man and the woman in turn driving the car, the actuality of the sequence shots indicates that it all really happened.

Thus the contradictory modes of discourse – the disavowal of the framing device versus the actuality of the sequence shots; the claim to authorial enunciation versus the industrial remanence of the project; the optimistic fantasy of modernity; the play with gender and genre – locate *Something New*, in contemporary critical terms, as a nodal document. This film becomes one of those texts that, as Giuliana Bruno writes, 'become part of a discourse of documents, placed within a network of other practices – a system of the space and duration of their occurrence, coexistence, transformation, recurrence, remanence, transferability, from the zero degree on, at all levels of dispersion, diffraction and contradiction.'[112] In this chapter, with its emphasis on social, biographical, and institutional contexts, its consideration of genre and gender in relation to the technologies of modernity, and the contradictions of enunciation and authorship, I have tried to demonstrate the capacities of Shipman's industrial projects to sustain readings within just such a discursive range of dispersion, diffraction, and contradiction.

chapter five

The Girl from God's Country

Eking out a living by taking on industrial projects, Nell Shipman and Bert Van Tuyle were determined to mount another feature that would capitalize on Shipman's promotional sobriquet, 'the girl from God's country.' Nell Shipman Productions raised the financing for *The Girl from God's Country* (1921) in Spokane, Washington. Although the company was trading on the star's earlier success, raising funds was far from easy. In this period of renegade entrepreneurship, fraud was an ever-present danger for the investor in films. Already Spokane financiers had been defrauded twice by stock-selling movie ventures that left town without producing a film.[1] Nell Shipman Productions had gathered a local board of directors and issued stocks for sale at a dollar each. Van Tuyle tried to talk the board of directors into a financial advance before the stock sales, but they insisted that the entire budget of $250,000 had to be raised first. Although in her memoir Shipman does not recount the financial details, in the fictionalized *Abandoned Trails* she constructs a scene in which Joyce (Nell) addresses the board 'enthusiastically, prettily, her big eyes dwelling on each man as if he alone must be the saviour,' citing the swiftly vanishing snow as the reason for urgency.[2]

The Girl from God's Country (presumed lost; seven-to-nine reels; copyright 25 September 1921) was a large-budget, long, epic feature, complete with airplanes, fires, and an earthquake. A film that was instrumental in Shipman's career – some blame the bankruptcy of Nell Shipman Productions on *The Girl from God's Country* – it precipitated the move to Priest Lake, Idaho, where *The Grub-Stake* (1923) and *Little Dramas of the Big Places* (1923) were made. Because *The Girl from God's*

Country is lost, it cannot bear the analytic scrutiny that can be applied to the surviving texts.

Although the text does not survive, there are many traces and echoes of the film, not only in Shipman's memoir and in *Abandoned Trails*, but also in reviews, trade paper notices, newspaper articles, and catalogues. From these traces we can approximate the circumstances of the production, reception, and institutional consequences of the project.

Shipman had written a script that not only took advantage of a setting similar to that of the successful *Back to God's Country* but also included magnificent effects, a dual role for herself as heroine, and an opportunity for her to fly in a plane. The American Film Institute Catalogue summarizes the plot:

> Carslake, a millionaire airplane manufacturer, his daughter, Marion, and her fiance are on a hunting party in the North. There they meet Neeka, a halfbreed girl who saves Carslake from the wrath of her grandfather, who recognizes him as the betrayer of her mother. Unaware that she is actually his daughter, Carslake adopts the girl and takes her to California. Otto Kraus, Carslake's competitor in trans-Pacific flight, enlists Neeka's sympathies for his efforts when she and Marion quarrel over social blunders, and he obtains the secret of 'solidified gasoline,' which Carslake himself has gained fraudulently from a demented inventor. The inventor's mind is restored when the hangar is set afire, and Neeka, realizing she has been duped, rescues him. Carslake's pilot is injured, but Neeka aids her sweetheart, a blinded aviator; Kraus is defeated in the competition and drowns after a fight with Neeka.[3]

Shipman played the parts of both women, undoubtedly with equal melodramatic gusto, alternating between a blonde wig and pale make-up and a dark wig with dusky make-up. 'I had achieved the ultimate of an actor's desire,' she wrote, 'twin characters shot in double exposure' (*Heart*, 89). The double exposures were produced by shooting a scene with one character, and then rolling the film back and shooting the same stock again with the second character occupying the other half of the screen. In *Abandoned Trails* Shipman mentions the tricky technical effect, displaying not only her understanding of the cinematic process but also her own consummate professionalism as an actor: 'The Bedroom Scene!

The difficult double-exposure where, in the role of the Breed-Girl she choked her rival, the Blonde-Girl, – also played by herself. God, but that scene had been tricky! Hours of re-take, matchless precision of action, – moving exactly on counts so that the dual characters would turn, speak and dove-tail their every gesture.'[4] 'I'd a theory about the twin roles,' wrote Shipman in her memoirs. 'They must be different from the skin out. Smell different, too. I'd scurry to my bungalow dressing room at Mr. Mayer's studio where a placid Negro maid waited, wardrobe laid out, everything ready. We'd strip me, put on a brand new make-up for each take. Back and forth we went: from the blonde's lacy nightgown to the brunette's costume, from blonde wig to brown braids' (102).

The lavishly budgeted film was produced on a grand scale, with an 'expensively salaried cast and crew' and extravagant action set-pieces (91). The $10,000 mansion interior set, shot in a studio owned by Louis B. Mayer, was one such extravagance. It came complete with a grand staircase and 'a forest' of 'fancy lamps' (104). Shipman's stunning wardrobe included 'the fashionable Sport's attire affected by the Blonde and the inevitable beaded buckskin and wool for the half-breed Brunette' (89).

Both Shipman and Van Tuyle were behaving with flagrant egotism: 'Its producer took it and herself seriously. The contract with the Finance Company read so-and-so: no interference, no editing other than what she decreed, etc. What Lola wanted Lola damn well got! She wore a handsome, leather, fur-trimmed coat and carried a brief case ... She hired and she fired. She afforded rages if there was incompetence ... The budget was slopping over' (*Heart*, 103–4) The animal trainer was also making extravagant purchases of exotic creatures, 'all of no use in our North American wildlife films, but so cute!' (104). Shipman here castigates her own behaviour, but Tom Trusky's note suggests that Bert Van Tuyle was also 'relentlessly indicted ... for fiscal irresponsibilities.' Trusky quotes a Spokane newspaper article that 'opens with the charge: "... the stockholders and directors [of producer William Clune's company] got the film [*The Girl from God's Country*] finished despite the fact that it did cost twice the amount Van Tuyle glibly assured the company directors would be required"' (172–3n).

The rival transpacific airplane plot was written into the script, Shipman admits, because she had developed a love of flying: 'I fell in love with the sky as I floated on my back in the water' when swimming at

Nell Shipman as half-sisters, in *The Girl from God's Country* (1921).

Venice Beach. 'On this afternoon when I saw my first airplane, flyers were barnstorming nearby, advertising a flight over the bay for five dollars. I swam to shore, climbed into my 1912 Cadillac in my 1915 bunchy wet bathing suit, drove the few blocks to the stamp-sized airfield and invested my five dollars. That did it, as it has for most of us ... I determined to someday get me fly-time. The chance didn't come until later when I wrote planes into my own opus for my own company. How I fitted such an improbability into the script would make a serial writer blush.' The flight sequence was expensive to shoot: two planes were involved, with stunt pilots and the rental of an airfield; 'the overhead was running near $10,000 per day.' Insurance had been taken out on the star (93–4).

The production of the airplane sequence was thrilling for Shipman. Two small single-seater First World War biplanes (known as a Jenny, with wings made from fabric stretched over wooden frames) flew side by side, wingtip to wingtip. With the Bell and Howell lashed securely in place, cinematographer Joseph Walker flew in one, sharing the single seat with the pilot. In the other, Shipman stood up 'and acted for the alongside-camera-plane' while pilot Frank Hawks, costumed in helmet, goggles, and silk scarf, doubled for Boyd Irwin, who played the blind aviator. Shipman was filled with admiration for those 'unbelievable, seat-of-the-pants flyers' who managed, without intercoms, to narrowly avoid collision as they banked and dropped through the clouds, keeping 'perfect formation with Joe cranking and me registering silent excitement.' Shipman was proud of the innovative footage: 'We got miles of flight stuff and, in that pioneer day, it was remarkable.' But there were dangers: When pilot Hawks was forced to make a 'frozen-stick landing,' the old Jenny 'fetched up against a fence and turned ass-over-teacup.' Shipman fancied that the producer watched the stunt flying 'with a speculative gleam in [his] eye,' as the sizable star insurance that the syndicate had taken out might render her more valuable dead than alive (94).

The end of the flight sequence required Shipman to climb down a ladder dangling from the plane onto the domed roof of a tower, thence to climb through a window to enter the interior set 'where Al Filson, playing the father of my blonde twin, was up to some hanky-panky' (94). She did not actually do this stunt from the plane; instead, she swung off a ladder hanging from a crane carefully kept out of camera range. However,

Joseph B. Walker, cinematographer, in the rear cockpit of the Jenny, shooting *The Girl from God's Country*.

the climb through the window was hazardous enough. Shipman narrowly escaped injury: 'sliding down the dome and entering [the] set by a window, I managed to fall and bang my rear-end, painfully. That there was not a permanent injury to my spine was due to what we called in the family the Barham bottom, a British example of ample sit-space' (95).

Shipman continues the description: 'Now, according to the script, this dome-set at the airfield was to be shaken down by earthquake. I don't remember how I worked that in but there being everything overboard but the kitchen stove it figures. The dome was an elaborate piece of set-building. It had a long outside flight of stairs down which Ed Burns was to carry my grandpa, the guy who invented the canned gasoline. The idea was to collapse the entire tower just as the hero, heroine and Gramps reached the ground. It was to be on fire, a seething caldron of flames following the earthquake' (95).

The fire got out of hand: 'It blazed too soon, too much. We were at the top of the outside steps, Grandpa acting unconscious, Eddie toting him, me stringing along behind. I saw the dome set collapse while the staircase remained flimsily intact but only for a few seconds. Then it started to tilt like a ladling spoon pouring us into the caldron. Eddie made a huge leap and got himself and Grandpa to the comparative safety of the ground. My own jump was spectacular. On the film it showed me reaching ground just before the staircase completed its dive.' Meanwhile, inside the hangar, the varnish on the wings of the airplanes, thought to be inflammable, blazed out of control (95).

In addition to the excessive studio set-pieces, they shot outdoor scenes on location: 'That I wrote the scenario for myself and presented myself with not only unlimited flying time but many weeks on location in the High Sierras at Kings River Canyon, must be considered sheer opportunism' (89). The location was remote – a long drive from Los Angeles over the Rim Route to Merced, Bakersfield; a dirt road to the edge of the canyon, where they left the motor vehicles; and then a two-day trip by horseback into the canyon. The rushes went out this way to the laboratory, a courier returning once a week with reports, mail, and fresh raw stock. Although Shipman was certainly used to the penury of remote locations, on this production they had an enormous support crew: 'We were said to have the largest outfit of wranglers to help us known' (90).

The earthquake / fire sequence in *The Girl from God's Country*.

Scriptgirl and Nell Shipman on location, filming *The Girl from God's Country*.

Still, the accommodations were not luxurious by any means. The star had her own private quarters, but it was no more than a cabin, and the wilderness was at her door. In her memoir Shipman recounts waking up one morning as a wild skunk climbed through an open window into the cabin. Her greatest worry was that her costumes would be ruined and that she would be shunned by the crew as well as by the two leading men with whom she had to play love scenes in her dual roles. She managed to keep her collie Laddie quiet in the bed while she opened the door with a long pole, 'hoping my friend [the skunk] might take the hint. He did' (91).

Meanwhile, a blizzard was hovering. If they did not manage to finish on time, they might be snowbound for the winter, but they 'had one last, difficult and rather dangerous scene to shoot before [they] could Get Out' (91). The heroine was to go down a white water stretch of the Kings River in her hollowed-out log canoe. Shipman had insisted on a real hand-hewn dugout rather than a birchbark or factory-made canoe, justifying the extravagance in terms of safety and realism. A birchbark canoe, she knew, would be too flimsy to survive the white water and rocky riverbed, and a camouflaged ready-made would register 'varnish-shiny factory-trim.' The dugout took weeks to make, using an old-fashioned adze and burning the inside. Eighteen feet long, cut from a thick pine trunk, the canoe was a very heavy piece: 'It took all the horses in camp to haul the craft from the forest to the river's edge.' Shipman was thrilled with the dugout: it was her 'dream boat'; it reminded her of her 'homeland of the great Northwest'; besides, 'it was beautiful. And so real!' (93).

Shipman's description of the canoeing sequence is dramatic:

The camera set-up for my ride over the rapids in my dugout canoe was on top of a big black rock which jutted out into the fast-running stream and brought the lenses mighty close to my face while I whirled past. It had to be me. If I didn't swoop by too fast, I'd register. No audience nowhere no time could holler 'Double!' The dangerous part of the stunt lay beyond the narrow rock-bound pass, out of camera range. Here the river got king-size and boisterous. The log canoe would swoop. But once past, it was in real white water which boiled and spumed hellishly. They decided to put a breakwater of pine trunks across this – boughs upstream, like a cheval-de-frise. The supposition was I'd tangle in this and come to a stop. Some of our crew and many of our cowboy hands were planted near to pull me out if the canoe overturned, which it surely would. The two leading men waited on the black rock, Eddie [Burns] stripped heroically to his trunks. He claimed I'd not even reach the set-up and he planned to dive to my rescue. Not in the script; but it sounded good. And he looked wonderful. Behind the worried director, Bert Van Tuyle, and his assistants, the even more-worried cameramen and their assistants, the pair of unconcerned tripods and the gleaming Bell and Howell cameras, loomed our Nemesis, the Head Ranger. Behind him, over the canyon wall, fanning up like the ebony fingers of an evil Genie – the storm. It was peering at us, at this silly little group of ardent fools so determined to risk life, limb and their jobs for a strip of celluloid not much longer than would tie a box of candy.

The moment was tense. It was our last shot for this location. The sun was setting. The light was getting low. Lower than Joe's [cinematographer Walker's] spirits. He was gnawing his fingernails. A few more minutes of shouted instructions, dire warnings, and we'd be sunk. Do or die. I knelt in my great, long, log canoe. I took up my great, long, hand-hewn paddle. I grasped my great, long, scared courage. (92)

Despite Shipman's determination, the scene failed. The heavy dugout ground to a halt on a rock midway through the run: 'No pivoting, whirling, spectacular stop to topple me to a watery grave! More of a sedate hang-up, on a submerged rock. I squatted, like someone in an overflowing bathtub, as waves of Kings River poured into her. Weeping with frustrated rage, I banged my hand-hewn paddle on her unwieldy hand-hewn gunwale and watched the sun go down.'

Shipman spent the following summer editing the film in the bungalow next door to her house at Highland Park, California. This was before the invention of the Movieola, so the editing process involved running the film through a projector; without a splicer, the editor cut the frames with a razor blade or scissors, scraped off a thin strip of emulsion and then glued the cut frames together 'with "stickum" smelling worse than nail polish' (115). Tom Trusky quotes a newspaper article that charges that it took Van Tuyle and Shipman 'as long to cut the picture – nearly four months – as they promised to take up in the entire production' (104 n). From the many hours of footage, Shipman 'cut

Working on *The Girl from God's Country*, Bert Van Tuyle wrote the caption for this photo: 'Making night scenes in the North Woods by the aid of flares. 60 dozen flares were packed in on horses for this work.'

and ran and re-cut until the footage was down to a reasonable 12,000 feet' (96). That puts the running time of the film at about two hours.

Shipman wrote rather proudly that the film was 'too long for a top half of dual bookings.' She described it as 'a real sockeroo, twelve reels of whizz and bang' (104). *The Girl from God's Country* premiered at Clune's Broadway Theater in Los Angeles on 11 September 1921. It was advertised as 'the greatest screen spectacle of the year,' with Shipman's name over the title and the promise of 'Clune's Augmented Concert Orchestra' and 'Rennie Becker at the mammoth organ.'[5]

In *Abandoned Trails* the opening of *The Girl from God's Country* is described as a somewhat qualified success. The foyer of the cinema was filled with bouquets of roses, and in the audience was 'Myer' (a thinly disguised name for Louis B. Mayer), who is described as 'an important magnate, a Producer whose opinion of the picture was of the utmost importance.'[6] Shipman blames a loud compliment from an old friend for disrupting the continuity for the audience, after which 'Myer, elaborately examining his wrist watch, pled a conference and left.'[7] Nevertheless, the end of the movie was greeted with applause and shouts of the star's name: 'it was their sincere tribute to the actress who had certainly put her all into their evening's entertainment.' When the star took a bow, 'A cheer greeted her. Someone thrust a sheaf of roses into her arms, someone hurried her down the aisle to the stage. The Orchestra Leader ... helped her to the stage and she stood there, sparkling-eyed, laughing, tears trembling on the edge of the laugh, holding out her hands to the applauding audience.'[8]

In the memoir, Shipman writes that 'everyone liked it because there was something in it for everyone to like!' (*Heart*, 104). An anonymous writer in *Wid's Daily*, a trade paper, reviewed the film positively:

There is certainly enough romance and thrills in 'The Girl from God's Country' to have filled a full-sized serial. So wide a range of material does it contain that with very little filling it would easily have made a production of fifteen episodes. As it is 'The Girl from God's Country' is crystallized romance and drama condensed in a single offering ... Many new thrills are introduced into this offering and the old hackneyed tricks carefully avoided. This, added to the general form that the picture takes, makes it unique and out of the ordinary ... In an early reel of this varied production

Miss Shipman introduces some very amazing wild animal work. She pets and feeds leopards, bears, wild cats – in fact, everything from a skunk to a lion. Among the thrills are included a fire, a rescue of a drowning man, an earthquake, a jump through a glass roof from an aeroplane, a race in the air, a parachute jump, a fight in the sea and an aeroplane transfer rescue. And these are only a few of the tense moments in this thrill-a-minute production.[9]

Notwithstanding this largely positive assessment, Tom Trusky cautions that reviews were 'mixed.'

The running time was a significant problem for the film: a Spokane newspaper article notes that 'Van Tuyle and Miss Shipman refused to cut the picture down from nine reels to the market requirements and threatened suit if any move in this direction was made. They acted in a way that the company had to cancel their contract and take the picture and have it put in shape so that it could be released.'[10] Evidently furious that the film was taken out of her hands and re-edited for distribution, Shipman writes, 'Van Tuyle and I caught it on general release in Santa Ana cut to nine reels. Murdered, slaughtered, senseless – well, perhaps it never boasted much sense but it did hang together. Not at 9000 feet!' She claims to have sent a full-page ad to every trade paper in the country advising exhibitors not to book the 'cruelly cut catastrophe' (104–5).[11] It may be significant that the *Wid's Daily* review cites a length of 'about 7,000 feet' – just a little over an hour long and considerably shortened from even the 'slaughtered' length of 9000 feet (about ninety minutes) that Shipman saw in general release. By the time of the review, the film was being sold as an F.B. Warren Corporation production, but Trusky notes that the film 'did not make money and soon disappeared' (*Heart*, 173n).

In retrospect, Shipman saw *The Girl from God's Country* as flawed by 'the cliff-hangers, the stereotypes, the utter lack of structural motivation.' Not only expensive, it had been 'so overloaded with twin stories for the twin heroines, so crammed with frenetic action that no character ever stopped to be. It leaped from one episode into the next: dog sleds to airplanes, earthquakes to snowslides. It was fun to make, but cost us dearly.' Of her own performance, she wrote: 'I was acting hell-bent, probably overacting' (102–3).

Shipman worried that she might have been 'black-balled in the business' because she had taken out the trade paper ads imploring theatre owners not to book the film: 'Would-be sandlot producers did not buck theater owners, big time Studios, Louis B. Mayer or Bill Clune' (105). Clune took over distribution of the film, 'and the financial results, for [Shipman], equalled zero' (117).

'Breedgirl'

It would, of course, be extremely interesting to see *The Girl from God's Country*, particularly in relation to questions of the representation of race and cultural identity, for in the film Shipman takes the part of an 'other' for the first time in her films. It was common in the silent cinema as well as in the sound era that non-white protagonists would be played by white stars. Lola Young suggests the material and ideological consequences of this prevalent practice: 'The casting of white people in [non-white] roles actually confirms the notion of racial superiority both in terms of the obvious – the part does not go to a [non-white] person – and the less apparent – the assumption that "whiteness" provides the "base" for portraying the complexities of human subjectivity.'[12]

In his book on the tradition of minstrelsy, Eric Lott takes a somewhat different position on the effects of white actors performing in blackface. For Lott, the imaginary racial transmutation involved in white actors taking the parts of other raced characters is less an articulation of difference than speculation about it. He suggests that race is imagined to be mutable, and that the burden of its construction is briefly thrown off, blurring the line between self and other.[13] For Shipman to take the role of the 'other' and to make her the heroine suggests a complication of meanings that ricochet rapidly around the space of construction.

Although there were few African-American actors getting black parts in the period, minor Indian[14] characters were regularly played by Native actors, especially in the many westerns made in the silent era.[15] The New York Motion Picture Company employed a troop commonly known as the 'Inceville Sioux,'[16] and James Young Deer, Redwing Young Deer, and Chief Dark Cloud were well-known Native actors in the Indian films that were among the most popular subjects of the silent era.[17] D.W. Griffith, who directed about thirty films that featured Indians, occasionally used Native actors in starring roles.[18]

It is possible that the minor Indian characters were played by Native actors in *The Girl from God's Country*, although there is no evidence either way.[19] There is reason for doubt, however. 'Notawa,' one of the secondaries in the film, is played by a white woman, and, only a few years later, when Shipman was making the low-budget short films that became *Little Dramas of the Big Places*, she cast one of the ranch hands as an Indian in *Wolf's Brush* (1923; presumably lost). Lloyd Peters, the ranch hand turned actor, was evidently so proud of the costume that he includes in his memoir not just one but two full-page photographs of himself standing with his arms folded across his chest and looking out into the distance with a serious expression. He is wearing long hair, beaded gauntlets the length of his forearms, and trousers that have flaps down the legs covered in what appear to be buttons. The second photograph is captioned, 'I played the Indian in "Wolf's Brush."'[20] On the dust jacket of the book there is an unidentified close-up of Peters with a very menacing expression in his furrowed brow and down-turned lips – as stern a visage as that on any wooden cigar store Indian. In both photographs Peters wears a band around his forehead – the headgear that had been invented by Hollywood as a fastening device for the wigs with their long braids. It appears that Shipman did not avoid consistently the pitfalls of either cross-race casting or hackneyed stereotypes.

Most writers describe silent films as representing Native Americans in a monolithically negative fashion. Hartmut Lutz mentions *Ramona* (d. D.W. Griffith, Biograph, 1910) as one of the few 'honorable attempts to stem the tide' of the deluge of movies depicting Indians as subhuman creatures in the silent period, along with *Heart of an Indian* (1913), *Call of the North* (1914), *The Dawn Maker* (1916), and *The Vanishing American* (1925).[21] Although D.W. Griffith is often cited as treating Indians sympathetically in his western family romances, Gregory S. Jay by no means concurs; he argues that Griffith's Indians are represented as primitive (though noble), incapable of adapting to the complexity of modernity, and therefore doomed, and aestheticized to produce poeticized sentiment for the white spectator.[22]

Roberta A. Pearson argues that 'the silent screen reflected and refracted the complex and contradictory position and representation of Native Americans within contemporary U.S. society and culture.'[23] As evidence, she offers examples of texts that valorized 'Native American

Lloyd Peters, in costume for *Wolf's Brush* (1923).

lifestyles as superior to that of the white man,' justified their land claims, and discredited anti-Indian characters.[24] Daniel Francis rightly points out that the valorizing of Indian lifestyles was a legacy of the 'noble savage' image from centuries of philosophy as well as fictional representations. The notion that 'Indian character and culture had something positive to teach Euro-Canadians' was particularly brought into play in the early decades of modernism. 'Indians were identified with the freedom, healthfulness and simplicity of the natural world,'[25] and were promoted as offering an alternative lifestyle in summer camp movements such as Ernest Thompson Seton's League of the Woodcraft Indians for boys.[26]

On the other hand, the frontier theory, which saw Natives as simply inhuman and deserving only of extermination – the only good Indian is a dead Indian – was 'part of a widespread popular discourse' in the United States.[27] Ian Angus suggests that the 'limitless outward rush into the wilderness' that characterized the American ideology of the frontier involves a domination of the wilderness (the well-known wilderness/garden dialectic): 'wilderness is turned into civilization without limit.' Moreover, what is actually new, 'the living of the frontier, escapes articulation and falls into the silence of violence.'[28] Rather than a frontier, Angus argues, Canadian social history has been articulated around something like a 'garrison mentality' (Northrope Frye's phrase): 'the garrison exists in the wilderness and constructs a border behind which it can retreat to attain order, identity, and self-protection. ... It is not a frontier in the sense of a receding line of confrontation between civilization and savagery.'[29] Homi Bhaba usefully suggests that the oscillating recognition and disavowal of racial, cultural, and historical differences always mark colonial discourse, which certainly characterizes the history of Canada not only in relation to Britain and France but also in relation to the First Nations of the country.[30] Francis points out that Canadians prided themselves on the fact that they, unlike their American neighbours, did not subscribe to the frontier theory and did not engage in the extermination of their Native population. Yet, the Canadian government advocated assimilation, which Francis argues amounted to the same thing.[31]

In Canada, it is impossible to consider the representation of Native peoples without encountering the North-West Mounted Police – the red-coated Mounties. 'One of the great romances of Canadian history, ... the Mounties came to stand for the very essence of our national character – a healthy respect for just authority.'[32] In Mountie narratives (histories as well as fiction), the Mounties miraculously quell the unruly Indian savages who, fuelled by unprincipled American whiskey traders, are constantly on the verge of wholesale uprising. This romance entails colonialism – 'Our mission is to raise the Flag / Of Britain's Empire here, / Restrain the lawless savage / And protect the Pioneer'[33] – and the erasure of the past. History begins here, and the Indians who are born in this historical moment 'share many of the characteristics of children ... It was the job of the police to take their hands and guide them gently toward the light.'[34] Ruled by their appetites, superstitious and credulous, the Indians are easily cowed by authority. The lone unarmed Mountie confronting a gang of angry Indian braves is a common trope in the popular literature.

The confrontation scene is a key element of the Canadian mythology that constructed Canadians as different from and morally superior to Americans, particularly in relation to the frontier theory and the issue of violent force. One important story in Canadian history is the arrival of Chief Sitting Bull in Canada less than a year after his victory over General George Custer at Little Bighorn (1876). In this frequently repeated tale, a lone Mountie rides unannounced into a camp of five thousand Sioux. He offers his hand to Sitting Bull, who, the story goes, is so nonplussed by the courage of the officer that he agrees to live in peace in Canada. Another example depicts a large troop of American cavalry escorting two hundred disaffected Cree back to Canada. At the border the cavalry is astonished to be met by only four Mounties, who successfully lead the Cree back to their territory. 'Writer after writer offered [these incidents] as proof positive that the Canadian approach to the Indian "problem" was superior to the American.'[35]

Writers of popular fiction seized on these stories from the 1870s dime novel until well into the 1940s cinema. Popular on an international scale, the Mountie narratives served not only Canadian ideology, but also chronicled the triumph of white civilization in general over the wilderness. The imaginary Indian, 'child-like denizen of the plains and forest,' was crucial to this ideological project.[36]

Shipman undoubtedly had grown up on these stories, as Canadian children have then and now, and there can be no question that she was familiar with the novels of Ralph Connor, who had an exceptionally successful writing career. He produced a book a year and became a household name in both Canada and the United States. Connor's *Corporal Cameron of the North West Mounted Police* (1912) and *The Patrol of the Sun Dance Trail* (1914) mixed fact and fiction in historicized stories of the Mounties and the Indians, the latter presented as 'wild, savage people, gullible and inept in their relations with White traders and pathetically addicted to alcohol.'[37] The certainty that Shipman knew Connor's work comes from the fact that her first husband, Ernest Shipman, produced a film adaptation of *Corporal Cameron of the North West Mounted Police* (1921). Although Nell and Ernie were divorced, they remained in contact, so Nell surely knew of his film.

Despite the failure of Ernest Shipman's production, films featuring Mounties were popular in the United States from 1909 until the 1940s, when their attraction apparently died out. Some of Hollywood's biggest stars appeared in these films, including Nelson Eddy and Jeanette MacDonald in *Rose Marie* (MGM, d. W.S. Van Dyke II, 1936) and Gary Cooper in *North West Mounted Police* (d. Cecil B. De Mille, 1940; shot on a Hollywood backlot). Needless to say, the Hollywood films tended not to replicate the Canadian ideological project, but rather rewrote the history of Canada in American terms, depicting, for example, Sitting Bull and the Sioux nation as looting and burning and massacring innocent white settlers in Canada – events that never took place.

Canadians nevertheless have been well served by the glorious romance of the Mounties. It has managed to create a history that claims its beginnings as the arrival of white colonialists and validates the dispossession of western Natives. The Mountie narrative also constructs an allegory of the extension of civilization into the wilderness while exemplifying the propriety of governmental policies of assimilation and what amounted to apartheid for the First Nations. Moreover, the myth affirms Euro-Canadian cultural values (the primacy of the law and the subservience of the individual to social order, as well as the putative impartiality of British justice) and – not coincidentally – constructs an identity for white Canadians as distinct from Americans.[38] Ever since the nineteenth century, and particularly in the face of the inundation of the world with American popular culture since the First World War, the construction and maintenance of a distinct Canadian identity has been a crucial component of government cultural policy and our own colonized egos.

I have no intention of dwelling on the question of stereotypes, despite the widespread use of the concept, especially in cultural criticism that deals with issues of race, gender, and ethnicity. As Steve Neale argued so long ago in an article that remains valuable, the limitations of the concept of stereotypes are immense and 'can actually block the productive analysis of the bodily differences central to categories of race and gender.' Because stereotyping is applicable solely to the analysis of character and characterization and must be seen as 'a repetitive structure that is relatively constant from one text to another,' the critical use of stereotyping ignores the specificity of particular texts and 'drastically underestimates' the multiplicity of their systems and operations. Stereotyping also implicitly assumes a pre-existing reality against which the stereotypes are to be measured, valorizes reader/spectator identification as ideologically and politically progressive, and privileges realism over the structures of difference and signification.[39]

But, just for the moment, it is necessary to consider character and characterization in relation to the plot of *The Girl from God's Country*, if only because that is all there is available as the film is lost. In *The Girl from God's Country*, Shipman sets the character of Marion, the blonde society girl, in motion on a hunting party. This should be indication enough of the construction of her character, for Shipman wrote more than once that her heart panged whenever she heard a gunshot in the forest or saw the dead carcass of a hunted animal. Shipman described Marion as a 'Society Sister ... [a] snooty-nosed, patrician Blonde'[40] and as 'indolent,' 'rich,' and 'bitchy.'[41]

The contrast between the wealthy snobbish blonde and poor but heroic Indian sets into place a cascade of dualities. On one hand, the assaults on the colour line (Eric Lott's phrase), played out by the same actor in dual roles, conjure up a kind of racial flickering, simultaneously producing and disintegrating the marks of race and difference. At the same time, the effort of corporeal containment in the racial masquerade that is literally smeared on the body (with make-up) brings with it the threat of intermixture that is furthermore underlined by Neeka's status as biracial. And although Neeka is the real heroine, and thereby provocative and transgressive in her strength, nevertheless the connotations of the power of an 'inferior' race are undermined because she is played by a white actor who implicitly demonstrates an ironic distance between self and the persona she performs. The final tier of the duality fountain is the role played by 'class prickliness' (Lott's phrase), now inflected with questions of race: well-bred Marion versus 'breedgirl' Neeka.

Neeka, the biracial heroine, rather than her blonde half-sister, is the one who saves the day. As a character, Neeka must have been imbued with Shipman's characteristic courage, wilderness knowledge, strength of will, and physical beauty. Such a construction would be demanded from a Shipman vehicle. After all, Neeka is the girl from God's country; Marion simply journeys to God's country for a hunting party. That Neeka is 'duped' by Otto Kraus may simply be a factor related to her femininity, reminiscent of the generically overdetermined and almost pathological femininity of the character of Dolores in *Back to God's Country*, who stupidly drops the gun in the snow in the moment of gravest danger.

However, one cannot help but shudder at the prospect of the 'social blunder' scene: was it played for comedy on the part of Neeka, or snobbish hautiness on the part of Marion? How would the 'Breed-Girl' be represented in such a scene? Would she seem to be justified in her attack on her 'rival,' or perceived as a wild savage creature? A note in the memoir suggests a bit of both:

> So here was *The Girl From* [*God's Country*], the dual role, blonde and brunette, confronting one another, quarreling – the indolent rich one sipping her morning coffee in a luxurious bed and, before the scene finished, having herself choked by her infuriated sister ... My brown half-breed hands, attached to my brown half-breed arms, crossed the invisible line which, as everyone knows, has to have the film in a double-exposure. I seized the white throat of that bitchy blonde who was myself in a wig and choked, hard. The same hands grabbed the coffee cup and pulled it back across the invisible line, clenching and smashing the china in a savage rage.[42]

We must infer that scenes like this would combine comedy and violence in a virtuoso display of physical performance. Such acts of performative irruption involving unruliness, comic set-pieces, physical burlesque, or 'savage' animation produce multiple meanings. While they insistently iterate the body as the place where racial boundaries are both constructed and transgressed, their inevitable outcome, according to Eric Lott, is to secure the position of the white spectator as the superior, controlling figure. Such dangerous moments of pleasurable disorder depend on a triangulated structure in which the white actor in 'blackface' shares the joke about the absent third party with the white spectator. At the same time, they are titillating in their ambiguity, as the humour/spectacle offers both a denial and a pleasurable conversion of racial fears.[43]

Such contradictions in the construction of heroic femininity with textual markings of race and sociality offer plentiful opportunity for speculation. Rather than confining ourselves to characterization or speculating about the lost film document, however, we may find some more material clues in a novel that Shipman wrote later using the character of Neeka.

Get the Woman and the Moral Structures of Melodrama

Get the Woman[44] is not a novelization of *The Girl from God's Country*, although there are a few overlapping tropes: the character of Neeka, the biracial woman from the north; a blonde woman from elsewhere; a blind man; a scene in which Neeka and the blonde woman fight, with Neeka's hands on the other woman's throat; and the melodramatic narrative structure. Although the plot, setting, and diegetical era bear no resemblance to the film (according to reviews, copyright plot outlines, and Shipman's own descriptions), the novel, like the film, situates questions of race at its centre.

Get the Woman belongs solidly within the melodramatic tradition. Peter Brooks has famously pointed out that melodrama is an essentially democratic form, in which the humble of the earth stand up to overbearing tyrants and express home truths.[45] Other writers have argued that melodrama is an essentially bourgeois form that confirms the values of the status quo.[46] All agree, however, that the form elevates the poor or the powerless – and especially women – to central positions.

More importantly for our purposes in the discussion of racial identity,

Brooks, inaugurating a trend in contemporary writing about the subject, has also argued that melodrama is a form in which we find a key encounter of the body with meaning.[47] Melodrama articulates an aesthetics of embodiment, in which the most important meanings have to be inscribed on and with the body.[48] Brooks traces the aesthetics of embodiment to the origins of melodrama in the French Revolution, and argues that the loss of a system of assigned meanings was followed by one where meanings have to be achieved; they must be the product of an active semiotic process in which the body is newly emblematized with meaning. In melodrama, the body has a new centrality as the site of signification: 'the melodramatic body is a body seized with meaning.'[49]

Although Brooks's theory is addressed to theatrical melodrama, later critics have utilized his ideas in relation to other melodramatic forms and in different ways – notably issues of the excessive rhetoric of melodrama and a resulting attention to the non-verbal, the ubiquitous emphasis on emotions and bodily sensations over rationality, and Geoffrey Nowell-Smith's influential psychoanalytic reading of the hysterical body of the cinematic text.[50] Brooks writes that the body becomes the place for the inscription of highly emotional messages that cannot be written elsewhere, cannot be articulated verbally. In melodrama the expressionistic body is usually a woman's body, on which desire has inscribed an impossible history, a story of desire at an impasse;[51] or, as Simon Shepherd puts it, the body is marked or moulded by the structure of causality that determines its existence.[52]

The 'problem' of *Get the Woman* is precisely the body of the heroine, who is a 'breedgirl.'[53] Her body is inscribed – 'memory re-enacted in the body'[54] – with her familial origins in transgressive sexual desire and miscegenation. Neeka LaRonde, daughter of a Native mother and white father, lives with her Indian half-brother, Miscou, in the tiny northern village of Neepawa. Neeka is lithe, beautiful, friend to animals, and replete with wilderness skills. Her virtue is demonstrated through her care for animals and is apparent, according to the melodramatic 'moral occult' (Brooks's well-known term), through her humble social status, located primarily in her racialized body: 'The body is never situated in innocent naturalness, free of acculturation; rather its physical features derive from and are scripted for a role within the relationships of morality and power.'[55] As Neeka herself explains, the racial hierarchy of the

North values pure blood, either Native or white. Miscou's parents, for example, were a Native princess and a chief; his blood is of the best, the oldest in the country. Neeka's parents also, each in their own purity – her mother a Native princess, her father a French-Canadian gentleman – were all right. But Neeka is just a 'common little breedgirl.'[56]

Out on the trail one day, Neeka comes across a sled in which she finds the frostbitten and near-dead body of Daisy Dell, a blonde woman from the south. Brooks has pointed out that in melodrama women's sexuality is aligned with criminality. He explains, rather instrumentally, that this association again arises from the origins of melodrama in the French Revolution and the figure of Marie-Antoinette, whose sexual immorality appeared inextricably linked to crimes against the Republic. Hence the melodramatic convention of the sexualized, and thereby criminalized, body and the necessity to read crimes as bodily.[57] It is no accident, therefore, that Daisy is wicked: she is a dance-hall girl and prostitute. Her professional use of her own sexualized body aligns her immediately with criminality, and the reader knows from the prologue that she has fraudulently obtained the map to Neeka's father's gold mine and that she plans to use it for her own ends. The coincidence of Neeka finding Daisy, who holds the key to Neeka's inheritance, is the first of the many instances of the 'providential patterns' that inform the melodramatic moral universe of the novel.

Not cognizant of Daisy's background or motives, Neeka and Miscou take her into their care and nurse her back to health. They are entranced with her shining blonde curls, her beautiful lacy clothes, and her seductive perfume. She soon comes to dominate their lives.

Very shortly, a Mountie, Robert Carlyle, arrives with a handcuffed murderer in tow. In Carlyle we find the embodiment of the Law, another frequent trope of melodramatic convention. Because melodrama privileges so-called common humanity above class difference, it also locates truth in deeply felt emotions rather than the discourses of dominant institutions. Hence the frequent confrontation of the individual with the law,[58] the institutional articulation of the 'repressive state apparatus' (Althusser's phrase).

Neeka is immediately attracted to Carlyle, for his body also exemplifies his heroic virtue: his tall, strong, masculine corporeality attests to his upright morality, and his golden hair signifies his 'pure' cultural heritage. Carlyle is appropriately and generically attracted to Neeka as well, but he finds out that, despite the delicacy and grace that suggests that Neeka's background is 'of the better class of French-Canadian,' she actually belongs to 'that unfortunate, socially doomed hybrid – a half-breed.'[59] Carlyle therefore quells his budding ardour and accepts Daisy's invitation to come home for dinner. The evening produces a tangle of confused and charged emotional vectors: as Daisy flirts outrageously with Carlyle, Neeka tries her best to be happy for them; Miscou observes Daisy and Carlyle morosely; Carlyle admires Neeka; Miscou and Daisy reunite; and finally, succumbing to his manly desires, Carlyle kisses Neeka, who allows herself to hope for pure love despite her own mixed blood. Although this scene is by no means written for laughs – this is no French farce – it belongs squarely in the tradition of comedy.

Although many writers have dealt with melodrama as a lower form of tragedy, arguing a serious public role for melodrama's interest in tales of personal truth,[60] Jacky Bratton has noted that the element of comedy is far too often overlooked. She argues that melodrama is a heteroglot, and calls up Bakhtin's definition of the heteroglot as a system of languages that mutually and ideologically interanimate each other. She notes the socio-ideological function of contending and contradictory discourses – the comic elements counterpointing or underlining the moral dialectic – as deliberate mediations performing ideological and hegemonic work in the text.[61]

Although Bratton is concerned with the function of 'low' characters, elements of farce, comic accents, extra-literary language, and the like, her work is more generally suggestive. It may be productive to read a wide range of melodramatic devices – especially of the sort found in *Get the Woman* – as predominantly comic rather than tragic. Not only the low characters, but also narrative devices and moral world-view, partake of the comic tradition: the providential patterns of coincidences, twists of fate, and the intervention of nature; romances, doublings, and mistaken identities; the appeal to nature over artificial and institutional constraints; the emphasis on sentiment and true emotion over rationality; and the happy endings.

From the Shakespearean comedy of the novel's dinner scene, which even includes music and dancing, melodramatic complications ensue. In disappointment, Neeka releases Carlyle's prisoner, who is killed by

Neeka's malamute, Giekie – another intervention of providence or nature – thus absolving Carlyle of the necessity of arresting Neeka. Carlyle proposes, but Neeka rejects him out of anger and runs to the woods. Refusing to be constrained by expectations of propriety or the repression of emotion, Neeka's volatile behaviour here is reminiscent of the eighteenth-century narratives of sentiment, which Shepherd notes as one of the sources of melodrama.[62] As a 'child of the forest' whose actions speak from true emotions, Neeka embodies the honesty of natural sentiment.

Carlyle departs for the south, asking Daisy to convey to Neeka his message of true love. While Neeka is away, Daisy reveals the treasure map to Miscou and, conspiring together to steal Neeka's birthright, they plan to wed. A mysterious blind man arrives. Neeka returns from the woods just in time for the large multiracial marriage celebration, at which Daisy lies to Neeka, telling her that Carlyle had left no message. After a confusion of identities, in another fortuitous coincidence, the mysterious blind man reveals himself to Neeka as Kippewa, Daisy's biracial guide on the route north.

Concealing his own nefarious designs on Neeka's birthright, Kippewa tells Neeka of Daisy's shady past and loose sexual morality, and that she has stolen the map to Neeka's father's gold mine and left the guide for dead. The celebrants observe Neeka choking Daisy in anger. By the end of the day, Daisy is dead. To protect Miscou, whom she believes to be the culprit, Neeka writes a confession in the church register, claiming that she is the murderer, and then flees.

The conflict with the Law is the central trajectory of the narrative. Carlyle's task of solving the mystery maps onto what Tom Gunning calls 'epistemania,' the desire to know all, to unearth the truth behind appearances.[63] As Carlyle attempts to track Neeka, he wanders into the uncharted wilderness. Camping out, he receives mysterious gifts of freshly caught fish and meat to sustain him, although there are no tracks to indicate how they arrived. The Natives are convinced that Neeka is a ghost, having died and reappeared as a 'loup-garou,' a werewolf. This is only the first appearance of the uncanny in the novel, a trope from nineteenth-century gothic melodrama.

Miscou's fate, which we discover in the next chapter, is the next episode involving the uncanny. Following Native custom, Miscou has buried his bride in the wilderness with all her worldly possessions. Driven mad by the death of Daisy and protected by Natives who see him as a kind of sacred legend, Miscou appears to be an eery figure from the netherworld. He stays to haunt Daisy's burial grounds, incessantly playing demented, discordant tunes on his battered fiddle.

Alone in the wilderness, Neeka survives, with Giekie's assistance, a harrowing battle with a pack of wolves. This is the first of what Tom Gunning calls the 'sensation scene.' At the centre of melodramatic structure, the sensation scene is addressed to the body and the senses, physical and emotional sensation, rather than moral cognition or rational processes. Played out on a large scale and designed to thrill, its spectacle and technical virtuosity require explosive measures of excitement and motion, as well as attention to verisimilitude. For Gunning, the spectacular sensation scene confirms the melodramatic mode as a dialectical interaction between moral significance and excess, which is aimed at non-cognitive sensations, thrills, and strong affective attractions.[64] The wolf scene, described in electrifying detail, fulfils all these functions, including the demonstration of Neeka's heroism once again.

After a near-death experience complete with visions – another visitation of the uncanny or otherworldly – again the hand of providence intervenes, as Neeka stumbles by fortuitous coincidence upon the remote cabin where her father and his mining partner had lived. The cabin is stocked with supplies and a letter leaving the partner's share of the mine to Neeka. She and faithful Giekie befriend a tame bear, apparently the miners' pet, who wanders into the cabin at the end of the winter. Determined to find Miscou and bring him back to the cabin, Neeka leaves in the spring with the bear and the dog.

The trio eventually meets up with Carlyle, who takes Neeka as his prisoner. In this extended central passage, Carlyle embodies the official rational discourse of the Law, with its obsessive desire to discover the truth from a legal and scientific perspective.[65] He is also the bearer of the Logos, for he torments himself ceaselessly about the claims of 'Duty' and 'Service' versus the emotional demands of his own heart. And here we find the extended debate that articulates the moral and emotional dilemma that so many writers find to constitute the generic socioideological foundation of melodrama.

Shepherd argues that at the heart of melodrama is the question of the individual in relation to the law. In melodrama the conflict is produced as natural versus institutional discourse, and in this ideological matrix the organization of suspense not only foregrounds the tension between differing knowledges and narratives, but, most importantly, it also specifically cathects the irruption of natural truth into the apparent logic of the law.[66] And this is precisely the ideological debate that Carlyle and Neeka carry out.

Upon completion of Carlyle's disquisition on 'the meanings of such words as "Honor," "Duty," "Society," and "Justice,"' Neeka assures him that she cares nothing for such notions, which she sees as man-made 'word-traps':

> She did not care, she said, for any of these things of which he had told her. They were as dry dust to her heart and the idle puffing of hot and empty wind to her ears. Once upon a time she had believed in them. Indeed, they were not unknown to her, for the Church, her friends, the McDonalds, her own father had taught her just such words: 'Honor,' 'Duty,' 'To be a good girl.' It was an old story and an older lie!
>
> Living alone in the wilderness, like a hunted creature, she had come to learn that these things – this Code – of which he spoke, were a man-made contrivance. It was very like the steel traps men put out on the Line to snare innocent furred animals. And there was no difference, really, between men and animals except that the former were the more sly. They trapped animals with steel but, to catch each other, they invented words.[67]

In such ways the novel polarizes the competing moralities of civilization and education versus 'forthright and honest' nature. Here we find a centuries-old vision of the 'noble savage' as an uncorrupted child of nature, celebrated by artists, authors, and philosophers such as Montaigne, Lahontan, and Rousseau.[68] Although in *Get the Woman* Carlyle by no means represents the corruption and moral decline of European and new world cultures, of which the figure of the noble savage often operated as a critique, Neeka's vision of the 'civilized' world with its 'word-traps' maps closely onto such a problematic, as well as the eighteenth-century narratives of sentiment. While Neeka certainly embodies the image of the noble savage and its critique of civilization, nevertheless I would not hasten to reduce her to the instrumentality of a simplistic and reductive stereotype. Distrust of the Logos has never been historically limited to a connection with nature or the noble savage; rather it has been a part of western philosophy since the Greeks, and endemic to the moral occult of melodrama.

Neither would I leap to align Neeka's view with anti-modernism, although certainly her (and Shipman's) emphasis on the forthrightness and honesty of nature nestles comfortably in the embrace of the concept, which attended the anxieties of urban modernity, of the wilderness as Arcadia.[69] Shipman was evidently perfectly capable of taking up the technologies of modernity (the automobile, the cinema) while at the same time espousing the spiritual and physical benefits of living close to untouched nature far away from the modern metropolis.

In this connection, Tom Gunning writes, 'One could claim that melodrama has always argued for the emotional needs of its characters against the desiccated discourses of established power: corrupted religion, law or hypocritical morality.'[70] Shepherd further notes that in these melodramas, the Law is a crucial institution because it is seen to address individuals from the outside, to turn subjects into objects by inventing narratives about them. In this case, in line with melodramatic convention, the evidence against Neeka is merely circumstantial. Because Kippewa knows that she wears Daisy's clothes, his identification of Neeka as the murderer results from this knowledge and the fact that the murder weapon was the scarf that Neeka was wearing – a 'narrative' indeed.

Finally, Carlyle determines to throw propriety and ambition to the wind for love. Even though marriage to a lowly breedgirl would ruin his career and his family connections, he declares his troth. Together they stay in Eden Valley, where they live for a time in romantic bliss, which is compromised only slightly by the handcuffs that imprison Neeka.

The French-Canadian trapper Jules, Neeka's old enemy and the wicked blind man's accomplice, who is tracking Neeka in search of the gold, discovers Neeka and Carlyle. But suddenly, a flash forest fire rages through the valley. Carlyle, crushed by a large fallen tree, is saved by Neeka, who commands the bear and the dog to remove the tree just in the nick of time. This exciting scene bears multiple marks of melodramatic convention. Here, as Brooks has said, 'Nature is under the command of rhetoric.'[71] Nature becomes an active agent in the narrative, participating in the achievement of justice – another uncanny event in which providential patterns prevail. At the same time, the thrilling and suspenseful forest fire provides another sensation scene. The raging and death-threatening fire fulfils its spectacular function, and, with another intervention from nature, eliminates the threat of the couple's exposure: the wicked trapper goes to a bloody death from attacks of hordes of mosquitoes in the swamp.

Brooks writes that, in melodrama – a literalistic realization of the importance of the body as the site of signification – the bodies of victims and villains must unambiguously signify their status. The virtuous body is frequently sequestered, constrained, and unable to assert its innocence and right to freedom.[72] As it turns out, Neeka has confessed to the murder to save her brother, who she believed was the culprit. Eventually, of course, Neeka solves the mystery: Daisy's murderer was Kippewa, the mysterious blind man. However, Brooks adds, the narrative cannot reach its dénouement until the virtuous body is freed and explicitly recognized as bearing the sign of innocence, a sign often inscribed on the body itself.[73] Finally, in the last throes of the melodrama, as the threads of the mystery continue to unravel, they discover Neeka's true identity. Neeka is revealed not only as 'white,' but also as of the most socially valued heritage. As it turns out, her mother was a descendant of British aristocracy, and the Native woman thought to be Neeka's mother was actually her nurse. Neeka's and Carlyle's grandfathers went to Eton together.[74]

Brooks reminds us that melodrama strives for moments when the repressed content returns as recognition. He invokes the phrase 'You! My father!' as exemplary of such a moment. In *Get the Woman*, the equivalent phrase would be 'Her! My Mother!' – the body again acting out as the crucial site of signification.[75] The liberal happy ending afforded to Neeka and Carlyle not only resolves ideological contradictions, but also dispenses with them absolutely by revealing that the racial impediment to their union was a mistake all along. Neeka is white! Neeka and Carlyle marry and set off for the idyllic cabin in the North. Finis.

While we may abhor such a conclusion for its flagrant racism, it is important to contextualize the ideological operations of the narrative within the socio-political assumptions of its time. As Chuck Kleinhans has pointed out, melodrama is usually strongly time-bound to its moment of production; it uses the social commonplaces of the time as an unthinking referential and moral norm in a way that is 'both its power and its liability.'[76] We may be able to unpack something of this appalling resolution by looking at other forms of popular racialized narratives of Shipman's day.

Miscegenation and the Tragic Mulatta

The questions of race, cultural heritage, class, social hierarchy, and sexual identity that drive the melodramatic plot of *Get the Woman* are multiple and complex. The plot involves characters who range across a multiracial grid from the 'pure blooded' characters of British, French-Canadian, and Native-Canadian extraction to the biracial Metis. These racially or culturally identified characters inhabit a particular matrix of sociality that is informed by conventions not only of melodrama but of conflicting local hierarchies: despite her analysis of the racial hierarchy of the North, which attests that the 'pure' blood of both white and Native is respected, Neeka dominates her Native half-brother because of her white heritage. As a figure of hybridity, Neeka is the character around which the textual markers of race, ethnicity, and gender circulate in the novel. Central to an analysis of this text are the discourses surrounding racial identity, miscegenation, and signification of cultural difference.

Well before the period of slavery, there were significant taboos against miscegenation and the progeny of mixed-race marriages. Lola Young traces 'Negrophobia' (Frantz Fanon's term) back to Elizabethan times, when 'blackness' was seen as 'some natural infection.' It was thought that sexual union between 'separate species,' as sub-Saharan people were thought to be, would result in infertile children. With the invention of the concept of 'race' in the nineteenth century, a more sophisticated version of the Elizabethan belief found traction in the notion that blood varies from race to race and that the mixing of bloods is undesirable. By the end of the nineteenth century, theories of natural selection were used to validate the belief that 'superior' groups would be detrimentally transformed by mixing with 'inferior' groups.[77]

Anxiety that interracial sexual activity led to social, moral, and physiological decay and degeneracy persisted well into the twentieth century. In 1927 there was an attempt to enact legislation to prohibit interracial sexual intercourse in Britain,[78] while Canada got around the problem in the twenties by enacting immigration legislation that effectively excluded blacks.[79] In the American film industry in the 1930s, the representation of miscegenation, or sexual relationships between white and black, was expressly forbidden by the North American Production Code of the Motion Picture Producers and Directors of America.

Discourses around miscegenation are variously inflected with issues of race, gender, and class. Taboos around working-class white women having sexual contact with black men are articulated differently than those prohibiting contact between wealthy Caucasian women and Asian men, for example.[80] Other considerations were applied to relations between American men and Asian women, who were considered appropriately 'feminine' and assimilable.[81] In the United States during the period of slavery, sexual relations with black women labourers and slaves were considered the right of the ruling male elite, and legislation was passed to protect white men's property from being inherited by the children of interracial relationships.[82]

Similarly, in Canada, British men sent to manage the Hudson's Bay Company trading posts in the North were allowed to take Native women as their 'country wives' without prejudice to their marriages in the home country.[83] The Indian Act of 1876 implicitly condoned Native men marrying white women: the man retained his Indian status, which applied likewise to his wife and children; in contrast, if a Native woman married a white man she lost her Indian status. This legislation remained on the books until 1985.[84] In another example of the prohibition against miscegenation, the White Women's Act, designed to prevent interracial intimacy, prevented white women from working in Chinese establishments.[85]

American notions about miscegenation vacillated ideologically as well as historically, as Jane Gaines points out. During slavery, 'Negroes' with white blood (usually fathered by the white master with a female slave) had a social advantage amid their peers, and their masters had an economic advantage in the possibility of demanding a higher price for slave property with white features. During the period of reconstruction following the Civil War, the connection between white likeness and economic success prevailed; later, as black society absorbed white cultural biases, so too did the connection between light skin and social status.

In the twentieth century, however, white society abruptly withdrew such favour; no fraction of Negro blood was acceptable. For African-American communities, the valuation of white blood eventually became politically offensive,[86] especially for African nationalists in the seventies, but preferences for light skin, Caucasian features, and straight hair still persist in the dominant culture, as any flip through the television channels or music magazines will attest.

The 'science' of eugenics, developed throughout the late nineteenth and well into the first half of the twentieth century, also argued the value of 'pure' bloodlines. Eugenics was embraced on a global scale and for many different reasons, and was not limited to Nazi ideology, as is commonly thought. After the breakthrough of modern biology around 1900, eugenics and racial hygiene took on a scientific cast, and its investigation occupied researchers who saw the new science as the redeemer of the western world. Eugenics societies were established in Britain, Canada, and the United States by the end of the 1920s, but the movement was much more widespread than membership in formalized groups. Feminists, health-care workers, legislators, scientists, and progressive radicals were engaged with eugenics in a variety of forms.[87] Central to the development of modernity as it was enmeshed with modern industrial and social revolutions, the eugenics movement was dedicated to the task of adapting humanity to a social ideal through biological means. Attention to health, diet, exercise, nudism, birth control, and sex manuals were some of the benefits – particularly for women – of eugenics. The consequences arising from notions about racial purity were far more dire, as the example of Nazi ideology and practice makes clear.[86] The 'science' of eugenics fell into disrepute following the Second World War.

Sander Gilman writes suggestively about the contradictions and oscillations of ideology and history in relation to miscegenation. Invoking psychoanalytical conceptions of identity, difference, and otherness and the infantile splitting of objects, the world, and the self into 'good' and 'bad,' he sees the construction of identity as imbricated with the projection of difference. Otherness may be invested with qualities of both good and bad (as in the 'savage savage' versus the 'noble savage'), but central to the process of the construction of identity is the creation of distinct categorizations that assist in the production and maintenance of an illusory order in a fragmented world. To disturb the boundaries of those demarcation lines is to reactivate the anxiety that the creation of other-ness was designed to alleviate.[89] As Young puts it, 'Having constructed racial difference as Otherness, "intermixing" becomes an unthinkable act, any desire for which has to be repressed. Scientific racist ideologies, racial myths, and stereotypical characterizations in theatrical, literary and visual culture are enactments which materialize from the cycle of repression and projection, as are individual, institutional and state rac-isms. Embedded in this psychic process are distortion, ambivalence and contradiction and it is underpinned by guilt and denial.'[90]

In American literature, one of the nodal figures around whom such distortions, ambivalences, and contradictions circulate is the 'tragic mulatta.' The term mulatto was used throughout the nineteenth cen-tury: 1850 censuses from Virginia, Ohio, and Tennessee identify resi-dents as mulatto, although by 1900 the term was no longer applied.[91] The literary 'stereotype' of the tragic mulatta was first articulated in the 1930s by Sterling Brown,[92] and the contours of the figure have been sys-tematically detailed ever since.

Although Brown traced the first tragic mulatta to Cora Brown in *The Last of the Mohicans* (1826) by James Fenimore Cooper – and thus makes Shipman's 'breedgirl' at home in this context – the character type has been cited elsewhere as originating from short stories by Lydia Maria Child, 'The Quadroons' (1842) and 'Slavery's Pleasant Homes' (1843). The tragic mulatta of abolitionist literature is a light-skinned woman of mixed white-and-black parentage. Typically, she is the daughter of an enslaved mother and a slave-owning father. Sometimes, she is ignorant of her mother's race and status; she believes herself to be both 'free' and 'white' until events following her father's death expose her true heritage. Remanded back to slavery and deserted by her lover, who is usually white, she dies the victim of male sexual predation. This portrait of the mulatta heroine as a sympathetic, helpless victim generally depicts her as pious, obedient, and domestic, hopelessly struggling to be pure, and notable for her beauty, sensitivity, and moral excellence. As a figure, she launched a serious critique of slavery and illustrated the gross injustice served her at the hands of the white master.[93]

During the Harlem Renaissance, the tragic mulatta theme was some-what revised. Rather than simply dying a tragic death, the mulatta protag-onist becomes disillusioned with the white world, in which she has been attempting to 'pass,' and returns to her black community. Nella Larsen's *Quicksand* (1928) and *Passing* (1929) are the most famous of these revised tragic mulatta tales, which are informed by the exploration of the psychological state of the black persona and the desire of early-twentieth-century black authors to change black literary representation.[94]

Although issues around miscegenation in American cinema are closely tied to the history of slavery and tend to concern themselves with intermarriage or procreation between white and black races, from the earliest days of cinema there has also been a strain of border-crossing melodramas utilizing motifs of Mexican, or interracial combinations of Native, Mexican, and Anglo progeny. An early example of the cinematic depiction of the tragic mulatta, here born of Irish and Indian parents, is *Ramona: A Story of the White Man's Injustice to the Indian* (d. D.W. Griffith, starring Mary Pickford and Henry B. Walthall, one reel, Biograph, 1910). The film was a retitled adaptation of *Ramona*, the famous novel by Helen Hunt Jackson (1884). In this 'foundational fiction' of the American Southwest, Jackson sought to do for the 'Indian' what Harriet Beecher Stowe had done for the 'Negro' in *Uncle Tom's Cabin*.[95] The novel was extraordinarily successful, with more than three hundred printings, numerous stage productions, and four screen adaptations between 1910 and 1936. It was attended also by nonfiction publications, a popular song, tourist sites, product tie-ins, and real estate developments, with businesses, streets, and even a town named after it.[96]

Ramona (played by Mary Pickford, wearing long dark hair and Mexican dress and shawl) is the foster child of the Moreno family, wealthy Spanish Americans who live in a 'Great Spanish Household' (intertitle). To the family's dismay, Ramona falls in love with Alessandro, a Luiseno Indian (played by Henry B. Walthall with a headband around his forehead, long dark hair, peasant shirt, and a woven band around his waist). When Ramona discovers that she is not Mexican, but rather half-Indian and half-Scottish, she elopes with Alessandro. Melodramatic tragedies ensue, including the couple's banishment from their home and land, the death of their child, and Alessandro's madness and, finally, his death. But there is a happy ending for Ramona: the faithful son of the Moreno family (in clipped beard and short hair, wearing full Mexican nobility gear – a short jacket with epaulets and lots of silver down the seams of his pants) rescues Ramona. They marry, relocate from California to Mexico, and raise a family.

At the centre of the novel is the biracial female protagonist who circulates within the text, between families, races, husbands, and nations, as Chon A. Noriega puts it, 'as a marker of social change and racial-cum-legal hierarchies.' The Mexican-Indian becomes 'almost the same but not quite' through miscegenation and assimilation, but, as Noriega suggests, 'despite her potential *racial* claims to whiteness, Ramona cannot exceed her *cultural* construction within the terms of Spanish colonialism – hence, her exile to Mexico.'[97]

Hartmut Lutz cites several more films that feature Anglo–Indian interracial love. *The Devil's Doorway*, (d. Anthony Mann, 1950) includes a romance between a white woman lawyer and a Native war hero; in *Broken Arrow* (d. Delmer Daves, 1950) a white man marries a Shoshone woman; Elvis Presley plays a half-breed in *Flaming Star* (d. Don Siegel, 1960); and *Two Rode Together* (d. John Ford, 1961) features a biracial couple. Needless to say, their love cannot be, and usually it is the Indian partner who dies.

Clearly many of the tropes of the tragic mulatta narrative could be found in Shipman's film, *The Girl from God's Country*. The central figure of the mixed-race protagonist alone compels such a reading. Young argues that the tragic mulatta embodies racial/sexual transgression, and that she is thereby doomed 'to live in confusion and fear.'[98] It is highly unlikely, however, that Shipman would have written for herself a starring role of such abject characteristics. The Shipman heroine is certainly susceptible to fear in the face of danger, and intermittent confusion or doubt can assail the melodramatic twists of the plot, but otherwise, it is inconceivable that Neeka should be portrayed as a tragic victim. As in other Shipman vehicles, essentially all partaking of the comic mode, the female protagonist must control the narrative with demonstrations of true heroism. Other commonalities with the tragic mulatta abound, however, including the melodramatic portrayal of the mixed-race protagonist as pure and noble, mistaken assumptions about the breedgirl's parentage and the eventual revelation of her true heritage, parallel romances, difficulties of assimilating to an unwelcoming culture (the 'social blunders' that her white sister derides), the romance with a white man whose social status appears to exceed her own, and, in the absence of the text, who knows how many more?

Stories of the tragic mulatta frequently featured a white sister or friend. Immediately we can see a connection with Shipman's two versions of the Neeka story, in both of which the trope of sisterhood or doubling of the female figures is found. In *The Girl from God's Country*, the two women are literally sisters, with a common father. In *Get the Woman*, although the women are not related by family, they share a house and a pivotal moment of the plot – the wedding and murder scene – is a melodramatic case of mistaken identity or doubling. Often in American critical literature the trope of sisterhood is read as a sign that these tales are ultimately more concerned with issues of white female identity and empowerment than with black women's lives,[99] but such is not the case, as it turns out, with either of Shipman's texts.

The Girl from God's Country does not share the resolution of the tragic mulatta narrative – either death, as in early versions, or return to the black community, as in the later approach. Certainly there is a 'happy' ending for Neeka in the film. Adopted by her wealthy white father and living in comfort in California, she is accepted by her white boyfriend and situated in the narrative as the heroine on every count – solving the mystery, saving her boyfriend's life, defeating the villain and thereby restoring her father as the winner of the competition. Notwithstanding the conventions of melodrama, which have a tendency to culminate in a happy ending that is not only impossible but that the audience knows is impossible,[100] a happy ending in a Shipman film *is* a happy ending, as it is propped consistently on the genuinely dauntless characteristics of the Shipman heroine. Thus while *The Girl from God's Country* may play on the familiar trope, the construction of character, adventure plot, and narrative resolution resolutely eschew the conventions associated with the tragic mulatta.

Get the Woman, on the other hand, maps quite closely on the tragic mulatta narrative. The figure of the mixed-race protagonist, who is portrayed as courageous, intelligent, beautiful, and spiritually pure, is at the centre of the narrative, and her mixed-race heritage situates her at the lowest rung of the social hierarchy, as she is quick to point out. A love affair with a white man of considerably higher social status is the hinge of the plot, and for most of the narrative the romance appears to be doomed precisely on the basis of her racial heritage.

Neeka nurtures Daisy and idolizes her golden curls, lace-trimmed clothes, and exotic perfume. She immediately assumes, when Carlyle comes for dinner, that he will fall in love with Daisy, and she accepts that as just, given her own racial make-up, homely garb, and her darker skin and hair. She sees herself as inferior to Daisy not only in beauty but also in social status. Despite her poor background, lack of education, and her own knowledge of her shameful profession, Daisy also assumes her social privileges on the basis of racial hierarchy alone. From Daisy's point of view at least, the privileges of subjectivity and empowerment apparently reside with the white character, although her assumptions are belied eventually by the twists of the narrative.

Just as occurs in *Get the Woman*, the trope of sisterhood involving a doubling of the woman figure is accompanied often in tragic mulatta literature by disguises and mistaken identities. Although such melodramatic plot devices may tend to confirm the racial hierarchy, at the same time they may suggest that the visible markings of race are unreliable cultural constructions. In this connection, the novel takes a double turn of the mistaken identity trope in relation to Daisy's death. When Neeka borrows Daisy's clothes for Miscou's wedding, the blind man mistakes her for the white woman on the basis of the tactility of the lacy scarf she wears and the perfume emanating from it. Here we find an example of what Lola Young raises as the question of the 'certitude of ocular proof' of race: 'The faith in identifying racial groups by selected phenotypical characteristics is shattered by what may be seen as the fallibility of ocular proof and visual knowledge.' She further suggests that the practice of casting white stars in non-white roles in the movies (as Shipman did for herself in *The Girl from God's Country*) 'would seem to point to the discardability of one of the main signifiers of racial difference.'[101] The momentary interchangeability of the two women, from the point of view of the man who, because he is blind, has no access to the ocular indications of race, suggests the racial liminality frequently invoked in discussions of 'passing.' Young also underlines the necessary connection to gender involved in these 'passing' narratives: 'the racially liminal subject who represents a dissolution of the line between white self and [non-white] other must be figured through a woman to ensure that the white masculine ego-ideal remains intact.'[102]

It is impossible to contemplate such blurring of racial identities in Canada without encountering the figure of poet Pauline Johnson. The daughter of a Native chief and a white woman, she was raised in a middle-class home on a reservation and received all the benefits of her father's standing. She became a celebrated poet in the late nineteenth century, giving much-publicized readings in theatrical settings. Race was decidedly hybrid and performative in Johnson's case, as she costumed herself as a Victorian lady for the first act, and then came out after the intermission in full Native buckskin (complete with a scalp hanging at her waistband) for the second act. Johnson performed all over North America and Europe, and even met Queen Victoria. She resented her status as a curiousity, however, and was always puzzled by the fact that her 'non-Native' poems were not as accepted as the colourful 'Native' material.[103]

In contrast to Pauline Johnston's performance of biraciality, Neeka's racial liminality is figured in another way in the novel, in the episodes in which she lives as an Indian in the forest. She puts on Indian dress, practises highly developed wilderness skills, catches fish with her bare hands, marks a trail invisibly, and travels through the forest without leaving tracks. The other Indians see her as one of their own. If Neeka is capable of living from both sides of her parentage at will, it is apparent that racial identities may be experienced and perceived as discontinuous and fragmented and that the boundaries of race are more porous or illusory than usually thought.

Jane Gaines usefully cautions that 'in the determination of social rank, we cannot easily extricate one sign of difference from another, and in American society, race seems to encompass a multitude of distinctions.'[104] Any fix on the visible/invisible dialectic based on skin colour is undermined, however, along with the ideological challenge to ocular proof, in the workings of the narrative of *Get the Woman*, for it is Neeka who is mistaken for Daisy, not the other way around. The 'breedgirl' can 'pass' for white, but the white woman is never mistaken for an Indian at the narrative level. While 'race' may encompass a multitude of distinctions, the ideological direction of the narrative renders 'whiteness' as fixed, essential, and ineluctable.

Tragic love affairs are endemic to miscegenation narratives of whatever racial configuration, for the doomed romance structures a narrative insistence on the dangers of miscegenation, whether or not it ends in death (as in the classic tragic mulatta tale). By no means limited to black-and-white sexual relations, there are countless examples in American films, including *Broken Blossoms*, a film that Shipman admired, and the many other Hollywood films involving Asian characters that Gina Marchetti discusses.[105]

Parallel romances frequently accompany the trope of 'sisterhood.' Gina Marchetti usefully points to the frequency of parallel love affairs in western literature (e.g., *Wuthering Heights*) and the ideological issues dealt with through this structure. Unresolvable ideological problems within one romance, she argues, may be displaced onto the other, where they find 'a certain equilibrium and sense of closure.' The death of the first tragic couple offers a critique of the social without changing it, as the sense of the inexorability of fate takes precedence over any plea for reform. The second couple, however, 'absorbs the social criticism of the first, weakens it, and allows for its accommodation within a slightly modified social order.' Offering a dual and therefore ambiguous perspective on sexual taboos, one couple provides the tragic punishment for transgression while the other enjoys the liberal happy ending.[106]

In the parallel romance of *Get the Woman*, between the white woman, Daisy, and Neeka's Indian brother, Miscou, the conventional melodramatic articulation ends in tragedy involving murder and madness. Unlike the more frequently encountered death of the racialized body, however, it is the white woman who dies in the Shipman novel. Rather than a motif of inexorable fate, Daisy's violent end comes as a result of her duplicity and criminality. Therefore any social critique of the prohibitions against miscegenation is mitigated by her construction as a 'bad' character, unless we would argue that her sexual immorality leads her to the ultimate sexual transgression, that of transracial and miscegenational relations with Miscou, the 'full-blooded' Native. Nevertheless, although it is Daisy who dies, the tragedy is ultimately Miscou's, not only because he has lost his beloved (a frequent trope of the miscegenation narrative) but also because, like Alessandro in *Ramona*, he descends into madness.

The tragedy of this couple is structurally effective as a warning to Neeka and Carlyle principally as a result of its location in the narrative: Daisy's murder takes place immediately following Carlyle's confession of love for Neeka. Thus, Daisy's violent end and Miscou's madness must be seen, as Marchetti argues, as a structural warning to Neeka and Carlyle of the dangers of interracial love. Of the other couple, Carlyle especially continues to agonize over the cultural and social ramifications of his passion for the 'breedgirl.' Although his misgivings are rendered in terms of his own career, family, and urban sociality, the death of Daisy continues to be a narrative motivation as a result of his belief that Neeka is the murderer.

Such narrative transpositions both propel the narrative and resolve ideological contradictions. Another of these transpositions is Shipman's version of the captivity tale, which is frequently found in narratives with racial issues as the axis. Captivity narratives are common in representations that involve Indians, usually involving the capture of the helpless white woman by the brutal savages. Issues of cultural difference, territoriality, gender, and racial boundaries ideologically activate such narratives and, in the American Western, often justify the massacres of the Indians. Captivity tales also underline gender roles in patriarchal terms, offering warnings to the woman who would stray from the homestead and thus functioning as cautionary tales for independent-minded women as well as justifications of racism. Marchetti notes the continuing popularity of captivity tales in the twentieth century, which 'seem to blend together all those things that made these tales compelling in the past: their exploration of cultural, ethnic and racial identity; their examination of women as markers of cultural limits; and their uncanny ability to project values and vices internal to a culture onto the alien to maintain a racial hierarchy of difference.'[107]

In *Get the Woman*, Neeka becomes the 'captive' of the Mountie in the central sequence in which he continues to investigate her criminal status and determines to do his duty. Abundant irony attends this device. Here is the noble Indian-identified woman (in moccasins and doeskin dress) as the captive of the white man, an ironic reversal of the trope of captivity often found in representations that involve Indians. A further irony is that, although Neeka is Carlyle's captive, it is she who must guide, protect, and finally save him. In one of the climactic moments of the plot, the forest fire in which Carlyle's life is at risk, tension is screwed to the sticking point by the captivity device: Neeka is in handcuffs and, as a result, has a very hard time saving him.

At the same time, mere ironic reversal cannot erase the ideological vectors of the situation. Cultural difference is relentlessly explored in this sequence of *Get the Woman*. Ideological differences regarding sexual

morality, religion, Law, ethnicity, cross-species likeness, and 'civilization' versus nature, are the continuing topics of discussion between the
couple, as they struggle with their forbidden passion in Eden Valley.
Luckily, Neeka's voice speaks as forcefully and convincingly as Carlyle's:
differences are highlighted but, for the moment at least, they are neither resolved into conventional hierarchies nor spuriously eliminated.

As for patriarchal gender roles, they are challenged by reversal and
then restored. Carlyle is, after all, the Law, the spokesperson for the
Logos, and – as Neeka so fondly hopes – is to be the Father as well.
Though debilitation, even helplessness, may intermittently mitigate the
Law, the restoration of order comes about through the heroine's
agency. This is consistent throughout Shipman's work: the domestic
heterosexual couple becomes a family as a result of the woman's desire,
but only after the man has proven to be vulnerable and the woman
heroic.

Representation of Difference

In the prose text of *Get the Woman*, race, class, and social standing are
represented by the realist textual markings that indicate idiosyncracies
of speech in both dialogue and narration. There are many contradictions in the racial schema at this level of representation. The characters
are represented very differently through spelling, grammar, and the
phonic representation of accent. At the apex of status are the characters
whose speech is represented without grammatical, spelling, or phonic
inflection. Factor McDonald's wife is said to speak correctly (she is
teaching Neeka to say 'these' and 'those' rather than 'dese' and 'dose');
Carlyle's speech is also grammatical and conventionally spelled. With
one significant exception, the speech of all the other characters is characterized by the use of phonic inflection, local phrasing, slang, and
incorrect pronunciation or grammar – signifiers of class, cultural heritage, or social status.

Many of the locals, including Neeka, speak with a French-Canadian
accent, which is phonically and grammatically represented. An unnamed local, a comedic low character, for example, exclaims 'By gar,
she got his man, that Mountie!'[108] The Scottish factor is described as
speaking with a distinct Scottish burr, although primarily idiosyncrasies

of usage are represented, as in 'Ye'll no want the burr I have in my tongue.'[109] Daisy's speech signifies her class roots and lack of education; she comes from a poor white rural family who lived on a farm in the United States, and she ran away at age eighteen for a life of prostitution and dance halls. She swears ('Aw! Go to Hell!')[110] and makes grammatical errors ('He's a man, ain't he?').[111]

In passages of direct discourse, Neeka is relentlessly depicted in difficulty with speech. Here is an example: 'That is jus' what I do to go to my Miscou! ... Jomp in my sled an' one-two-three! I be there to give heem one beeg surprise!'[112] In melodramatic tradition, it is precisely Neeka's inability to speak that is the evidence of her truth; her body – her bearing – takes over from words as the reliable guarantor of meaning.[113] Concomitantly, the representation of speech and speechlessness is instrumental in the social and familial acceptance that Neeka enjoys when she finally meets Carlyle's mother, the British woman who speaks to Neeka in French. As Neeka recalls: 'At first we were so funny! She would look at me so sharp and speak, all quick, in French.' But then they bond forever when they pray together in the expression of the devout body.[114]

There is one significant caveat concerning the representations of the competing discursive formations. Although Neeka's accent, uneducated grammar, and patois vocabulary are represented in passages of direct speech, her 'thoughts' are rendered with conventional spelling and grammar and a poetic use of language that maps onto the narrator's own voice. We can read this in several ways, as the narrator elevating Neeka's interior voice to heights of complex eloquence of which she is incapable in speech, in a valorization of Neeka's intelligence and philosophies, or – more instrumentally – as simply a translation of Neeka's thoughts from her own language, presumably French, which contrast markedly with the ungrammatical crudeness of her speech in English. Both readings tend to confirm Neeka's status as speechless and therefore melodramatically virtuous.

The privileges of grammar, conventional spelling, and phonic illusion seem, at first blush, to align with conventional western social and racial hierarchies. The significant exception in the novel is the representation of Native speech, which contrasts markedly with studies of representations of Indian characters that invariably castigate popular forms for their depiction of Indian speech. Daniel Francis writes that 'the movie Indians usually spoke a form of drunken English consisting mainly of "How" and "Ugh." Occasionally they spoke an actual Native language, or something that sounded like one.' He relates one instance of a film that simply ran the English soundtrack backwards to depict Indian 'gibberish.'[115] The title of Gregory S. Jay's article on D.W. Griffith's treatment of Indians offers another example from the intertitles of *Romance of the Western Hills* (d. Griffith, Biograph, 1910): 'White man's book no good.'[116] Hartmut Lutz writes that the language spoken by Indians in the movies consisted of a specially invented 'Indianlect' or 'Garble': 'It included grunted monosyllables and idiomatically flawed rudimentary English that characterized the speaker as silly and of sub-standard intelligence and linguistic competence. In the majority of cases, however, Indians were mute and silent, uttering nothing but screaming war cries when charging to an attack.'[117]

In *Get the Woman*, according to the narration, the Natives speak in their own language to each other. When these moments occur in translation, they speak in grammatical and highly formalized English. After Neeka has said ('in their own tongue') 'Miscou never, never mus' drink!' Miscou replies 'Who is to say an Indian shall not drink? Do we say what the white man shall or shall not do? Here, in our own country, shall he say what we must do?'[118] The formally grammatical use of the verb 'shall' marks Miscou's speech as intelligent and sophisticated. And here are unnamed Natives who believe that Neeka has become a werewolf: 'Tomorrow I will seek the man who searches up and down our valleys and I will tell him we have seen the ghost of Neeka. Then will his hunt be ended and our game no longer disturbed by his restless feet.'[119] While the structure of such sentences imitates a conventional understanding of Native speech patterns (cf. Chief Joseph's famous line, 'I will fight no more forever'), it also contravenes the stereotype of the Indian in cinema and popular culture. The formality and dignity of the representation suggest the nobility of the Native speaker. And while we might once again dismiss such representation as another instance of the noble savage stereotype, it is worth pointing out that the depiction also accords precisely with Neeka's analysis of the racial and social hierarchy of the North as respecting pure white and Native blood equally.

This brief description of racial and cultural identity through the representation of speech suggests that there are multiple competing discourses in this literary text. This pattern of signification persists throughout the novel, producing a vividly realistic representation of local patois, educational status, and racial and cultural heritage. In this regard, Kleinhans argues that such realist narration constructs a dialectic that is potentially more progressive that 'the negative determinism of naturalism.'[120] Bratton also points to the confrontation between dominant literary language and the extra-literary, between the more 'natural' characters and formulaic representations of generic virtue and villainy. Rather than the frequent reading of excessive rhetoric as signs of the unconscious efforts of the text towards repression or as mere signifiers of its low-brow address, Bratton argues that the heteroglossial voices of the text must be read as signifiers of real contradictions.[121] Contradictory, ambiguous, and oscillating, the work of the text keeps such heteroglossial voices in play until the final page – when silence falls over the land.

'Race' and Narrational Configurations of Virtue and Villainy

At the level of plot and melodramatic characterization, *Get the Woman* produces a more complicated matrix of racial identity, villainy, and heroism than, for example, *Back to God's Country* or *Something New*. In *Back to God's Country*, the white men who humiliate and kill the Orientalized Asian immigrant and maltreat forty dog-generations are characterized by the intertitles as savage brutes, and the boat captain villain and his accomplice, the trading-post factor, are their direct descendants. The Metis and Inuit characters are complicitous only as they do the bidding of the white male villains. The villainy/heroism vector is aligned in *Back to God's Country* predominately along gender and species lines, with the white woman and the dog as proponents of moral virtue, physical prowess, and courageous heroism. In *Something New*, by contrast, villainy/heroism is aligned directly and simply with racial alterity, with the Bad Hats (the Mexicans) as generically villainous others marked by conventional cultural signifiers.

In *Get the Woman*, however, villainy is shared by the white woman who conspires to steal Neeka's birthright, the Metis guide who murders Daisy, and the French-Canadian trapper who is Neeka's enemy because of his cruelty to animals and who colludes with the guide Kippewa. Heroism is centred in Neeka, who is believed to be of biracial descent until the conclusion, and Carlyle, the upright British Mountie. Neeka's heroism consists equally of her wilderness skills, kinship with nature and animals, courage, self-sacrifice, and integrity. For his part, Carlyle is supported in his limited heroism – as in all Shipman's work, the female character is the ultimate hero – simply by his generic manly strength.

The supporting characters, all racially marked in a variety of ways, are situated in connection to villainy in complex relation to their cultural heritage. Neeka's Native half-brother, for example, transgresses his noble racial heritage briefly in his collusion with Daisy to steal Neeka's inheritance and in his marriage to the white woman, but he reverts to his culture in his response to the murder and thus becomes a kind of sacred legend for the other Natives. On the other hand, Neeka's father and his partner, both French Canadian, are on the side of the angels throughout, while the Hudson's Bay Company factor and his wife, both of Scottish extraction, not surprisingly align themselves with Carlyle, and show conflicted loyalties in relation to Neeka. Thus we find white women along with white, French-Canadian, and Metis men on both sides of the heroism/villainy equation, while the Native man oscillates.

These examples point to ambiguities in the novel's view of the hierarchy of racial identities in relation to moral value at the level of the plot. Another form of contradiction can be found in the contrast between the diegetic racial hierarchy and the valuation of the characters produced by the structure of the narration. The tiny Keepawa outpost apparently ascribes to Neeka's analysis of the northern view of race, the equality of 'pure blood.' Miscou is thus respected by both Native and non-Native neighbours, and the French-Canadian trapper, despite his villainy from Neeka's point of view, is economically valued by the community and accepted as an equal member, along with British Carlyle and Scottish factor. This is the diegetic value system in relation to racial and cultural heritage.

The construction of the narrative, however, takes a rather different view. The third-person narrative voice clearly values Neeka over all the other characters and, as the central character, her heroism and nobility are entwined precisely with the mixture of bloods that drives the melodramatic plot. Moreover, even though she is pitied by the community for her hybrid racial heritage, she is loved by her neighbours and the priest because she ascribes to Christian beliefs (praying in church, for example, and confessing in the church register to Daisy's murder). In contrast to the Christian values of the local inhabitants, however (although consistent with the conventions of melodrama), the narration clearly exonerates Neeka's 'natural' morality, her 'instinctual' response to sexual desire, her lack of concern with the formalities of religious marriage, and her pantheistic approach to nature.

Moral virtue here is defined in complex terms. Rather than the conventional melodramatic morality pitting feminine sexuality against sexual purity, as a simplistic Daisy as bad girl/prostitute/gold-digger versus Neeka as virginal good girl might suggest, Neeka's sexuality flows spontaneously and as naturally as that of the animals in the forest. A brief illustration: when Neeka and Carlyle eventually meet in the woods, Neeka takes a strand of Carlyle's golden hair, makes a wedding band for herself and proceeds to plan for a baby. No waiting for a church ceremony for her.

Rejecting bourgeois institutional repression and instead sympathizing with the free flow of Neeka's emotions, the narrative consistently absolves her of blame for the outcomes of her uninhibited spontaneity. For example, when she releases Carlyle's prisoner in a fit of anger, the narrative conspires structurally, with a tossed-off explanation regarding the dog Giekie's participation in the death of the prisoner, to deliver Neeka from the necessity of punishment.

At the same time, narrational sympathy also extends to the generic moral conundrum in which Carlyle finds himself. Although the sensations and emotions of other characters are described by the omniscient narrator, Carlyle is the only character besides Neeka whose inner workings are represented in detail and at length. From time to time Carlyle's thoughts are voiced through direct speech, rather than described in the third person, as in this passage when he meets Neeka for the first time: 'He was thinking: "Lord, how pretty she is!" Aloud, he remarked ...'[122] Often the narration takes up Carlyle's voice indirectly, as in this passage, when he discovers that Neeka is a Metis: 'As he expressed it, after, he felt as if his heart had plunged down the lift in one of those towering skyscrapers the Americans were building in New York.'[123] The use of the British term 'lift' for elevator and his reference to 'the Americans' signify that the narration, although third person, speaks in Carlyle's voice. When he must track Neeka as the murderer, his incessant reworkings of the dilemma are voiced in this way at great length, often with the two modes of signification combined. Here is one relatively brief example: 'At mention of the girl's name all the longing he had thought buried leapt into the light and at knowledge of her danger the desire to protect her, save her, at any cost, fogged all other thought. Duty? What duty had he except to that girl? What duty save to his own heart? ... "So that is the sort of rotter you really are!" he mused, brought up sharply by this stabbing honesty. "You'd cheat the Law, dishonor the Service and take her away – for yourself!"[124] Carlyle's internal moral debates are given a lot of room in the text, indicating their valuation within the narration. His dilemma is protracted over chapter after chapter following his reunion with Neeka in the forest, for until the very end he is not sure whether she killed Daisy or not. Page after breathless tortured page, melodramatically punctuated with dashes and exclamation marks and riven with rhetorical questions, situate Carlyle's consciousness as privileged in the narration in relation to that of all other characters except Neeka's.

The narration centres Neeka's consciousness, giving her thoughts, emotions, experiences, and philosophies extensive play, especially in those chapters in which Neeka is alone in the wilderness. The narrator shares Neeka's poetic responses to nature in paragraphs of empathetic description, and her perceptions, capabilities, and determinations are consistently valorized. Here is an exemplary passage that finds Neeka alone in Eden Valley as the winter is coming on, contemplating death: 'Death, she thought, could not catch her, or was it she who could not overtake him, win his priceless gift of peace? If Death was to be found, surely he would be up there in the Arctic, by the bones of her dead father! He was no longer something to be feared, but a Lover, a glorious, mystic Lover in whose arms she would find happiness. This was the song the wild geese sang to her lonely, embittered heart on the shores of the jewel-lake in the hidden Valley of Eden.'[125] Thus in terms of the construction of narration, the lovers are given equal verbal facility and equal time, as it were, in the representation of consciousness and the valorization of points of view.

In terms of structure, therefore, the privileging of consciousness as a narrational device produces an equalizing effect that belies the racial disparity at the level of (most of) the plot. Nevertheless, this parity unravels with the dramatic realignment of racial identities in the final pages of the narrative, in which the historic western hierarchy of racial identities is fully re-established, as Neeka discovers that her mother was white after all.[126]

Happy Ending

'Giekie, in the bow, shifted uneasily. The drip-drip of the paddle had ceased again and the canoe floated in a dream lake, a silvered silence from which the last, lingering touch of rose receded. Somewhere a loon called, softly. Giekie looked over his shoulder and groaned. It was as he feared – the Lovers were kissing!'[127]

The happy ending that evacuates the contradictions of the racial dilemma again underlines the potential resonances of melodrama with the comic, rather than the tragic, mode. As Jacky Bratton argues, conventional melodramatic devices are not to be taken seriously all the time: they are self-conscious, intertextual, and self-referencing within the reader/audience's knowledge of the genre. Readers are expected to recognize the standard tropes and enjoy them, relishing the turns of plot and their own expertise of anticipation. Indeed, as Bratton insists, such participatory pleasure need not discredit the work's moral assumptions.[128]

That last generic sentence – 'the Lovers were kissing!' – unfailingly brought a catch to my throat when I was a kid reading nurse novels. A bodily response that combined adolescent eroticism and wish-fulfilment, this catch in my throat was the culminating pleasure of the read, a true jouissance. At this point I am reminded of Jane Shattuc's 'good cry,' the equivalent emotive response to the melodramatic tragedy. Shattuc provides a powerful argument against the contemporary inclination to distance ourselves from the effects of melodrama through the concentration either on its complicity with bourgeois ideology or its ironic or contradictory value: 'Having a good cry represents the potential for the disempowered to negotiate the difficult terrain between resistance and involvement.'[129] In the comic mode of melodrama, rather than the good cry at the tragic end, the ecstatic catch in the throat allows for the pleasure of recognition and – at least for the moment – the mutual conjoining of desire.

As we have seen, the plentiful incongruities of the novel arise from the melodramatic grid of villainy/heroism in relation to cultural heritage and class and extend to the narrational privileges of representation of consciousness and the significatory practices of representation of speech. The generic values of melodrama overcome conventional institutional and western morality, and the construction of the heroine reverses conventional western racial hierarchies, but the 'happy ending' of the comic mode reinstates the racial agenda of the dominant culture.

Perhaps these 'contradictions' make the fantasy of the appalling conclusion more palatable. With that last line – 'the Lovers were kissing!' – Shipman's novel simultaneously worries the issues of race and cultural identity and provides erotic and joyful generic satisfactions. Without diminishing the racial problematic, we can relish the intertextuality and self-referencing of the mode and our identificatory participation as readers. At any rate, the moment of reconciliation of the irreconcilable cannot last beyond that flash of jouissance, the catch in the throat.

chapter six

:: :: :: :: ::

The Grub-Stake

Close to broke after the fiasco of *The Girl from God's Country*, Nell Shipman and Bert Van Tuyle had to sell the house in Highland Park, California, as well as the new car that they had bought in the first flush of the
financing. The furniture, baby grand piano, and heirlooms were put in
storage while the couple set about to raise money for another feature,
The Grub-Stake (1923; titled *The Romance of Lost Valley* in Great Britain,
and re-released as *The Golden Yukon* in the United States, 1927). As had
been her practice since the beginning of their partnership, Shipman
gave Van Tuyle credit as co-director, although she wrote the screenplay,
played the leading role, and edited the film.

The Grub-Stake

Shipman plays Faith Diggs, the daughter of a retired New England
sailor, Skipper Diggs. Faith takes in laundry and works in an art supply
shop. She makes a bit of money on the side by modelling for artists, her
buxom corporeal riches modestly covered by her enormously long hair
(a wig), until the day comes when she must sell her hair to buy medicine
for her father. Enter the villain, Leroy, a well-dressed, older man, gambler by trade. After Faith fends off his sexual advances, she proposes a
deal for a grubstake, through which Leroy would back her to open a
laundry in gold-rush country. Faith and Leroy get married, although
Leroy, who has a wife already, knows that the marriage is a fraud. Off
they go to the Klondike. Leroy is planning to market Faith's luscious
beauty in the sex trade and, at the same time, to get her dad out of the
picture with an overdose of his sleeping medicine.

Driven to desperation when she discovers Leroy's dastardly design, and further led astray by a crazy old prospector, Malamute Mike, who promises to take them to his gold mine 'at the end of the rainbow' (intertitle), Faith gets her ailing father into the dogsled and drives the team into the 'snow-silenced' wilderness (intertitle). Somehow they are separated and Faith stumbles off, wading through snow up to her thighs, sliding down mountain crevasses, injuring her leg, and getting hopelessly lost in a fierce blizzard – all just wearing a cotton blouse and a skirt! Of this plot device, Shipman wrote: 'I do not recall how Faith manages to lose herself in a blizzard, wallow in drifts to her neck, dodge ice-cakes like in *Way Down East,* but leave it to her writer. She does it.'[1] Faith then happens upon a cave inhabited by a hibernating bear. At first frightened, she relaxes when the bear greets her with a friendly lick on the face. Presumably she spends the rest of the winter there (in her blouse and skirt), for when she emerges, it is spring, which fortuitously passes almost immediately into full-leaf summer with ripe berries to eat.

A series of animal and wilderness scenes occupies a central portion of the film, until Faith is rescued by a young man, Jeb, who takes her to her father. Skipper is now in the care of Faith's old dance-hall friend, Dawson Kate, coincidentally the young man's mother. Eventually Leroy arrives and reveals that his marriage to Faith was legal after all, as his wife had already died. This plot device adds a bit of tension, which is relieved when Faith engineers Leroy's fatal fall from a cliff just in time to allow Faith and Jeb to marry.

For the dénouement, there are more lyrical animal scenes – frolicking bear cubs, a coyote nursing her pups, a mother duck with her brood trailing her in the lake – and an ending similar to that of *Back to God's Country.* Shipman later described the ending in ironic terms: 'At least it had a sockeroo finish! The final scene, shot before we quit the Spokane Studio and found our way to the nether-most reaches of Nowhere, was pretty good. It brought to customers that dimple we aim to create so it may cup their shed tears. "Spring Came to the Valley" piped the subtitle and we saw Faith and Jeb standing beside a rustic cradle in their rustic cabin gazing fondly at a rustic baby' (*Heart,* 110).

The screenplay that Shipman wrote, as she later admitted, was a pretty old-fashioned melodrama: 'Fact is, viewing the scenario from the wrong end of time's telescope, *The Grub-Stake* bears a strong resemblance to a Soap Opera! Perhaps the great-great-grandfather of them all! "They ain't done right by our Nell!" "Run for the roundhouse, Nellie, they can't corner you there!" The transfer to the Northwoods, cheek-by-jowl with the Real Thing, did not immediately transform the melodramatic tradition of my years as a Curwood heroine' (*Heart*, 106).

Production

The film was shot in Spokane, Washington, in the Minnehaha Studios owned by Dorothy and Wellington Playter, old friends from the days of *Back to God's Country*. Although a couple of features had been shot there in the past, the studio was floundering. With the assistance of the businessman father of Dorothy Playter, Shipman and Van Tuyle raised the financing by enlisting three hundred subscribers. Something of a joint venture, the film was intended not only to refinance Nell Shipman Productions, but also to revitalize the mostly idle studio. As Shipman wrote, 'this picture was a real "grub-stake" gamble ... for a prospector who *must* strike it, *must* pan out!' (*Heart*, 106).

Some of Shipman's other old colleagues were with them. Lillian Leighton and Walt Whitman, who had played Notawa and the inventor of the solidified gasoline (respectively) in *The Girl from God's Country*, were back on board as Dawson Kate and Skipper Diggs. Joseph B. Walker was shooting the film, with Bobby Newhardt as second camera and Bill Dagwell as assistant.

Shipman and Van Tuyle raised a budget of $180,000, the lowest since *Back to God's Country*, and nowhere near adequate to support the production expenses. The Klondike interior sets constructed in the studio were large and expensive. The dance hall was an elaborate set, with fancy private boxes complete with draperies in upper-floor balconies along two sides. At the front of the hall was an orchestra pit, a stage with a painted scenic backdrop and a proscenium outlined in lights. Flanking each side were two long wooden bars, fully stocked. The set was constructed on an outdoor stage covered by a retractable tarp in case of rain, under which hung a row of large silk light diffusers and truss-beams strong enough to hold cables and lights.[2] When the dance-hall scene was shot, according to Lloyd Peters, who was one of the production carpenters and later joined them in Idaho, there were three hundred extras on set, although in the film there appears to be fewer. The extras included 'dance hall girls, rough men they picked up on skid row, professional barkeepers, and game table flunkeys. Mingled with all of these were the real actors, some with lesser parts, others hired to dance and sing and some to fight' (*Lionhead*, 26). They also built the principal cabin set in the indoor studios, including all the furniture. The carpenters had to cut the timber themselves from a woodlot at a nearby farm, hauling two truckloads of logs to the studio. Two smaller cabins were built on the lot outdoors, and in the studio they also built the façade of the waterfront buildings, an apartment, and the artist supply store and studio (*Lionhead*, 29, 30).

The storm scene was rigged on a hillside and shot night for night. An airplane engine and two fire hoses provided wind and rain, and two batteries of Klieg lights were wired to make the lightning. Lloyd Peters recalled that they 'worked all night filming scenes in the rain, (artificial, that is) but it was just as wet, and you should have seen us by morning! Poor Nell! In one scene she was fleeing from the villain, trying to escape up a steep path with the rain blowing in her face. She ended up crawling in the mud on her hands and knees. It made a wonderful picture, but by morning she looked like a half drowned mud hen' (*Lionhead*, 33).

The producers moved the entire zoo from Highland Park and built cages for the birds and animals as well as a 'five hundred dollar' beaver pond on the grounds of the studio (*Lionhead*, 38). The cast stayed at an expensive hotel, where Shipman and Van Tuyle occupied a suite, and everyone 'ate high on the hog.' Shipman 'played Madame Producer to the hilt,' marching around in her leather coat and carrying her briefcase, but privately she was terrified – 'scared cold-silly inside.' She knew she would have to face 'the inevitable day when we'd run out of money and the shares must be assessed to pay for production delays, [and] unsettled weather, which snowed when we didn't want snow or melted when it must lie in Klondike drifts.' When that day came and Shipman had to meet with the grumbling stockholders – 'the toughest audience [she] ever faced' – she was saved from having to muster a sob by a Canadian rancher who rose from the group and testified that he had invested in *Back to God's Country* and made 300 per cent on his money. The production continued (*Heart*, 106).

After six months of shooting the interiors in the studio and the few exteriors with actors, the zoo was shipped down to Priest Lake, Idaho.

Using the carpenter shop at the studio, workers had built about two hundred new transportation cages as the old ones were in 'pretty bad shape and would not hold up for another move' (*Lionhead*, 38). Shipman and Van Tuyle had nearly run out of money, and still owed the actors two weeks' salary, although they expected they would be able to pay everyone when the film was finished and an advance had been acquired on distribution. As Shipman wrote, 'this was pretty much the way *Back to God's Country* ended its shooting schedule, the company broke and the animal sequences still to be made' (*Heart*, 111).

Reaching the towns of Priest Lake by rail and Coolin by car, the cast and crew moved by motorboat to a small hotel – 'a clapboard summer resort shack' – at the north end of the lake, twenty-two miles away (*Heart*, 112). Peters described the hotel as 'a large hulk of a house with its rough unpainted siding and its flat dormers, extending out of the roof two stories above the sandy beach ... A screened porch extended across the front of the house and faced the dock' (*Lionhead*, 61). Luckily it was more inviting inside than it appeared from the outside. 'Plain but comfortable,' the hotel 'consisted of a large combination living-dining room, a large kitchen and servants' quarters, a pantry and a long stairway to the upper floor, with a layout of eight rooms.' With so few rooms, some of the crew had to sleep on the screened porch (*Lionhead*, 62).

The transportation cages with the animals were ferried across the lake on a huge barge towed by local landlord Sam Byars's steamboat (*Lionhead*, 55). Shipman and Van Tuyle hired Lloyd, Raymond, and Paul Peters, a family of carpenters and helpers who had also worked for them during the Minnehaha Studio shoot, to build runs and shelters for the animals and cabins for the humans. The only technical staff by this point consisted of the cinematographer, Joseph Walker, and his assistant, Bill Dagwell.

The location shoot was demanding. For the cliff-hanging sequence, they had to climb to the top of the highest mountain in the region, Mount Lookout. The pack horse carrying the camera equipment began to buck on the way up and 'didn't stop until every camera was lying all over the place' (*Lionhead*, 74). The company had to make camp overnight on the mountainside, wake up well before dawn, and climb over granite boulders 'half as big as a house' to get a sunrise shot of Lionhead Mountain with its flat sheer cliff face a thousand feet high (*Lion-*

head, 79). Dummies and long poles were taken to the top of the cliff, where a ledge was built overhanging the crater, 'five hundred feet straight down.' The cameras were mounted around the rim of the crater, positioned to get the shot of the ledge and the side of the cliff. 'When they got ready to crank, they gave a signal to trip the ledge and down it came, falling into the crater. The villain went over with the ledge and Nell was left hanging onto a root' (*Lionhead*, 80).

Several weeks were spent filming the animal scenes. One of the scenes called for Shipman to be menaced by a wolf. 'In the scene, Nell was sleeping on the ground in the wilds of the North. The wolf was supposed to steal up on her and sniff around her head.' For this they used a large Siberian wolf that had been tame enough that 'you could pick it up and carry it under your arm if you were strong enough' (*Lionhead*, 85). But on the day of the shoot, the wolf lunged at Shipman, snapping at her face. Someone finally got a choker rod on him and forced him back into his pen: 'From that day on he was completely wild.' They finally had to destroy him (*Lionhead*, 86).

When the animal scenes were finished, Shipman returned to Hollywood to edit the material. With two cameras and multiple takes on each scene, they had shot 50,000 feet, to be cut to 11,000 feet – a meagre shooting ratio of less than five to one. Shipman and Van Tuyle convinced a laboratory on Sunset Boulevard to back the project to the point of a show print; in return for the cutting room and the laboratory services, the lab would hold the negative until it was paid off. Shipman edited the film in a hot little room on the third floor: 'sweating in the heat, dizzy from the chemical smell of the film she handled, cutting, splicing and running over and over, in a small projection room.'[3]

Shipman was proud of her editing skills: 'One afternoon I found a stranger at my elbow as I cut film and thought, "The sheriff!" but it was Doug Fairbanks' brother, visiting the lab as manager for his famous Star. He said that he did not think there was an actor in the business capable of doing what I did. Maybe not, at that time. Nowadays only Union Cutters and Editors may touch a picture.' The lab provided a splicer, so Shipman had an easier time than on the edit of her previous film, and considered her frame joints to be 'improved.'[4] Nevertheless, without a Movieola, let alone a flatbed Steenbeck (both invented later), the process was quite arduous. The film had to be run back and forth using hand-cranked rewinds, and the viewer was a small square of illumined glass: 'matching lip movement, eye direction, exits, entrances, close-ups to long shots' was a painstaking procedure with this equipment. Shipman was happy with the results: '*The Grub-Stake* was showing up good in the first, second and third rough cuts so I was fairly cocky,' she wrote. She was pleased with the work of the lab technicians as well; they performed 'miracles with color, using sepia with a silverish tone to overlay a warm pink tint. The snow looked violet in the shadows and the conifer trunks blushed rose under a silver sheen.' Meanwhile the cast was suing them for the two weeks back salary and trying to attach a lien to both the negative and the print. 'I could look from a window to Sunset Boulevard and see one of my best friends park behind the sheriff's car, ready to identify me. At different times others took over the job of surveillance. It was rather cruel, also short-sighted because to tie up the picture meant no distribution deal. A lawsuit could not squeeze blood from an impounded movie-turnip or turkey' (*Heart*, 114).

The lab stood behind Shipman, blocking the cast from advancing past the first floor and denying that she was on the premises. 'And so we worked though that hot September, ran the stuff at night, cut and edited and made changes. If we spotted the enemy waiting outside I'd exit via the fire escape and scuttle up an alley to a furnished cottage in what was called a "Bungalow Court"' (*Heart*, 114). Shipman wrote later that she 'rather enjoyed the stealthy exits via rear doors and the quick dashes to and from the building but in the end she was caught and must admit her identity'[5]

There were other money troubles as well. At Priest Lake, where the animals were kept, 'food was low, cash nil. Horses were to be driven in over the trail to be slaughtered for winter feeding. The estimate for grub to carry us through totalled $3000, plus the freight costs' (*Heart*, 114). Shipman and Van Tuyle arranged for credit with a friendly trucker who would haul the feed from the railroad to Coolin, and the man who owned the barge that would carry it to the camp would also wait for his money. But Sam Byars, the owner of the rented camp, was not so easily assuaged. Their debt relationship with Byars would have dire consequences in the future, but for now Shipman decided to ignore it in the interests of getting on with finishing the film.

When Van Tuyle failed to raise the money for a sales trip to New York, they pawned the furniture and Shipman family heirlooms stored in Los Angeles: 'The fares east were paid for by the baby grand, boxes of books, some paintings and the family silver' (*Heart*, 115). Shipman climbed out onto the fire escape for her last stealthy exit with the twelve reels of *The Grub-Stake* 'packed in tins like pie containers' for the trainride on The Chief.

In order to keep up an appropriate profile as Hollywood producers, Shipman and Van Tuyle stayed at the Astor Hotel in New York. But Van Tuyle had suffered a grievous blow to his ego: 'The fact of the need for haste, for a quick advance to Grub-Stake the outfit at Priest Lake, the blow to his pride of that company attachment we'd dodged tied a knot in nerves already stretched thin' (*Heart*, 116). Van Tuyle got sick. As a result, Shipman had to handle the trade screening for distributors on her own.

In *Abandoned Trails*, Shipman writes that it was the fashion then to put on an expensive preview lunch, preferably at the Ritz, with elaborate gifts for the press. She depicts them instead as peddling the film from door to door on Film Exchange Row.[6] In her memoir, on the other hand, she recalls that *The Grub-Stake* was screened in a projection room at 729 Seventh Avenue, a building that Shipman describes as 'offices of Biggies and Quickies, Film Magnate[s] and State's Rights Shoestringers.' About a dozen men formed the audience on whom Shipman's future hinged. There were a few representatives of trade papers, but most of them were 'sports-jacketed, sportsminded gentry of the Film Industry, prone to slump in the hard seats, squirm, exchange gossip and golfing dates, pay attention to their neighbors, their finger nails or give vent to an ill-concealed belch.' Shipman sat in a seat in the back row under the beam of the projection light, her heart in her throat: 'no one who has not gone for broke, all out, all the way, with his backer's bankroll at stake, knows what it means to watch the unreeling of twelve-thousand feet of film which carries his colors to victory or defeat.' At the end of the screening, most of the audience left without a word: 'they all made hasty exits from the screening room, seeming relieved that the ordeal was over. Some nodded to me as they passed but mostly I was ignored. It was over. The threadbare poke of specimen gold-dust had been assayed by experts, spewed out upon the counter, weighed and, I was sure, found wanting.' Returning to the Astor, where Van Tuyle was in bed, Shipman had to tell him about the reaction to the film: 'It looked as if we had a turkey' (*Heart*, 116).

But almost immediately a phone call came from Fred Warren, a partner in the American Release distribution company: 'He said he liked the picture very much. Why kid us? It was good holiday fare: homespun, exciting, made attractive by the animals and the scenery. He'd like to have it. Would we come to his office on 42nd and talk?' (*Heart*, 116). Van Tuyle still couldn't get out of bed, so he instructed Shipman to write down the list of questions she must ask. Although Shipman had done nearly everything else in the film industry, she had never negotiated a deal for international distribution of a feature film. Distribution of the other films had been handled by the studio (Vitagraph for the early films, First National for *Back to God's Country*) or by partnering producers such as William Clune, who had taken over the release of *The Girl from God's Country*. Now Shipman, burdened by fears for her future livelihood and by the normal trepidations of the director waiting for her creative work to be judged, had to negotiate with a hard-nosed, knowledgeable film businessman. Warmly praising her 'new baby,' promising to spend money on advertising and prints, place the film in prestigious venues, and ensure 'stellar billing' for Shipman, Warren snowed her big time. He estimated a gross of 'at least a half-million' and requested that she make personal appearances with the film to promote it. Of course she would do 'anything to make our picture a great big beautiful box office success!' There would be no advance, however: 'The nut paid, we'd get ours' (*Heart*, 117). The contract was drawn up then and there, and Shipman signed it before she left Warren's office.

Ruefully admitting that she had been 'green as grass,' Shipman told the sad tale of the aftermath. When she got back to the hotel that same afternoon, the calls started coming in 'from every one of the major distributors.' To Shipman's surprise, they had all liked the film and wanted to make an offer. When she blurted out that she had assumed they did not like it because they had left the projection room without saying anything, one buyer replied, 'Don't be silly, Sweetie, we never say anything at a Trade showing. You must know that!' (*Heart*, 117). The best of the deals that got away, Shipman wrote, was one from Metro that offered an advance of $75,000.

Shipman and Van Tuyle were living at this time in Byars's hotel at Priest Lake, where they planned to remain permanently after they built their own camp. Shipman had fallen in love with the territory when they had gone there to shoot the animal scenes for the film. She instantly recognized it as her 'Ultima Thule, the one spot in all God's world where you belonged, where your roots could go deep into soil which would forever nourish you' (*Heart*, 110). Her intention was to continue to make her films there, and she had plans already for the next project, a series of short films to be called *Little Dramas of the Big Places*. Van Tuyle was already engaged in trying to raise the financing for the project.

At the end of the winter, Shipman made personal appearances with *The Grub-Stake* in Portland, Seattle, and Tacoma: 'On its face this was to help bookings for *The Grub-Stake* but the inside fact was the $1500 per week I'd get' (*Heart*, 124). The trek out from Priest Lake to collect the money 'was a tough trip.' They had to go to Coolin by snowshoe and dogsled, and by canoe when a Chinook wind opened the ice. When they got to Coolin, a team and wagon on runners took them to the railroad, and thence to Portland.

For her arrival in Portland, Shipman wore the beautiful Hudson's Bay parka with the wolverine hood that had become her trademark garment since *Back to God's Country*. She found the city 'plastered with 24-sheet billboards in color' – all photographs of her. 'Me! Me! Me! I had not known such a kick since the morning when driving to work at Vitagraph I stopped across from a big poster on Sunset Boulevard which said in large black type "Remember her in *God's Country and the Woman*? Now see her in *Through the Wall*," and my name in even bigger letters.' Fred Warren had kept his promise about her billing, for her 'name [was] at least four feet high and it came first, "IN" not "With"' (*Heart*, 125).

But these personal appearances were no easy star turn. Shipman appeared five times a day at the end of the film, with dogs Lady and Tex posed at her side. Tex knew his part, and went into it without prompting, allowing Shipman to steal a handshake and a kiss as she 'swung [her] moccasined feet soubrettishly.' She told little jokes – such as the one about the 'Chinaman running from a Bear sniffing his tracks: "You like-um tlacks, I make-up plenty,"' and another about the Englishman who worked on the film driving a dog-team and said 'Porridge' instead of 'Mush.' Shipman ended the act with some Robert Service verse.

There were some full houses, but the supper-show was usually half empty (*Heart*, 126).

In *Abandoned Trails*, Shipman portrays the episode with considerably more affect and self-revelatory details. She describes herself as 'babbling' the Service poem selected as 'atmospheric' while 'hiding boredom and self-disgust.' She is lonely, and her position, standing near the screen as she waits for the film to finish, distorts the image into 'strange, elongated objects.' The audiences in 'the vast chancel of a modern movie Cathedral' are hypnotized with the 'ceaseless play of light, shade and movement,' and to her they appear 'petrified; like the painted figures on a back-drop which depicts the interior of an Opera House.' Into this chasm her voice 'dropp[ed] like a pebble into this silent lake ... thin and eerie ... It was with difficulty she kept her routine off the treadmill of monotonous repetition.'[7]

In Tacoma the performance had escalated almost into vaudeville. Other performers were added to the bill, including a soprano who was drowned out by the dogs who set to howling when she hit a high note. In Seattle – where the Shipman family had lived for a time – the local Elks honoured her, as her brother was a member, and a newspaper ran a contest with a gold nugget as the prize. As usual putting a positive spin on these publicity appearances, in the memoir Shipman writes that she enjoyed the gig: 'There must be some Carney show blood in me for I like publicity stunts,' she wrote (*Heart*, 126). In the novel, on the other hand, she writes that 'she considered that to show-off thus, without benefit of playwright, was the lowest rung on the theatrical ladder, – lower even than the poor freaks who exhibited their monstrosities in circuses.'[8]

The $4500 fee for the personal appearances was all the money Shipman collected from the film. Fred Warren and his American Release Company went into bankruptcy, and *The Grub-Stake* was lost along with the company's other assets. Hardest for Shipman was that, just before filing for bankruptcy, American Release Company had sold the British rights for $4000: 'There wasn't a chance of us clearing a dime' (*Heart*, 154). Although Shipman received no compensation for the British rights, there is 'some solace,' as Tom Trusky says, for viewers and scholars of the present day – if no consolation for Shipman herself – because it was as a result of this foreign sale that *The Grub-Stake* is preserved: the

British Film Institute has retrieved and restored the only surviving print, found in Britain (*Heart*, 180n).

Shipman had her own print of the film, and for some years she would earn a little money by offering the film and the personal appearance of the star to local theatres (*Heart*, 143). Five years after its production, and apparently without Shipman's knowledge or financial benefit, *The Grub-Stake* was recut to seven reels, retitled and rereleased as *The Golden Yukon* (1927).

Family Ties

Shipman wrote adventure scenarios, with cliffhangers (literally in *The Grub-Stake* – Faith hangs from a quickly loosening branch after the death of Leroy), coincidences, verge-of-death situations, threats to female virtue, plucked heart-strings, rescues, escapes, and happy endings. The plots often constructed the family romance along the way, and the happy endings featured the heterosexual couple in matrimonial bliss, either heading off to start a family (as in *Something New*, *The Girl from God's Country*, and *Get the Woman*), or with a family already underway (as in *Back to God's Country* and *The Grub-Stake*). In this way, as in so many others, Shipman's scenarios situate themselves squarely within the conventions of melodrama and popular cinema.

What seems unusual in Shipman's work is the representation of the parental family. Although the heroine usually enjoys marriage partnership and motherhood as an adult, there is never a trace of similar parental reciprocity in her background. In most of her films, a maternal figure does not make an appearance until it is time for the heroine herself to assume that role.

The adult women in Shipman's films never have a mother. In *Back to God's Country*, Dolores lives with her father in a cabin in the forest, and he is young-looking enough that on first viewing it is easy to assume that he is her husband. In *Something New*, the adventures of the brave young single woman protagonist come as a result of her visit to an old uncle, who lives alone. The heroines of *The Girl from God's Country* and *Get the Woman* eventually reunite with their fathers, but their mothers are long dead. *The Grub-Stake* features an elderly sick father to whom his daughter, the protagonist, is fondly devoted. In the surviving examples of *Little*

Dramas of the Big Places, the heroines are single women living alone, and the parental figure is removed to a fond position as honorary (if not biological) 'Grandpap.' The title of *The Clam-Digger's Daughter* hints pretty strongly that this will be another father-daughter scenario, and it is. Youthful fathers who exhibit fond affection for their rampantly Oedipal daughters, old uncles, or avuncular prospectors stand in for the family in Shipman's films, which tend to evacuate the mother altogether, except when Shipman herself plays the heroic mother to her own son.

Shipman thus replays the classic Oedipal scenario, in which, as Freud would have it, the daughter's trajectory into patriarchal womanhood involved renouncing her mother as love object and turning instead to the father. Fantasies of sexual relations with the father were eventually to be replaced with a father-substitute, a male lover or husband, and the woman could achieve her own desire for the phallus by giving birth to a son. The marginalization of the mother is seen in Freudian theory as a necessity for the normative development of the heterosexual woman.

The Grub-Stake is the only film in which this classic Oedipal trajectory is reworked. Rather than the virile youthful father seen in *Back to God's Country,* who is conveniently killed off by the villains to make way for the lover of similar build, in *The Grub-Stake* the father is old and sick. His daughter, Faith, provides nurturance and care for him, rather than vice versa; Faith also supports him financially, and for the first half of the film he occupies the position of almost a child. As they make their escape from the villain via dogsled, the father is too weak even to walk, and must be bundled like a baby into the sled, which Faith drives. Moreover, the character of the father is constructed partly sympathetically, and partly comically. His background as a New England sailor inflects his speech incongruously in this first urban and then landlocked wilderness terrain. His salty dialect colours his every verbal expression and renders him more childlike than fatherly, more comically cute than sage.

The suave well-dressed husband, another Oedipal figure who appears to be considerably older than Faith, is also repudiated in the screenplay. From the outset, Leroy's sexual designs on Faith are apparent, and in the near-rape scene that sets their relationship in motion, she makes it very clear that Freudian Oedipal fantasies are not part of her character. She rebuffs his advances forcefully; in fact she socks him in the jaw. She insists on a businesslike arrangement of a real grubstake, in which he would finance her laundry business in return for a share of the earnings, and accuses him of not taking her seriously because she is a woman. By a melodramatic turn of the plot, they are married – as Shipman wrote later, 'in deference to the Hays Office,' presumably to account for a young woman travelling with an older man (*Heart*, 109).

As the plot thickens and Faith becomes virtually indentured to a job as a dance-hall girl, the representation of feminine sexuality is comically contradictory as it is pushed to the level of the masquerade. Rather than the free-flowing naturalness of sexuality and corporeal ease that marked Shipman's previous work (especially *Back to God's Country, Something New*, and *Get the Woman*), Faith is naive about the new requirements of sexual display. In the dance hall, where most of the other dancing girls are dressed in matching outfits, femininity is constructed in artifice, literally performative. Faith must wear the highly fetishized costume, make-up, and fabulous hat that Leroy provides for her, which contrast markedly with the casual, loose-fitting dresses, simple blouse, and high-waisted skirt that construct Faith's sartorial system for most of the film. Shipman's critique of the 'unnaturalness' of patriarchal expectations and the performativity of conventional representations of feminine sexuality is thus inscribed in the narrative in the depiction of Faith's naivety and ineptitude.

When the moment arrives when Faith finds love in the wilderness, it is with a young man of her own age who seems to have skills that equal hers. Unlike the husbands of *Back to God's Country* and *Something New* (and, tellingly, her partner Bert Van Tuyle), who are injured or fall ill in the moments of greatest tension, Jeb manages just fine. He finds Faith in the wilderness and reunites her with her father, proving himself to be an appropriate mate in the egalitarian partnership of modern marriage. As a landscape painter, he shares Faith's sensitivity to the beauties of nature.[9] Their suitability for each other is depicted also in parallel intercut scenes of fights: as Jeb holds off the villain's gang outside, Faith struggles tooth and nail with Leroy inside the cabin. Shipman is terrific in this scene. She lands many blows, bites Leroy on the wrist when he has her in a headlock, and throttles his neck in close-up. The fight goes on and on until Jeb arrives just as Faith is about to go down in defeat.

Surprisingly, Jeb not only rescues Faith, but he also brings into her life the closest figure to a mother that we find in Shipman's work. Faith gets a husband and a (surrogate) mother in one fell narrative swoop, wringing a variation on conventional expectations of genre. Some theorists have argued that the 'missing mother' is endemic to the comic mode: Naomi Scheman points to 'the apparent paternal parthenogenesis of comedic heroines' and notes that classical romance requires, rather than the discovery of one's parentage, the acknowledgment of fathers and the mandated repression of mothers.[10] *The Grub-Stake* not only reunites the daughter with the missing mother, but happily circumvents incestual father-daughter desire by reinstalling the father's proper relationship with the mother. And what a mother. Although in the seventies we might have been inclined to read Kate as the patriarchal mother who inducts Faith into the conventional feminine role and provides a mate for her to boot, the narrative of *The Grub-Stake* contrarily insists on a rhetoric of reciprocal female bonding in a context of professional collegiality. The emphasis here is on work for women, independent subjectivity, and egalitarianism not only between husbands and wives but also between mothers and daughters. This mother, who was first a friend, is another of Shipman's complex modern figures.

E. Ann Kaplan was one of the first to identify the roots of cinematic maternal melodrama in the nineteenth-century cult of true womanhood inaugurated by the Industrial Revolution. She argues that the form of maternal melodrama that featured the maternal sacrifice theme and dominated the early cinema, like the sentimental novel, 'gave illusory veracity to the social institutions and division of labour essential for the success of the Industrial Revolution ... but at the same time, the fiction functioned to satisfy first, unconscious male desires for the idealized pre-Oedipal Mother (the child in these novels is usually male), and second, unconscious wishes to punish the Mother for her sexuality evident in her betraying the child with another man.'[11] Kaplan cites D.W. Griffith as 'the director who established par excellence ... [the] self-sacrificing, pure, passive Mother figure' in films such as *Mothering Heart* (1913), *True Heart Susie* (1919), and *Way Down East* (1920).[12]

Especially in the 1980s, there was a prodigious flow of scholarship and study of the melodramatic mode, and much of this work centred on the maternal melodrama, with strong emphasis on the mother-daughter relation. Some of this material reworked or challenged Kaplan's argument. *Stella Dallas* (d. King Vidor, 1937) and *Mildred Pierce* (d. Michael Curtiz, 1945) have received most of the attention. Feminist theoretical work predominantly emphasized the question of spectatorial identification with the point of view of the mother either happily sacrificing herself for the class mobility or being done in by the selfish independent desires of the daughter (*Stella Dallas* and *Mildred Pierce*, respectively).

Linda Williams invokes Simone de Beauvoir to explain the devaluation of motherhood in patriarchal culture and the mother's resultant attempt 'to use her daughter to compensate for her own supposed inferiority.' The common device of 'significant mirroring' found in the woman's film and the subgenre of maternal melodrama results initially in the mother gaining a vicarious superiority by association with a superior daughter but finally feeling inferior. The problematic of the mother-daughter relationship thus becomes a paradigm for woman's ambivalent relationship to herself.[13] The melodramatic mode, which rewards virtue among the powerless and often situates itself within the domestic (feminine) sphere, becomes an important matrix of female wish-fulfilment.[14] Williams's journey through feminist theories of representation and maternality (Laura Mulvey, Nancy Chodorow, Luce Irigaray, Adrienne Rich, Julia Kristeva) concludes with Jane Gallop's notion of a dialectic between the maternal unrepresentable and the paternal already-represented as a way out of the theoretical bind. *Stella Dallas* is Williams's test case for the representation of motherhood – or its 'ultimate unrepresentability in any except patriarchal terms' – and its possible readings by female spectators.[15]

Working through issues of fetishization, the masquerade of femininity, specularization of the female body, and identificatory structures with their multiple and conflicting points of view, Williams concludes that even if the film 'resolves' the multiple contradictions in the final moments 'the 108 minutes leading up to this moment present the heroic attempt to live out the contradiction' and position the female spectator in identification 'with contradiction itself – with contradictions located at the heart of the socially constructed roles of daughter, wife *and* mother.'[16]

As the surrogate mother to the father's daughter, Faith, and biological mother to her own son, Jeb, Dawson Kate is neither the phallic smothering mother who must be condemned and marginalized by her son nor the sacrificial victim who is inferior to her daughter, nor is she the emblem of true womanhood who inducts her daughter into patriarchal femininity. A hybrid and contradictory figure, she is a bit of everything. While Jeb believes that she runs the post office in Dawson, Kate sacrifices her virtue by working in the dance hall in order to finance her son's education as an artist. Counselling and nurturing Faith, Kate becomes a negative mirror to Faith's innocent virtue (and hence moral superiority), but, unlike the fetishized masquerade of Stella Dallas or Doane's narcissistic over-identified feminine,[17] Kate is a 'He-woman' (intertitle). She rolls her own cigarettes and puffs away while Faith gapes in astonishment, and when her son is holding off the villain's henchmen, she steps in to take over, gun in hand, swearing that she is capable of 'holding off this gang of curs' (intertitle), and thus allows Jeb to rescue Faith from her fight with Leroy. But when Jeb is about to find out his mother's true profession, it is Faith, the surrogate daughter, who must rescue the mother by falsely claiming to have received letters in Kate's post office. Finally, the phallic 'He-woman' resituates herself in femininity by taking Faith's father as her own lover. In this androgynous character, who provides oscillating figurations of (conventionally gendered) masculine and feminine characteristics, we may find Shipman repudiating her youthful horror of homosexuality;[18] more likely, she is complicating and interrogating precisely those gendered dualities.

Willams's argument challenges Kaplan's and Doane's rather more monolithic notions of female spectatorial identification: 'It is a terrible underestimation of the female viewer to presume that she is wholly seduced by a naïve belief in these masochistic images, that she had allowed these images to put her in her place the way the films themselves put their women characters in their place.'[19] Multiple, hybrid, and liquid, Kate represents not only the contradictions of womanhood and motherhood, but also their apparently infinite and functional possibilities.

Kaplan has also posited a group of fictional texts as 'resisting' maternal women's films. These films, in Kaplan's terms, neither condemn the terrain of the emotional (i.e., 'femaleness') and the aesthetic of melodrama, nor value the masculine sphere over the feminine. While these texts may take the male/female bipolar structure of the social formation for granted, the 'resisting' text 'remains in passionate identification with heroines' and raises moral/political issues within the narrative, especially relations of power and institutional structures.[20]

Kaplan notes that Lois Weber was unusual in exploring male/female emotions from a psychologically sophisticated point of view, rather than cleaving to the plot-oriented melodramatic structures characteristic of her day. We can make no similar claims for Shipman, for there is virtually no evidence of psychological complexity or emotional subtlety in *The Grub-Stake* or her other films. With few exceptions, Shipman's love relationships happen suddenly and barely even dramatically; they simply occur as the exigencies of the formulaic plots require. Neither does Shipman's work tend to question conventional cinematic language or to found a new one. However, we can make claims for Shipman that are similar to those that Kaplan makes for Weber. Like Weber's, Shipman's texts 'remain in passionate identification with heroines' and 'disturb the established hierarchy of discourses that privilege the male at least to the extent of permitting us self-conscious access to the patriarchal feminine discourse.'[21]

Unlike Weber, Shipman also positions her heroines as the ones who drive the narrative: her women evince powerful desires and wills 'that dislocate the male order.'[22] In the cases of both Dawson Kate and Faith Diggs, these desires are economic as well as social/emotional. For Faith and for Kate, the character's motive is first of all to provide for herself and her father/son and thereby achieve social independence, and thereafter to achieve appropriate familial stability. The desires of both women figures are happily realized in the new family that is established in the conclusion of the film – a familial group that includes two grandparents, two parents, and a baby.

Kaplan questions the degree of 'resistance' that can be ascribed to Weber's texts. Weber, in Kaplan's argument, 'keeps safely within the semiotic patriarchal codes, dividing her female characters into good/ bad images in the familiar Hollywood manner.'[23] Such a practice has been apparent also in Shipman's melodramatic lexicon in the case of *The Girl from God's Country* and *Get the Woman*. The doubled figures of the women characters in both cases were cast along good/bad lines, where class privilege, shallow materialism, and lack of relational generousity were condemned in the former, and loose sexual morality, duplicity, and thievery were punished by death in the latter. In *The Grub-*

Stake, however, the principal women characters are never pitted against each other in terms of a moral hierarchy: they seem equally and multiply positioned in relation to institutional structures, moral codes, and social/class formations. Faith's acceptance of Dawson Kate's friendship and tutelage in the dance hall, and her subsequent sympathetic false testament regarding Kate's profession, suggests not only the general democratic liberalism of Shipman's social and moral vision but also the repudiation of patriarchal moral dichotomies that constrain women within the virgin/whore dialectic.

Kaplan continues her questioning of Weber's resistance, arguing that 'Weber has no vision of any alternative to the positioning of woman as the unquestioning nurturer and general care-taker.' She justifies Weber's acceptance of the patriarchal sex-role division as the only ideology available at the time: 'Even the suffragettes by and large were not questioning the division of labor, or the burdens placed on wives and mothers,' she writes.[24] While it is true that many of the early maternal feminists strategically traded on motherhood to achieve their own political ends, arguing their moral superiority and suitability for political power as a result of their nurturing instincts as mothers, it does not seem to be the case that such an argument was monolithically accepted either among feminists or in the culture at large. In the early twentieth century, the birth control movement was well under way, resulting in the decline of birth rates and numbers of children in families. Many women at the time carved out a very different kind of life for themselves. Gertrude Stein was one of the first women to enter medical school specifically to advance the 'cause of women,' although she left before graduating to chart a very different life for herself as an avant-garde writer and doyen of the cultural world of Paris in the teens and twenties. Even if they did not consciously claim feminism as their motivation, many women rejected patriarchal expectations of motherhood and gender assignment. Djuna Barnes, also a writer, was one of many who constructed new androgynous or lesbian sexualities in a cultural climate that blew the raspberry at the dominant sexual and social ideology. Luisa Casati in the same period ditched her older husband and stashed her daughter in boarding school to pursue a life of wild corporeal transformation and multiple lovers.[25]

While these three examples hail from the privileged middle and aristocratic classes, we can see other patterns in working-class, black, immigrant, and poor families. Families headed by single mothers formed 20 per cent of the population in this period. A fraction of this group were widows; most had been deserted or divorced, or had never married. Between 1910 and 1920 the single-mother sector was large enough to require most countries to enact motherhood pension laws, albeit with stringent eligibility requirements. But the state did not enforce a monolithic notion of the sanctity of motherhood across all sectors: African-American slave mothers had virtually no rights over their children; and, in Canada, Native mothers were forcibly separated from their children with the advent of the church-run residential schools. 'Patriarchal ideology' as a state apparatus was contradictorily inflected with class and race, and has continued to be so.[26]

In the early twentieth century, unruly daughters who were rejecting traditional modes of behaviour were enough of a social 'problem' that juvenile courts were flooded with cases of delinquent teenaged girls who were challenging traditional family roles and expectations. Urbanization and the expanding wage-labour economy increased opportunities for young women – especially working-class women – and gave them unprecedented freedom from family and community restrictions.[27] Many women in the 1910s and 1920s were practising diverse sexualities and social moralities, modes of leisure and mobility, professional careers or wage labour, and forms of motherhood that challenged patriarchal norms.

Certainly for Shipman, in her films as well as in her own life, creative achievement, economic independence, social mobility, and sexual equality were central to the vision of contemporary womanhood that underlies all her narratives and portrayals of women and male–female relationships. Shipman does not merely 'expose the codes that constrain [women],'[28] she presents an alternative vision in which women are actively engaged with the contradictions of narrowly defined patriarchal controls.

Kaplan has explained that, even in the resisting maternal woman's film, women are rarely seen working outside the home because 'the discursive field was still, even in the 20s and 30s, not such as to make the independent career woman a possible positive construct.'[29] Recent studies of silent film and female spectatorship suggest otherwise, however.

Ben Singer's work on serial queens – independent and competent career girls, for the most part – and Shelley Stamp's study of women moviegoers articulate a rather different mapping of female protagonists within popular cinema and the economically independent employed female audiences of the movies.[30] In this context, the mother figure of *The Grub-Stake* is, like the heroine, a 'new woman.' Dawson Kate may instruct Faith Diggs about the sex trade, but she also provides for Faith a modern son who has been raised by a mother for whom a profession was not only a necessity but also provided her progeny the freedom to become an artist (Jeb is a painter of pictures). As an independent professional woman (albeit in the sex trade) she has a house in the forest and a handsome son who loves her.

House and Home

Mary Ann Doane and a host of others agree that the place of melodrama and the woman's film is the domestic sphere. Doane argues for 'a rather strict mapping of gender-differentiated societal spaces' in the family melodrama.[31] In what she calls the 'paranoid woman's films,' Doane cites the woman's space within the home as constituting a threat to her life. The woman is confined to the domestic sphere, and its terrain – the bedroom, the staircase, the window – 'becomes the analogue of the human body, its parts fetishised by textual operations, its erotogenous zones metamorphosized by a morbid anxiety attached to sexuality.'[32]

Shipman's work cannot be categorized primarily as domestic melodrama, as its emphasis is on adventure and crisis produced by the wilderness landscape and its human and animal populations. Nevertheless, in *The Grub-Stake*, the most domestic and familial of Shipman's films, there are some interesting resonances with questions of the house and home.

Several different kinds of domestic spaces are depicted in the film. The first of these domestic spaces is the bare little room in the urban apartment building that Faith shares with her father. The dad's wheelchair, a laundry hamper, a bare wooden table, a straight-backed wooden chair, and a threadbare little window-curtain furnish the space. This sparsely furnished and unadorned space is reminiscent of the hovel inhabited by Lucy and Battling Burrows in *Broken Blossoms* (d. D.W. Griffith, 1919), a film that Shipman admired. It serves not only as a signifier of poverty, but also as an indicator or the relationship between father and daughter. Although it is clearly their living space, it is also a place of work for pay, as Faith takes in laundry here. Set decoration does not include accoutrements of cozy domesticity – no dishes or cooking utensils, no pictures on the walls or rugs on the floors, not even a throw cushion. Clothes hang from hooks on the wall. The only decorative object is a large model of a ship. The room's principal article is a ship's lantern whose large size and functional design signify its status as industrial equipment rather than domestic furnishing.

This object, incongruous within the domestic space, functions paradoxically as an indicator of the relationship between father and daughter. Every evening at dusk, as Faith is on her way home from her job, Skipper Diggs lights the lamp as a welcoming beacon for his daughter. A sign of Skipper's care and love, the lamp also speaks to Faith's responsibility for her child/father, as he is confined to his wheelchair by the window. After a day of futile job-searching, Faith pauses by the harbour and gazes into the black water in despair until the beacon in the window reminds her to come home. In this scene, all of the vectors of the father-daughter dyad – the memory of his commanding past as a ship's captain and the present reversal of dependence, his helpless immobility and her enforced wandering, his optimism contrasting with her despair, the dichotomy of their mutual love and individual solitudes – ironically become concentrated in this industrial rather than domestic object.

The lantern in the window may also be read as a marker of the destabilization of generic expectations that the film consistently effects. 'The window,' Doane writes, 'has special import in terms of the social and symbolic positioning of the woman – the window is the interface between inside and outside, the feminine space of the family and reproduction and the masculine space of production. It facilitates a communication by means of the look between the two sexually differentiated spaces.'[33] Significantly for Doane, it is the woman in the woman's film who looks through or waits at the window. In *The Grub-Stake*, however, it is the man who obsessively waits and looks through the window. In addition to the reversals of the daughter as provider and the father as the helpless child, the sphere of the home is the place of the passive male, while the outside world is the terrain of female mobility. The window not only marks the interface of the domestic and industrial world, but also cannot avoid being read as analogous to the cinema screen, which, in Shipman's world, women traverse in multiple directions. The beacon, analogous to the cinema projection beam, finds the woman outside her generic sphere and refers to Shipman's own profession, which places her outdoors in an industrial setting. For the female spectator, both the window and the beacon then function in multiple ways. The dilemma of the new woman in modern culture reverberates far more widely than the melodramatic narrational issues of domesticity and maternality, and is confounded also by economic and professional responsibilities along with the confusions, dangers, and freedoms of mobility in the world outside the home.

When Faith and the Skipper move to the Klondike with Leroy, he installs them in a cabin that is somewhat more comfortable. There is a round table covered with a cloth, a lamp, and other objects. A pretty hat hangs on the corner of a mirror on the wall, a pot-bellied stove blazes in the corner, and pictures adorn the wall. In the paranoid woman's film, Doane says, 'It is the male character who fetishises the house as a whole, attempting to unify and homogenise it.'[34] In Leroy's bourgeois and domesticated space, in which Faith believes herself to be the happy bride, it is certainly significant that the picture on the wall is an old-fashioned silhouette print of a 'lady' from the past, complete with long flowing skirt, lacy sleeves, and parasol. The image of hyper-femininity from a previous century says everything about Leroy's notions of patriarchal womanhood, and perhaps – somewhat ironically – about Faith's own gender ideals. In this cabin, here Leroy tells her that she must not take his name as her own, conspires with the servant to kill her father, and dresses Faith in dance-hall finery as part of his plan to indenture her into the sex trade. This domestic scene is the place of danger for Faith's happiness, her integrity, and her family, and – shades of the paranoid woman's film – it is this home that Faith must flee.

Bachelor Jeb's little home in the forest is another 'scene' altogether. A pretty little lakeside log cabin with shrubs growing near the door, its interior is the epitome of rustic domestic comfort. A large wooden armchair sits near the fire burning in the substantial stone fireplace, a gingham tablecloth drapes the commodious table, and a corner shelf holds knick-knacks and books. There are flowers in a vase, pictures on the wall, dishes, cooking utensils, teacups with saucers, tied-back flowered curtains at the windows, and even a basket of darning. In the bedroom, there is a large brass bed with pillows.

Here Dawson Kate, the 'He-woman,' finds respite from her work in the dance hall. Shedding her androgynous horse-riding outfit, she dons a pretty dress with a bow at the neck and an apron and sets to work to clean up the dishes while she awaits her son's return. A later conversation with Jeb is composed as a tightly framed back-lit two-shot of Kate in her armchair with her son kneeling at her side. She has become the perfect image of domestic maternal womanhood.

But by no means has Kate been ineluctably repositioned in patriarchal femininity, as most feminist criticism would have it. On the contrary, she remains capable of oscillating between modes of gender and subjectivity with expedition and alacrity. She is capable of abjection and heroinism, femininity and androgyny, maternality and romantic sexuality. She can leave her domestic space to stand down the villains and return to domesticity when she takes on a male partner of her own age.

The shelter that Faith finds in the wilderness is the extreme opposite of the cozy cabin that Jeb shares with his mom. When Jeb finds Faith with an injured leg that prevents her from travel, the pair providentially come upon Malamute Mike's gold mine and his miner's shack, where she holes up until he can return with assistance. This 'home' is a wreck of a place, a one-room jerry-rigged lean-to made of logs without chinking. Its windows are boarded up, its door falling off, and it is inhabited by a pair of owls and a nest of skunks. The furniture is rudimentary at best – a rickety handmade table and a flimsy wooden bench. Dust flies from every surface when touched. Ironically, this is where Faith finds not only romance but also her fortune.

These four different domestic spaces function ironically as signifiers. The spare, industrial object of Faith's first home paradoxically signals care and nurturance; the bourgeois, hyper-feminine accoutrements of her second mark her danger; the coziest, most comfortable of them all belongs to the bachelor artist; and the most derelict is the place where Faith finds love.

Finally we come to the rustic cabin with the rustic cradle and the rustic baby. Faith and Jeb by the cradle, Kate and Skipper in matching armchairs – are they all living together as an extended family? Are they in a new house or Jeb's cabin? The relatively short duration and medium focal length of the shot make it difficult to tell. There are different curtains at the windows and an additional armchair, but the same tin lantern hangs by the same door as in Jeb's place. Whatever: Functional and iconic, the ending shot – a pan that joins the family together in one space – is a simple image that continues to play out the imbrication and equalization of gender roles in the ideal family. Jeb and Faith are equally centred in the frame, gazing down at the baby in the cradle, and Kate fondly touches her husband's arm while Skipper sits in the chair knitting (!).

Lionhead Lodge

Shipman, Van Tuyle, the small crew, and the animals stayed at Byars's Forest Lodge for almost a year, until the film was finished, and they found the land down the lake at Lionhead Bay, where they built a camp. Shipman called it Lionhead Lodge. This was the most stable physical habitat Shipman's family had had in some years, and for Shipman, in her memoirs, it remained the place she called home. The memoir predominantly takes place here and ends with the move away.

A far cry from the Astor Hotel in Seattle or the Highland Park establishment, at Lionhead Lodge there was no housekeeper, no grand piano, and no indoor plumbing. Shipman's first 'house' on the site was a one-room log cabin, a temporary shelter until the larger cabin was built – the one seen in *Little Dramas of the Big Places*. Along with the runs and shelters for the animals, there was a boathouse that was used as a cookhouse, a shack where the animals' food was kept, and tents for the hands to sleep in. Eventually a warehouse, a main headquarters, and living-room cabin, a bunkhouse, a film and cutting room were built, as well as two cabins for the cinematographers and their families (*Lionhead*, 126). Another private cabin was built for Shipman to write in – this one with a fireplace (*Lionhead*, 147).

The house that Shipman shared with Van Tuyle and her son, Barry, was, in terms of its rustic context, relatively grand. Walls of hand-hewn logs, fitted tightly together and trimmed with birch bark, supported a cedar shake roof. The floor of the building was made of tamarack blocks, standing on end, fitted together and polished. The tables, chairs, and bedsteads were also handbuilt from birch poles and cedar bark, and, according to Lloyd Peters, one of the carpenters, 'they were fancy' (*Lionhead*, 147).

There was a large combination living and dining room, a special room for Shipman, an office for Van Tuyle, a kitchen with a large oven for baking bread, and two bedrooms. Here, in their last years of their partnership, Shipman and Van Tuyle clawed their family life out of the wilderness. Barry had returned from military school, as they could not afford the tuition any more. He became an active and productive member of the family team, catching fish to be dried for animal fodder, helping Shipman with household chores, and pitching in with the animals.

Shipman's memoir and her autobiographical novel, *Abandoned Trails*, suggest a family life that was not only much more arduous, but also much less egalitarian than the idealistic family structures she portrays in her films. In the novel Dirk (Van Tuyle) is plagued with his frostbitten toe – at least that is his excuse for staying up all night smoking cigarettes and drinking to excess, bouts of foul temper, and increasing complaints to Joyce (Shipman) about everything under the sun. He also never accepts the boy as a son, and as his pain and bad temper increase, he takes it out on Stanley (Barry). When ten-year-old Stanley has made a child's mistake, Dirk yells at him to 'Wipe that smirk off your face or I'll wipe it for you!' And when Joyce intervenes to protect the boy, he yells at her: 'That's right! Stick up for him! Let him get away with murder, like he always does!'[35]

Passion was gone from the relationship, Shipman admits in the novel, and in one episode Joyce flirts with infidelity when she has to take shelter alone with a young man on their way back from town in the winter. She wilfully charms him, but soon checks her sexual impulses and manages the star-struck boy into gentlemanly behaviour. Dirk is consumed with jealousy, however, and cannot let it go. It begins to corrode their relationship even more. They fight bitterly.

Money troubles, disappointment, and the sheer hard labour of keeping Lionhead Lodge going were getting Shipman down. She felt old at thirty, and when she looked at her hands, she saw swollen joints and coarse red wrists 'like a charwoman's' (*Trails*, 189). To brighten her spirits and boost her ego, at one point she concocted an enormous picnic, inviting all the surrounding populace for a free day at Lionhead Lodge to see the animals and meet the movie star. To prepare for the picnic, she rose at dawn to make hundreds of doughnuts by hand, sunk the last of their cash into meat for a barbecue, and spent the day glad-handing the visitors. They came by the hundreds, ate all the food, and responded to the event as to a visit to a theme park.

Shipman devotes an entire chapter in *Abandoned Trails* to a conversation with a woman at the picnic in which Joyce finds it hard to fathom her own degree of masochism in her relationship with Dirk. The two women diss their partners roundly, but the conversation turns serious when they admit to each other their own complicity in the dysfunctionality of the partnerships. The movie star is as debilitated by lack of self-esteem as any contemporary woman. In the conversation, she says, 'Sometimes, when I come to the table with a heavy platter of stew and I see Dirk sitting there, waiting, – one of the men, waiting for his woman to serve him ... why, it comes over me in a terrible rush that that is all I am good for.' The phrase 'one of the men, waiting for his woman to serve him' suggests her own astonishment that the couple has become fixed in the mould of patriarchy, and at the same time indicates the contrast with her own ideals. She swears that 'it is only temporary,' that it will pass and 'she'll be herself again.' But, at the same time, she has to admit that 'from a standpoint of feminine psychology,' she somehow enjoys it (*Trails*, 150).

Joyce's friend Nellie identifies the masochistic syndrome: '"Martyrdom," said Nellie, briskly. "Not one of us but enjoys playing that game. Stretching ourselves out on the arms of the cross we've erected for ourselves – or let our men-folk raise for us!"' But Nellie firmly warns Joyce against such indulgence, while still allowing an explanation in terms of emotionality: 'Most every woman's "cause" is a lost one, because her own heart is the battleground and the stake.' The scene closes with Joyce expressing her admiration for the older woman. 'Joyce thought; "This woman knows. She's been down to the gates, her back has been to the wall – the deadfall 'you can't climb over.' And she is alive. Vitally so"' (*Trails*, 150).

As for motherhood, in the novel the heroine eventually packs the boy off to school in Spokane with the first money raised for the movies that became *Little Dramas of the Big Places*. She 'hardly missed him,' she wrote, 'she was so busy and it was a relief not to have the child riling Dirk. Now she could keep camp affairs on a smoother track and devote more time to her pictures and writing' (*Trails*, 243). In this autobiographical novel, the vision of matrimonial partnership is very different from that in the films or in the fiction of *Get the Woman*. Essentially a tragedy of lost ideals and hopes, *Abandoned Trails* takes on the representation of cognition and psychology that Kaplan finds necessary for the resisting text, and confronts the challenge of the traditional woman's position in marriage. In contrast to the memoir, in which Shipman exonerates Van Tuyle and castigates herself for business errors, in the novel Joyce begins to doubt her judgment in her choice of partners, and blames Dirk for their troubles: 'In this strange partnership Dirk was still "boss" though the woman was far from being blind to his mistakes, his tyranny and the Dutch obstinacy which, time and again, brought them to the brink of ruin ... Three times he had come to an impasse in the business relations of the companies formed to finance Joyce's pictures and three times she had stood by him, against the others and, in the end, thrown up the sponge; lost everything for which she toiled and walked out, empty-handed' (*Trails*, 123). The novel ends with Joyce's decision to break up the relationship and the business partnership.

In the films, on the other hand, while Shipman makes no attempt to extricate her women characters from conventional attributions of nurturance, maternal instincts, or desires for heterosexual romance, she is able to restructure those desires and outcomes to form an ameliorated vision of maternity in the context of an egalitarian marriage partnership. Despite the absence of representation of cognition or psychological analysis, for women spectators these women protagonists provide points of identification with more or less contradictory figures, similar to most humans. And in these plot-driven narratives in which psychology does not play a significant part, the achievement of successful agency for women is fairly easy to come by, according to the formulaic conventions of the defeat of the villain and the happy ending for the heroine.

This is clearly the upside of the narrational system of the melodrama in the comic mode. The absence of psychological investigation or emotional subtlety has the advantage of evacuating impediments to the generic workings of the formulaic scenario. As long as the plot acquieces to melodramatic narrational codes, characters and relationships apparently need not conform to prescribed psychologies. It appears that the aesthetic of melodrama is more porous and malleable than usually thought, and much less locked into the prison-house of patriarchal ideology than many feminist critics have argued.

It is unnecessary to claim Shipman as a utopian thinker. Her films need not be read as proto-feminist or ahead of their time. The unanimous response of the potential buyers to *The Grub-Stake* suggests just the opposite: the film does not appear to have been seen as a revolutionary document. The consignment of the era to a monolithic patriarchal ideology of womanhood and motherhood (as Kaplan would have it) clearly underestimates the multiplicity of available and acceptable representations of psychological and social possibilities at the time. Distributor Fred Warren's assessment of the movie as 'good [homespun] holiday fare' indicates that its vision of the domestic unit, work for women, and romantic partnerships was by no means acceptable only to progressive adults but rather was suitable for family entertainment.

Sisterhood

In her memoir, Shipman mentions that she was saddened by efforts of the cast of *The Grub-Stake* to sue the production for owed wages, and particularly so because one of her best friends, Lillian Leighton, was a principal in the altercation. Leighton was the character actor who played Dawson Kate in *The Grub-Stake* and had also performed as Notawa in *The Girl from God's Country*.

Leighton and her mother had been 'such good friends to me for so long,' Shipman wrote, they had crocheted for her 'a stunning shocking pink dress with a deep fringe, a labor of love which swung as it swished on stage for my personal appearances.' In the descriptive details and sensual language (the fringe swinging and swishing with her bodily movement), one can sense the corporeality of the memory of friendship embodied in that dress. The presence of the memory still lingering in her own body is palpable as Shipman writes the memoir over forty years later. Shipman was not simply saddened by the 'odor of a decayed friendship,' however. Perhaps even more importantly, Lillian Leighton was 'among the very few women who seemed to like [her]' (*Heart*, 115).

Given the reworking of the characteristics of femininity, heterosexual romance, and maternality in *The Grub-Stake*, it is notable that instances of friendship between women are rare in Shipman's work. From time to time the Shipman heroine may have a woman friend or ally. Presumably the two women characters in *The Trail of the Arrow* were fast friends, and in *The Light on Lookout* (1923) the protagonist's best friend, a woman visitor, arrives from the city. Both of these were short films, and *The Trail of the Arrow* is lost. In the novelized version of *Under the Crescent*, the series that Shipman wrote first as a movie serial in 1913, the heroine befriends a spunky and capable local woman with a baby; the two women assist each other in their adventures and escapes. These are the only examples of female bonding in Shipman's work prior to *The Grub-Stake*, and Faith's friendship with Dawson Kate in that film is the only representation of companionship between women in a Shipman feature film.

In *Abandoned Trails*, on the other hand, Shipman includes two episodes involving 'sisterhood.' One illustrates the heroine's kindness to another woman, a young German immigrant who lives a life of drudgery and loneliness in the nearby village. The kindly movie star tries to befriend the girl outside a village dance party, offering her the ticket that the girl could not afford to buy, and encouraging her to come in to dance. The villagers despise the girl simply for being foreign and treat her with open contempt; they also gossip that she has been seen down at the marsh with the village crazy. Seeing their reaction, Joyce is horrified. She had thought the village to be 'a kindly, homey little place,' but now she sees its ethnocentric parochialism. Wresting her thoughts away from the lonely girl, Joyce speculates on the village's response to her own plight, the derision she assumes they express now that they know she is broke and in debt. The girl disappears from the narrative at this point, to return chapters later with the news of her suicide, which offers opportunity for Joyce to express pity, remorse, and anger at the 'meanness' and 'lies' of the villagers (*Trails*, 216).

This gesture of sisterhood has a dual function in the novel. In the tradition of the eighteenth-century sentimental novel, it indicates Joyce's nobility of spirit, as she is able to sympathize with the plight of the downtrodden and despised, and marks her superiority to the viciousness and stupidity of the villagers. In the construction of heroic femininity, the episode works in exactly the same way as the incident with the Inuit women in *Back to God's Country*. Exploited, ridiculed, and the object of

jingoistic contempt from brutes who fallaciously consider themselves
superior, these abject women – the German girl and the Inuit guests on
the boat – provide opportunities for the heroine to enact her sensitivity,
generousity, social and political understanding, and truly superior
morality.

At the same time, in both works the heroine is incapable of effecting
change on behalf of her sisters. This is a bit dodgy. It suggests that the
protagonist is the exceptional woman who can fend for herself and
achieve success while her sisters go down to defeat by the patriarchy,
and at the same time it affords her the opportunity to display her heroic
and noble humanity in her remorse. As Sally Potter's analysis of the figure of Mimi in *Thriller* (1979) suggests, the woman who dies – even of
natural causes – becomes the murder victim; but in Shipman's case, the
narrational beneficiary of the women's death is the heroine rather than
the hero. Yet, in both cases, the episodes allow the narration to challenge the laws of patriarchy and its servant racism/xenophobia and to
represent their consequences for all but a few women. In *Abandoned
Trails*, the girl's death instigates a page-long rhetorical tirade on the
injustice of solitude and drudgery augmented by the cruelty of small-
town bigotry: 'Alone, day after dreary day ... Eating her bitter bread,
alone. But not alone! A hundred taunting faces jeered at her from the
blackened walls and evil tongues jangled like tuneless bells in her frightened ears' (*Trails*, 217).

In *Abandoned Trails* and *The Grub-Stake* another female friend
emerges, an androgynous woman who is neither the victim of patriarchy
nor completely eludes its grasp. Dawson Kate in *The Grub-Stake* and Aunt
Nellie Horstadt in *Abandoned Trails* are both tough, admirable women
who can do anything a man can do and be women as well. In many ways
they could be seen as a possible future for Shipman, had she continued
to live in the wilderness.

The narrational voice of *Abandoned Trails* is filled with admiration for
Aunt Nellie: 'She had made history and spoke with the tolerant authority of a woman who had lived her life and not simply let it blow over her
covered head.' Rumoured to have killed an intruder with a sawed-off
shotgun, Nellie admits to having horse-whipped a woman who tried to
steal her man. Stout, large-bosomed, and 'a battered wreck of a woman
but still valiant,' she rolls her own cigarettes, drinks her liquor straight,

and curses 'like a mule-skinner.' But Joyce senses about Nellie a past that included 'red plush furniture, picture hats, ostrich feather boas and iced champagne' and 'men in grey derbies and red cravats' who once 'bowed at the crook of her little finger.' Even now, 'at the touch of a troubled hand,' she turned 'womanly, sweet and compassionate' (*Trails*, 144–7).

Some of the protagonists in *The Grub-Stake* had been modelled on characters that Shipman remembered from her time in Alaska when she was an adolescent touring in vaudeville. The old prospector Malamute Mike was a figure Shipman had seen dragging an empty rope and believing his lead dog was still with him; the painter Jeb was based on 'a real live artist who did incredible sunsets with a palette knife on boards.' Dawson Kate was also a real person, 'Heart-of-Gold in dancehall finery' (*Heart*, 106). It is interesting that Shipman wrote *The Grub-Stake* before moving to Priest Lake, for Dawson Kate and Aunt Nellie are cut from the same cloth.

Nellie Horstadt was based on Shipman's friend Belle Angstadt, who lived eleven miles down the lake at the Lone Star ranch. 'Known and loved throughout the region' as 'Aunt Belle,' she had also once shot a man – 'a former boyfriend gone mean.' When Shipman arrived at Priest Lake, Belle 'was verging on an old age' but 'she was spry and the firm manager of her spidery, ex-prospector husband, Uncle Harry. Usually in winter she lived in a Priest River cottage with a mended front door, wrote squibs and verse for the local newspaper, fed, cheered and consoled every friend and, it can be said, was the greatest, biggest "heart of gold" to step from the real life pages of wild West romance.' In the memoir, Shipman also tells the identical story, recounted in *Abandoned Trails* down to the detail of the feather in her hat, of Belle/Nellie whipping a rival with her riding crop (*Heart*, 127).

Belle Angstadt 'had comfort, advice and a welcome exchange of wit' for her friend, and one time counselled Shipman to be patient and stay with Van Tuyle despite the loss of his 'good nature' due to his diseased foot (*Heart*, 137). Angstadt is a frequent presence in the last forty pages of the memoir as her friendship with Shipman 'grew to many meetings, exchanges of confidences and much shared laughter' (*Heart*, 127). When Shipman left Lionhead Lodge for the last time, she collapsed into a coma brought on by depression and exhaustion. After being 'blacked out' for five days, the first friend she saw was Angstadt in Spokane. Even then, Angstadt had kind words for Van Tuyle, but Shipman was not to be dissuaded. The second last passage in the memoir is a letter to Belle from Shipman, now in New York and embarking on a new life.

Unlike Angstadt, who remained a dear friend, Aunt Nellie disappears from the novel and from the protagonist's life when Joyce doesn't heed her advice to leave the ranch and Dirk. Without the comforts of friendship, Joyce endures another winter of the wilderness, animal starvation, crippling debt, failure, self-degradation, and the torments of her crazed partner. Finally, in the last pages of the novel, she leaves her home, her beloved animals, and her lost dreams to 'follow her new trail, unmapped and strange. Free, at last, of self-torment, stripped of everything save tolerance, she would follow it bravely and meet her destiny at the Trail's End' (*Trails*, 311). Joyce is alone.

I'd Rather Be Alone

In the memoir, as in the films and novels, Shipman represents the central female figure as predominantly alone in a world of men. Although the wilderness settings of the films and novels may account for the preponderance of men in the diegetical populations, and the shoestring budgets of most of the films required that the number of characters be kept to a minimum, the almost exclusive solitude of the woman protagonist is still a notable feature of Shipman's work.

Shipman's trademark animal scenes, which feature in every film except *Something New*, also help to underscore the sense of female solitude. The bucolic scenes with the bear or baby skunks in *Little Dramas of the Big Places*, *Back to God's Country*, and *The Grub-Stake* are Shipman's spectacular star turns, and she is invariably alone onscreen with the animals. These moments of spectacle featuring the solitary star performing transcendent feats have little narrative impetus and no function of relational motivation in regard to another character. As such, they are highly unusual in star-driven vehicles. When Douglas Fairbanks swung through the window or flew off on his magic carpet, he was motivated by love – the need to rescue a woman or defeat an adversary. Even Fred Astaire had a dance partner, an audience, and an orchestra playing along. In Shipman's films, by contrast, the scenes of the protagonist bravely befriending a giant bear, facing down a cougar, beating off a pack of marauding wolves, or tickling a porcupine on the chin are made doubly spectacular by the fact that she is unassisted, alone, and a woman. The status of these scenes, functioning to halt the narrative for a moment of spectacle, and their repeated use in publicity material ensure their endurance as touchstones of Shipman's work.

Janey Place argued long ago in relation to the femmes fatales of film noir that it is not the preposterous or conventional endings that we remember or treasure from these films, but the transgressive woman figure who dominated the narrative up to the moment of closure.[36] In her argument regarding maternal melodrama, Linda Williams also de-emphasized the endings that 'reconcile the irreconcilable' in favour of 'the 108 minutes' that came before the final moments. Similarly, I would argue that with Shipman's work the narrative trajectory culminating in the inevitable heterosexual coupling that closes the story is less compelling or memorable than the scenes of the solitary woman braving the wilderness.

Shipman is the only human being on the screen for about one-third of *The Grub-Stake*. In the second act Faith wanders off to gather wood, inadvertently slips down a snowy crevasse, and has to forge through deep snow, sometimes on all fours. She ends up lost and alone in the woods. Before she finds shelter with the hibernating bear, she encounters threats from a cougar and a wolf and rails at nature when a spectacular lightning storm strikes. When she emerges from the cave in the spring, another lengthy episode follows her journey through the forest – her leg still not healed – as she and the bear forage for food. Delivered from the winter and provided for by nature's bounty, she apologizes to the universe for her previous anger, enjoys the pleasures of the frisky animals and babbling brook, and seems content to be alone despite her debilitating injury.

Later in the film is the dramatic sequence in which Kate's true trade is almost revealed and Faith lies on Kate's behalf. Immediately after the exchange, Faith recoils from Kate's touch on the shoulder and walks to the door of the cabin. When Jeb moves to accompany her outside, she says to him 'I'd rather be alone' (intertitle) and exits for another solitary scene. This is a moment of great anxiety for Faith. She has been apprehended by a Mountie, who has tracked her as the thief of Leroy's dogteam; they remain in Kate's cabin only because Skipper is still too frail to travel, and the Mountie has hunkered down to wait with them until he is well. Faith must be despairing for her future. She walks outside, raises her arms to the sky, roils around for some time, and finally throws herself to the ground. Fade out.

The next morning, dawn brings to Faith the knowledge of 'the only way out' (intertitle). While Jeb and the Mountie sleep on the ground outside, she slips out of the lean-to and walks into the lake up to her knees. She writhes around and angles her body into expressions of turmoil, despair, fear, and doubt. She turns to look at a far-off place and, before you know it, she is clambering up the mountain, apparently preferring a plunge off a cliff to a watery grave. The scene ends as Leroy and his henchmen arrive to jump the claim to the gold mine, and another sequence begins.

These scenes are intriguing for a number of reasons. The scenes of Shipman in the wilderness with wild animals are, of course, Shipman's trademark and the principal evidence of her star quality. Equal to any Disney or television nature show, the images of the wild animals in their natural habitat were – as Fred Warren's assessment indicated – among the main attractions of Shipman's films. They are also gorgeously shot by Joseph B. Walker: the wide shot of the valley as the mist rises in the morning, the dappled light in the glade entered by the wild deer, the sparkling water and perfectly composed vignette of the beavers at 'their morning toilette' (intertitle), Shipman prostrate on a verdant bank whose every leaf is etched in silvery light. As editor, she allows these shots to play fully, lingering on them sufficiently for the spectator to develop a moment of lyrical contemplation. In these beautiful shots, Shipman's professionalism, love of nature, and cinematic aesthetic are in full evidence.

It is in these sequences also that the display of the woman's body is most significantly inflected with sensuality and affective emotionality. Shipman seems to relish these moments, throwing herself into the performance with great energy, striking melodramatic 'points' when alone, and interrelating with the animals with playfulness, tenderness, and sensitivity. These scenes contrast sharply with Shipman's performance of love scenes with humans, through which she passes rather perfunctorily, perhaps because of Van Tuyle's jealousy. Her relationship with the ani-

Alone at dawn, in a melodramatic posture, *The Grub-Stake* (1923).

A typical Joseph B. Walker shot, with dappled lighting and fine detail.

mals and with the forest is performed with almost erotic sensuality: tender little kisses for the deer, great slurps of the bear's tongue received with a blissful smile, a tree embraced with the full press of her body, the languishing indolence of her relaxation on an ivy-covered slope.

The narrative of film theory from the seventies and eighties has been a history of the gaze, dating from Christian Metz's articulation of the 'three looks' of the cinema: the look of the camera, the looks exchanged between characters, and the look of the spectator at the image.[37] The spectator's gaze necessarily identifies with that of the camera and, in psychoanalytic theory following from Metz, maps onto the protagonist's look through the suturing processes of classical narrative. Feminist theory gendered that gaze, arguing that the cinematic symbolic was structured along the lines of the masculine unconscious such that the woman's body was fetishized and specularized to confirm the subjectivity of the male and his control of the Word and the Law.

In the psychoanalytic model of spectatorship that has come down to us from Mulvey's famous essay, the iconicized image of the woman's body is relayed through the male protagonist's gaze, constructing a relation of voyeurism (and hence a precisely defined sadism or sense of mastery) between spectator and fetishized image of woman.[38] There have been several variations rung on this model, notably Doane's notion of the woman spectator's narcissistic over-identification with the figure of the woman, a concept that has been propped on French feminist psychoanalytic theories of the closeness of the woman to her body.[39] Most of this theory has dealt with film texts produced in the Hollywood sound period marked by dialogue-driven narratives, invisible continuity editing, point-of-view shots, and the suturing processes of the classic realist style. While this approach now seems dated, and its psychoanalytic underpinnings have been shunted to the margins of film theory, I still find some aspects of the operations of the gaze useful for textual analysis.

Shipman's films were made in the period before 'decoupage classique' was developed. Nevertheless, there are some interesting points of overlap and some significant differences in textual strategies. Shipman's textual practice is especially interesting in relation to her own work as leading actor and the deployment of her body as affective instrument of performance.

As I have suggested in the consideration of *Something New*, the subjectivities of the protagonists in Shipman's films tend not to be indicated by spectatorial access to their visual perspective. Point-of-view shots are rare, although telling when they occur, as in shots of Bill/Van Tuyle from the unnamed Writing Woman's perspective. In *The Grub-Stake*, perspectival editing with eye-line matching is also rare. The scene in which intercutting between reaction shots is most pronounced, for example, is the one in which the Mountie reveals Kate's true profession and Faith must lie to cover for her. The film cuts back and forth between Kate, Jeb, the Mountie, and Faith as the dramatic moment is dilated to the peak of tension. The angles of the shots, however, do not privilege any of the characters' point of view. Instead, each character faces the camera directly to register his/her emotion. Here there is little evidence of a controlling perspective in terms of textual operations, and the narrative situates the spectator in identificatory relation equally with Kate, Jeb, and Faith.

Similarly, in only two of the scenes in which Faith goes off by herself are there other viewers represented. The first is the scene in which Jeb discovers Faith in the forest. Contemporary deployment of conventional film language would lead us to expect a shot from Jeb's point of view as he comes across Faith and then a shot of him from her point of view when she becomes aware of his presence. Instead we have a third-person shot of Faith nursing her injured ankle in the stream, a shot of Jeb from another angle, and a return to the earlier shot for Jeb's approach. The merely functional narrational strategy positions Faith and her predicament in direct relation to the camera/spectator's omniscient gaze, privileging neither character's point of view.

The second is the scene in which Faith rises at dawn, presumably to commit suicide. Her exit from the cabin and her walk into the lake are observed by the Mountie, but camera angles and shot focal length do not match his point of view. The textual operations emphasize long shots and affect-laden mid-shots from omniscient narrational angles, rather than positioning the spectator in eye-line-matching identification with the Law. In this way, we might find – with Kaplan – *The Grub-Stake* to be a resisting text, as the enunciative apparatus eschews alignment with patriarchal discourse and its legal state apparatus precisely in its moment of surveillance and control.

In all of the other scenes in the film in which Faith is alone, we find either the perfunctory narrational omniscience of the camera's gaze or

Faith's direct address to the camera/spectator. Although Tom Gunning's thesis of the 'cinema of attractions' was developed to describe the effects of stylistic practices that predated the development of narrative, we can see some echoes of it in *The Grub-Stake* in Shipman's use of direct address and display of wonders, not only the animals, but her own bodily exhibitionism. Gunning's taxonomy of formal strategies used in the primitive cinema encompassed not only the sheer revelation of the fascinating attractions filmed, but also the abrupt transitions, fragmented or non-existent narration, gags, outrageous reliance on trick effects, and self-conscious display of technique. Gunning stressed 'exhibitionist confrontation' and 'direct stimulation' that appealed to a modern urban viewer who was rapidly becoming used to a 'culture of distraction.' The concept has thus been employed to construct a vision of spectatorship in which fragmentation and displacement at the level of cinematic style result in a visceral, bodily involvement of the viewer in the experience of shock, attraction, and astonishment. The illusion that permits a distanced identification with the action on the screen gives way to an immediate bodily response in the spectator.[40]

At her most heroic and dramatic – declaiming to nature, interacting with the wild animals, responding lyrically to the picturesque landscape – Shipman offers her body to the spectator's gaze not only as an 'attraction' in itself, but in a cinematic discourse that is disjunctive and calls attention to itself as it momentarily arrests the narrative. Furthermore, one can only imagine the effect of these images in the absence of an original tinted print. Shipman's description of the 'miracles' that the laboratory performed with colour, 'using sepia with a silverish tone to overlay a warm pink tint' can only suggest the luminous opulence of the details that 'blushed rose under a silver sheen' (*Heart*, 114). Her language here evokes the sensual, almost erotic quality that the scenes of her alone in the forest must have been able to evoke, particularly if one is mindful of the painterly qualities of Walker's cinematography. This, I would argue, is not a visual erotics of voyeurism or fetishization (the gendered notion of the woman as specular object of desire constructed in seventies and eighties feminist theory), but rather an intersubjective relation between the spectator and the image that renders what Laura Marks refers to as 'haptic visuality.'

A form of vision that calls into play the sensory qualities of touch –

what Marks calls 'the skin of the film' – haptic visuality has been ascribed to the surface textures of the image as it diffuses, striates, or
interferes with optical visuality.[41] My experience of viewing *The Grub-
Stake* maps precisely along this sense of the term, for I have been working from a duplicate of a video produced on a tele-cine chain, little
better than pixel-vision with a smear of vaseline. However, this is not the
image quality that I refer to, despite its materiality in my own spectatorial experience.

Rather than the haptic as a critique of vision, or springing from a suspicion of the limits of vision, as Laura Marks has argued informs much
of the haptic qualities of art-video, these images from *The Grub-Stake*
glory in the proprioceptive and kinaethesic sensuality of vision. As
Marks writes, 'the erotic capacities of haptic visuality' call into question
'cinema's illusion of representing reality by pushing the viewer's look
back to the surface of the image.'[42] Despite Walter Benjamin's famous
argument about the loss of 'aura' as a result of the potential for infinite
mechanical reproduction of the image, anyone who has ever seen a
carefully restored and tinted print of a silent film shot on monochro-
matic stock by a cinematographic artist such as Joseph B. Walker can
attest to the auratic and sensual power of the image. Luminous and
detailed, these images invite 'a caressing gaze.'[43]

Marks rightly cautions against the temptation to conflate the haptic
with the feminine, as in Luce Irigaray's glorification of women's pleasure in touch over vision. Nevertheless, Marks argues that haptic visuality may be a feminist visual strategy, and goes so far as to suggest that 'it
is not coincidental that a number of haptic images are made by daughters of their mothers.' She cites *Seeing Is Believing* (video; d. Shauna
Beharry, 1991), 'in which the artist's camera searches a photograph of
her mother, following the folds of the silk sari in the photograph as they
too dissolve into grain and resolve again.' She argues that these images
evoke 'a tactile mirror stage' and calls up Gaylyn Studlar's theory of masochistic identification, in which the film viewer gives her/himself over
to an entire scene – sometimes literally a shimmering surface – rather
than identifying with characters. Marks goes on to argue that 'haptics
draw on an erotic relation that is organized less by a phallic economy
than by the relationship between mother and infant' in a 'labile' play of
identification and immersion.[44]

It is certainly tempting to read *The Grub-Stake* in such terms. Here we find the compelling combination of the lustrous surface of the image, the scenario of longing for the absent mother, and the images of Shipman's solitary body in the depths of the wilderness. Moreover, these are also the scenes of her most affective moments of performance. She contorts her body in angles of abjection, flings her arms to the sky, twists her shoulders into poses of frustration or relief, throws herself to the ground, or turns with exquisite slowness from the vista that has claimed her lyrical contemplation. In some scenes, she appears to have been influenced by Lillian Gish's performance in *Broken Blossoms*. In that film especially, Gish became famous for the wresting of affective emotion from her body, as she twirled around in frenzied despair in the closet, obsessively twisted her hands together in fear, bent her body with the force of desire for the doll in the window, or cowered and recoiled from the brutality of her father. Shipman, in fact, imitated Gish's performance in some early scenes of *The Grub-Stake*, especially the hand-twisting motions and the frenzied twirl. In the dramatic scenes of solitude, in which Shipman rails at or placates nature, contemplates beauty or despairs for her life, Shipman's performance peaks with Gish-like kinaesthesia. These scenes are composed in direct address to the camera/spectator, constructing an immediate and deliberate relationship between audience and star.

Vivian Sobchack gets at this in a somewhat different way by noting the interactivity of the viewer with the image, as opposed to the passive voyeur that characterized the spectator of earlier film theory. Eschewing the traditional metaphor of the cinematic image as window, frame, or mirror, Sobchack identifies a dialogic participation of the viewer in cinematic space, emphasizing the 'sensible' qualities of the 'lived-body' of the spectator. As opposed to Lacanian psychoanalysis, which posits a subject constituted by and positioned in language, Sobchack suggests a semiotic phenomenology to describe a subject that constitutes speech and always-already holds the power of authorship; she emphasizes the lived-experience as perceptive and expressive.[45] As for the 'being seen,' Sobchack argues that the body's animated display makes sense of the world 'through its sensible presence in the world';[46] she thus constructs spectatorship as an interactive exchange between image and spectator, which Marks casts as ' intersubjective eroticism.'

Although Sobchack suggests this rubric as a model for the 'film's body,' which she defines as the irreducible relation of the viewer and the visible image as well as the material existence and linguistic operations of the film, I would suggest that the dialogic relation between spectator is at its most sensorially intense when the 'film's body' is overlaid with the 'intending body-subject.' In those scenes in *The Grub-Stake* in which Shipman's sensual and heroic body displays itself in a shimmering exquisite space, as Sobchack writes, 'we recognize the moving picture as the work of [a] ... sign-producing body-subject intentionally marking visible choices with the very behavior of its bodily being.'[47] In other words, the intersubjective experience of the film (through perception and expression of the lived-body – 'the address of the eye') is the pleasure of embodiment, the rapture of synthesized vision.

The enunciator of the discourse as director and point of identification for the spectator as protagonist and the authority who has set the film's body in motion and subject/object of vision, Shipman asserts her lived subjectivity through her perceptions and expression, and invites the spectator to gaze directly at her body in all its heroic magnificence.

Blood on the Archive Floor

Rather than a two-dimensional image on a screen, Nell Shipman's body, impinging materially on the documents of her life as preserved in the archive of her effects, imparts a lived energy and evokes a visceral animism that can be sensed through contact with these inanimate records. This is not simply the evidence of her struggles to regain a foothold in the Hollywood economy – the letters and clippings – which have their own empathetic cathexis. I mean here the sense of the body of the subject[48] as perceived through the sensorium of the researcher.

Anyone who has done research in an archive has experienced this. An example from the distant past, when I was doing my MA on Emily Bronte: I'm willing to bet that anyone who has worked on Emily Bronte has become cathected on that little phrase, 'the pill'o potate,' the phrase Emily shared with her sisters to describe the scullery maid. And there, in the British Museum, were the very notebooks in which she had written that phrase, with her tiny drawings, delivered to me in gloved custodial hands. It is impossible to describe the thrill of receiving the little notebooks – to actually touch what she had touched. Or the reception of Gertrude Stein's notebooks in the Yale Beinecke Library, those French school children's exercise books in which Stein wrote longhand every night and which Alice B. Toklas typed into manuscript the next day. I can still feel the texture of that newsprint paper today: smooth and soft, it allowed her pen to fly across the pages. The size of the writing – approximately four words per page – also indicates the speed and energy of her composition and renders a sense of Stein's body at work that is material and tactile, perceived through the skin of the researcher's hands. As Ashley Montagu wrote in his pioneering work on the sense of touch, 'its sensory elements induce those neural, glandular, muscular and mental changes that in combination we call an emotion. Hence touch is not experienced as a simple physical modality, but affectively, as emotion.'[49]

Although notebooks such as Bronte's and Stein's can be photographed and perfectly represented in facsimile quality photographs, those images can never reproduce such affective sensations. It is the difference between the photographed body on the screen or paper and the sense of the body of the subject as perceived and cathected in the archive that I am on about now. And here we have another difference between the Bronte and Stein notebooks and Shipman's archived effects, for the sense of Shipman's lived body is mediated through a machine. Shipman wrote hundreds of letters as well as novels and screenplays on her Underwood typewriter, claimed as her instrument of enunciation and delivered visually in *Something New* (1920). In that film we can see her body completely engaged with the machine as her fingers tear across the keys, perhaps hyperbolized in a parodic expression of her customary practice. But when we hold those letters in our hands, a startling sensation occurs. At the end of every sentence there is a hole in the paper.

Unlike the computer keyboard, on a manual typewriter the comma and period were on the same key. So to produce an end-stop, one had to hold down the shift key on the left and press the comma/period key on the right. Similarly when a capital letter was required, the shift key was held down on the left while the letter key was hit. Without the fluidity and ergonomic ease of the electric keyboard, on a manual typewriter that action required a level of attention that to some degree halted the flow of the writing. And every time Shipman typed a capital, the letter jumped up half a line, and when she came to the end of a sentence, she hit the period key with such force that it left a hole in the paper.

Roland Barthes's notion of the punctum as an element of the analysis of photographs operates here in its most literal sense. Barthes wrote of the punctum as a point of identification (memory, nostalgia) in connection to a detail of the photograph that situates the emotional connection in relation to time and affect. His choice of terminology was metaphorical in relation to the photograph, for the moment he describes strikes to the heart or point of the recollection that the photograph instantiates:

> A Latin word exists to designate this wound, this prick, this mark made by a pointed instrument: the word suits me all the better in that it also refers to the notion of punctuation, and because the photographs I am speaking of are in effect punctuated, sometimes even speckled with these sensitive points; precisely, these marks, these wounds are so many *points*. This second element which will disturb the *studium* I shall therefore call *punctum*; for *punctum* is also: sting, speck, cut, little hole – and also a cast of the dice. A photograph's *punctum* is that accident which pricks me (but also bruises me, is poignant to me).[50]

In connection with Shipman's effects, the term is no longer metaphorical, but absolutely literal. Punctum derives from the Latin verb – *punctere* – that gives us the word *punctuation*. As Barthes points out, it also means to puncture or to prick. The holes in the paper that Shipman produced by the force of her body on the machine astound with the materiality of the force of punctuation.

We connect with Shipman's body through those holes in the paper. That it is Shipman's body that we contact, rather than a simple fault in the machine, is proven when we read a letter from Shipman's husband written on the same typewriter. His capitals do not jump nor do his periods make holes in the paper. The sensation of Shipman's body, her energy, her thrust, is transmitted therefore – albeit mediated by the machine – from her fingers to the fingers of the researcher. The sensation of contact with her body through the researcher's body can never be reproduced even in facsimile quality photographs of the letters, and

[4 .18.39]

" Son, son, " said Ma Liberty, ever so many times, graciously
waving her Torch......

Tuesday 18

Dearest Wooz

Am sitting here on what I hope will be the last anxious
seat; and really it isn't anxious, because I know its alright now.
I8ve got a wire already written to go to you today, and I8ve
written the letters to go with money to the car, etc, so while
that is a dangerous thing to do, I'm all ready for the deluge....
Firemen will be nothing compared to us going into action!

It was supposed to happen yesterday. Agreed upon Friday
Saturday - after banking hours! - it had to ride over until Monday
(another week-end!) and then on yesterday the Market did handsprings
and our Broker was sick into the bargain and didn't come to town
at all. We nearly died, but Peeley actually saw the check on a desk,
togeher with the agreement, so we really were sure. Today it was
set for noon, and he's just phoned to say he's having lunch with
Broker and Lawyer, at one o'clock. So I'm filling in the actual
last hour by writing you.

You will have had the wire -- which I wrote on purpose for
display -- and which I know you will understand. You told me in a
past letter you'd pull it in some such way. Now, the money we're
getting today is merely an advance, or loan, from the Broker who is
underwriting the production. It was got on the proposition that you
and I must be started on the continuity, you must be wired, so to
give notice, etc. etc. And the man saw the light. This advance goes
back to him when the contracts and all the law business is done.
The lawyers say this will take about 12 days. But we are safe, because
there is enough to bring you on, pay the most pressing debts, get
ourselves started to work.

I haven't the faintest idea how soon you can get off, but
thought on the strength of that wire, you might whoo-hoo them. That's
why I put in about the ' legal ' thing. They can imagine its something
with an estate, or something. That s better than a sick mama.
We've counted on your needing cash to repay Republic but hope you'll
be able to leave your last salary with Beula. Your salary can start
from the time you get here. I've earmarked $ 200.00 per for five
weeks for the continuity. After that we'll try and keep it the same
through the picture, but we have to remember every dollar we shell out
comes off said opus. But I know you won't worry. Now that it's
really come.   I'll want you to pay Rex the forty and bring the
typewriter.   Your actual fare is a bargain... $ 123.00 round trip,
plus 14 pullman, plus your eats. The trains are not the fastest but
pretty quick. They leave twice a day. You'll have your return ticket
so you'll be safe on the May 23rd date at court.

When I think of your really getting on a train, and arriving,
and of our going to work on that beloved story..... I nearly die!
Get all teary and excited. You will make the start just as soon as
heaven will let you, won't you?

The last weeks of waiting have been unbelievable ... day to day,
hour to hour.... and I couldn't do anything except sit here, wondering!
I8ve gone mad a couple of times but I8m alright now; just a little

Although the jumping capitals are apparent, the holes in the paper are
unreproducible even in an archive facsimile.

stands in a specifically affective relation to cathected desire. This is neither Laura Marks's 'caressing gaze'[51] nor Vivian Sobchack's dialogic
relation between spectator and the 'sign-producing body-subject intentionally marking visible choices with the very behavior of its bodily
being'[52]; nor is it exactly Benjamin's 'aura' of the original artefact,[53]
although something of that aura pertains. It is, on the contrary, actually
(though I hesitate to use the word) and experientially – rather than
metaphorically – tactile and emotional.

From the haptic visuality of her body on the screen to that sense of her
vigour and strength and the urgency of her composition in the writings,
one achieves a visceral sense of Shipman's body in motion. The desire is
not to inhabit her body, not to taste what she tastes or smell what she
smells, but to recognize her body in its expressive fullness. That hole in
the paper – a sensorial and proprioceptive absence – paradoxically
redounds not only to her absence but also to her lived presence.

Film theorist turned archivist Marc Vernet noted the affective imme-
diacy of archival research when he wrote about the decision to make
archival material available to more than a privileged few via digital
media. He writes, 'Then I began to consider the substantial pleasure
associated with handling, with great caution and respect, these tangible
traces of the past. There is, if not an erotic dimension, at least a certain
affect that is beneficial to research and necessary to the desire at the
heart of cinema study which cannot be replaced by viewing videodiscs or
CD-ROMs. This is not simply a respect for original documents, imbued
with the aura of history. There is something equally important at work
which forms a part of the researcher's emotional response.'[54]

Vernet goes on to note that this emotional response is contingent
upon the rarity of the document: 'Confronted with the kind of historical
object that tends to disappear, it is as if the researcher has encountered
the last member of a species on the verge of extinction. The document
demands attention and care, a protective attitude, to the degree that it
is perceived to be rare. We experience this emotional state because we
believe we hold the last trace, the last copy.'[55]

Vernet's emphasis on the significance of rarity to the production of
such emotion is reminiscent of the story of the collector who thought he
had a unique book. When he heard of the existence of another copy, he
hastened to buy it and destroy it. This story, by now a legend of collect-

ing, is recounted by Jean Baudrillard in *The System of Objects* (1968),[56] and commented on by Susan Stewart in her work on collecting. In the possession of a unique object that has acquired particular poignancy since the onset of mechanical reproduction, the collector, Stewart argues, gains control over repetition by defining a finite set, and in the process destroys labour and history. Stewart sees such an approach to collections as the antithesis of creation.[57]

Contrary to Vernet's reticence about the erotic dimension of research, I would argue that not only is that affective sensation unreproducible and unrepresentable, but certainly it belongs to the realm of the erotic. One way of reading the erotics of archival research is to emphasize the desire of the researcher to possess or consume the subject, the sense in which Susan Stewart evokes 'longing' as both the desire for the lost object and the nominative sense of a belonging, appurtenance, or acquisition. The collector, she suggests, has an uncontrollable urge to take and keep, an urge towards 'incorporation' for its own sake as an attempt to erase the limits of the body.[58] The pleasure of the souvenir – the magical trace of a past experience – is dependent upon others, upon the system of images within which the corporeal body has been transformed into a fetish or point of representation. The collection such as that found in archives or museums, on the other hand, is abstracted by classification – a controlling, ordered system that masks desire through quantification. 'The dialectic between hand and eye, possession and transcendence, which motivates the fetish, is dependent upon this abstraction ... Thus the collection is ... the most abstract of all forms of consumption.'[59]

When the collection contains the effects of a beloved subject whose possession or consumption is utterly abstracted – cardboard boxes numbered, hidden, briefly displayed, retrieved, and hidden away again – the tension of the collection for its custodian, Stewart suggests, strains altruistic commitment to display and use value, on the one hand, with containment, control, secrecy on the other. Researchers partake of similar 'uncontrollable urges' towards hoarding, privacy, and possession. However, even beyond the narcissistic desire to defy mortality, to extend the limits of the body by collecting or consuming, may be the necrophiliac thrill of contact with the dead body of the loved subject, a reaching beyond the grave. Is this what that hole in the paper ultimately signifies?

On the contrary, C. Nadia Seremetakis asserts that the contact of my fingers with that hole in the paper is a moment of birth. The sensory landscape, she argues, is neither stable nor fixed but inherently transitive, demanding connection and completion by the perceiver. The completion/connection with the sensory artefact is a mutual insertion of the perceiver and perceived in historical experience. 'It is a *poesis*, the making of something out of that which was previously experientially and culturally unmarked or even null and void. Here sensory memory, as the meditation on the historical substance of experience is not mere repetition, but transformation which brings the past into the present as a natal event.'[60] Here we can read the erotics of sensory contact with the lost object as a truly celebratory and creative act.

This is, after all, what the researcher longs for – to bring the subject back to life.

Speaking of the inadequacy of science or medicine to describe the ideosyncracies of the corporeal, Claire Denis[61] said recently that we tend to forget that films are produced *through* bodies, including not only the body of the cinematic apparatus, but also the visceral urge of the author/director to express her/his fullness of desire, and the contortions of the bodies of the actors onscreen as they demonstrate the pain of performance at the same time as they are watching their marks and biting the blood capsule on cue, all the while assailed by the wafting odours of the sweat of the crew under the heat of the lights and the food on the craft services table.[62] My interest in Nell Shipman's body, and the erotic thrill of making contact with it through a hole in the paper, comes down precisely to this: the sensation of her body at work.

:: :: :: :: ::

chapter seven

Bits and Pieces

We must take a little dip back in time for the beginning of this chapter, to pick up a short film that Nell Shipman made almost immediately after *Back to God's Country* and before *Something New*. After a brief consideration of *A Bear, a Boy, and a Dog* (1920), we will return to the Idaho years to consider the last films that she made there. Situating Shipman's films within a brief history of wildlife films, this chapter concerns itself with the use of animals in Shipman's work. Issues of wilderness consciousness, anthropomorphism, women's involvement with animal care movements, and new scholarship in ecofeminism arise.

Shipman had purchased the zoo of wild animals used in *Back to God's Country* as part of the severance agreement after the dissolution of her partnerships with Ernest Shipman and James Oliver Curwood. According to Shipman, most of the animals still lived with their trainer, Felix (Doc) Graff at his place in Azusa,[1] although Tom Trusky can find no evidence of the establishment.[2] Along with the North American wild animals that were featured in *Back to God's Country* as well as the later films, the collection included a little East Indian honey-bear and a Siberian wolf. Shipman continued to collect more animals along the way. In *Abandoned Trails* she describes the trainer himself as offering her a gift of two small Panama deer to add 'to our family,'[3] and the zoo eventually became the largest privately owned collection of wild animals in the United States.

After *Back to God's Country*, Shipman and Bert Van Tuyle moved to a new house in the Highland Park area of greater Los Angeles. There, Brownie the bear's residence was carved out of the hillside and came complete with a large patio, a dining table, and an overhead shower. Whereas small animals such as raccoons, squirrels, chipmunks, a skunk, and a desert rat named Ignatz had runs and cages, a small grey desert fox was not caged, preferring to ride on Shipman's shoulders. Bobs and Babs, a pair of wild bobcats, had the run of the house.

Shipman delighted in taking bear and dog for rides downtown in the back seat of her car:

> Bear and Collie used to ride in the back seat of the old National without leashes, each with a head thrust out as they took the breeze. The effect on even the sparse traffic of that day was bedlam. I'd park downtown and go into a store, like Bullock's or Robinson's, on Seventh, and leave the pair in the car. Guarded by Laddie, Brownie would stay in the back seat but would perform gymnastics, chinning herself on the top brace or standing on her head to clown for the sidewalk audience. Laddie only hammed for a camera. He knew exactly when he was in focus for a close-up and the moment he spied a tripod gave his best profile to the lens. Parked at the curb on Seventh Street he looked indulgently on as Brownie made an ass of herself for free. The police asked me not to bring the bear downtown. She tied up traffic.[4]

Collies and Wildcats and Bears, Oh My

In her memoir and in *Abandoned Trails*, Shipman tells the identical story of the sibling bobcats who had the run of the house. 'Their pet trick was to leap from the top of the piano to a person's shoulder. This was disconcerting to human visitors who suddenly found themselves wearing handsome live fur pieces.'[5] Dramatizing the incident with considerably more colour, *Abandoned Trails* finds the protagonist sitting decorously at the grand piano playing her favourite theme song until she is 'rudely interrupted by the landing of a weight, like a thrown ball, on the shoulder of the pianist.' It turns out to be one of two spotted wildcats, who are playing on the Chinese rug beneath the piano. Complaining aloud, 'Oh, those dratted wildcats!' the housekeeper sniffs, thinking 'How anyone can bring themselves to pet wildcats, let alone bears!' The protagonist gathers up 'a tawny armful,' promising to put them in their cage.[6]

Shipman had grown up with pets, especially dogs. When her parents were elderly they had three dogs that walked with her father every day. In the fictionalized account of her father's death in *Abandoned Trails*, Shipman recalls that the three dogs 'went ahead of him, like heralds, or traffic cops clearing the way.'[7] Laddie, the little collie that became Brownie the bear's mentor and Barry's companion, stayed with her father through his death, from the day he fell to the sidewalk when they were out on a walk: 'Laddie was with him and the dog set up a howling over the big, crumpled form ... It was apoplexy and [her father] never spoke coherently again. He seemed to know Laddie only and the collie stayed by his bed, refusing to move until he was dragged away, howling.'[8] In the affecting scene wherein Joyce (Nell) mourns her father in *Abandoned Trails*, she turns for comfort to the two Great Danes who had played Wapi in *Back to God's Country*. Waiting to cry until her husband was out, she went to the top floor where Tresore and Rex were chained in a deserted storeroom, 'fastened so that they could not rend one another but, as Joyce sat between them, each dog could reach her. Tresore came first. She felt the great weight of his head on her lap and heard his murmuring whine, low pitched and more than human in its understanding. She clasped her arms around his corded throat, felt the warmth of him, read the sympathy in his eyes and, at last, began to cry. He licked her hands, blotting the falling tears.'[9]

In the novel Shipman represents the dogs as having putative human thoughts. As they comfort her, she imagines 'these two hated rivals who waited only to tear at each other' agreeing to a temporary flag of truce; they even have a concept of death and heaven. Shipman renders their voices in direct speech: 'This human thing we both love is in trouble. Something belonging to her has gone over to the other side. She is ignorant and does not know she will see this person again. We know more than she does and if we will just keep still she will hear the beat of our hearts and know that we understand. Sympathy helps to cure sorrowing humans. It is one of their many weaknesses.'[10]

Domestic pets are not the only creatures that evince cognition and emotion. Of the bear, Shipman writes: 'Brownie, the cub, was a born clown. She bubbled humor like uncorked champagne. Mischievous is too weak a word. Her stunts were premeditated, carefully worked out routines performed with eclat, spontaneity and the essence of comedic timing.'[11] Shipman describes the bear as almost as dear to her as her son; she 'could not imagine life without the brown bear and a picture lacking Brownie in a leading part would invite failure.'[12]

In *Abandoned Trails*, Shipman devotes almost an entire chapter to Brownie's delightful playfulness, describing an incident that involves Brownie's 'private shower,' which Joyce turns on to fill the bear's drinking dish. Joyce then leaves the faucet on while she goes to fetch her son for lunch. Meanwhile, Dirk (Van Tuyle) arrives in the car. At this point, the housekeeper comes screaming from the garden, soaking wet. '"Drat the creature!" she was crying. "Did it on purpose! Put her paw over the faucet and turned the water slap-bang onto me! ... When I tried to dodge she'd shift her foot and hit me with the stream."' Shipman's delight in the animal's antics is evident in the language she uses here: 'Brownie, seated on her behind, blinking in the last rays of the sun, aimed her spout of water straight up so that it fell in a sparkling shower about her fat shoulders; for all the world like a stout old lady in a brown fur coat posing for a fountain figure!'[13] As the scene proceeds, first Joyce and then Dirk approach the cage to turn the faucet off. Brownie drenches them both. While Dirk curses the bear for ruining his business suit, Joyce collapses in laughter. At last the faucet is turned off, and the chapter ends with Shipman's fond imagining of Dirk's final rapprochement with the bear:

> 'Come here!' he commanded. She came slowly from the corner, eyes on him, head swaying, doubt in her mind whether to hit and run or kiss and make up. She sniffed and licked the outstretched hand, looking up at him with the pupils of her small eyes rolled so far over they were like quarter-moons. 'Bad, bad girl!' he repeated. 'Grumph!' she swore, fetching him a clout on the side of his leg and galloping for her den, ears back. Dirk managed to spank her, smartly, before she disappeared and, in a moment, she was out again; repentance on every feature. But now he feigned indifference, turning his back and pretending to be busy with the water faucet. The bear climbed to her table, craning her neck to reach and kiss him. 'Oh, you pet!' he said, putting an arm about her shoulders ... She caressed his cheek with her tongue, making a crooning love-noise, like an ardent bee.[14]

As well as Shipman's fondness for the animal, her estimation of

Brownie's abilities of cognition, emotion, self-awareness, and expression is evident in every sentence of this passage. A similar regard for the potential for animal subjectivity informs many of her films.

A Bear, a Boy, and a Dog

While Shipman was trying to find investors for the new feature *The Girl from God's Country,* she was also trying to hang onto Joseph Walker as cinematographer. When he was getting low on funds, 'she dashed out a one-reeler story about a boy, dog and a bear to keep [him] busy. [He] was to direct, photograph and have complete charge of making it. In turn, [he'd] receive half the profit.' Walker's version of the arrangement for creative control may be as they discussed it, but Tom Trusky credits Shipman and Bert Van Tuyle as directors, with Walker listed only as photographer.[15] Walker's story goes on: 'The cost would be very little – we had plenty of short ends of film on hand, Nell supplied the bear and dog, and in exchange for running the picture in his theater free for one week, [William H.] Clune [owner of Clune's Broadway Theater in Los Angeles] offered the services of a twelve-year-old singing lad, Sonny Howard ... between shows at his Broadway theater.'[16] Trusky gives Clune credit as producer.[17]

A Bear, a Boy, and a Dog (1921, 20 minutes) is one of many one- and two-reelers that Shipman wrote and directed independently. Referring to them as 'bits and pieces, "fillers" made while we waited for my percentage of the take on the big picture [*Back to God's Country*],' Shipman disparages their distribution sources as 'Poverty Row Independents' and their exhibition venues as 'small-time State's Righters' (i.e., the southern circuit).[18]

Originally entitled *Saturday Off* and shot in 1920, the little film was retitled *A Bear, a Boy, and a Dog* and copyrighted in 1921.[19] The delightful comedy stars twelve-year-old Sonny Howard, her favourite collie, Laddie, and Brownie the bear. Although Shipman usually starred in the films with her pets, in *A Bear, a Boy, and a Dog* she appears only as an extra, wearing a large hat shielding her face and sitting with her back to the camera. In contrast to the framing device of *Something New* (1920), which situates her as writer/enunciator of the tale, sitting at her typewriter and smiling conspiratorially into the camera, her presence/

absence in *A Bear, a Boy, and a Dog* could be seen as a disavowal of authorship. I would prefer to read it instead as a modest act of generosity, giving the eponymous trio their rightful status as stars, not to be outdone by the more famous face of their director. They are the only featured players, and the title indicates the equal weight of the three characters in the film.

And 'characters' they are: as well as the boy, of course, both the dog and the bear are autonomous subjects in the narrative, capable of a range of emotional responses, problem solving, and the formulation of strategy. This seems to be an essential Shipman authorial note: that the animals act on their own, apparently without instructions or orders from human masters. Shipman articulates their thoughts through intertitles. The bear's sad reflection on his state, for example, comes close to poetry: 'And this on a September day with the wind whispering in the wildwood,' he sighs from his cage in the zoo (intertitle).

The film begins with the introduction of the three characters, each confined on a beautiful September Saturday: the boy by his chores, the dog left tied to a tree as his mistress drives off, and the bear, in 'the saddest prison of all,' the zoo. Just as the dog is barking 'I want my liberty' (intertitle) and the boy decides to go on strike, the bear's cage door is inadvertently left open so that Brownie can also escape. As Laddie wriggles his head through his tight collar, the intertitle takes the dog's voice: 'If you scrooge back your ears this doesn't hurt ... much.' In the one-reel adventure, Brownie raids the boy's house and eventually meets up with the boy and the dog, who have left for an adventure in the woods.

The heart of the tale is the friendship that develops among the trio, eventually culminating in a sentimental tableau of the three of them, all entwined together, sleeping in the woods. Of course burglars/villains are apprehended through their efforts, and all seems right in movieland until practicality overcomes sentiment in the end, when the poor gentle bear is sent back to the zoo.

The film contains a wonderful surprising moment when Brownie chases the boy up a tree and then climbs right over him. The stunt wasn't in the original script, relates cinematographer Joseph B. Walker in his autobiography. The first draft had Brownie as a bear in the wild who chases the frightened boy up a tree in a scene in which the extreme fear in the boy was played up.

Brownie liked chasing the boy; this became a game and a new kind of romp, but she balked at climbing a tree. We had to resort to scaring her.

Bert ran after her beating a metal disk. Brownie wasn't used to this kind of treatment. She tucked her tail and made haste. When she got to the tree she scampered up it in fast clawing strides – and upon reaching the boy she didn't stop, she clambered over him and kept going till she could climb no further.

There, clinging to a spindly branch, Brownie remained, looking down at us more frightened than the boy ...

When Nell saw the scene run in the projection room, she couldn't stop laughing. Then and there she rewrote the script and turned it into a comedy, allowing us to utilize that fantastic shot of Brownie clambering over the boy.[20]

Not particularly remarkable, this charming little film is one of many that Shipman turned out, and it happened by luck to be preserved in excellent print condition. It belongs to a tradition of dog films that is as long as the cinema itself, beginning with early Edison films such as *Laura Comstock's Bag-Punching Dog* (1901). In a series of Happy Hooligan films produced by Edison over five years, Mannie, Laura Comstock's dog, plays a tramp's nemesis in titles such as *The Tramp's Dream* and *Pie, Tramp and the Bulldog*. These were by no means the relatively sophisticated narratives that Shipman's work developed. The scenario of *Pie, Tramp and the Bulldog*, for example, is only slightly more complex than its title. After the dog prevents a tramp from grabbing a pie cooling on a windowsill, the tramp returns on stilts to outsmart him – to no avail. The dog jumps out the window and the two exit with the dog clamped to the tramp's pants.[21] And that is that.

Another dog film, *Rescued by Rover* (Cecil Hepworth, 1905) makes it into the history books as one of the earliest complex narrative films. In the one-reel adventure, a dog, exercising his own initiative and intelligence, has to rescue a kidnapped child. Another early narrative is *Playmates* (Edison, 1908), a story about a child and her faithful dog companion. When the child gets sick, the dog, dressed in a costume and given a pipe, informs the parents and stays with the bedridden girl. Despite the doctor's fatal diagnosis, the dog prays for the girl and effects a miraculous cure.[22]

The developing dog-movie genre, to which Alice Guy Blaché contributed *The Detective's Dog* (1912), continued through the many Lassie and
Rin Tin Tin films of later decades, not to mention the dreaded Disneys.
Shipman's films are notable, however, for her light touch with the intertitles that reveal the animals' thoughts and representations of speech.

Trail of the North Wind

This same loving and humorous understanding of animals is evident in
virtually all of Shipman's other extant films. In *Trail of the North Wind*
(1923) a malamute named Nugget (played by a malamute named Tex)
saves the day, in another heroic display of animal subjectivity. He demonstrates first his determination and skill by wriggling free from his sled-
dog harness, and goes on to track the missing Dreena and Billy (played
by Shipman and son Barry) as they stumble through the snowbound wilderness. When he finds them, he 'installs' them (intertitle) in a little
snow shelter until he can rouse two woodcutters to their rescue.

As in *A Bear, a Boy, and a Dog*, a similar insouciant subjectivity informs
the intertitles. His intentions signalled to the spectator by a quick cross-
fade to Dreena and Billy in their snowy lair, Nugget approaches two
woodsmen, then runs away and returns a couple of times. While the
men stand there looking perplexed, Nugget barks (in intertitles) 'Come
this way! Can't you understand dog-English?'

The impetus for the plot of *Trail of the North Wind* – a simple tale of
wilderness travail – is grandpa getting caught in an animal trap. Billy
comes across him in the woods and sets out to get help. Shipman's sense
of cinematic drama provides a number of thrilling and/or comic
moments, most of them shot in real time. In a long comic scene, for
example, Billy tries to climb up onto a donkey's back so that he can alert
Dreena to Grandpap's injury. He throws himself again and again
towards the donkey's back until he finally manages to climb onto the
large animal's neck. When he finally gets up there, he is facing the donkey's tail and has to turn himself around to face the head, slipping
several times down the other side in the attempt. To cap off the scene,
when Billy is at last in the saddle, he finds he has forgotten the rein,
which is tethered in front of the donkey's head. Finally he is able to set
off for help. The entire scene is shot from a static camera at a sufficient

distance to signify the actuality of the effort and the lack of off-screen assistance, indicating Shipman's grasp of the grammatical significance of both focal length and non-edited real time, as well as the dramatic effect of actuality that they produce.

In addition to demonstrations of Shipman's sense of drama and the grammar of film, *Trail of the North Wind* showcases her wilderness skills and environmental consciousness. As Dreena and Billy set out on the dogsled across the snow, for example, a series of wonderful panoramic shots of the dogsled with its passengers crossing the screen doubles the protagonists in mirror image: they are reflected with crystalline clarity in the dark open waters of the lakeshore. Although the cinematographer on *Trail of the North Wind* was Bobby Newhardt (once Joseph. B. Walker's assistant), this is something of a reprise of a shot that Joseph B. Walker had used in his promotional film about the 1918 Maxwell. Walker's shot, of the car perfectly reflected in a pool of water with a ramshackle wooden building behind it, was introduced by an intertitle as 'A mirror in the desert – one of nature's whims.' The *Trail of the North Wind* image, unlike Walker's, is not marred by a building in the background, but suggests the magnificent untouched wilderness in its breadth and lack of human habitation.

As they continue their journey, the dogsled and the humans range in a tiny moving line across the centre of the frame; they are dwarfed by the snow-covered reaches of the wilderness and the open sky behind them and reflected in the clear dark pool that takes up the lower quarter of the frame. The nature cinematography here is reminiscent of the tropes of nineteenth-century landscape painting that had figured so influentially in depictions of the wilderness cherished by the newly founded environmental protection groups such as the Sierra Club and the Wilderness Society. Snow-covered mountains, magnificent old-growth forests, and reflecting pools of water with the human figures carefully placed within the composition are motifs that came to signify positive landscape images for environmentalists and conservationists. Compositional elements often included recessive planes, 'prospect' symbolism, and the sublimely vast panorama, with the human figure of inconsequential size in relation to the grandeur of the untouched landscape. These tropes are evoked in *Trail of the North Wind* in the long travel sequence that occupies the centre of the narrative, particularly in

the wide shots, somewhat akin to Claudian frames – typical compo-
sitions of French landscape artist Claude Lorraine, in which the vast
landscape minimizes the human element.[23] Shipman's sense of the
landscape as monumental and the human as an 'atom' (intertitle) in
this universe is visually played out in shots in which the figures are mere
tiny traces, visible only because of their movement in a straight line
across the frame.

As Dreena and Billy head out across the frozen snow-covered lake,
panoramic wide shots effect more than a reference to the compositional
traditions of landscape painting and photography; they also signify the
actuality of the location and the dauntless skills of the protagonist. The
adventure unspools before us without fakery, sets, or rear projection –
and clearly on the first take, for the snow stretches before them
untouched, track-less. To underline the actuality of the settings and
their dangers, in the memoir Shipman describes a scene of driving
across 'the bad ice, Barry in the toboggan. We came to an open space
where black water seeped. I was afraid the lead dog might balk and the
load go under but one after the other they jumped, harness taut. The
small sled bridged the gap and I followed, only wetting my mukluks as
the crunching ice sloughed off. Not much of a scene I suppose, but it
was real. We did it. The camera caught it.'[24]

Eventually Billy slips off the sled into a patch of open water and
Dreena must rescue him. Close-shots now detail without cuts the
attempts to leave the icy water: Billy slips under the surface; Dreena
leaves the sled to assist him, slipping into the water herself; the two
struggle against the ice that cracks before them as they try to gain a foot-
ing; together they eventually crawl on all fours to safety. Finally on solid
ice with Billy, Dreena wrings the water out of her long dark hair. A wide
shot reveals the sled moving off into the distance as the dogs desert
them, leaving Dreena and Billy having to make the rest of the journey
on foot. Wide shots again testify to their crossing through thigh-deep icy
water that is ringed with deep snow, and their trudging through snow
up to their knees with a blizzard raging. Such 'real' scenes, caught on
the first take or not at all, form a significant element in the lexicon of
adventure in the wilderness and the respectful admiration for the ele-
mental landscape in which the films are located.

In these scenes, the actuality of the setting and of the struggle is delivered to its melodramatic full. Later, when Dreena and Billy become mired in the heavy deep snow, narrative conventions of shot variation allow for a beautiful close-up of Shipman as Dreena, her dark tresses covered in snow ringing her face. Shipman's love of the wilderness setting, evident in the close-up of Dreena, reverberates also in the memoir when she writes of another scene, 'A simple piece of business but, in the frame of white bending the graceful cedars, the low light sparkling on cones and twigs, bark, moss and powdery snow ... I thought there was something which made a Moving Picture.'[25]

The boy has fallen again and is too weary to continue. Dreena pleads with him to carry on. Meanwhile Nugget the dog has slipped, of his own volition, from his sled-team harness; he is on their trail. When he finds them marooned in the blizzard and unable to go farther, Nugget takes over the rescue. Except for the momentary inability of the woodsmen to understand 'dog-English,' the narrative winds up expeditiously.

Trail of the North Wind hinges around communication with nature in all its aspects. Dreena, the heroine, is identified first as the 'story-girl' because she listens to the 'voices of the wilderness' – the babbling brook, a bear sniffing the air, and the personified North Wind himself – and translates them for people. Intertitles: 'The Big Bully, roaring down from his mountain lair, bent tree and sapling to his wanton will ... But one day, he met a human atom who dared defy him ... [Cut to Dreena at the edge of the lake, shouting and waving him away: she defies the North Wind in its first rages and forces it to retreat.] He rumbled his way home, vowing some day to return ... Picture him waiting for the fates to weave their drama and cast him as the villain.' Here Shipman personifies all aspects of nature. In the memoir, for another example, she describes a nearby peak as 'our ... mountain-neighbor' who looks 'better groomed' than usual, its slopes covered with blueberries in summer.[26]

Nature is an overwhelming force in Shipman's work, rendering the human element tiny and inconsequential. The effect is underlined in the *Trail of the North Wind* intertitle that describes Dreena as a 'human atom' – humanity reduced to a particle in the universe. The reference to the discoveries of contemporary physics situates Dreena in the context of modernity; she is no throwback to an earlier or less developed time. She is wearing tight breeches and knee socks, carries a backpack, and has her longish bob held to her head with a bandanna. She is a thoroughly modern woman out by herself for a hike in the woods, her only companion a dog. Despite the grandeur and sometimes frightening force of nature, she not only shows no fear, but rises at times to defiance.

Thematically central to the drama, such demonstrations of Shipman's wilderness consciousness get dramatic traction through the emphasis on interspecies connection. What hurts the animal also hurts the human, and it is clear that sympathetic communication and respect would prevent all such injuries. The moral of the story is told with a smile, as Dreena sends a trap to a watery grave, never to be used on animal or human again. Here again, for the ending, the wide-shot is of an idyllic almost-spring lake, with the old man, the boy, and the heroic woman rowing to its centre in a small wooden skiff. In a shot that would be an appropriate image for a Wilderness Club calendar, at first they are small 'atoms' in the panorama. Soon they come closer into view as the characters apparently concur on the fate of the brutal trap. Only as the narrative concludes does the shot cut to a close-up as Dreena drops the dreadful trap into the water, intercut with a close-up of Billy smiling in agreement. Fade out.

Trail of the North Wind belonged to a series called *Little Dramas of the Big Places*, of which it seems at least five were begun but only four completed. Only three are extant, the first three filmed. They were made in the remote wilderness of Idaho after the fiasco of *The Girl from God's Country* (1921) and the completion of *The Grub-Stake* (1923). The two-reel dramas were made on minimal budgets and usually featured amateur actors – friends and neighbours – in leading roles: 'Most everyone around the lake would be actors and, of course, the animals.'[27]

Animals in Silent Movies

Since the earliest days of the cinema, animals have been subjects and featured players. In 1877, with an apparatus of multiple cameras operated by trip wires and electronic shutters, Eadweard Muybridge revealed many kinds of animal motion, including the heretofore unknowns such as that galloping horses lifted all four feet off the ground. Muybridge also staged a tiger attacking a buffalo at the Philadelphia zoo, 'setting a precedent,' as Alexander Wilson notes, 'for the sacrifice of animals that became a standard in TV entertainment.'[28] To film the motion of birds in flight, the French physiologist Étienne-Jules Marey invented the chrono-photographic gun in 1882, recording the first moving images of animals in the wild. Thus, not only were animals involved in cinema from its formative stages, but in turn the motion picture camera played a key role in the development of the science of biology.

Animals were also features of the cinema as commercial entertainment from the beginning. The commercial debut of Edison's kinetoscope in a midtown Manhattan 'parlor' in April 1894 featured a short film called *Trained Bears*. Charles Musser notes that the entrance charge of five cents, the fashionable location of the 'parlor,' and the 'non-offensive' subjects (tempering the rougher subjects of earlier Edison productions that catered to the homosocial world of men) brought in the middle class, including women.[29] An example of this softening effect is *Boxing Cats* (1894), described in the Library of Congress catalogue as 'a very interesting and amusing subject.' In this parody of the sporting world's manly preoccupations, two cats in a miniature boxing ring wear tiny boxing gloves; a man holds them up so that they seem to be balancing on their hind feet and trading blows. *Prof. Harry Welton's Cat Circus* was another similar offering,[30] as is *Trick Bears* (1899), a short film that reveals a number of large bears, one of them wearing a kind of granny cap and shawl, and the others at times wearing bits of costumes and performing stunts at the behest of trainers wielding long poles. They sit up on chairs, dance around, and generally perform like circus bears.

The Edison films catalogue describes another film, *Fun in Camp* (1899), as 'showing a group of soldiers and Red Cross nurses being amused by a number of small children who are riding upon the backs of trick bears. A remarkably fine picture, with U.S. Infantry camp in the background.'[31] About half the film depicts the infantry camp (two tents with a campfire in front) with some soldiers sitting around until three large bears, walking on all fours, stroll into the camp with their trainers. They seem to be the same bears as in *Trick Bears*; certainly the trainers are the same, wearing the same hats and carrying the same long poles. One of the trainers gives a small child a ride on a bear's back. The turn to 'non-offensive' subject matter catering to a wider audience can be seen in this film in the combination of children with the bears, signalling also the appeal of animals and nature in popular culture.

Wilderness and wildlife literature was already topping the best-seller literary charts in the first decades of the century, especially the realistic wild animal stories of Jack London, whose hugely successful *The Call of the Wild* was adapted for film by D.W. Griffith (Biograph, 1908). A critic for the *Mirror* commended the film for 'the particular elements that go to make up a successful moving picture.'[32] Literary naturalists such as Ernest Thompson Seton created in the animal story a genre that corresponded to the artistic, educational, and recreational values prized by the urban middle class in their reverence for nature.[33]

One of the first attempts to market large-scale wildlife films in commercial cinemas was *Roosevelt in Africa* (1910), featuring former president Theodore Roosevelt, an amateur naturalist and conservationist, hunting big game in the African Congo. Sponsored by Andrew Carnegie on behalf of the Smithsonian Institute, with a mandate to collect specimens of African flora and fauna, Roosevelt's year-long expedition was recorded by cinematographer Cherry Kearton, a famous naturalist-photographer from London.[34] As one of the first commercial animal features, this trophy-hunting film corresponds to the developmental taxonomy of the animal story outlined by Charles G.D. Roberts, one of the early writers of animal stories. Roberts suggests that such primordial tales, dating back to drawings on cave-walls, are the first stage of the genre: 'Perhaps the most engrossing part in the life-drama of primitive man was that played by the beasts which he hunted, and by those which hunted him ... They furnished both material and impulse for his first gropings toward pictorial art ... We may not unreasonably infer that the first animal story ... was a story of some successful hunt.'[35]

In contrast to Roberts's assertion that a principal merit of such stories was their verisimilitude – 'they were convincing'[36] – none of the footage of *Roosevelt in Africa* caught Roosevelt bringing down game, nor was Kearton successful in his attempt to secure the first motion pictures of lions in the wild. Instead, a still of a lion was cut in. One reviewer described the shot as 'flatter than a pancake. It looks like a dead lion, or a poor wash drawing.'[37]

Roosevelt in Africa was not the first film on the subject of Roosevelt's famous hunting activities; his adventures shooting mountain lions in Colorado were the basis of *Terrible Teddy, the Grizzly King* (d. Edwin S. Porter; Edison, 1901). In the first scene of the film, which 'opens in a very picturesque wood,' a man spots a mountain lion up a tree. 'He kneels on one knee and makes a careful shot. Immediately upon the discharge of his gun a huge black cat falls from the tree and Teddy whips out his bowie knife, leaps on the cat and stabs it several times, then poses while his photographer makes a picture and the press agent writes up the thrilling adventure.'[38] What the catalogue does not mention is that the hunter is dressed in a bear suit and his two companions have hand-lettered signs hanging around their necks, one saying 'my photographer' and the other 'my press agent.'[39] Based on a cartoon series from the Hearst Corporation's New York *Journal*, this burlesque not only played to the working-class audience that later derided *Roosevelt in Africa*, but at the same time underlined a scepticism about the world of naturalism and conservation.

Roosevelt espoused conservationism, naturalism, and a middle-class ideology that emphasized a strenuous life and families of at least four children. In the context of the anti-modernist reaction to the galloping industrialization and urbanization of twentieth-century culture, Roosevelt worried that '"men of his class were threatened by the physical and moral effeminacy of modern times" ... Fearful that man overly civilized by industrial society would lose the "great, fighting masterful virtues," he championed the wilderness as the place to restore "vigorous manliness."'[40] Framed as the anti-pode of civilization, the wilderness was deemed to hold curative powers that could soothe anti-modernist anxieties about industrialized metropolitan life.[41]

Roosevelt's 'naturalism,' in the form of big-game hunting, was not without its critics. In 1907, after Roosevelt killed a bear, the *New York World* gave nature writer William J. Long a front-page column headlined 'Calls Roosevelt Bear Killing Pure Brute Cowardice.'[42] Opposition to cruelty to animals was by no means new to the twentieth century: thinkers as diverse as Plutarch, Pythagoras, and Montaigne had all written on the subject in preceding centuries. The late eighteenth century gave rise to the organized movement that attempted to define precisely what cruelty to animals would be, and introduced the more radical idea that non-human animals could have rights. The first laws against cruelty to animals were passed in England in 1822, the year the Society for the Prevention of Cruelty to Animals was founded. The debate existed so visibly that by the 1840s (when Queen Victoria's support brought about a change in the name to Royal Society for the Prevention of Cruelty to Animals) to advocate laws on the behalf of animals ceased to be considered the work of revolutionaries or fanatics. 'What Roderick Nash has described as the progressive expansion of natural rights to include not only oppressed classes of humans, but also animals specifically and nature in general, was not an unknown strain of revolutionary thought in the late 18th century. The idea was that a truly reformed society would liberate not only the unenfranchised, but also oppressed and exploited animals.'[43]

Another Edison film that indicates an alternative take on cruelty to animals, big-game hunting, and (probably not without politics) the exploits of President Roosevelt is *The 'Teddy' Bears* (d. Edwin S. Porter, 1907). A complex work of irony with a jarring shift in tone and referent, the film is based on a well-known hunting party in which Roosevelt refused to shoot a bear cub. The incident inspired a toy manufacturer to produce a stuffed version of the spared cub, and by 1906–7, thousands of 'teddy' bears were being sold each week. *The 'Teddy' Bears* was advertised as 'a laughable satire on the popular craze.' Here is Musser's description of the film: 'It starts out as an adaptation of "Goldilocks and the Three Bears" and works within the framework of the fairy-tale film. For the first two-thirds of its running time, the life-sized teddy bears (actors in costume) are the subject of an endearing children's film. Suddenly the picture moves outside the confines of the studio, changing moods and referents. The bears chase Goldilocks across a snowy landscape until "Teddy" Roosevelt intervenes, kills the two full-grown pursuers, and captures the baby bear.'[44]

The film clearly operates in a complex satirical mode, imbricating the sentimentality of the teddy bear craze, the anthropomorphism of the fairy tale, and Porter's sardonic view of Roosevelt's hunting as a manly and heroic pursuit. While *The 'Teddy' Bears* does not use real animals (instead inserting a sequence of animation using stuffed bears), it comments on a cultural milieu that emphasized the benefits of closeness to nature and familiarity with wildlife, particularly because they reinforced 'family values.'

Gregg Mitman situates *Roosevelt in Africa* in this socio-political milieu as well. In the reformist era, educational and religious leaders regarded natural history films as an important vector in the moralization of movies. Films with animal subjects were part of this moralizing movement; they were 'entertaining in the best sense of the word and at the same time rich in educational value,' reinforcing social values in their devotion to offspring and home-building. They also connected to the anti-modernist back-to-nature movement of the first decade of the twentieth century, which saw 'the emergence of environmental preservation organizations such as the Audubon Society and the Sierra Club, the federal [American] government's preoccupation with conserving the nation's natural resources, the push for nature study in the public schools, and the growth of landscape architecture.'[45]

A commercial failure, *Roosevelt in Africa* generated responses that seemed to divide along class lines: in working-class districts the film was slammed. One exhibitor complained that 'anybody could take a .22 rifle and go out in the sagebrush in Idaho and get more excitement hunting jack rabbits.' A reviewer in *Motion Picture World*, on the other hand, noted that the film seemed to be appreciated by a 'more intelligent class of people,' such as that found at the Broadway houses that catered to the middle class rather than 'the shopgirl trade.'[46] It was becoming clear that anti-modernism and its concomitant values such as conservationism were class-based, with the urban middle-class intelligentsia more concerned about vanishing nature than were the poorer under-classes.

As Mitman remarks, however, the dismal box-office returns of the Roosevelt film made clear that audiences wanted drama even more than authenticity or education. Catering to this desire, the Selig Polyscope Company of Chicago restaged the African expedition using a vaudeville actor with a talent for Roosevelt impersonations. *Hunting Big Game in Africa* (1909) featured a melodramatic re-enactment of stalking a lion in the jungle and faked a scene of the lion being shot. The success of the film led Selig to establish a game farm in Chicago, where over the next five years he produced a series of immensely popular animal films, including *Alone in the Jungle, In Tune with the Wild,* and *The Leopard's Foundling.* These films were sensational 'blood curdling romance[s] of the dangerous animal infested jungleland of Africa.' The popularity of these productions, combined with Selig's sensationalistic appeal to 'base' emotions and the sacrifice of authenticity for melodrama, was worrisome to reformers who were concerned that wholesome, educational material would not be able to compete commercially. As Mitman remarks, the films also pointed out the difficulty of distinguishing between wholesome education and bawdy entertainment.[47]

Especially in non-narrative films, exotic wildlife from tropical jungles was the biggest draw. As Alexander Wilson notes, 'itinerant nature photographers and filmmakers ... abandoned North America for "undiscovered" lands that could still support narratives of exploration and domination. Africa – the continent, but also the film location that has conflated so many cultures and biographies – was an obvious destination, as were other amorphous and historical places, like the South Seas.'[48] Exotic wildlife films were also a source of controversy about authenticity: 'The boundaries between the real and the fake were not always easy to discern; the eye alone could not be trusted to distinguish the authentic from the artificial.'[49]

Integrity and trustworthiness soon came to be regarded as essential attributes of the cinematographer and producer. Mitman suggests that 'authenticity embodied more than just a faithful representation of wildlife, as if that itself was unproblematic. It also depended upon whether the photographer had experienced the thrill and danger of the hunt while capturing wildlife on film.'[50] Expressing his opinion of the hierarchy of bravery on the hunt, cinematographer Cherry Kearton wrote that 'It is much easier, much less dangerous, to shoot a lion, after your boys have led you up to him ... than it is to creep close to that lion and take a moving picture of him.'[51] Such spiritual participation of the hunter in the hunt (whether great white hunter or, in the twentieth century, cinematographer) has traditionally been an issue: the 'country gentlemen' – from the British aristocracy in earlier centuries and the wealthy industrialists of the twentieth century – who almost solely formed the hunting class sought to represent hunting as a sport that lent nobility to its participants ... It represented a kind of return to nature, was evidence of a vigorous relationship with the wilderness – much as Izaac Walton's *Compleat Angler* had argued for fishing in the [seventeenth] century. Hunting was an act of leisure which revealed the physical and spiritual health of the hunter, a man at the top of society who could yet easily descend to and return from an apparently primal activity.' As Oerlemans points out, and the films about Roosevelt so amply demonstrate, most of the people who argued in favour of 'humane treatment of animals did so with the explicit premise that humans are far superior to animals, and that cruelty to animals needs to be avoided primarily because it reflects poorly on our moral supremacy.'[52]

Strangely enough, this long-standing notion of the nobility of the hunt propelled the big-game-hunting film into a privileged scientific form. Despite their attention to 'the thrill of the action, the final triumph of the human actor' rather than to 'the peculiarities or the emotions of the beast protagonist,' Charles G.D. Roberts saw an interest in scientific inquiry as a reasonable outcome of such hunting stories: 'The inevitable tendency of these stories of adventure with beasts was to awaken interest in animals, and to excite a desire for exact knowledge of their traits and habits.' He sees this development in the animal story as 'altogether admirable and necessary' and – writing as he was at the turn of the century – values the camera for its assistance in revealing 'the truths of wild nature.'[53] Commenting on the predominance of the technologies of the visual in modernity as they shape our attitudes towards the human and non-human worlds, Alexander Wilson takes a rather different view:

> The metaphors we use to talk about the act of photography are strangely revealing: we take pictures, we capture or even shoot something on film. These are metaphors of the hunt, an activity that in modern urban culture retains few of the meanings it has in traditional societies ... Most popular representations of nature are organized around the eye, an organ that is itself surrounded by ideologies encouraging a separation of the human individual from the natural world ... The camera, with its insistence on perspective and the narrow field, exaggerates the eye's tendency to fragment, objectify, and estrange ... At the same time, the snapshot transforms the resistant aspect of nature into something familiar and intimate, something we can hold in our hands and memories. In this way, the camera allows us some control over the visual environments of our culture.[54]

Wilson's emphasis here is on fragmentation, objectification, estrangement, and control of nature as a result of photography. A sequel to *Roosevelt in Africa* brought these cultural vectors into sharp relief. The combination of North American cultural traditions, Western imperialism of nature and geography, control over otherness, and the eye of the camera are all imbricated in *Lassoing Wild Animals in Africa* (1911). The film featured Colonel Charles 'Buffalo' Jones and two Mexican cowpunchers who went to Africa to rope and capture wild animals. Kevin Brownlow reports that Roosevelt said 'They make my own efforts look like thirty cents.' The cowboys, wearing sola topis instead of Stetsons, charged after animals such as warthogs, roping them with expertise and dragging them before the camera and then releasing them after they were photographed. One of the most dramatic confrontations was with a lioness: after a long chase and dangerous struggle, the cowboys still could not manoeuvre their horses close enough to her to use their lassos, so they resorted to using a pole to slip a noose around her neck.[55]

Everyone knew the camera could lie, so the scrupulous integrity of the cinematographer had to be guaranteed. Roosevelt himself vouchsafed the authenticity of *Lassoing Wild Animals in Africa*, emphasizing the courage, prowess, and gallantry of the cinematographer, Cherry Kearton: 'In moving pictures of wild life, there is a great temptation to fake, and the sharpest discrimination must be employed in order to tell the genuine from the spurious. My attention was particularly directed toward Mr. Kearton's work because of its absolute honesty. If he takes a picture it may be guaranteed as straight.'[56]

By the 1920s, Hollywood had come to realize the commercial potential of wildlife films. Metro Pictures, which in 1924 merged with Goldwyn Pictures and Louis B. Mayer Productions, found in Martin and Osa Johnson a nature-photographer team who did not quibble about authenticity versus commercial success. Since 1910, the husband and wife team had had immense success on the Orpheum Vaudeville Circuit with travelogue lectures illustrated with slides and motion pictures. As Kevin Brownlow writes, 'They laced their sensational material – and much of it was sensational – with scenic and comedy material, but they had no scruples about authenticity.' Their first travelogue-adventure film, *Among the Cannibal Isles of the South Pacific* (1917), 'photographed at the risk of life,' was commercially successful, due primarily to the contrast between the photogenic, petite Osa and the cannibals and headhunters of Malekula, and to titles replete with racial slurs and gags. When the Johnsons took a projector and portable generator back to Malekula to show the film to its stars, they roared with laughter. Martin Johnson subsequently wrote to the president of the Pathescope Company, which manufactured the Peerless projector he had used: 'it would have done you good to see the Peerless and the generator going over mountains and into valleys, on the backs of savages, and at night to have seen hundreds of cannibals squatting around the devil-devil grounds, watching the wonderful things they never dreamed of before. Many a time the trees and houses would be full of human heads – dried – all about us.' Despite the Johnsons' delight in the film, a cable from Robertson-Cole, marketers of their films, changed everything: 'The public is tired of savages. Get some animal pictures.'[57] The Johnsons' response was a quick turn: they found their metier as wild-life filmmakers.[58]

Despite the Johnsons' flim-flam background and lack of experience in wildlife photography, by the time they hooked up with Hollywood they were being touted as conducting themselves 'according to the standards of this new world of science.' Their next film, *Jungle Adventures* (1919), was successfully marketed through tie-in advertisements for adventure clothing at New York department stores. Especially with such commercialization of the films, authenticity required testimonials. They got Carl Akeley, an authority on African wildlife, taxidermy, and museum display, and inventor of a lightweight movie camera fitted with a long-focus lens that revolutionized wildlife photography in the field, to sign a testimonial that their next film, *Trailing African Wild Animals* (Metro Pictures, 1923), was 'free from misleading titles, staging, misinterpretation, or any form of faking or sensationalism.'[59]

Trailing African Wild Animals combines naturalism with narrative, building around a story of the search for a lost lake teeming with wildlife. Not lost at all, the lake in fact was well enough known that an outpost of the Boma Trading Company had been established there since 1907. And, despite the testimonials, scenes of danger and suspense were staged, and animals were often provoked into action. 'In a carefully crafted climactic scene, the heroine, Osa, drops the camera for her Winchester rifle and rescues Martin from the charge of an elephant without a moment to spare.' Mitman relates Osa's escapades to the earlier staged Selig wildlife films with 'beauty and the beast' themes, indicating that Hollywood cinematic conventions were well in place.[60]

In their next film, *Simba* (1928), the Johnsons incorporated conventions from Jack London's realistic animal stories, relying upon the inscription of distinct personality traits to highlight individual animals. In addition to the eponymous lion, other wildlife characters were given names, a practice that Mitman notes as helping audiences to identify with the animals, creating associations between wildlife and domestic pets within American culture, and adding a familial and intimate sense of life on the veldt.[61] Species typecasting added comedy and drama, pitting, for example, the 'timid' giraffe against the 'cruel, sneaking' hyena. This sort of stereotyping of animals, according to Charles G.D. Roberts, is another stage of development of the animal story: 'and so, as advancing civilisation drew an ever widening line between man and the animals, and men became more and more engrossed in the interests of their own kind, the personalities of the wild creatures which they had once known so well became obscured to them, and the creatures themselves came to be regarded, for the purposes of literature, as types or symbols merely.'[62]

It is almost needless to add that human and racial stereotypes are rampant as well, with native Africans portrayed as 'half-savage.' Mitman points out that until well into the 1950s, natural history films of Africa often portrayed the continent's indigenous people with less dignity and integrity that that of the majestic species of African wildlife. Racial sight gags and gender stereotypes are also in full play, not only with the shots of bare-breasted young African women but with the white heroine as well. Take the final climactic sequence of *Simba*, for example: after bringing down a lion, Osa prepares an apple pie for dinner in the camp! Mitman's assessment of this concluding sequence concurs with many critics who argue that Hollywood depictions of the emancipated American woman, replete with courage and self-reliance and often facing danger, frequently demonstrated that the heroine's newly realized freedom actually revitalized life within the domestic sphere.[63]

In addition to the obviation of animal alterity through stereotyping and imperialistic domination of the foreign by Western culture, such nature films are frequently critiqued for their commodification of nature as an object for consumption. From the time that the Johnsons made their films, nature films have been large-budget productions using large crews, camera blinds, sets, the latest in cinematographic technology, and, in the later period, helicopters and remote sound. The effects of this technological overload, as Wilson suggests, can tend to promote an illusion of mastery or detachment: 'In films nature is easily constructed as a resource or commodity to be consumed as scenery ... Usually in these movies we're supposed to be able to sit back and "view" nature without becoming involved in it ... In other words, nature films traffic in images that are ordinarily invisible. Our ability to produce these films of "life in the wild" is an index not only of our power over nature but also of our distance from it.'[64]

The success of *Simba* induced the Fox Film Corporation to finance the Johnsons' subsequent feature, *Congorilla*, and the Johnsons to give up any pretensions to science. They had 'found in nature a commercial commodity that capitalized on the entertainment industry and enabled them to participate in the fame, luxury and leisure of Hollywood society.'[65] Between 1917 and 1937 the Johnsons made nearly thirty immensely popular adventure movies, shot mostly in Kenya or New Guinea.[66] 'The influence of the Martin Johnson pictures was considerable. Their wide acceptance by a public normally averse to educational films led to Hollywood incorporating more and more documentary backgrounds.'[67]

The combination of sensational drama, travel, and adventure in the Johnson films opened the floodgates for a Hollywood industrial model of wildlife films. Other films in the twenties combined drama with wildlife, sometimes including claims to 'authenticity' and sometimes not. Ernest Schoedsack (later to produce and direct *King Kong*, 1933) and Merian Cooper produced *Grass* (a Paramount release, 1925), which depicted the gruelling confrontation with nature of the Bakhtiari people as they shepherded – barefoot – their enormous herds from the plains near the Persian Gulf, across the Karun River and the Zardeh Kuh mountains to their summer pasturelands in central Persia. Brownlow reports that one of the few English phrases the Bakhtiari were taught was '"Don't look at the camera." No one understood the word for camera, so the phrase became "Don't look at me."'[68] Spectacular wilderness cinematography and a romantic vision of a primitive relationship to nature were not enough, however: the film's 'lack of individual characters and limited use of comedy failed to captivate the interest of the moviegoing public. Voted the worst picture of the year by Princeton students, *Grass* ... earned ... a modest return on their initial $10,000 investment.'[69]

Chang: A Drama of the Wilderness (d. Cooper and Schoedsack, Paramount, 1927) was much more successful. This time out the team combined the romantic theme of the struggle against nature with the life of an individual Lao family, including husband, wife, and two kids. The 'natural drama' includes predatory beasts that kill the family's domestic animals and threaten the life of the protagonist. The climax brought breathtaking footage of a stampeding elephant herd shot from a pit covered with logs at ground level, intercut with aerial footage.

Like the Johnsons, in *Chang* Cooper and Schoedsack personalized individual animals for emotional identification and dramatic character development as well as comedy. Mitman cites 'the mischievous antics of the family pet, a white gibbon named Bimbo, cute scenes of an adorable mother honey bear and her cub, and an obstinate baby elephant.'[70] The Lao family was of course contrived, cast from local actors, and the preparation of the log-covered pit for the elephants' destruction of the village indicates that the animal scenes were staged. Brownlow's assessment of the film is superlative: '*Chang* is the audience picture supreme. Its slow start lulls them into condescension; its savagery takes them unawares. The rhythm builds, with sights unfamiliar despite the hundreds of wildlife pictures since, to a climax that belittles such publicity terms as "stupendous." As a piece of film craft, it is masterly and stands far beyond the other documents in that regard.'[71] The film was nominated for an Academy Award and returned enormous revenues in urban centres, 'where the back-to-nature movement flourished ... among city dwellers in search of arcadia.'[72]

Persuaded by the success of *Chang* that the combination of entertainment and education was viable, William Douglas Burden cast Ojibwa actors in *The Silent Enemy* (d. H.P. Carver, Paramount, 1928). The fully scripted drama, set in the 'primeval forests' of northern Ontario and Quebec, pits the Ojibwa nation in a 'race against time, starvation and the harsh Arctic winter,' as they attempt to intersect with the great caribou migration across the Canadian barren lands. Many of the props had to be made, including wigwams, canoes, fur clothing, and sleds. A young man training to rival the tribe's great hunter, a wise chief who dies, the chief's tender-hearted daughter, and an evil medicine man who uses false magic are the dramatis personae.

Animal scenes included intimate footage of a wolverine, a fight between a mountain lion and a bear, and timber wolves attacking a moose, with the great caribou migration as the climax. Unfortunately for claims to authenticity, the caribou migration was staged with a herd of reindeer, the smaller and semi-domesticated Eurasian relative of the caribou. Unfortunately also, a few of the actors turned out to be problems.

Molly Spotted Elk, who played tender-hearted Neewa, was well known to New York socialites who frequented the speakeasy clubs she danced in, and Chief Buffalo Child Long Lance, who cut a striking figure as the loin-cloth-costumed hunter, was already the toast of New York society as the author of a best-selling autobiography, *Long Lance* (1928). It turned out that the autobiography was largely fiction; Long Lance himself was of mixed African-American, Catawba Indian, and white parentage and had assumed the identity of a Blackfoot member of the Plains Indians of Montana.[73] Paramount considered *The Silent Enemy* to be a problem picture – educational but not entertaining enough – and dumped it on the small-town third-run circuit with disastrous box-office results.

The primary locale for the circulation and reception of nature movies, steeped in anti-modernist sentiment, frontier and wilderness mythology, and fears for 'the end of nature,' was the industrial metropolitan centre that was so quickly developing in the first three decades of the century. As Wilson writes, 'Wildlife movies are documents of a culture trying to come to terms with what Bill McKibben calls "the end of nature." Their short history is one of intricately overlain traditions: animal fables, technological fetishism, dissident science, sea and adventure stories, and conservationism. Nature is alternately (and sometimes simultaneously) understood as refuge, community, and commodity.'[74]

Of the industrial formula of wildlife films developed in the silent period after the Johnsons, Alexander Wilson comments that 'Today [these] movies seem an embarrassing amalgam of bad anthropology, natural history and adventure – a formula that has meant "box office" right up to *Raiders of the Lost Ark*.'[75]

Anthropomorphism

In her memoir Shipman remarked, addressing the reader, 'I beg your belief and I repeat: animals have a keen sense of humor and *they can think* [her emphasis].'[76]

Debates about anthropomorphism (often linked with sentimentalism) have been common to discussions of representations of animals in virtually every medium and throughout history. Anthropomorphism, a concept extensively dealt with in theological literature regarding the philosophical difficulties of 'humanizing' the supreme deity, extends to animals in the sense that we commonly ascribe human characteristics of emotion or thought to animal appearance, behaviour, and consciousness. This has been a ubiquitous motif of animal and wildlife films throughout the twentieth century, although tastes and tolerances have oscillated through different periods.

As noted earlier regarding animals in silent films, the authentic representation of nature was already an issue of debate in the early part of the twentieth century. Naturalist literature such as Ernest Thompson Seton's *Wild Animals I Have Known* (1901), which went through sixteen printings in four years, was criticized for sentimentalism and anthropomorphism. The boundaries between fact and fiction, science and drama were at issue. Animals of all kinds were endowed with human values, and sentimentality was rife. American President Theodore Roosevelt took it upon himself to criticize the representation of animals in stories by Jack London and W.J. Long, calling them mystifying '"nature-fakers." If London and these others really understood nature, Roosevelt charged, they wouldn't go about humanizing animals in such preposterous and unbelievable ways.'[77] London returned the volley, challenging Roosevelt as 'homocentric' and a '"rank amateur" unschooled in the principles of evolution that insist on an intimate "kinship" or strict unbroken continuity between animals and humans.'[78]

Oerlemans tempers the argument this way:

Anthropomorphism at its most obvious, as in much children's literature, strikes us as naive or quaint, a sign of a charming delusion, perhaps. Yet it is difficult to imagine a perfectly neutral representation, one which prohibits or forestalls this kind of imagining; perhaps only the most grotesquely neutral of representations, say a map of a specific animal's anatomy, succeeds, but only by literally exploding the object. Abstractly considered, the problem of how we are to view animals neutrally, to see them as they are and not as they are like us, probably has no solution. We cannot, finally, distinguish those features of their being (emotions, desires, etc.) which are truly theirs from those with which we are familiar because we experience them ourselves.[79]

Alexander Wilson suggests that wildlife films 'did something far more than reveal "nature's mysteries": they spoke to us of a living and intelligible world beyond the fence of civilization, a world we could enter at will and experience in something like human time. The stories and memories of the non-human world were meant to stand in for the stories and memories of our human world, and vice versa.'[80] Oerlemans concurs: 'Recognizing animals as a part of the landscape can distance humanity from nature in allowing us to regard the "bestial" and instinctive as being other than culture; or it can bring us closer to nature, since countless similarities between animals and humans have been recognized, even above the protestations of religious thinkers like Descartes (who argued that animals were equivalent to machines).'[81] Mitman adds that the fascination with nature in the early part of the century was not based on the contact with nature enjoyed by the farmer whose livelihood depended on the land; 'instead, nature offered a place of regeneration and renewal for a growing, managerial middle class with increased leisure and money to pursue the luxuries of country life previously confined to the rich.'[82] Wilson goes on: 'Sure, the wildlife movies were the fantasy preserves of an older order, tales of hidden places supposedly untouched by the dislocations of modern society. But they also functioned as lived myths of freedom and space, helping to give shape to the cultural and environmental politics of the coming decades. As such they were part of a long and distinguished tradition of North American nature stories.'[83]

Oerlemans argues that the attempt to render animals as genuinely other – as having an energy and presence not possessed or even understood by the humans around them – may be figured as giving the animals expression, 'by [representing] them as possessing and communicating emotion, which we might recognize as a form of anthropomorphizing.' Rather paradoxically, he argues that to allow animals expression in this way, even to raise the issue of anthropomorphizing, is also to begin to entertain the possibility that animals can be considered to exist as individuals, to possess some kind of consciousness and self-consciousness, or, more simply, to be subjects.[84]

Charles G.D. Roberts's views may have been the greatest influence on Shipman's approach to animal subjectivity, as his work was hugely popular in Shipman's day. He wrote over twenty books, all of them enjoying multiple printings and publishers. *Kindred of the Wild*, for just one example, went through twenty-two printings in just under thirty years, and copyrights were held by seven publishers. In a treatise on the animal story that prefaces *Kindred of the Wild*, Roberts traces the developments in the genre from its earliest days, using as the basis for his argument theories that were developing at the time in the sciences of psychology, biology, and sociology. He specifically repudiates earlier theories based on notions of 'instinct' and 'coincidence' that had been used to account for the appearance of rationality in the non-human world. The combination of the new technologies of observation, the science of biology, and psychological studies of 'mental intelligence,' he argues, had 'forced [men] at last to accept the proposition that, within their varying limitations, animals can and do reason.' Invoking the new literature of personality, he writes: 'We have suddenly attained a new and clearer vision. We have come face to face with personality, where we were blindly wont to predicate mere instinct and automatism.' For Roberts, the authors of contemporary animal stories 'may be regarded as explorers of this unknown world, absorbed in charting its topography. They work, indeed, upon a substantial foundation of known facts. They are minutely scrupulous as to their natural history, and assiduous contributors to that science.' Rather than challenging in any formal textual or diegetical sense the issue of anthropomorphism, Shipman's blithe representation of the consciousness of animals may be read as participating in what Roberts defines as 'a psychological romance constructed on a framework of natural science.'[85]

As Oerlemans writes, perhaps it is the concept of anthropomorphism itself that is at fault: 'In seeing signs of subjectivity in animals, we are not necessarily projecting human qualities onto them, but recognizing in them natural attributes which we share with them. Writing this sympathy off as merely the projection of human characteristics – which the very introduction of the concept of anthropomorphism has the effect of doing – errs not only in its underestimation of animal being, but in its extraordinary exaggeration and deification of human being. One of the effects of this anthropocentrism is to cut us off from the animal, and perhaps the entire natural, world, to turn it into a purely material and phenomenal realm, set in contrast to the spiritual one of human being.'[86]

In contrast to Alexander Wilson, who argues that 'nature is in part a human construction after all,'[87] Oerlemans rather more elegantly suggests that anthropomorphist tendencies in the representation of nature undermine easy distinctions 'between nature and culture, being and non-being.' Wilson concurs that 'at the very least ... anthropomorphism allows animals to be addressed as *social* beings, and nature as a *social* realm ... Anthropomorphism is thus not a program, but an historical and strategic intervention, a step on the way to understanding that the wall between humans and the natural world is not an absolute. It is permeable, movable, shifting, able occasionally to be leaped over.'[88] Oerlemans concludes that 'it is not so much the cultural construction of nature but rather the construction of a concept of culture that has reified human being to the exclusion of all other life in nature.'[89]

Adamant about the necessity to explore 'the real psychology of animals,' which he sees as the final stage of development of the animal story, Roberts criticizes popular authors for their tendency to impute a specifically human psychology to animals. He castigates Kipling, for example, for humanizing animals: 'their individualisation is distinctly human, as are also their mental and emotional processes, and their highly elaborate powers of expression.'[90] In this regard, Shipman's representation of animal psychology can be differentiated according to the medium in which she is working. In her writing, she is as guilty as Kipling or Marshall Saunders (author of the best-seller *Beautiful Joe: An Autobiography* [1894]) of imputing highly complex thoughts to animals, as can be seen in the passage about the dogs' thoughts of the afterlife quoted near the beginning of this chapter. As Roberts puts it, 'depiction of animals' 'reasoning powers and their constructive imagination are far beyond anything which present knowledge justifies us in ascribing to the inarticulate kindreds.'[91]

In Shipman's films, on the other hand, despite the inscription of animal 'voices' in the intertitles, the representation of animal behaviour indicates something akin to what is now referred to as biocentric vision, which attempts to collapse the 'cardinal distinctions between animal and human ... [and] aims not simply to justify feeling for animals, but to open up the potential for feeling like animals. Animal life is seen as possessing a purity of desire, a fullness and self-sufficiency, that humans lack.' Roberts expresses it this way: 'the motives of real animals, so far as we have hitherto been able to judge them, seem to be essentially simple, in the sense that the motive dominant at a given moment quite obliterates, for the time, all secondary motives.'[92] In Shipman's films, the alterity of the animal world resides in its direct relationship to a spontaneous and unmediated relation to desire and experience.[93]

The Light on Lookout

In *The Light on Lookout* (1923), the animals are deployed in ways that intersect with such issues of anthropomorphism, human culture, and animal 'psychology' and alterity. Another short subject (approximately eighteen minutes), *The Light on Lookout* is prefaced by a title that attests to the film's location in the 'wilderness of Upper Priest Lake, Idaho.' It was shot by Bobby Newhardt, and stars Shipman, Dorothy Winslow, Ralph Cochner, and Brownie the bear. With a conservationist subplot involving an old-growth forest and timber thieves who capture the honest lone woodsman, the main trajectory of the narrative involves a romance in which a wolf is instrumental and, at the climax, the intervention of Brownie the bear.

In this film, animals are found in their natural woodland habitat, and are treated as others. No animals speak in the film (via intertitles, as in *A Bear, a Boy, and a Dog* or *Trail of the North Wind*), nor are they invested with 'character,' independent cognition, hermeneutic strategy, or abstract reason. The film thus challenges the modes of animal representation found in earlier Shipman films and in her novels.

The film begins with Shipman's customary authorial trope: a woman alone in the wilderness. The character, Dreena, walks through the woods, nuzzles a bear, spots a marmot or some mink-like creature in its nest in a hollow tree, and proceeds through various idyllic vistas until a large evergreen tree comes crashing down through the forest. Eventually she comes to an enormous old tree – which she hugs! Close-up of Shipman, her cheek pressed to the deeply crevassed bark of the tree. At this point the handsome woodsman, Jim, approaches with his long two-handled saw, and a little 'seed' of romance (intertitle) is sown. Before romance can germinate, Lila, Dreena's friend from the city, comes to visit. Dreena sees the spark between Lila and Jim, and, after a little disappointed sigh, she carries on.

At this point the plot develops rapidly. Dreena 'bribes' a wolf (intertitle) to help her further the romance between Lila and Jim by first giving the wolf a treat and then placing another on a tree stump overlooking the place to which she leads Lila. She has strategically placed Jim nearby, and tells him repeatedly to stay there. When Lila sits down to rest, the wolf approaches to retrieve the food. Lila is terrified, and Jim jumps out of his hiding place to rescue her.

This is the first nodal point of a relation to animals that has not been apparent in the other films dealt with in this chapter. Although the wolf is a real wolf, rather than a dog in disguise (as was the practice in many other films, with dogs standing in for wolves – with their ears tied back or their fluffy tails oiled down), the animal is clearly somewhat tame. Yet Shipman by no means treats the animal like a pet, nor is it represented as having anything approaching the subjectivity of the dogs in *A Bear, a Boy, and a Dog* or *Trail of the North Wind*. The wolf simply responds to a morsel of food. It 'acts' from its own autotelic nature, rather than performing for the camera, as Shipman insisted the collie Laddie and even Brownie the bear were accustomed to doing.

Significantly, it is the human's response to the presence of the animal, rather than any unusual or 'human' behaviour on the animal's part, that creates the drama. The anthropomorphist tendencies of the earlier films are not in evidence here. Rather, it is precisely the alterity of the animal as an animal that functions in the drama. Although the wolf functions causally in the progression of the tale, the animal is not represented as having any agency or as belonging to any socially instrumental or cognitively informed category. Neither is there any suggestion of the sort of interspecies extrasensory communication that informed the relationship between the woman and the dog in *Back to God's Country* or in *Trail of the North Wind*: in both films the dog sensed the heroine's plight and, of its own volition, broke free of its chains to charge to her rescue.

In *The Light on Lookout*, Shipman seems to ascribe to the notions of species hierarchy that have been assumed in Western culture since Aristotle, a spectrum of development that puts some animals closer to humans and some at the other end, closer to the primitive.[94] Although related in species, the dog and the wolf have traditionally been seen as antinomies on the savagery, loyalty, altruism, and intelligence scales. However, it is worth pointing out that the wolf is depicted in Shipman's film in a very different way from the more usual representations of the beast as a vicious predator. As Wilson notes, the wolf has become synonymous with the archaic: 'As a figure of the primitive, the wolf has been invested with the most savage and barbarian characteristics. It stands in opposition to everything that is meant by civilization.'[95] Again, Theodore Roosevelt figures in the characterization of the animal, for he had sent cinematographer J.B. Kent to Wichita National Preserve to document a man capturing a wolf with his bare hands. *Wolf Hunt* (Oklahoma Natural Mutoscope Company, 1908) pits John Abernathy against the wolf, struggling to the (wolf's) death, the man's hands around its throat.[96] As Rod Preece puts it, 'the much maligned wolf received almost universal bad press.'[97] Plato expressed the view that those humans who have chosen to live in 'injustice and tyranny' would be reincarnated as wolves.[98] We need only think of well-loved children's stories like 'Little Red Riding Hood,' 'The Three Little Pigs,' or 'Peter and the Wolf' to find the cultural heritage of *canis lupus*.

Barry Holstun Lopez writes that 'we create wolves ... In the wolf we have not so much an animal that we have always known as one that we have consistently *imagined*.'[99] Lopez's *Of Wolves and Men* is a fascinating book that charts the place of the wolf in the imaginary, always emphasizing the contradictory twin images of the wolf as ravening killer and nurturing mother (as in the legend of Romulus and Remus). Still the principal beat is the wolf as a figure of greed, lust, and deception. The ancient Greek legend of Lycaon, who was changed into a wolf by Zeus, persists to this day in the scientific name for the eastern timber wolf, *Canis lupus lycaon*, and in the psychoanalytic term lycanthropy, the name for a kind of melancholic delusion. 'The wild man and the werewolf alike were metamorphosed from formidable forces in the pagan imagination, through the grotesque, almost psychopathic imagery of the Middle Ages, to become the derivative, often impotent and pathetic caricatures we find in movies and pulp literature today.'[100]

Notwithstanding the popular epithet of the 'lone wolf,' this animal is often seen in various forms of representation – whether folkloric, literary, or cinematic – in marauding packs, attacking deer, moose, or caribou; the snarling, slavering, gaunt predators are the apogee of the viciousness of the wilderness. Their gloomy, haunting howls at night strike fear into the hearts not only of conventional human protagonists, as in the 1953 remake of *Back to God's Country*, but also of other animals in the forest. Pointing out that the wolf, as a half-light hunter seen at dawn and dusk, has for centuries stood for things in transit, Lopez emphasizes two apparently contradictory aspects to this notion: 'The first is the wolf as a creature of dawn, representing an emergence from darkness into enlightenment, intelligence, civilization. The second is a creature of dusk, representing a return to ignorance and bestiality, a passage back into the world of dark forces ... His howl in the morning elevated the spirit ... His howl at night terrified the soul.'[101]

Hated and feared, the wolf has been shunted to the margins, both physically and culturally. Erwin A. Bauer writes that, two hundred years ago, the wolf was the most widely distributed mammal on earth: 'Absent only from deserts, rain forests, and the highest alpine reaches, wolves roamed everywhere across North America, Europe, and northern Asia.' Today in North America wolves have been completely eradicated from the entire United States, except for Alaska and small populations in a few other states, although there are significant populations in northern Canada from Labrador to the Yukon.[102] Wolves have also been hounded to extinction throughout most of Europe – none are left in Great Britain – and their populations have been substantially reduced in India as well as in the Near and Middle East.[103] Alexander Wilson reminds us that for decades into the late 1980s, many Canadian provinces and American states had official wolf eradication programs. These programs were carried out on a bounty system, with aerial gunning safaris and bait laced with strychnine, cyanide, and a nerve toxin (sodium monofluoro-acetate).[104] Lopez notes the 'prejudice against wolves' that from the Middle Ages on was fixed 'in the human imagination so solidly that it was not until the twentieth century that the human imagination could produce a new wolf.'[105]

It was not until Canadian naturalist Farley Mowat wrote *Never Cry Wolf* (1963),[106] later produced as a fairly traditional wildlife movie (*Never Cry Wolf*, 1983, a Disney co-production), that such representations of the wolf were challenged widely. Mowat wrote sympathetically about wolves' social organization, mating, and nurturing behaviour. Although now considered dated and romanticized, Mowat's work was an early entry into the contemporary wolf literature that is now a significant industry.[107]

Shipman's deployment of the wolf in *The Light on Lookout* is conceivably a direct retort to Jack London's popular literature, which obsessively revolved around the wolf. Though the idea of the beast was cast as admirable in London's fiction, nevertheless the wolf consistently figured as 'brute nature' – wild, fighting, uncivilized machismo. Shipman plays on a reversal of representational conventions regarding the wolf's predatory and savage nature. Alone, rather than in a marauding pack, and looking quite well fed and well kempt, with fluffy clean fur and a sweet little face, the animal simply steps into Lila's vicinity and eats the bit of food placed strategically beside her. Lila's reaction to the wolf's presence is the traditional cultural response: extreme fear. The wolf does nothing to provoke her or to suggest that she is to be ravaged limb from limb. Her response to the wolf, although immediate and apparently spontaneous, has been honed through cultural representations of the animal. Moreover, Jim's heroism in the moment is brief and extremely easy to come by. There is no heroic struggle: he simply shoos the animal away, and the wolf exits without a sign of a snarl or even a backward glance.

Paradoxically, Shipman's depiction of the wolf, its nature and its effect on the 'stranger from the city,' redounds once again to the heroism of Shipman as protagonist and enunciator. As trainer of the animal and enunciator of the tale, Shipman has inscribed herself in the key role of the person who not only shows no fear, but also knows that fear is unnecessary. As protagonist, she can coerce the animal into doing her bidding, not through 'mastering' nature, but through a biocentric understanding of the animal's autotelic nature, its spontaneous and unmediated relation to desire. Show the animal where food is to be found, and expect it to return to that spot: that is all there is to it.

The episode involving the bear is somewhat different. We know the bear is tame: we have seen Dreena with Brownie in an earlier scene, as she strolls through the woods, lolls about, and affectionately plays with the bear. As a species, the bear is an apparently tamable creature, capable of complex forms of relationships with humans, as countless representations have demonstrated, from the trained bears of the Russian circus to those featured in the early Edison films. There is no more sophisticated example of this relation in literature than Canadian novelist Marian Engel's *Bear* (1976),[108] in which a woman living in the woods has a loving and sexual relationship with a bear. In this tour de force of gradually accrued biocentric sympathy, the female protagonist must learn to understand the bear's nature, including the possibility of its absolute alterity. At first she anthropomorphizes the bear, wilfully indulging herself in romanticizing nature in all its aspects. But when the bear is aroused and rakes her back with its claws, she finally has to come to terms with the 'bearness' of the bear, and to learn not to expect the bear to have human qualities or to serve as a symbol for her – even of the unknown.[109] The novel inspired Canadian multimedia artist Joyce Wieland to make a small bronze sculpture of a woman and a bear in a passionate embrace.

Shipman's relationship with Brownie bears no resemblance to the intricacies of interspecies passion that Engel depicted, for the displays of affection in the Shipman films go no further than a slurping animal tongue on a human cheek or the playful nibbling of a furry ear. Even these less graphic representations of interspecies desire, however, suggest a degree of communication with the animal that had never – to my knowledge – been expressed in cinema until Shipman's work.

In *The Light on Lookout*, Shipman treats the bear as her pet, and it does her bidding. No bait is involved in the relationship between the woman and the bear; this is a privileged relationship, involving Shipman's particular and spectacular skills with wild animals. Because the lone woodsman has been captured by timber thieves, the eponymous light on lookout, which Jim promised to send out every night to his sweetheart, has been dark. Shipman climbs the mountain for the rescue. After investigating the situation, she hides and sends the bear into the tent to effect Jim's release. The bear ambles into the tent at her command and the predictable outcome is hilarious: the creature scares the daylights out of the bad guys. A comic scene in long-shot has the tent rocking and shaking as the thieves tussle with the bear while Dreena releases Jim from his bonds.

The Light on Lookout was part of the series called *Little Dramas of the Big Places*, the second extant film of the series. Among the last films that Shipman was able to complete as an independent producer, it repeats the formula of shoestring independent production, heroic femininity, wilderness setting, and generic deployment of wild animals. It is useful also as a touchstone for understanding an aesthetic sensibility in which the enunciation of authorial identity explicitly connects nature and the animal world with feminine heroism.

Women and Animals

Since the mid-1980s, with the rise of eco-feminism, a flood of feminist literature has dealt with animal rights, the relation between women, animals and nature, and the development of appropriate theoretical rubrics to assess this traditional relation. Scholars have examined the treatment of animals in literature; the Western cultural alignment of women with nature, and the concomitant 'othering' of both; somato-phobia (fear of the body and its processes); feminist vegetarianism; and connections between speciesism and sexism, vivisection and pornography, and biocentrism and feminism. Although much of this writing has been published in ephemeral literature, such as the *Feminists for Animal Rights Newsletter*, academic journals and publications have also taken up the issue. *Signs* devoted two issues to a debate on feminism and animal rights,[110] and a number of prominent scholarly books have emerged in the nineties, ranging across disciplines such as philosophy, science, literature, and feminist theory.

Josephine Donovan outlines the historical context of feminist theorizing about animals. From Aristotle on, the ideological justification for discrimination against women has been premised on women's relation to animals and nature. Women's bodies have been seen to intrude upon their rationality, which has been, for much of Western philosophy, the defining requirement for membership in the moral community. Women, along with animals and non-white men, have been excluded from the rights of public citizenship until the twentieth century.

Feminist responses to this historical alignment of women with animality have varied. The first approach, as Donovan outlines it, rejects the equation of women and animals, arguing that women are distinctly human. Mary Wollstonecraft stressed that women, like men and unlike animals, have intellects and rational minds. Likewise arguing, in *The Second Sex*, that women must transcend the physical, material level of existence, Simone de Beauvoir inspired several generations of modern feminists to affirm women's rationality over biology.

Some other feminist theorists have argued against rejecting the woman-nature connection, citing the Western philosophical tradition of transcendent dualism as the root of an ideology that emphasizes the connections between the human and the divine and thus justifies domination of nature and the despised body.[111] Recently, this approach has spiralled into a theory of feminism as a transformative philosophy that embraces the amelioration of life on earth for all natural entities.[112] As such, contemporary feminism carries on the history of animal rights activism from the eighteenth century, which moved from legislation against cruelty to animals and on to protectionist laws for children and women in the workplace and against abuse of children in the private sphere. In such a history, the movements that concentrated on antivivisectionism, animal rights, protection of children, temperance, women's property rights, and suffrage may be seen to culminate in the eco-feminism of the late twentieth century.[113]

Women have been prominent in movements against cruelty to animals even before the founding of the VSS (Victoria Street Society for the Protection of Animals Liable to Vivisection) in Britain in 1875. Over the past century, antivivisection and other animal rights movements have been dismissed as the sentimentality of old women or, alternatively, celebrated as a women's movement. The much older SPCA (Society for the Prevention of Cruelty to Animals) also had a majority of women members, as indeed did most of the major philanthropic movements of the nineteenth century. Queen Victoria was a prominent supporter. Women's participation in these movements was typically attributed to their greater sentimentality, a notion rooted in the traditional association of women with emotion rather than reason, and with nature rather than culture. However, women were seen to play an important role in the moral reform that came to be necessary in the aftermath of the Industrial Revolution and, even more crucially, with the advent of modernity. 'Animal welfare was, for some, part of this civilizing role.' Philanthropy also provided a useful entry for women into the public sphere, as the feminists of the late nineteenth and early twentieth century clearly saw; moral reform, it was hoped, would mean the abolition of double standards of morality for men and women.[114]

The strands linking first-wave feminism with animal welfare, sexual purity movements, and campaigns against compulsory vaccination, ovariotomy (sometimes referred to as 'spaying' of women), and the Contagious Diseases Act in Britain are tangled in complexity. Many of these concerns were echoed in contemporary fiction, especially in the 'New Woman' novels of the 1880s and 1890s. In fact, the term 'New Woman' is attributed to Madame Sarah Grand, didactic novelist, sexual purity campaigner, and antivivisectionist.[115]

The campaign for animal welfare was jolted into a new social force in 1903 with the 'brown dog' episode. Two women medical students attending their first lecture reported that they had seen an unanaesthetised '"brown dog of the terrier type" struggling in agony' in a cutting operation. A sensational trial ensued, and a statue commemorating the brown dog was erected in Battersea, coinciding with the establishment of the Second Royal Commission on Vivisection in 1906. The statue was destroyed in the Brown Dog Riots of 1910, but the controversy was so well known and so well remembered that a new statue was erected in 1985.[116]

Although public sentiment against cruelty to animals was also strong in the United States early in the nineteenth century, the founding of institutions and passing of legislation came later than in Britain. The ASPCA (American Society for the Prevention of Cruelty to Animals) was founded in 1866 and rapidly gained widespread support. The American Humane Society, a national organization, was founded in 1877. By 1907 every state had an anti-cruelty statute on the books, and by 1923 the laws were expanded to include a wide gamut of issues, including cruelty in filmmaking.[117]

Links between the women's movement and animal welfare activism continued through the struggle for suffrage and well into the twenties. In 1920, Virginia Woolf took up animal welfare and aligned the issue specifically with women. Edwardian fashion for women had featured large hats that were resplendent with exotic plumage. The Plumage Bill (Britain), designed to halt the traffic in exotic feathers and the resultant environmental and wildlife desecration, was defeated in parliament. Woolf lashed out at the newspaper columnist who had blamed women's desire for adornment for the failure of the bill; she ascribed its failure rather to the fact that there was only one woman member out of sixty-seven in Parliament. She also explicitly tied the plumage trade to male hunters, who 'are the very scum of mankind.' She painted a vivid picture of the cruelty of the hunt, with its decoys tied to stakes and many more birds wounded than captured. Because the plumage is at its most colourful in the mating season, she writes, 'we must imagine innumerable mouths opening and shutting, opening and shutting, until – as no parent bird comes to feed them – the young birds rot where they sit.' And a final almost unimaginable cruelty: 'But perhaps the most unpleasant sight that we must make ourselves imagine is the sight of the bird tightly held in one hand while another hand pierces the eyeballs with a feather.' Woolf's language is polemic, and she admits that it is 'embittered by sex antagonism.' A short and powerful piece, it is now seen as a forerunner to her feminist classics *A Room of One's Own* (1929) and *Three Guineas* (1938).[118]

Shipman undoubtedly was aware of these movements and these events. Sent out to Canada by his family as a remittance man before Shipman was born, her British father had grown up in this milieu, and Shipman herself was an avid newspaper reader, as her letters repeatedly demonstrate by commenting on contemporary news events and headlines. She knew well that the success of her films was generically founded on the wild animals. In Britain especially, writes Tom Trusky, Shipman's reverence for nature and her kindness to animals lit an affectionate spark in a period that was rife with outrage about the mistreatment of animals in many American silent films.[119] Her own view of an essential connection between femininity and nature is evident everywhere in the films and profoundly informs the representation of domestic and wild animals.

From a present-day standpoint, such an essentialist construction of femininity, bound by and to nature, must be critiqued, of course, especially as it ties in to 'some grand crosscultural narrative of women's identity with nature.'[120] The limits of a discursive creation that reifies the identity 'women' in relation to an equally static 'nature' need articulation in respect to their theoretical implications, particularly the binding of women to their roles as caretakers, to their own bodies as their principal source of identity, and to the unproblematized concept of identity itself as a theoretical stake. For eco-feminists, the political ramifications of privatizing environmental consciousness must also be a concern.[121] However, although Shipman in many ways evinced the ricocheting discursive vectors of progressive modernity, she was neither a postmodern theorist nor a political activist; her works popularize and disseminate the diverse constellation of ideas that were current in her time. Equally proud of herself as a woman and as a lover of animals and nature, she represented her convictions with tenacity, conviction, and creativity.

Little Dramas of the Big Places

In addition to *Trail of the North Wind* and *The Light on Lookout*, Shipman seems to have finished at least two more of the *Little Dramas*. *White Water* (1924) revolves around a wilderness writer who comes to a lumberjack town and finds two hungry orphan boys, whom she takes in as her own. In her memoir, Shipman mentions another (untitled) film, shot at the Lone Star Ranch, eleven miles away. It hinged around a sick neighbour for whom a doctor had to be fetched. Shipman comments on the dramas: 'The slender plots were woven around such incidents, how we overcame obstacles aided by the animals and friendly humans. I thought the things had simplicity and charm, a sense of movement, of getting there in time. As a writer friend put it, "Get 'em in a tree, throw rocks at 'em, get 'em out of the tree."'[121]

Wilderness production conditions were austere in the extreme. For *The Light on Lookout*, for example, the high, snowbound Lookout Mountain had to be climbed, shooting on the way up and at the peak. According to her memoir, on the journey Shipman is more concerned for her partner, Van Tuyle, than for herself. Although she is 'cheerful' about the prospect of having to 'hoof it to the base of the Lookout crater and make our winter camp there,' she worries that the pain in Van Tuyle's toe, from the *Back to God's Country* frostbite, is increasing: 'would my partner be able to make the climb? In summer the trail was long, rugged and very steep; in winter, a leg-pulling effort, five miles straight up' (*Heart*, 124).

Finally at the peak, the small crew pitched their winter tents for a week-long shoot. In the memoir Shipman recalls the 'monument' that remained from the production. It was 'in the crater of Mt. Lookout, where we spent a week in the middle of winter in tents buried under the snow and, after the tents were up, a latrine came next. Burlap was strung in a triangle around the tops of three pines. Came spring and hikers to the mountain's top would spot this strange triangle of sacking perched high above. They'd ask if it were a blind for hunters when the forty-foot treetops touched the snow. I am certain they were informed it was only the John where the Movie Star sat of a morning' (125).

When the *Little Dramas* were finished, Bert Van Tuyle took them to New York to sell them on the distribution circuit. Pathé, 'the best of the short subject distributors,' turned down *Trail of the North Wind*: 'There was no villain except Nature on the rampage. No sex ... The exhibitors and Pathé wanted the menace to be a man.' The series was finally sold to Lewis J. Selznick for distribution (128–30).

The Priest Lake period lasted only two years, but they were two years of continual struggle. Money was a constant problem. The memoir repeatedly mentions Shipman's hatred of debt, the kindness of suppliers who let 'their accounts run without complaining,' and a visit from the Sheriff 'to nail a paper on the storehouse door.'[125] This was the first attempt to attach a lien to the zoo.

Keeping the animals alive in the winter was arduous. The memoir includes many details of netting fish for smoking and drying for animal food; they made dog biscuits with hundred-pound sacks of flour, cornmeal, bran, and rye mixed in a trough with water hauled from the lake. A daily routine involved cutting away the bad parts from the three tons of carrots and apples that had been hauled in during the fall (132).

During 'the winter of near-famine,' when they were shooting *White Water* at a logging camp, the film crew was treated to noon dinner. 'They served four kinds of meat, three sorts of pie, potatoes in jackets, without jackets, mashed and swamped in gravy thick enough to walk on, mounds of bread, rolls and muffins' (132). Shipman's detailed memories of the meal, recounted nearly fifty years later, indicate the contrast of the luxurious meal with the penury they were accustomed to.

In the memoir, Shipman's devotion to the animals is a constant refrain:

The animals! How they race through the rosemary-drenched pages of my remembrances! What a scurry of flying feet they bring to me, like an echo. What a banner of waving tails, eyes bright at sight of a loved human! O welcome, welcome! You have come home! ... [Brownie's] greatest happiness – besides acting for the camera – was to sleep curled up beside me on pine needles, my head on her rump, my arms embracing her ... Sweet of heart and sweet of spirit, rosemary for Remembrance!

Being in a sense so alone with the animals, serving them, maintaining the soft-spoken image which arrived punctually with their food and the conversation and petting each one expected and learned to love, made communication between us a natural and easy thing. It must be that they possess a sixth sense of understanding ... with this treasured silent dialogue (136).

By 1925, the dashing production manager Bert Van Tuyle was gone, Nell Shipman Productions was bankrupt, and the landlord sent the bailiff to seize the animals. There were reports that some of them were starving and showed signs of maltreatment, although Barry Shipman denied that any animals starved at Lionhead. Shipman owed $795 to her landlord, Sam Byars, who sought retribution by seeking a court-ordered auction of one hundred animals – 'the first time,' according to the *Spokesman-Review*, 'that a wild animal zoo was ever offered on the auction block on court orders.' Shipman, now in New York, succeeded in blocking the auction, and her wildlife collection was eventually consigned to the San Diego Zoo. The *Priest River Times* (18 June 1925) noted that 'about 40 animals and birds' were sent south, including 'dogs, bears, deer, wildcat, wolves, skunk, eagle, rats, possum, coon, and other small animals.' Brownie the bear was in this shipment. Tresore, who had played the heroic Wapi, had been poisoned the year before; Shipman suspected that the wicked landlord was the murderer (182–3).

Shipman never lost her love of animals. In her old age, long after her company had gone bankrupt and her wild animals were dispersed, countless numbers of dogs and cats lived with her in her house.

chapter eight

⁛　⁛　⁛　⁛　⁛

Tissue-Paper Tower

As recounted by Shipman in the memoir and in *Abandoned Trails*, the scene of the last Christmas at Lionhead Lodge in 1924 is worthy of any melodramatic scenario. It features son Barry, home for the holidays from school in Spokane, Washington, Bert Van Tuyle, Shipman wearing evening clothes, high heels, and perfume, and a twenty-two-year-old actor, Ken Sidney – Sid – from New York who had come to Lionhead Lodge for a career in the movies. As the radio plays music and the candles gutter, Shipman and the young man begin to dance and then to flirt. Van Tuyle, drunk and crazed from the pain of his gangrenous foot, raves madly as he points a gun at Shipman. 'Numbed and stunned,' she passes into a state of dissociation: 'I might have been watching a series of subtitle cards turned into a soundtrack ... I suppose the entire scene came close to a movie and I could not achieve complete realization of its meaning.' In her 'high-heeled pumps, silk stockings and crepe de chine dress,' she stumbles towards the lake to kill herself. Barry follows, screaming, and eventually gets her to the surreal shelter of a 'partially roofed, half-walled "set"' they had built for one of the *Little Dramas of the Big Places.*

At dawn, Shipman and Barry watch Van Tuyle and the young man take off in the dogsled, heading for the hospital. Relief all around, until, later that day, Van Tuyle reappears. With thirteen-year-old Barry holding off Van Tuyle with a .22 rifle, Shipman and Barry lock themselves in the bunkhouse for the night and, fearing that Van Tuyle has murdered Sid, leave quietly on snowshoes at first light. When they reach Belle Angstadt's Lone Star Ranch, they find out that Sid has left 'for Coolin and civilization.' With that, 'the melodrama fell to pieces at once and for all time.'[1] When they finally arrive in Spokane, Shipman collapses for five days.

According to Barry Shipman, Sid and Shipman were together for a time in Spokane.[2] His story accords with the version in *Abandoned Trails*, which portrays Sid as respectful of Dirk but madly in love with Joyce, who saw him as a 'White Knight.' In any case, the affair did not last long. In New York later that year, when Barry asked Shipman about Sid, 'she smiled and passed it off. "The last time I saw him was in Spokane," she said.'[3] The trip from Spokane to New York was floated on the sale of her diary, in three installments, to the *Atlantic Monthly* (March–May 1925). With the $200 netted from the sale, she was heading down the 'come-back' road.[4]

Apparently Shipman did not intend to leave Idaho forever, although after an appointed last meeting with Van Tuyle in Spokane – 'on his knees, pleading, in tears' – that partnership was finished.[5] Planning to go to New York to refinance and then to go back to Lionhead Lodge to continue making movies alone, she had a new project already, a feature to be called *The Purple Trail*, in which she would once again play Neeka the 'breedgirl,' with a Mountie in pursuit. The deal did not go through, however, and in the meantime the animals had been consigned to the San Diego Zoo, undermining an essential generic ingredient of her film production.

By February 1925 Shipman had settled in an old brownstone on Madison Avenue, just a block from Thirty-Fourth Street. Not a fashionable address by any means, the house was apparently divided into rooms with kitchenettes. Shipman made friends with two artists living on the ground floor, and they in turn introduced her to Charles Ayers, a portrait painter from New Hampshire. A big, handsome man with a football player's physique, Ayers was a 'very physical man' and 'a lovely guy'; he adored her and was a great lover.[6] Within a few months, Shipman and Ayers were married and living in the artists' colony at Old Lyne, Connecticut. Carlos, as Shipman called him, was constantly painting her portrait, always with a cigarette hanging out of the corner of his mouth.

By this time, Shipman's first husband, Ernest Shipman, was back in the movies as a promoter. They had somehow remained in contact, and Ernest had made friends with Charles. It was Ernest who enticed them to Florida the first time, notifying them of the boom there and intent on possibilities for Nell's return to pictures.[7] By the next spring, Nell and her new husband were in Florida and she was pregnant at the age of thirty-three. On a whim they left for Spain and found a lovely old two-story cottage with a garden filled with flowers, a grape arbour, and an orchard with fruit trees of every species. The six-month lease cost them $122.50.[8] Twins Daphne and Charles were born 3 May 1926, in Spain.

Back in the United States later that year, they lived with Ayers's relatives in New Hampshire for some months, but November 1927 found them in Sarasota, Florida. In March 1928 Shipman performed in the Ringling Brothers Circus annual pageant, playing the part of Sara de Sota, daughter of the famous explorer. Ernest, who had some connection with the Ringling Brothers, had set this up. Barry Shipman recollects that 'on the final day of the festivities, Nell, gowned in white satin, pearls and feathery plumes, was brought to the pier in a festooned barge where she was met by an escort of honor. Seated in a guilded [sic] chariot drawn by six camels, accompanied by glittering circus horses and their riders, Nell was paraded before thousands of visitors and citizens.' Although Shipman was apparently pleased with the publicity, the gig did not pay. Neither did Ayers's paintings bring in any money. This caused both financial and emotional problems: like the male protagonists in Shipman's films, and former partner Van Tuyle in life, Ayers collapsed under pressure. He found it 'impossible ... to work when conditions were adverse.'[9]

Shipman had been hoping that her reputation as a star would land her acting jobs, but she was so poor that she could not even afford photographs for promotion and did not have adequate clothes to wear for auditions. According to Barry Shipman, his mother was not trying for jobs as a director during this period. Ironically referring to herself as 'Princess Running Deer,' she had lost her nerve.[10] Instead, she supported her husband and family by writing plays, magazine articles, and novels. In addition to the *Atlantic Monthly* article that got her to New York – 'The Movie That Couldn't Be Screened' – short stories and articles on wild animals were published in *Field and Stream*, the *Humanist* (Britain), and various other papers. A story about Florida history, 'The Tamiani Trail,' was published in a number of Florida newspapers.[11] Playing 'Miss Narbo' (thinly disguised name for Greta Garbo) with son

Barry backing her up as a messenger boy, she made a bit of money with a play, *Are Screen Stars Dumb*, that ran for a week in the Olympic Theater in Miami.[12]

By 1930 she was back in the money. Dial Press published a children's book that she had written, *Kurly Kew and the Tree Princess* (1930), followed in the same year by *Get the Woman*, which *McCall's* magazine serialized under the title *M'sieu Sweetheart*. With the advance on *Get the Woman*, Shipman paid for an exhibition of Ayers's paintings at a gallery in Pasadena before leaving for New York for the publicity launch that billed her as 'the most exciting author of outdoor fiction since James Oliver Curwood!'[13] She followed up this success quickly with the publication of *Abandoned Trails* in 1932 (also by Dial Press).

Reviewing *Abandoned Trails* for the *Los Angeles Times*, Lillian C. Ford describes Shipman's writing as 'dynamic,' offering 'thrill[s] ... because of the keen Northwest winds that blow through its wilderness scenes.' But beyond the 'stirring' wilderness scenes and the 'excellent rendition of Hollywood life,' the significance of the book, writes Ford, lies 'in the clash of character and the development of the ambitious young woman who gallantly meets defeat but never accepts it ... It strikes deep into the heart of the modern woman, who is constantly betrayed by her emotions while constantly competing for honors in a world still controlled by men.'[14]

Abandoned Trails did not match the success of *Get the Woman*. Barry Shipman blames its failure on lack of publicity from Dial Press, which 'was cutting back on sales expenditures,' and because *McCall's* turned it down on moral grounds: 'The heroine of the story was not married.'[15] Broke again, Shipman lived for a while in Mabel Dodge Luhan's house in Taos until she and Ayers went to Canada, where Shipman was researching a book about Alaska.[16]

By this time Barry Shipman was grown up. He worked briefly as a dancer in the chorus of movies such as *Paramount on Parade* (d. Dorothy Arzner, Paramount, 1930), *The Vagabond King* (d. Ludwig Berger, 1930), and others. On the basis of his 'reputation,' he ran a dance studio for a while, teaching local girls at a dollar per lesson, before he got a job on the Republic backlot. He soon got a contract writing Republic serials, and managed to set his mother up to write a Gene Autry movie.[17] But, he says, 'she couldn't do it.'[18] Perhaps the stoop was too low, or her fear too great.

In 1929 she turned an idea that she 'stole' from her son[19] into a screenplay, *Wings in the Dark*, featuring a protagonist based on Amelia Earhart, the famous aviatrix with whom Shipman was acquainted through Earhart's husband, George Palmer Putnam (of Putnam Publishing).[20] By resurrecting the idea of the blind aviator from *The Girl from God's Country*, she managed to write in a part for a seeing-eye dog. The screenplay was apparently a 'collaboration' with Philip D. Hurn, with whom she worked on several projects. She wrote about her association with Hurn in a 1933 letter to Barry, telling him that [Hurns] has 'got most everything of mine now and wants more ... He took "Mary" [another project] away last night.'[21] In November 1934 she mentions *Wings in the Dark* again: 'The continuity of Wings in the Dark is in and its [*sic*] a peach of a piece of work and going to do both Hurn and myself lots of good. Its [*sic*] a swell aviation story, with some dog ... and they are spending real kale [money] on it ... I am very pleased that they have, really, followed the original all but word for word.'[22]

When *Wings in the Dark* was released (d. James Flood, Paramount, starring Myrna Loy and Cary Grant, 1935),[23] she was disappointed to find they had not followed the original that closely. Paramount had all but eliminated the seeing-eye dog element, leaving merely 'some ears poking up in the bottom of the frame. Instead of the motivating psychology of the dog-man-girl, with its human heart and uplift motive, we had dreary stretches of dialogue through which everyone was very restrained and polite.' And Shipman has no respect for Myrna Loy as an actor: 'she is very charming ... but she is a bread-and-butter drawing room Mary Astorish gal, who, in our picture, is the perfect example of what the well dressed young aviatrix will wear but had just about as much emotional heart as a clothes dummy. Never once did she make you believe that ... she was really a flyer – a sweet but almost tough little sport who worshipped airships and aces – and not a nice girl who played at flying for fun. To me she muffed line after line of the swell dialogue.'[24]

After nearly ten years of marriage, Shipman and Ayers separated in the summer of 1934. Suffering depression and artist's block, Ayers had come to dislike New York, Shipman's friends, and 'the general ferment.' Shipman wrote to Barry about the end of the relationship: 'My own position is very clear. He knows it is entirely washed up and off on "strong free wings" and he is not resentful, only slightly puzzled, still "in love" but lonely and hoping that what I saw will come true, he will find "some-body."'[25]

After she sent Ayers packing, Shipman moved to a 'little dump' at 244 West Tenth Street in New York: 'one small room with a fireplace, very cozy, cutely furnished and colorful, with a hole which is a kitchenette (meaning it has a shelf with an electric plate) and a bathroom ... The rent is 40.00 ... I am stalling all bills, though they are catching up with me.'[26]

Stalling creditors, writing new screenplays, and always trying to raise new financing, Shipman had already – before 'the Big Break' [with Ayers] – fallen 'very deeply in love'[27] with Amerigo Serrao, a baron (according to Barry Shipman) whose grandfather was the prefect of Rome and whose father was an attorney for the British government in Italy. Serrao had had a brief career in the movies (1927–31), but was a bit down on his luck.[28] Nevertheless, he was 'fun to be with, witty, enthu-siastic, and eternally optimistic.'[29] Seely, as he was called by the twins, also went under the names Arthur Varney,[30] Grover Lee, and Peter Locke. According to Barry Shipman, the alias Arthur Varney was taken on for 'professional reasons ... because the Hollywoodians couldn't pro-nounce' Amerigo Serrao.[31] 'There was some reason for believing that at least one "alias" had to do with avoiding alimony payments,' adds Barry Shipman.[32] Grover Lee was the name associated with bad debts, as Ship-man's letters over many years to her son indicate. Soon Shipman and Serrao were living together and – inevitably – moving frequently, leaving creditors in their wake wherever they went.

With Serrao, Shipman bounced around America for close to twenty years, moving from one town to another, living on the pittance that her father had left her.[33] They were unutterably poor. Barry sent them a 'fiver' from time to time, but they were very low. One of Nell's letters to Barry begins, 'Many thanks for the fiver! It surely did just pop in in time. The night before I'd remembered a dollar on deposit at the lend library, and withdrawn that ... the last one in their till.'[34]

Shipman went through enormous depressions, verging on nervous breakdowns. Desperately worried, Serrao wrote to Barry in 1938: 'On the debit side we have the 200 note, the rent, the locals bills, and Nell's state of mind, which has me more frightened than anything in all my previous years ... Nell has been in bed since Sunday. Barry, its [sic] breaking my heart. She is ashen, and just lays there not saying a word, staring at the ceiling, burning up with fever. Today, for perhaps the first time in my life I have felt that civilization is a great handicap – I wanted to go out and hold up a bank, smash somebody in the face and take, take, take.'[35]

Despite the depressions and the horrors of dire poverty, Shipman continued to write. At first she wrote scripts based on old ideas, topical newspaper stories, or new social trends. Wherever they moved, they tried to drum up projects. Shipman's modus operandi was to research the local history of each stopping place and try to pitch a film based on her findings to the town council, the Chamber of Commerce, or the corporate elite. She always had a pocketful of projects to flog. As Barry Shipman writes, 'As the next four years went by it appeared to be a case of a Dreamer being nourished by another Dreamer. The only substantive results were Nell's scripts, stories, plays, pageants, musicals and Historic Extravaganzas – with titles and themes too numerous to include here.'[36]

Running from debts and unpaid rent, they had 'learned the art of the one-toothbrush move.' Between 1935 and 1939 they virtually disappeared.

Letters, We Get Letters

This chapter differs from the preceding ones by offering excerpts from Shipman's letters from one year, 1939. These letters paint a portrait of a committed filmmaker who, although she has not made a film in fifteen years, shows no signs of giving up, and makes every attempt to continue to be optimistic. In 1939, Shipman sends letters to her grown son approximately every five days, writing with almost pathological frequency and in maniacal detail. She tells of the projects she has under way, her negotiations with investors, bankers, and studios, and her hopes for the rebirth of her career.

In 1939, she and her fourth partner move six times. Their addresses include a rooming house, a hotel, and a penthouse (with blessings heaped upon the landlady who accepted their deposit in the form of a cheque). Because her trusty Underwood typewriter has been pawned for $40 and remains in California, for a time she has a rented typewriter. When they can no longer afford the payments, she has to write by hand;

when there is no money for stationery, she writes on the back of old movie call-sheets.

Except for occasional bouts of 'the dumps,' Shipman keeps up a tone of optimism that sometimes seems heroic and at other times seems almost delusional. But the passionate commitment to the projects, the world of filmmaking, and the business of production are not delusional: this is her life. And its disappointments, frustrations, depressions – along with its highs and hopes – are the stock in trade of the independent filmmaker to this day.

January

The beginning of this tumultuous year finds Shipman and Serrao on a journey south, as usual short of money: 'Have 50.00 left and may be okay but doubt it,' writes Shipman to Barry. She is hoping that he will send some 'mazuma' (cash): 'Of course if I find we can make it I won't wire.' She promises, in a postscript, 'You'll get it back me lad – !'[37] By the time Shipman and Serrao get to Memphis, they have ten dollars left, so had 'actually spent $83 for *2000* miles.' She signs the letter with 'Hold Everything Boy – its going to be okay.'[38] Although they are on the road, she buzzes with excitement about the prospects that the coming New York World's Fair holds for show business: it would feature broadcasts on both radio and the brand new medium, television. She is already pitching the organizers: 'This will be settled about Wed. – I mean, our doings.'[39] She has revived an old contact, Hal Haskins,[40] to help her on another project, 'Fear Market.' Although many projects are in the pipeline, this one seems most likely to go.

February

Shipman and Serrao surface in New York. The letter of 10 February 1939, typed on plain paper from 'Hotel Holland, West 42nd,' is the first of many reports on the state of the various projects seeking production. It is quoted at length to convey a sense of the length and the obsessive minutae of the letters, which total almost one hundred pages of manuscript in a single year. She writes in a dynamic personal voice full of anecdotes, colloquialisms, and endearments, always with that incredible focus on the projects. In this letter she refers to a number of projects, including 'Fear Market,' and a magazine article based on the screenplay ('a "literary" version') that she is hoping to sell to *Cosmopolitan* magazine.

I'm very sorry it's been so long, and it hasn't been because of nothing happenings, nor of wanting to wait until it actually did, because I do know that even the daily whoo-hoo keeps one bucked up and silence is deadly. But it's that I first got a helluva cold, really grippe or flu, and during it thought I ought to get into a 'literary' version of Fear Market, which I did, and pounded this rented machine [the typewriter] daily until I couldn't look a letter in the face. That's the truth of it. Yesterday I finished and today it will be in the dear little hands of the no 1 associate ed. of Cosmopolitan, which might mean some pretty quick action. It happened thusly; unbeknownst to me, Seeley[41] picked an agent out of the sky (literary) a Mrs Champonois [*sic*], whom Nan had once mentioned to him as being okey. He called her, charmed her and then found she knew me very well, was in fact the original discoverer, the Christopher Columbus (do you find when you've come off a long job that you can't write the most simple words?) quite an admirer and the one who staged the great McCall party for our Nellie, – a clambake still talked of in local circles. Well, she, and her son, were all agog and I met them and found them sold to the hilt on Fear Market. They like Cinderalla [*sic*] Town too, and agreed it should have a collaborator and be lengthened, and they like Angel's Flight, and agree I should re-write *that* when I can afford the time, and they think 'God Made the ...' the most beautifully written, etc, etc, and needing no re-write (I mean for publication) but harder to sell and will take more time. But Fear Market! They drooled over this one. It seems they are very close to the Hearst pubs [publishers], Mrs Cham having been an editor there before she took to 'representing.' So I felt it was up to me so to speak and went to it. It's come out alright, I think. They didn't want any changes just a re-write and polishing so it was fit for our readers. It's still a swell story. So thata is thata.

It's been wonderful to be here with Seeley, and I shall always be grateful for the chance to get out of the sandtrap ... think I would have died if it had gone on much longer, the dreary round of zero, but there has had to be the wait at this end, too. Buckley [a potential investor?] got back from Venezuela last saturday and since then no one has been visible, it's been one protracted meeting. You wonder what the devil they can talk about, day in and out and far into the nights. Is it an act? I mean, we could have done a complete continuity while they've been at it, bickering and snarling and figuring. Anyway, it's going on and, apparently is still in progress, because not a hide nor hair of [Hal Haskins] has been seen, nor have we heard from him. I am sure that when the smoke clears the dear old warrior will clump forth, ear phones and all, and say 'here it is' and I've felt guilty over the *other* 'deals' which have cooked and simmered and are, seemingly, popping this week-end.

No 1. is a Wall Street group willing to finance two pics to be made immediately, in France (the original Hueneme schemes, over which they are as greedy as ever). Following the two French pick-ups they would go on with Fear Market, here, at $125,000.00 The two French comedies are to cost $35,000 each. They are to be done without American names, but with what English speaking actors we can pick up over there, plus ourselves. I'll say more about the foreign pic situation later.

The No 1. gang had a contract already on its desk but Seeley wisely insisted upon a proposition in writing from them to us, first, and that is supposed to arrive today, so we can study it, mitt lawyers, and reach a decision by Tuesday. It seems, to date, to be all right. Not exactly generous but it's a job and a chance and it isn't for life ...[42]

In her ambitions to produce films, she is clearly prepared to ignore the anti-Semitism of the German-American investors, although she and Serrao are evidently not inclined to shoot in Germany, which was already at war in Europe:

No 2 on the fire is the damndest thing ever. Seeley, down in Wall street, was hailed out of a window by some long lost palsie. This led into an offer to go to Germany on practically our own ticket. He naturally refused, that is, he wouldn't commit suicide, but he countered with the Monaco, International idea; their money and their equipment (the best in the world) but English speaking actors of all nationalties and a base in Monaco, and a complete soft pedal [*sic*] on the German source. As a matter of fact, it's American-German. The rich boys over here have really got together to fight the propaganda and it's amazing what is being done.

Well, he more than made good before a committee and, it being found that not one ounce of the hated [Jewish] blood coursed through the veins of either of us (and let-me tell you this is no fooling! Even the strictly American Wall Street bankers (gang no 1) asked the same pertinent question!!!!!!!. My God, comes it the revolution! why, over this holiday, all the Germans and Am-Germans are getting together at somebody's country place and ourselves, known as the 'film-deal,' and two other American products, something like razor blades and rubber (!) will be discussed. Again, on Tuesday, we will learn the verdict. If it should happen (and we should take it) it might be a very extraordinary set-up. As Seeley's friend, the initial caller-outer of window, puts it, we could lay ten eggs in a row and they would still put up more dough. I think it hinges entirely on whether they will accept our unbendable decision that there must be no propaganda, no inkling of the Germanic source. We are *international*. I don't need to point out the full import of what that would mean, to us. The American side of this (I mean, the rich German-Americans) see it. The two real government reps (one of them actually heil hitler-ed Seeley, with salute and all) will hold out for our coming openly into Germany and saying so. We couldn't do that. We might make fine pictures but there wouldn't be a screen open to us, nor a job, for life.

I don't need to tell you to not repeat any of this, nor show it, because, if it should so happen that it *is* German, I mean, *their money*, the secret must be lost in the sands, forever ...

The French racket seems to be the one thing likely to get the Wall Street wolflets. Capital for Fear Market must come from other sources, I am afraid. Such sources as Hal [Haskins], or the rich pipples [people], unless it waits the outcome of the two initial Frenchies and their profits.

Charlie Glett[43] has been grand. He was very, very ill and full of operations, and the long silence of last summer was quite understandable, as I always hoped it would be. Now he is right where he was at the studios, and they are magnificent, and he, bless him, has had a splendid budget breakdown made on Fear Market. It's a service which costs all prospective customers a hundred bucks and Charlie presented it to us, keeping the bill himself. It's a lovely looking job, and amazing, considering they had no continuity. Minus cast, ourselves and story cost, it comes out at $75,000, which I am sure we can shade when we come to it, but it is absolutely complete, with extras and everything you can think of. It makes your mouth water to read it, and to see that studio, and to think what it would mean to prance in there with *everything* and turn out that picture! I thought it pretty swell of Charlie, don't you? We're putting F.M. [Fear Market] at $125,000. Naturally, a publication of it will help in every way, besides the cash, so we're hoping it will happen.[44]

Hoping that Barry will come east to work with her, Shipman offers various proposals over the course of the year. Sometimes she dreams of his moving permanently, with his wife and new baby, to work with her on all her projects, but here she just suggests a 'leave of absence' from his job at Republic writing *Durango Kid* serials:

Like we said; it's hard to make the plans until the mazuma [money] is in the fist. If it's Gang No 1 and the French pictures, pronto, there is to be story money on the line. I think you should get a leave of absence and just simply skitter, without saying too much about it. We'd do the scripts between here and Paris, and from then on. We'd all work in the things, clean 'em up as fast as possible, and be back. By then the weather will have broken (it is unbelievably awful, now; having never stopped snowing, raining, blowing and sleeting since I came) and the family might be here, at the dock, to meet you. From then on we're in the lap of the Gods, anyway. I am certain it would mean going right on with F.M., here, but, if it didn't, and Rep [Republic Studio] forgave you, you could go back.......... But, oh, darling, I hope you never will!

But let's leave it until the cash is in the hand. It's all so much easier, then.[45]

The end of the letter indicates Shipman's thoughts about the new medium of television and the conclusion of her attempts to interest the New York World's Fair in some kind of production for broadcast:

The Television is a dreadful disappointment, so far, though good Fredo will not have it so and still insists it will be made possible. Personally, I think they've met with a lot of stumbling blocks. They were in Washington and we heard, from other sources, that it was pretty much of a wash-out. Anyway, the song and dance has completely changed since Seeley was talked to. At that moment they were shouting the possibilities ... and offering him an immediate job, to go to Washington then and there. Now its [*sic*] all soft peddled. They will only telecast two hours per week. They will fill that bill with their own personelle [*sic*]. They may only sell about 10,000 sets, and those only in N.Y. There will be no telecast beyond the fifty mile radius of N.Y. (they didn't mention the coast where, naturally, they will be doing the same thing). If, and when, they sell more sets, and need more program, then ... etc. etc. ...

BUT their attitude, and outlook, on their own stepchild, is awful. Pinhole camera, peep-show stuff. They haven't the faintest conception of lighting, staging, production, story, anything. We saw the demonstration, the regular tourist show, and Seeley was televised, for my benefit. The damn thing is rather awful, as limited to this tiny screen, for the picture humps in the center, due to the *round* bulb inside the camera, which throws it out of focus on all the edges. It is however very clear and natural and, with lighting, quite possible. But, oh, the limitation of their tiny minds! Of course, I haven't talked to Fredo myself, yet, and I know, if I did, I would find that he realized the future, the great huge future. It is there. But it will have to come out of the home toy stage first. Someday it will be a medium of education in schools, and there will be news theaters you will go into to see what's happening all over the world, and live shows, and telecast movies, will be shown on huge screens.[46]

As she has no suitable clothes to wear to meetings with investors, she has borrowed a suit from Barry's wife ('I thank God I came and borrowed back the famous suit because I do not know what the hell I'd have done!'). As poor as they are, they make a point of going to the movies to keep up with the industry. 'The foreign picture situation is amazing. New York is scattered with long run French pictures, Grand Illusion, 22 weeks, Story of a Cheat, running, Heart of Paris, ditto, and revivals all over the place. And all these are *in French*, with those awful English titles hopping up at you. Chevalier's new picture, made in Paris, with a French director whom we've known in Hollywood for years, arrived this week. 'With a smile.' And it's swell.'[47]

Interested in the European imports because they have hopes for productions in France and Germany, Shipman technically assesses the films with unabashed Hollywood chauvinism:

All the others had left me dithered with their talent but sunk as to their photography, lighting and lab work. We had about decided that it must be something awful they do over there with all three. Then along came 'With a Smile' and we breathed again because here was one done by *Hollywood experience*, and the lighting, photography and lab work were all A no 1! So it's simply been lack of experience all along! Boy, did we sing in the street! Because that was the only bug-a-boo we had. It would have been pretty bad to have got over there, with all the talent in the world, and then turned out something like pea soup in a dark restaurant.[48]

A short paragraph in this letter mentions that Shipman has 'low spells, and panics, sometimes.' This little phrase does not begin to suggest the level of despair that Shipman experienced.

Two weeks later, Serrao writes to Barry that Nell had been in 'one of her dumps' but that she was out of it now, because 'Fear Market' is definitely going. There had been a great meeting with investors: 'Fear Market' has been beautifully estimated for immediate production, and the thing has even gone far enough to have a huge party, where Nell was placed next to the president of the bank that IS the finance of both the studio and the ERPI Company ... and *did Nell go to town*! It was quite a formal affair, evening clothes, top hats, etc and it finally wound up at the Stork Club from which place we exited at three a.m. woozy with champagne and the amount of money we had sat with. In the meantime the net result is that the Studio and the bank will go about $75,000, together, and I am busy as bird dog getting the other necessary $50,000 to make the opus.' Their dreams for the casting line-up include 'William Faversham, Jack Norworth, Richard Bathelmess [*sic*] and possibly Lillian Gish.'[49]

As a bonus, 'Strangely enough Angel's Flight has also struck the gong and there is a very serious discussion of serial rights with an advance on delivery of the first instalments, two or three.' And now 'we are coming out of the woods, kid, all of us ... My having brought Nell right into direct contact with all of it has done wonders for her. She now feels okay and full of ginger. She looks like a million and I think next week will see the start of the continuity for Fear Market. She will tell you all about the change of address, etc ...'[50]

Yes, another change of address. They have moved from the Forty-Second Street hotel to a rooming house in Greenwich Village. Serrao ends his letter to Barry with 'Give my best to Rex. Tell him we'll be sending for the typewriter pretty soon now.'[51] This is a refrain that will be heard throughout the year regarding the recovery of the pawned typewriter, buttressed by promises that the debt on the car will be paid off, and that Barry's loans will also be returned.

Shipman writes to Barry the next day, the day after his birthday. She has no money to send him a gift: 'Was lonesome for you yesterday, on your birthday. Didn't forget you, but hoped, all the early part of the day, we could send you a little wire with the price of a bottle of Scotch, to celebrate, but couldn't. And that made me feel sad and droopy drawers. So many birthdays and Xmases have gone by.'[52]

She mentions a little job that Charlie Glett got her: 'This was sub rosa and meant five hundred bucks, which was a god-send, but we're having the usual trouble collecting.' But there is a new investor on the line for Fear Market, a '"Mr. Staudel" [sic] ... a newcomer into our lives; a quiet little down-town business man who seems, at last, to have taken hold ... He seems the most sincere and honest person ever met and he has spent the last two weeks gathering together the people who (it seems) will be our backers. Next week, they believe, will see it in the bag, with ourselves incorporated and the story purchased.'[53]

Meanwhile, she is still trying to sell 'Fear Market' to *Cosmospolitan*, 'but it's to hold off until Monday ... If they don't buy it, it's set to go over to Red Book. But I am hoping for Cosmo, because it will be kudos for the story.' And the agent Mrs Champoinois [sic] 'has gone nuts over "Angel's Flight" and prays for the first 15000 words in literary form, swearing she can place it with Good Housekeeping ... And Doubleday-Doran are considering Cinderella Town, either with me doing it (as a book) or a collaborator ... There'd have to be an advance on that, and also on Angel's Flight, if it went over.'[54]

March

Shipman has decided they have to move from the Greenwich Village digs: 'this address won't do any longer because I have to see people, and be seen.' They move to the newly built Hotel St George, Brooklyn: 'It's a lovely place, the second biggest in the world, but outside of that, fine. With a view of the harbor, lovely rooms, the subway in its basement, *and* the biggest salt-water swimming pool back here! Also Gymnasium, etc. It isn't too expensive, or won't be under the coming circumstances. 'She adds, 'Now if I can get some bills paid, and buy some clothes.'[55]

Less than a week later, her optimism flags, as the hoped-for production contracts for 'Fear Market' have not come through. They are in debt for $200, and Shipman requests that Barry not give out her current address: 'It would be just as well if they don't know where I am.' *Cosmopolitan* has asked for two more weeks to make up their minds about 'Fear Market,' so the agent has sent it to *Redbook*. Shipman writes, 'I was no more disappointed than usual.'[56]

But Straudel, the wonderful new investor, has brought in a new pigeon, 'a strange sort of a duck ... someone so fantastic he is probable! A one-legged aviator from the British Indian Flying Corp, who has flown the Indian border ... This funny duck seems in touch with gobs of British money. He himself is slated to put up some front money for us, a down payment on the story, etc. It would be a salvation! ... There seems no question about my getting "Wanda" [the lead in 'Fear Market']. Nobody even thinks anything else! ... My God, how I look forward to that job ... both the continuity, the part and the picture! ... We are to be incorporated and things and it's all very business-like.'[57]

About two weeks later, still in high hopes, Shipman again promises son Barry a job on the current production: 'Am so dreadfully afraid of being premature and of building hopes that I am in danger of leaning too far the other way and may catch you all unprepared and off guard. You are being throughly sold to the "company" and the necessity of bringing you on immediately, both to work with me on the continuity and then continue with the picture has been so firmly established that the money for your expenses and salary is to come out of the first money up, as is the down payment on the story itself, to me ... There have been endless scares, starts, waits, seeming disappointments, etc. but I won't go into those today; They are so usual and we're so used to them now.'[58]

She asks him to phone, advising him to reverse the long distance charges and bill them to Grover Lee, the alias that Serrao used for his debt scams. Shipman wants her son with her from the start of pre-production: 'I would rather start the continuity from scratch with you along side of me ... I figure that with everything in our favor, and the original story as full as it is, we can do it in three weeks; at least at the end of that time we will have a script which can be broken down, even if we still have some final polishing on it ... Then, when we have it, I want you to continue thru the picture in a capacity I don't exactly know how to name except that you would be the "other me." A lot of the producer-ship details would fall on you, especially when I'm working in the picture; you would be general right-hand-bower.' She also has him in mind for scoring the picture as 'arranger and writer' and has her eye on 'a marvelous little piano.' She promises him, 'You will get screen credit on the continuity ... or "screen play," as I like it called, on the music, or partly on it, if you did it, and in [what] ever technical capacity you functioned on the staff. In other words, Shipman, Shipman and Shipman!'[59]

  Despite her optimism, a trace of doubt bubbles up: 'Regarding your leaving Republic caution makes me sort of squinch and say ... have it a leave of absence or something ... and yet I know this is nonsense ... I'm just hoping to God I'm not premature with this little booklet of ways and means because I feel, if it should lay an egg, now, I couldn't survive it. But there seem so many people now, all equally determined to put it over.'[60] Again, she sounds the refrain that will be constant throughout the year (and perhaps her life): 'The next week ought to see great happenings.'

  Two weeks later, things look good: 'Your salary has been agreed upon, at a "big" meeting (and, boy, were you sold! Completely, before your name was asked ... And then they asked if you were related to me and the awful truth exploded. And they didn't die. In fact Dr. Fromm ... remarked that "when a relationship presented such a real and unquestionable talent it was an asset, not a liability."' However, as Barry Shipman said, she had 'lost her nerve'[61] after the bankruptcy of 1925 and still harbours fears of a big studio project. This is clear from her own writing: 'I was privately afraid of the very modern hustle-bustle of the studio ... with its terrific formulae of "assistants," "speed," page-boys who follow you with telephone extensions, etc. ... I want to be off quietly by ourselves, where we can work out our picture under cover, make and rectify our mistakes and really be producers with ourselves.'[62]

  She is convinced that this picture will go: 'Things look wonderful, dearest. Seeley is now with the last of the "pigeons." ... He and his friend, who would count as one member of the syndicate, represent the last money needed. The rest is pledged.' But, as usual, the letter ends with a frisson of doubt: 'Do you think it has really happened to us, at last?'[63] Just in case, she has another project under way: 'Will be mailing you a copy of a new brain-child which I mothered ... It's about the Statue of Liberty and quite timely. It's called "Mother Liberty" and we think enough of it, – and are anxious to protect it by copyright, – that we've gone in debt to have it printed as a brochure ... We are going after it every way from the ace – magazines, show, pictures and syndicate. A ghost-writer will have to be put on it, I am afraid, if anyone really nibbles, excepting for pictures. It is a synopsis. Too expensive a Picture for us, but there are producers here looking for them.'[64]

April

In mid-April Nell writes, 'Am sitting here on what I hope will be the last anxious seat; and really it isn't anxious, because I know it's alright now. It was supposed to happen yesterday. Agreed upon [friday crossed out] Saturday – after banking hours! – it had to ride over until Monday (another week-end!) and then on yesterday the Market did handsprings and our Broker was sick into the bargain and didn't come to town at all. We nearly died, but Seeley actually saw the check on a desk, together with the agreement, so we really were sure. Today it was set for noon, and he's just phoned to say he's having lunch with Broker and Lawyer, at one o'clock. So I'm filling in the actual *last hour* by writing you. The last weeks of waiting have been unbelievable ... day to day, hour to hour ... and I couldn't do anything except sit here, wondering! I've gone mad a couple of times but I'm alright now; Just a little jittery. Which we both are. All that will pass like a cloud, now ... The "deal" will be okey. Neither Seeley or I will exactly make a fortune out of it but that's alright.'[65]

But, as usual, it doesn't happen. Later that night, she adds a handwritten postscript: 'Since I wrote it we've waited all afternoon for the man to come in and sign the check. He didn't come in.' Yet there's another flip in their fortunes, for while she 'died, here, a flat, calm little voice phoned "Mr Lee"' and left a message. '"The Bank had (today) passed the application for credit! Would Mr Lee come here tomorrow morning and arrange the details?!!!!!!!" This means the entire 125,000 to our credit, sans brokers, promotors [*sic*] ... *anybody*. We are nearly crazy with excitement.'[66] And as always, at the last minute, 'chances for touching big money have poured in from all sides and the most unexpected sources, among them a marvelous private bank and a Baron who was a big shot in Ufa (Germany). Through this last connection we may swing a deal for the next three ... bigger ones ... $300,000 each ... Cinderalla [*sic*] Town. Jungle Ship. God Made the Sea.'[67] A little bravado shades the last sentences of the letter; she has lost hope that Fear Market will be published: it 'will not be a magazine story and I'm really glad. Not sour grapes. It's a picture.'[68]

The ups and down are fierce: 'Have nearly gone nuts since that last letter ... The man's check was finally signed but dangled out in front of us, like bait on a hook. Then came the miracle of the bank. Okey and just as suspected. A $125,000 "overdraft." Then a frantic squittle after coin from a money-lender, so we could send for you and also incorporate (necessary for the bank business) ... Then, yesterday, into the picture is injected a brand new side ... the real principals, the lawyers who represent and handle the owner of the bank with whom we'd be dealing ... one of the richest men in New York ... and us without a bean and the hotel raising hell. Boy, it's been sumptin. I finally went under, screwball as anything. Had to stay in bed two days.'[69]

Meanwhile, the possibility of earning some fast money from 'Fear Market' has percolated to the surface again. The magazine deals are not quite off yet: 'Liberty is also considering "Fear Market."' This will be the last submission, because time is too short. It hasn't had a real turn down yet. Sat Eve Post liked it immensely but would have to have it done as a short story, or lengthened to a novel . They have never published its particular, and awkward, length. So now it's Liberty, or nothing.' Then, she covers herself: 'Personally, I hope it doesn't see print. I think it spoils it. It's a picture, and it has certain mystery elements.'[70]

By chance, she has come across 'the Alaskan novel ... and falling to pieces ... I gave it to the Champonois [*sic*], who are elated with it and, of all places, it is going to McCall's for consideration!!! I've called it "The Naked North" from some lines in a poem by Service. It has surprising guts and splendid action. It would make a great modern out-door picture; one of the best.'[71] This is the manuscript that Barry Shipman later referred to in an interview as the instigation for a trip to Canada when Shipman was still with Ayers. Clearly it was not under contract to *McCall's* when they made the trip.

As always, Nell has plans for another new project for television: 'Oh ...

oh ... oh ... Manana ... Mister Gilette razors is being brought from Boston, no less, for a final conference at N.B.C. over "Jungle Ship" as a half-hour, two-shows-a week. They, N.B.C, are peeing their pants. We are pretending to be cool. But, oh boy! And has our little adventurous Claibourne gone nuts over Jungle Ship? That is next Winter's picture. We're all to be on it, in a ship ... the Keys, the Gulf, ... etc.'[72]

They plan to move again, to a flat they have rented in Manhattan, at 203 East Fifty-eighth Street. Although the house is 'shabby and old,' the apartment is the entire top floor; it has 'seven rooms, of sorts,' and 'plenty of atmosphere.' It also has 'a real kitchen, with big frigidaire and stove, bath with shower, balcony overlooking yards with actual trees! ... lots of cupboards and, best, *exits*. No tunneling through other rooms.' When Shipman told her husband that she had managed to get the owner to reduce the rent from $85 to $75 per month and had taken the place, 'Seeley nearly died, of course, but he came round to it and now is very sold.' She plans to use it as an office and gathering place for the production crew: 'I'll furnish one room with desks, the piano, etc. ... A big long table for the dining room, mitt comfortable seats, so all the company can forgather ... and couches, and more desks.' She plans on a long lease.[73]

This time the move is not to a better address; it is motivated by the Hotel St George coming after them for back rent and a false credit rating associated with Grover Lee: 'We've liked it here so far as the hotel is concerned but the Credit has been someting [*sic*] awful. Figure they are the ones started the unfortunate investigation out there, account a bounced check and some delays in bills. However, they had no business asking those questions ... I needn't say for all of you to know nothing as to whereabouts, We will not leave a forwarding address here, just pick up mail ... Nuts to them.'[74]

Five days later: 'Wednesday next it will be signed! ... Today the final bugs were shaken out, the last holes shot, and tomorrow the agreement will be drawn-up, Monday we'll get it, and on Wednesday it will be signed by the principal. It is a complete re-issue and a new deal and it came about through the most intricate and sometime most difficult to follow trails.' The trails included moneylenders backing out, Wall Street disasters due to the 'war scare headlines,' new investors coming in, 'appalling disasters and apparently unsurmountable barriers,' and finally triumph as a result of Seely's 'unrelenting fight' and 'everybody's utter admiration for Fear Market.' It has happened just when they were absolutely flat broke: 'One day, when there were not even eats, Seeley kicked something on the pavement and it was three little one-dollar bills!' Shipman is convinced that those hungry days are gone: this deal 'means limitless finance if we make good.'[75] She thrills again at the thought of Barry coming from California to work with her and writes extravagantly, 'I think, now, you'd better fly.' She needs him for pre-production in May, because 'The hope is we'll be shooting between June 1st and 15th.'[76]

May

The planned move to the large seven-room apartment on East Fifty-Eighth Street has apparently fallen through. They have moved instead to a building downtown: 200 West Sixteenth Street, Penthouse A. This is the fourth move in three months. Serrao writes the news to Barry: 'It's a penthouse on top of a 22 story building, with a 180 foot terrace overlooking the Hudson and most of N.Y. The main living room, with six huge windows, is 40 feet by nearly thirty and very high. Grand piano, a big cabinet radio, lovely furniture, ultra modern kitchen, etc. etc, all complete and about as perfect a set up as anyone would want.' Not only 'the bargain of bargains,' it's also 'by far the most luxurious place we have had.' When Shipman discovered it, they moved in 'on a three or four hours notice (you know us).'[77]

More news about the 'Fear Market' deal: it was supposed to be signed on Wednesday, but had to be postponed because of a court hearing – Grover Lee's debts? – and now, because one of the investors is 'a *very big* city official,' it has gotten stuck in the crisis around the coal shortage that threatens to shut down the New York subway system. 'In the meantime everything that can be pushed without money is being done, such as distribution arrangements, tentative casting, etc.'[78]

In a postscript, Serrao assures Barry that he has sent a money order for $26.90 to Pacific Finance, the company that they owe for the car and that is apparently hounding Barry: 'I mailed it a few hours ago ... I was able to to do this because we finally moved out of that G-D- St. George [Hotel] which was very expensive and stupid.' Counting on an advance on the screenplay coming in 'within a matter of a couple or three days,' he promises to send more. Besides, 'only April [is] actually delinquent as May isn't yet.'[79]

The next day, Shipman writes a two-page single-spaced letter in an unusually breathless style. Into the middle of the letter, she drops this short paragraph: 'Yesterday Benny [Boyer] paid for himself by delivering a Paramount release into our laps. For five pictures.' A new paragraph follows immediately: 'I'll just let that stand alone, classic and serene, and let you savor it on your tongue, as we did last night. Frankly, we both wept slightly. Seeley on his way home, me when I heard it. Not that I'm surprised. I had no doubts – either for R.K.O or Para[mount] – but it's a wonderful thing to know it's sure, that our market is set ... far, far ahead. That our product will see plenty of screens ... big, beautiful screens.' Although Paramount has 'okeyed' Shipman, Seely still has 'to be sold' because of 'the damned "Grover Lee," which must be straightened out.'[80] Obviously, Serrao's debts under the Grover Lee alias are causing a problem.

After this news, the letter begins to break down into little excited phrases joined by ellipses, a style quite unlike her usual conventional sentences and paragraphs. Shipman is dreaming in technicolour in this letter. She rhapsodizes about acting again in the part that she has written for herself: 'When I think of the delicacy of that initial, key-stone scene between Wanda [her part] and Pat, of writing it, and of playing it ... I go all weak and hot and cold ... but I'll get away with all of it, ... and more ... thanks to everybody who will help, from the Angel to the make-up man!'[81]

There is 'a slight string ... attached to the release, but it's alright. The Paramount distribution head has an actress wife ... and she is to get Stella. But she is a professional, and Benny says, okay, so it's not so bad as it might be.' Shipman goes on to dream of the cast: who will play opposite her? In contrast to Seely's last letter, which said that 'we have corralled Richard Bennet' for the part, Shipman wants Paul Kelly, but 'Seeley doesn't think Paramount will take him.' She had also thought of John Boles, 'but the opinion is he is too old for me!' Richard Barthelmess is another possibility; after nearly twenty years of B movies, he 'has "come back" in a current Columbia picture with Grant and Arthur.'[82]

And the other projects too. For the Paramount five-picture release deal, she has a great list: Fear Market, Challenge to the Sun, Cinderella

Town, Jungle Ship, God Made the Sea – or maybe the final one should be Angel's Flight? Challenge to the Sun will be the next one out, to be shot in Arizona in October, and then on to 'Cinderella ... maybe Wyoming – Jackson hole – maybe Red River and Cimarron and Taos ... Jungle Ship ... the Gulf ... Key West ... The keys. Klamath! How glad we must be that we have lived so much ... and so many places! That we could discover, and mine, all this wealth of material ... stories done ... not to be 'thought up.' ... but all ready, eager to be made and so *make-able* ... How glad for all the bloody trail, the delays and disappointments, the wait for the right hour to strike!'[83] And so she goes on: 'So I can't be impatient or nervous or fusity anymore. You are coming ... all keen and keyed ... the release is ready ... the money will be ... even a swell studio, far from the madding Erpi ... Heaven can go on Waiting.'[84]

This breathless tone, as we learn in Serrao's next letter, written only seven days later, covers the blackness of despair. After a quick filling in of the news – 'one God Damned thing after the other, with delays, postponements and an apparent freezing of things in the status quo. By this I mean no step forward, no step backward' – Seely writes, 'I wouldn't worry one minute about it all if it wasn't for Nellie. *She is feeling it more than she lets on*; I can't be with her all the time because I have got to be on the job.' He fills the letter with details that he doesn't want Shipman to know, peppering it with asides like 'this is strictly between you and me' and 'which I carefully refrained from imparting to Nell.' On top of all the delays, they had a visit from the twins (living with their father, Charles Ayers) for the first time in a very long while; 'everyone was terribly pleased wth the day, except for the terrific emotional impact of this first meeting with the kids, which left Nell like a rag.'[85]

The deal was acquiring lots of wrinkles, including 'a protective clause' in the Paramount release agreement 'in the form of a cancellation to be exercised by them upon the delivery of each picture as to the ones to follow.' Nevertheless, he writes, 'I want to tell you that there are no dangers, but that the time element may be affected by a matter of a few days.'[86]

June

Shipman's next letter repeatedly betrays her anxieties over 'the drastic bills, the stalls, the scrambling from day to day to keep alive and not let *them know* ... And I've been so terrified that because of the terrific strain we'd show our hand and kill the deal ... It's hard to chatter ... hard to keep waiting and not go quite nuts. Thank God for the penthouse! I don't leave its luxurious beauty from one week to another! Can't in fact because I am now, literally, *naked*! We're stalling on seeing Paramount (release) and Columbia (ditto) and the studio and everything, because I can't be visible! Isn't it silly? But it's just a matter of hours now. The ... money has got to come ... even a part of it will do! That's the awful part, waiting for such a slather of coin when we only need a few hundreds to start the merry old ball!'[87]

In the midst of despair and worry that 'Fear Market' might not go after all, Shipman has come up with a new idea, based on a headline story about Jewish refugees fleeing Germany but refused permission to land in the United States: 'I don't know if you read about the SS St Louis, the Refugee Ship sailing around off Havana and Miami, with 709 poor devils on board who might not land? It was front page stuff here, with editorials and pleas, and last minute tries to save the passengers from going back to their hell in Germany. Along with any warm hearted customer I got excited, of course, only I insisted there was a picture in it.' She calls it 'Blue Barriers'; she has pitched it to Republic already, who have turned it down: 'As usual the regular studios shy off. There is a claim that propaganda stories are not so hot.' But she has found a Jewish investor from the south who has hooked her up with a 'book-maker' who swears he'll find the money.[88]

But she cannot seem to shake her depression: 'The days have dragged through such agonies of waiting and worrying I haven't had the heart to write; also it has still been a moment to moment thing, with wires written out to you ready to send, etc. Then the mere business of trying to keep alive, dodge creditors, etc. ... all the regulation activities of the very broke ... have ground me down to being sick most of the time.'[89]

Evidently very worried, Serrao writes a quick note to Barry: 'I think that it would be a very good thing if you sat down and wrote Nell a little line – nothing special – just to say hello and tell her you still love her. She has been rather ill – but principally sad. Though she hasn't said so, I think she has missed your even occasional letter full of fun and wise cracks. As the above is the principal object of these lines I won't add more, other than to say that she is much better, but silent, and I think she wouldn't like it if she knew of this note. As to business – I won't say a word – and don't intend to, until there is something to actually announce.' In the next sentence, grim resignation darkens the tone: 'I am still of the same opinion I was when I induced Nell to leave L.A. and still determined that from the moment she left there, we would work out our own salvation – without crying to anyone anymore – something that you will admit, has been adhered to.'[90]

July

Although Barry has written and cheered his mother up a bit, she still writes 'I guess the whole strain has been too much for all of us, and we've been more than a little screwy. Also sick ... Just general nervous muss-muss.'[91] Suddenly, things seem to have turned around. 'Blue Barriers,' the idea for the film about the refugee ship, seems to be a green light. A certified cheque for 'eighty-one thousand bucks' is sitting in the bank, ready to be cashed on Monday. Out of this will come the company's share, but 'we [are] in business and the picture in the works.' Shipman writes that when Seely heard the news 'he sat down and bawled.' The deal had almost fallen through, but when the backers tried to pull out, Serrao made a speech and one 'very important lawyer' was so impressed that he 'jumped up and said he believed in the picture and if we needed more money he'd put in 5 G's. Whereupon, all in one movement, our promoter, our own especial gunman, our *Producer,* arose and hooked the offerer by his arm, led him out, got it in writing and raised the ante 2500.00 in the space of two minutes flat.' Shades of the bad old days of *The Grub-Stake* – and, in fact, nearly every other movie Shipman had ever made. But here they are now, with 'an amazing crew – a studio dug up over in New Jersey, which I go to "okey" and a long list of assistants, cam-era-men, a studio owner who turns out to be an old timer of the Ernie-Nellie era, ... a Lab which now is ours ... etc. etc. etc. In other words, all the hurly burly of a picture, albeit a shoestring pic, going into the works.' At the same time, on the other side of town, 'the final contracts are being drawn up for "Fear Market" and the no 2 picture.'[92]

Of course, there is 'yet another picture deal': 'we are always looking to the future, to bigger budgets, *and other units.* That is always in the back of my mind, and events seem to be shaping themselves in the way of willing backers, with liquid money, studios, labs, releases both major and astonishing States Right markets, etc. etc. I'm tipping you off to this thusness so you may note the straws in the wind, handwriting on the wall, etc. etc. And be certain that there is a future with a very large F.'[93]

The only thing still in the way is 'Seeley's domestic difficulties.' I am uncertain whether this refers to unpaid alimony, which Barry Shipman suggested was the reason for one of Serrao's aliases, or the Grover Lee trouble over debts. In any case, Shipman writes that she it going to 'doodle it [herself] and stall somebody else.'[94]

Three days later, she adds a handwritten postcript to the unmailed letter, dating it 6 July: 'It's been signed sealed & delivered at noon today – that is, "Blue Barriers." More news later.'[95] When the weekend arrives, they still do not have the money. No surprises there; but the letter conveys much stranger news: Shipman plans to cast the original Three Stooges as refugees! What has this socio-political human interest story turned into? Here is a hint: 'We are going to use the original Three Stooges and, in the ship's concert scene – before they get to where they don't land – I want them to do a Yiddisher Rhumba, one as a burlesque female with huge maracas (?), another with a comedy concertina and the third with a push cart which has a miramba [sic] in it.'[96]

Another week goes by, and they are going crazy. A very poignant letter at this point deserves a long quote. Shipman writes:

All the accumulation of strain piled up and up until I went nuts, literally, and we has quite a time. The thing was catapulted, oddly enough, not by phones getting shut off, penthouse owners howling or any of the other dozens of doings – I've got more or less used to them – but by the fact that on Tuesday we went over to see an old deserted barn of a studio in N.J. and I went overboard on its possibilities and pranced about for hours planning its immediate workings. Then some last minute troubles arose in the BB ['Blue Barriers'] company and I thought we'd lost the picture, and I worked myself up to believe the other was gone too, and suddenly realized that the sight – and potentiality – of that 'our own' studio had carried me back exactly fourteen years.

Everything that has passed in that time telescoped and I was exactly back at that moment when I lost everything ... animals, studio, pictures ... the 'Nell Shipman Prods' in other words ... and I suppose I realized at last that the broken heart had not really mended and the mere thought of once more seeing that lettering, and what it implies, was enough to wipe out all the years between. All I could see was Brownie pacing her cage in the dawn and Laddie leaping against the closed door.

So I do not need to tell you how sick I've been for the rest of the week.[97]

Inevitably more stalls characterized the 'Blue Barriers' deal. Shipman recounts many ups and downs, including the story of Serrao's meeting with the bookie who has taken over the financing: 'Seeley meets him a one o'clock ... at the Astor. (eat at the automat.) It's been pointed out, by us, that all the banks are now closed on Saturdays, soo ... but the gambling guy sez he don't deal in checks, but cold, hard, cash, dough or kale. Well, we'll see what we see. We've decided if it's a stall or a racket we'll make a deadline of eleven Monday morning and then wash it up.'[98] She has reached the limits of her endurance: 'I can't go any further or stand any more. It would be a terrible shame to lose the little picture ["Blue Barriers"], and the loss of the payment would be almost unbelievable. There isn't one cent of it now which is not mortgaged. But there is a limit to what endurance can stand and I think I've gone far beyond it.'[99]

Her tone cheers up considerably as she describes the New Jersey studio to Barry. This is typical Shipman: at the thought of production, she can catapult herself into the most material of dreams, charging through the practicalities one by one, figuring out how much they will cost, how problems will be solved.

> Now, about the studio. It's quite ideal ... I mean, for us ... It was built along in the twenties, I imagine, and soundproofed later. It's a solid three story steel concrete building which must have cost plenty ... Originally it had a complete lab, plus projection room, etc., so there is a great deal of space we'd use for scenario and art depts, etc. Also the familiar line of offices and a quite amazing dungeon of dressing rooms, below stage, also carpenter shops, lofts, prop rooms, etc. The stage, proofed within the original glass walls, is not very big, neither is it tiny. About the average Republic stage, and fairly high. There isn't anything in Fear Market we couldn't set up in it, except the old theater interior itself, and that we intend doing at one of the two dark houses over in New Jersey. Considering how long it's been

closed up ... it's in very good shape ... Everything stands ready for installation. I think five laborers for five days, plus lights and phone, would move us in ... I don't need to tell you what such a spot means to us and our plans![100]

'Fear Market' has also been through its vicissitudes, but now has a new financier, a bank owner who will complete the deal: 'The 1st of August is set as the probable time for this to happen.' She again mentions one of her other planned projects, 'Mother Liberty,' which she compares to the story of 'Blue Barriers,' 'maybe put ahead another ten years, so that it is twenty years ahead, with all the "world of tomorrow" doings, which is always so fascinating.' She plans a 'really great climax where they rally in the good old fashioned American way to save Ma Liberty.'[101]

'I've kept the enclosed open since its date,' she writes a week later, 'hoping every day would be the one, so I could really send it to you as "done." This Friday last was the climax. We'd been put off until Wednesday, then Friday morning, then it was to be Friday night, with the guy going in person to somebody in Philadelphia, to "collect." There wasn't any doubt as to this, it was overheard and witnessed. So that seemed the answer. We made our final plans, even went to the store to pick out the birthday present delayed since May 3rd. Everybody was to be paid, everything fixed. On Wednesday the owner of the penthouse came to put us out and I'd talked her into relenting, the Railway Express had been stalled for the last time – they've had six months of it! I'd planned a pair of shoes and stockings and some lipstick and powder ... and these are not symbolic, they are actual done without. I can, now, no longer go on the street and I haven't for six weeks! I'm not hollering, simply trying to tell you what the final and last promise meant. At Six o'clock Goldberg [the banker] came in and said it will be ten days before Miller (the gambler backer) can get his money. There was no use bawling, though I did, and have, since. I did the only thing I could, which was to take Refugee Ship ["Blue Barriers"] away from them. Because simple pride and business judgement says you can't let anyone push around a property like that forever.'[102]

Despite the disappointment, she is determined to keep the project alive: 'We must save Refugee Ship ["Blue Barriers"] because with the move the president has made to have all the nations confer in Sept.

upon the problem of what to do with the German Jewish refugees this subject is going to be the most valuable we've ever struck. The papers will be filled with it. He has already come out on the local front pages and named it the most burning issue of the year! And I, having known that all along, have been pushed around by tinhorn four-flushers!'[103] A sign of hope remains: 'Meanwhile a very nice gent was here from Texas, the head of the firm owning all the Texas theaters. He booked Blue Barriers into all his houses on description.'[104] Predictably, the Texan does not pan out. In his next letter, Serrao refers to him as 'the unspeakable little rodent.' He 'left for Texas on Monday night at 11.45. He was due there yesterday at four. I should have heard this morning from him, but haven't as yet.'[105]

Serrao has pressing business for Barry, who has now moved up to a contract with Universal. The finance company Serrao and Nell owe for the car are bothering Barry again. Barry must be pretty fed up by this time, and Serrao approaches him with extreme politeness: 'Now then, I am wondering if you would mind very much to contact the gentlemen from the Pacific Finance office (the one who phoned you or called on you before – I forgot which it was) and merely say that you have heard from us ... that the matter is not deliberately being allowed to lag ... and that a little time will be necessary to conclude all our business ... you can explain, please, just how God Damned unbelievably we have been stalled by men and fate ... and that though we will try our level best to clear the whole thing at once by the 6th of August (when the contract elapses) we certainly would do so, happily, if granted a little while longer – say another month on the contract ... What I am trying to avoid is that they take any action ... Under no circumstance would I advise that they know Nell's address.'[106]

Serrao encloses a carbon copy of a letter dated 10 July enclosing the final instalments ($134.50). He has been unable to mail it yet.

August

'We were so glad to get your long spec del last sunday. Were scared when it came, because the morning before had brought an attachment from the garage [where the car has been stored since February] on the car! ... I know it's been a helluva time since I wrote, but the struggle has been pretty desperate and there wasn't any news worth handing on; none that wasn't a prospective run around. So I just kept quiet. Also have been sick a lot ... Felt worse of course because I couldn't send a present for the First Birthday [of grandaughter Nina, Barry's child].'[107]

That was Shipman writing. Serrao also encloses a note. 'As to the Pacific Company, all I can say is that according to promises made to Nell and myself jointly and individually, we should have money paid over to us within a day from now on the little picture. And even regardless of this there are, as you know, other matters pending, So, keed, if they call you up assure them that they are not forgotten, and that they will get their dough pretty darned soon – maybe as they are even talking to you.'[108] Shipman writes that 'Fear Market' is still pending and should be shooting soon, but 'I've had to ditch Refugee Ship for the time; every body with cold feet. But I still want it. Also Tomorrow is Thunder has good prospects – Challenge to the Sun to follow. So it looks as if we might get eating again, let alone pay a few bills. Have been desperately worried about the car (Pacific) but hope we can send it tomorrow. We owe four months rent! ... Forgive the ragged letter. The typewriter is shot ... also the people want it back, or their money! Aren't people odd?'[109]

September

Another letter, headlined '*Highlights from the world of sports*,' comes in the form of a list:

> Item no. 1. Pic called 'Face on the Mountain' 1st of so called little pictures, four of which to be made for Monogram release. Pre-production started so far as rounding up camera eqip, cast, etc. Expect finances to be settled this week in which event you will be sent for willy-nelly. Monogram release effected at very good terms ... Four pics will be financed by first, and are to cover a year's time. Company to be 'Nell Shipman Pictures' and all are to be 'typical.'
>
> No 2. After weeks of hedging, and with the first checks actually signed, old puddin-face money bags decides to let loose on some of it next Tuesday. This starts 'Fear Market' on road to recovery.[110]

September's letters are concerned largely with the possibility of the

United States entering the war and on Barry's plans to join up, but Nell manages to throw in a report on 'Fear Market' and the new trends in movies during the war:

Fear Market. The pre-production agreement was signed by Seeley, acting for me, last Friday. Mr P was to sign it and accompanying checks, Tuesday, after the holiday. We got through the three days somehow. Then he was called to Washington on important business. He gets back today – another Friday. The checks, everything, is waiting for him. Included $1500 which, as I said, covers your trip and salary on the script. Incidentally he is trying to make us cut down the budget because of losing the foreign market. This has been combatted. It's scraping the bone now. First effect of the war will be that the title must go overboard. Judging by the past the box-office need will be for flashy excitement, lots of comedy, glitter and gaiety. Pictures to 'take you out of it and yourself.' War pictures, heavy emotional things (Wuthering Heights) will be out until it's over. Also screw ball pictures. They resent too giddy an attitude ... It's a ripe time for a big spectacle with gobs of girls and comedy, like 'Crazy with Tahiti.' Which we are going to push with all our might with Billy Rose and his aquacade. Over three million people have seen it at the Fair, and it's a hit. A great big luscious swimming picture would be elegant. He has already been tackled and I have hopes ... if we get behind it.

Fear Market, under another title, is safe. It's 'human,' has pace, is non-controversial ... Also good box-office is just such a 'little gem' as 'Face on the Mountain' the New Hampshire Idol [sic]. That has taken a distinct uptrend since I wrote. We have formed an alliance with an old showman very highly thought of in the business ... one of the papas of serials, by the way ... named Frank McConnell. He came to see me and, as usually seems to be the case when I can get at them (which makes this lost time through poverty so very cruel) went overboard. He is raising the greater part of the money and supplying the release, and the program calls for four of them over a year – all the same caliber. They will cost about $39,000. All this is about to be put in the bag, and would have been accomplished this week, if – damn his eyes – he had not gone for a voyage over the holiday, on his boat, with guests (all 'important') ... It's nice that we have a partner who is well off, has large boats, etc. ... but oh God what a time to do this to us! However, he hasn't been sunk, and he will be back.[111]

This letter also mentions her new invention, a coin slot purse 'and other gadgets' attached to an umbrella handle. She calls it the 'Chamberlain Bank' after the umbrellas known as Chamberlains (named for the British prime minister, Neville Chamberlain) that have become so popular in the early days of the war. They have met 'and are doing biz with a man very close to all high and mighties of departments stores, related to Gimbels, Sax [sic], Bonwit Teller, etc. On a try, Seeley took it to him and he went nuts! He, in turn, takes it to a manufacturer of novelties and he goes nuts. They believe there is a real fortune in it! Of course they don't know we are broke and they've kicked it back to be patented by me, for my own protection.' The only impediment: 'we are held up for ten dollars to give to the artist for materials' to draw an illustration for the patent application.'[112]

Meanwhile, the money troubles continue to pile up: 'The owner of the penthouse came in yesterday, and we could face her frankly, she has been so amazingly kind. We owe her four months rent and she is letting us have the place for an extra [month] over the lease; all I guess because she "has faith." She sent me a ten spot one time, because she had just read the Atlantic Mag and was filled with admiration, or something. Anyway, its [sic] extra-ordinary that some funny elderly females have kept us alive ... nearly so. I'm sicker than I like Seeley to know, and very worried about it. It doesn't seem now to be something good news, food and a chance to go out on the street again will fix.'[113]

October

Headed 'Oct 1 (hurrah; our good month!),' Shipman's letter begins 'Was a bit too optimistic in last and, really, all of it was a bit too good! The situation has not changed, however, only its complexion and certain frontiers. MGM did not buy Refugee Ship. They all but did, at, probably 15,000 (wow) then discovered the West had bought "Flotsam" (Collier serial and important novel) and they'd bought "Escape" (Sat Eve Post and best seller) and also "Reaching for the Stars," all of these tremendously expensive properties and all anti-Nazi! ... Paramount turned it down without comment ... Columbia and Universal seem the liveliest bets. Both are waiting on the Coast.'[114]

On the umbrella front: 'The Chamberlain Bank umbrellas are waiting our finding a few dollars to start the patent hunt and finish the models. Then the largest umbrella mfg in U.S. is ready to dicker, on a royalty basis. Everybody thinks they are a knockout. I got scared of having the thing stolen as too many lawyers began to mix in it, so I simply had it said we were arranging the patents and models ourselves ... *meaning we will do so soon as we can.*'[115]

'Fear Market' is still hopeful: 'Downtown (Fear Market) stalled all week and we nearly went nuts, ... plus pennilessness and general starvation. Finally we said "do or die," "Fish or cut bait" and "... or get off the pot ..." taking a long chance that the duck would get sore and dump the deal, and our 184,000.00 bucks backing. He didn't. They swear they will get the first of the checks (they are divided in *four*, the 1500.00 for your services among them) tomorrow. This will start umbrellas, pay worst bills, buy me clothes so I can be seen, etc. It is very necessary I be visible!'[116]

As for the 'little pictures' and the connection with Frank McConnell (whom she refers to here as Fred J. McConnell) for the New Hampshire movie, 'They have had a hard time raising that initial $15,000. All week went by in meetings, strivings, missed dates and general damp drawers and what I now call Khaki Kaps ... you know, scooping up handfuls of it and plastering it on your head and letting it trickle in brown streams of remorse and woe ... But the old man (Fred J. McConnell) vows it will be in by Wednesday. He already has the release, the bank loan and the lab ditto.'[117]

'Meanwhile, over this week end, I've thrown a monkey wrench by deciding I will not make 'Face on the Mountain' as the first pic. This will cause a riot as they are all fearfully sold on it and it is pretty nice. But I am determined that if we are to make these "little" pictures they are to have something to set them apart from poverty row and Class C quickies. Only the budget is to be low. We must make them sincere, realistic, on the spot, without faking. Real "Nell Shipman's." As the weather got worse and the time more limited, Mac began swinging Process shots and going down to Virginia at me ... all the good old fakes. I fell for a few days then went back on my heels and have, now, thundered my "no." "Face" must wait until Spring. We must go up there to the Gap, the lake, river, farmhouses, elms, wells, stonewalls, birch groves, etc. mitt company, and really make a New Hampshire picture ... yaaas ...'[118]

Barry has sent Shipman a cheque for $25 for her birthday. She greets it with ecstatic gratitude: 'That was a very sweet and dear of you. I was terribly glad to get a letter, not having heard in ages, and when I opened it and found the checkles [cheque] I was werry werry pleased and happy. Indeed and indeed on Wednesday ... eatings ... drinkings ... poopings, the finger rampant! And there will be a real reason! On Tuesday Pop goes up to Poughkeepsie, (now the banking scene of our future) and gets the check, the cash, the mazuma, the dough, the *first* advance on Fear Market! Actually and really and I do not believe anything can stop it now. That was another reason why it was so wonderful getting the twenty-five! We didn't know quite how to get over until Wednesday! Now we can pay some bothering small bills and eat! *But* on Wednesday, I promise, the twenty-five will be re-possessed and spent on Whoopee! I think we will get very very drunk. What a birthday!'[119]

She is still hoping that 'Fear Market' will come through and that Barry will work on it with her: 'You see, the Tuesday money includes your fare and salary (four weeks) for Fear Market. The incorporation will be through in about ten days from then, with the balance of the money for the production ... $118,000.00. The deal is greatly changed over all these weeks, new faces, new money, ... but we come out the same ... and that we do come out, plus two pictures, and after this unchristly wait, is all due to the little man who has negotiated it every foot of the way and picked it up from the pavement every time it fell down.'[120] This optimism is mitigated later in the letter: 'Have been terribly sick ... for quite a long time. Flu and a nervous breakdown and things. Oh, quite awful. Am still not very well and that worries me because, suddenly, the load becomes terrific. But we'll manage! We must ... now!'[121]

A week later she writes again: 'This isn't whistling in the dark – everything is absolutely alright. But the pay-off didn't come on Tuesday, nor any of the following days, so I couldn't wire you, nor phone. There being no pennies, and the phone out of commission. It did seem that yesterday or today would deliver the check to us – it is signed and ready – but it couldn't be done. But we are sure Monday will do it. If it doesn't we will know just *when*. The deal is as good as gold and we are not being kidded, though it would certainly seem to anyone on the outside. And it's damned hard to explain to landladies and creditors!'[122]

In the previous letter she had mentioned a four-picture release deal with Grand National, but now there is another update: 'The four picture deal has been removed (again) from Grand National, who have gone broke (again) and been taken back to Monogram under the most astounding circumstances. I can't go into it in detail but it amounts to this – the U.S. Government loans Monogram a lot of $$$ so that they, in turn, finance us for the four pictures. This sounded so screwball and wild I couldn't believe it, but it's true. It turns out easier to get one or two hundred thousand than our pathetic little twenties! Soooooo! Having got on the inside track ... do not be surprised if you find us with some such picture as "Cinderella Town" completely financed, to follow Fear Market!'[123]

She had hoped to send a birthday present for Barry's wife, along with the $40 to get her typewriter out of hock, and the payments to Pacific Finance for the car, but these had to wait. Moreover, they have to move again: 'Will be leaving our beautiful prison penthouse on the 3rd. We owe, today, 500.00 in rent! Was there ever a more wonderful landlady? Thank God she'll get it!'[124]

November

'Just a note, the last on this machine! Am in a welter of packing because we have to give up the place on Friday. Don't know exactly where we'll go to hide until the tide turns but imagine it will be the old "Holland Hotel" West 42nd – because they know us and won't jump an advance rent.'[125] The typewriter died that day, in mid-sentence, and the letter is handwritten starting in the middle of the third sentence. The subsequent letters are written by hand, some of them in pencil.

A last-minute reprieve allows them to stay on at the penthouse: 'We are still at 200 W. 16th. The good angel owner is letting us stay until the 15th so we can get out of our miseries and not be "on the street." She has taken our note for the rent – $575.00! There are some wonderful people in the world.'[126]

In the next letter, Shipman voices, for the first time, the possibility that she might leave the film industry: 'For three days it all looked pretty awful and we nearly threw in the sponge, but Seely has snapped back again and is going strong while even I am forced to admit it's okay. If *it doesn't* – I mean in the last imaginable catastrophe, – then I am determined to drop out for keeps.'[127] Still, she does not imagine that the deal will fail. They have so many irons in the fire, something must come

The old typewriter pooped out!

[? Oct 1939 # 5]

Wednesday

Dearest

Just a note, the last on this machine ! Am in a welter of
packing because we have to give up the place on Friday. Don't
know exactly where we'll go to hide until the tide turns but imagine
it will be the old "Holland Hotel" West 42nd -
because they know us and won't jump an absence
rent. But— I'll drop you a line Friday night or,
if the news is good, will wire. I have put in
a dreadful week of waiting and now Callender
has followed Ingram to Albany where, tonight,
they are seeing the Lieutenant-Governor, to get the
money straightened out. Fortunately for us McG
has to have it or sink. I haven't a doubt
we'll get it and everything will be okay.
Further finance is being arranged to follow.
Jean Market, and Cinderella Town is the story.
Everything is just as I wrote you, only this
last damnable delay. Am heavily hurt but
sure you are riding it ease out there — I mean
that you are letting Nature take its course and
keeping on at O until you get the word
(and money) to jump.

Poor Luella (Sealy's mother) operated on today
for cancer of the breast. She's 76! It's only a
50/50 chance for her to pull through. This
heart helped! But will pull out, Bimbo. Days

ahead —
All my love,
Nell

'The old typewriter pooped out!'

through. For now, they have to move from the penthouse, as the land-lady's patience has finally expired. 'Have to leave here on Saturday morning and can be reached at the *Brevoort Hotel*, Fifth Avenue. We can get a room there until the storm blows over and then do better, I mean get better rooms.' She is still writing by hand: 'Sorry to still be writing by hand, but we are minus typewriter now as well as most everything else including eats.'[128]

Two days later, she is excited again about all the projects working out, money coming in, and Barry coming to work with her. The line-up of projects has changed somewhat, with a new project, 'One More Moon,' as the first one to be made with financing from local money and loans: 'This letter is more incoherent than I am if possible, but I'm pretty God Damn excited. I shall not even try to tell you the line-up because I can't even read my own writing, let alone eat, but it begins this way: "One More Moon" (fast as possible – $69,000 up next week); "Cinderella Town!!!" (immediately after – $125–$130,000.); "Fear Market" (In the early spring $125,000).'[129]

She promises – again – to send the $40 for the typewriter and the $134.50 for the car payments, as well as $200 for Barry as an advance on his salary and to pay for his trip east: 'You may have to come by train to save pennies but I hope not because, if it's by air, you could be here by Friday or Saturday. *If* it's by air you can ship the typewriter *if* it makes your baggage too heavy.'[130]

Still writing by hand, two weeks later Shipman thanks Barry for 'the 2 bucks.' They have spent it 'killing times at movies' to take their minds off their problems. But today is the day: 'Today, at 1:30, what seems to be the last of the Wolf of Wall Street meetings takes place and of course we are on the qui vive, whatever that is ... The finance now is for four pictures: "One More Moon," "Fear market," "Cinderella Town," "Challenge to the Sun" at different budgets ranging from 50, to 150,000. And it is understood that the arrangement goes on year by year – if – The option still holds on the Biograph Studios on a flat rental.'[131] She also holds out hope for a radio drama version of 'Jungle Ship': 'one of the brokers, our pet, has personally taken over "Jungle Ship" for the air. That is he will finance the recording job personally and we will sell it as a completed serial ... I am going to try and do an "Orson Welles" on it and both narrate and act.'[132]

December

'Today's interview took only 25 minutes & was apparently a new formality, all "business" having been done. This afternoon there is one more
meeting with a man who is supposed to put the "okey" upon the literary
side of it: read the scripts, etc. But he is an old picture man, married to a
one-time star, and a close personal friend of our broker's, so I think we
will pass. Anyway noone has ever thought the stories, particularly F.M.
[Fear Market], anything but "great." Apparently our endorsement from
inside the business has been 100%, which is consoling. No good saying
"how long" the technical formation of "Amelco" will take but it is understood it's to be fact. Meanwhile the money for making the radio things
may show up early next week. Oddity: the name of the firm putting up
the picture finance is Jos. Walker!'[133]

This last piece of news deserves some comment, although Shipman
does not choose to make any, undoubtedly because the import of the
name 'Jos. Walker' would be so well understood between Shipman and
her son that no elaboration would be necessary. But this 'oddity' says a
great deal not only about Shipman and the loyalty her friend felt for
her, but also about Joseph Walker's current status and his memories of
the person who gave him his start. Walker had become one of the top
cinematographers in Hollywood. Since he had last worked with Shipman on *The Grub-Stake* (1923), he had shot nearly one hundred films,
including many directed by Frank Capra and Howard Hawks (*Mr Deeds
Goes to Town*, 1936; *Lost Horizon*, 1937; *You Can't Take It With You*, 1938;
Only Angels Have Wings, 1939; *Mr Smith Goes to Washington*, 1939) and
numerous other hit films by major directors. He would continue shooting until 1952, by which time he had completed 142 films.

In her earlier letters, Shipman had not mentioned Walker as part of
the financing arrangements, so we have to assume that she did not contact him herself. With all the shopping of the projects from studio to studio, Walker must have learned of Shipman's straits and voluntarily
stepped in to help. Good for him. Doubly good for him: he does not
mention this kindness in his autobiography, although he devotes several
chapters to Shipman.

In the last letter of the year, Shipman writes,

It seems we must be done with 1939! What an awful year it has been for everybody in the world! It will be over soon, thank god! Well I think I can tell you safely that the new company is over the top yesterday, at six, we got the confirmation that the final wrinkles had been ironed out and the 'group' stood ready to finance the five pictures 100%. Two things only stood in the way: they must see evidence of Distribution before their money goes over the counter and 'if the U.S. goes to war they withdraw their support' ... The 'war' stipulation scares me but I cannot believe that will happen, at least not in years.

You will notice I said 5 pictures (if you can read this, which I hope you can!) ... I feel keenly that at the end of this dreadful struggle we have got real, solid backing and we must put all our weight into producing for that backing, and not scatter.

This situation is and has been quite unbelievable. We've lived on sandwiches brought in and coffee, I've had to accept a hand me down coat because I was afraid of pneumonia, now I can't go on the street any more for lack of shoes and stockings. It's hard to explain to business people! Already it's been asked 'Are these out at the elbow Producers?'

We've pawned everything in sight and sold books to keep eating, the hotel has carried us three weeks ... Somehow we've managed to share the sandwiches with actors and cameramen who look to us for future jobs. A good many times it has become so black we could not see light, but we are still alive – and we have our deal!

Only one man closely connected with the financial side of the deal knows the truth of our situation and he is as broke! But he is in the throes of selling 5 million barrels of oil to the British G. at $1 per barrel. He will help, out of his commission, and will also put up $5,000 for us to make all the platters for 'Jungle Ship.'[134]

In April 1940, Shipman writes to Barry on her new letterhead. Handsomely designed, it trumpets 'Nell Shipman Enterprises' across the top, and a bar down the side reads 'Presenting Jungle Ship, a Nell Shipman Production.' The address is 117 East 24th Street, New York, N.Y., but Shipman says in the letter that the address belongs to 'an angel' who has paid for the letterhead and lent her a typewriter.[135]

Jungle Ship, the radio drama that had started its life as a film project at least five years earlier,[136] is the only one of the projects discussed in Shipman's letters from 1939 that was ever completed. Financed by the 'angel,' a 'preview recording' of a reading of portions of *Jungle Ship*, on a huge sixteen-inch record dated 1945, resides in the Boise University Archives. The record was made by Columbia Recording Corporation, a subsidiary of CBS. There is no evidence that it was ever broadcast.

Post Script

I chose 1939 almost arbitrarily as a year of letters to be excerpted. It had been fifteen years since Nell Shipman Productions went bankrupt, and ten years since she had sold a script (*Wings in the Dark*, for which she received no credit). Any one of the dozens of letter files stored in the Boise University Archives Special Collections might have done just as well. Shipman wrote letters incessantly, even when she was down to old production call sheets for stationery, and she seemed to find money for stamps despite near starvation and sometimes homelessness. The news is nearly always the same – of projects floating and falling.

In these excerpts from the 1939 letters, I have excised the personal news – of the twins, who live with their father, Charles Ayers, and his new wife; of relatives and friends; new babies; illness. This is, after all, a working biography. What remain here are her heroic displays of (at times, delusional) optimism, her lively wit and imagination, and her constant attempts to reinstate herself in the film industry.

:: :: :: :: ::

chapter nine

Naked on the Palisades

Shipman's efforts to make it back into the movie industry never ended. Shipman and Serrao ceaselessly planned and attempted to flog projects, trying to get back into the industry. Barry continued to send them money, and Shipman and Serrao continued to move. There were times when they lived in the dark because the electricity bills remained unpaid, pawned borrowed jewellery ('Two dollars worth!') so they could eat, or rode 'the subway [at] nights because there was no sleeping place.'[1] But the projects for movies, television, radio, and theatre kept being written and the deals kept falling through.

The Clam-Digger's Daughter

In all these years of effort, Shipman succeeded in getting only one film made, *The Clam-Digger's Daughter* (1947), also known as *The Story of Mr Hobbs*.[2] Discovered recently in a British private collection, it now resides at the British Film Institute, missing the final reel.

The film hinges on an ecological disaster involving the erosion of the clam-beds in the absence of a breakwater. We must assume that this regional story set in Charles Bay, Virginia, is typical of the projects that Shipman and Serrao tried to sell to local investors as the couple boomeranged around the United States. The scenario that Shipman wrote involved a bitter old clam-digger whose livelihood was literally being washed away, his feisty daughter, a millionaire who owns a holiday home in the idyllic ocean location but has no care for the well-being of the local inhabitants, and a Latin American villain from a military dictatorship.

Although the directing and producing credits go to Lorenzo Alagio[3] and John M. McCool respectively, the film bears every trace of a Shipman project. First of all, there is the tell-tale family situation of the missing mother and the tomboy heroine. Mr Hobbs, the clam-digger, is very tight with his daughter, who is named Timothy – Timmy – because he wished she had been born a boy. He has taught her to fish and to clam, and she is a modern woman, laughing in a wind-blown close-up, wearing a striped tee-shirt and jeans with a rope for a belt. She is a girl 'with a love-song on her lips' (voice-over) because her sweetheart, Bob, is coming home from the war. Predictably, for Shipman, oedipal tensions cloud the homecoming scene as the boyfriend admits he would 'rather meet a Kraut tank head on' than her father.

The early scenes develop around the middle-class aspirations of the boyfriend, which clash with the father's passionate commitment to the local shellfish economy and his desires for his daughter to carry on the family occupation. With music swelling in the background, the father makes one of Shipman's 'sockeroo' speeches: 'That ocean, that miserable, cruel, greedy-gutted old man ocean, eatin' and eatin' and never satisfied, gnawin' at the land, tearin' it off in hunks and chunks, takin' away my island' – here his fist pounds his chest dramatically – 'I'm tellin' you I'd stop that ocean with my bare hands if I could, I'd stop it with my body' – choking – 'I'd lay down my bones and build me a fence if that way I could stop that devil ocean, that devil ocean.' And the soundtrack music swells to a climax.

The father has already tried to get the millionaire who owns the beachhouse to lend him the money – only $18,000 – to build a jetty to protect the island. But the rich man does not care. And now the clam-digger's daughter has a boyfriend who also does not care about the ocean and the fishery, who wants to make his career as a newspaper reporter and to use Pa's boat for tourist excursion trips.

Enter the Latin American villain, pitching the rich man for a $50 million loan for his army to stop the revolution in his country. When Timmy comes up against the millionaire's bodyguard, who has already punched Bob in an earlier encounter, Timmy – a genuine Shipman heroine – stands up to him, declaring 'Nobody is going to hit nobody I love.' They are run off the property. Bob – a typical Shipman hero – is about to give up, but Timmy is determined to save the day: 'There's more than one way to dig a clam or get a story.' Timmy is not only the more tenacious of the couple in the struggle, but she is also the sexual aggressor, cajoling Bob with enticements like 'Bob, honey, I heard tell that lovers could live on kisses.'

Crazed with anguish, Mr Hobbs kidnaps the millionaire in his boat, planning to murder him for revenge. Luckily, in a triumph of sisterhood, Timmy enlists the millionaire's wife in the rescue, and elicits a promise that her husband will pay for the needed jetty. The build-up to the climax involves Mr Hobbs's ensnaring the millionaire in a fishing net to trap him in a room that is going to be underwater at high tide. Meanwhile Timmy is on the way to the rescue, with some comic scenes to delay the climax: the boat running aground and the rich man's seasick bodyguard sinking up to his knees in the mud and moaning 'Why did I ever leave Brooklyn?'

Because the last reel is missing, the film cuts out abruptly, but the conclusion is predictable: Timmy will arrive just in time to prevent her father from becoming a murderer, and the rich man's wife will see to it that her husband puts up the money to save the clam-beds. It is not hard to guess what will happen to the Latin American from the military dictatorship; Shipman's postwar patriotism and sense of democracy, combined with the uninterrogated racism that permeated American culture, surely would have sent the mustachioed villain packing.

One of the more interesting features of this film is that Carreras, the Latin American fighting against the revolution, is played by 'Arthur Varney' – Amerigo Serrao. A heavy-set man, with dark hair receding at the temples and a big (fake?) moustache, smoking and speaking with a thick accent, he does a nice piece of broad comic acting. Shipman doesn't appear in the film.

Shot in black and white on a clearly minimal budget, the film has many scenes without sound effects, some post-dubbed scenes that are out of synchronization, local amateur actors,[4] almost exclusively outdoor location shooting, and other scenes shot with direct sound with unseen boats going by. It is the sort of movie that might have played on the B or C distribution circuit, along with low-budget films that are now cult classics such as *Detour* (d. Edgar G. Ulmer, 1945). As much like a silent movie as a late-forties production, with music that soars, swells, and 'mickey mouses' throughout and visual devices such as wipes and irises providing transitions, the movie suggests that Shipman remained embedded in her silent period formation.

The End of the Trail

Shipman and Serrao continued to move around the United States together until sometime in the 1950s, when they went their separate ways.

Late in her life, Shipman's son Barry notified her of the Motion Picture Relief Fund, an organization that assisted veterans of the film industry. Shipman wrote the organization a letter 'for the sake of a future,' although she assured them that she was 'not sick but so healthy it's shameful. Can still ride, swim, walk and work harder and faster than most juniors half my age ... Also, having since the "silent days" turned, first, writer, then independent producer, then back again to free-lance writer, am up to my whitened locks in projects it seems obscene to shelve and just to sit in the sun!'[5]

She has heard that the Relief Fund would 'help without one going to the House; in other words, staying available and doing business ... And that one may return this providential loan to the Fund.' She decries 'this horrible necessity of eating,' and hopes they will help her with a 'refundable loan.' Because she is living in New York at the time, she floats the possibility of coming to the coast, positing that 'once back there again I might intrigue an Agent into doing a spot of work for an old-timer. I still have my acting-pants handy and a make-up box alongside my work-worn typewriter.'[6]

According to Barry, the Relief Fund found that there was 'not enough information' in her letter. He counselled her to send them a 'date-by-date-name-by-name-pix-by-pix chronology,' to 'smash 'em with a backlog of pioneering movie work that should set 'em back on their rockers.' She should mention 'the Vitagraph period in detail,' the independent work, the book writing, titles of projects, dates, efforts, publications, 'all aimed at come-back and picture business.' He reminds her that she 'also lived – eked-out is the word – by selling quickie scripts to poverty road characters under other names (make up a few) ... Meanwhile the big picture never faded ... Plays ... Musicals ... Try-outs ... Interviews ... Encouragement to other thesps and writers' (ellipses in original). And he warns her: 'Don't DON'T – say anything that can be checked out differently.' Barry's advice concludes: 'Make it a document of brief, telling fact and dramatic understatement. It will be read to a board. Make 'em shit their pants!'[7]

In July 1963, Beatta Quinn, Social Welfare Department, Motion Picture Relief Fund, Inc., responded to Shipman's 'brochure.' Mentioning that for twelve years Shipman had written, directed, and acted in films (1912–24), Quinn writes: 'With the exception of 1929, when you wrote "Wings in the Dark" ... we cannot see where you had any further association with the motion picture industry ... We regret that you do not meet our eligibility requirements.'[8]

So perhaps this story of Nell Shipman's working life is a weepie after all. One friend, a colleague who read the manuscript, wailed that she was in tears at the Relief Fund story. Damn right. When I started this book, I told several people about this letter. One writer advised me to begin the book with it, even though Shipman would have been horrified at the thought of giving away the ending at the outset. Although Shipman's scenarios always ended with the triumphant heroine getting everything she wanted, I always thought I should end her story with that bleak bureaucratic dismissal: 'We regret that you do not meet [the Motion Picture Relief Fund] eligibility requirements.' Melodramatic adventure though it may be, her own life did not have a happy ending.

In the last moments of writing, however, I knew it was wrong both ways. This is just not the sort of scenario that Shipman would appreciate.

Here is the real ending.

True to her scripts and novels, Shipman – like her own heroines – was not in the least bit daunted by this setback. For the rest of her life, she kept tenaciously, and as obsessively as ever, shopping projects. In 1967, three years before her death, she conceived a 'multi-projected film plus live on-stage performance' complete with 'Aquadrome' that would celebrate the Southern Pacific Centennial with a pageant representing the upheaval of 'The Golden Pass,' from 'the bowels of the earth' – in animation – and then 'how man came, 25,000 years ago, of the aborigines and their life in the ... bountiful valleys of the sun, of the first white explorers, the prospectors, hunters, pioneers ... the first break-through over the impossible road between Banning, Cabazon[9] and Whitewater Station ... and then the coming of the Rails ... In the finale of the show we see the Legend of the Pass as it is lived today ... all that is modern in the development of the communities where the people are dedicated to the "golden life."'[10]

At the age of seventy-five, Shipman still had an agent who was sending out her proposals. In one letter, to the Beverly Hills office of William Morris, the agent notes that a script for 'The Catnip Mouse' was intended for Jack Lemmon, although Bob Hope and Phyllis Diller 'could be integrated also.'[11] The agent also had at least two other Shipman scripts.

A letter from the agent makes it very clear that Shipman is being a bit too high-handed in her expectations and demands: 'You have hinted that you want a big agent to handle CATNIP, etc. Well, you are welcome! I do not care! ... I'm not a fool, Nell.'[12] Still generating scripts, Shipman was as active – and apparently as feisty – as ever.

Shipman moved to a little house in Cabazon, California, where she lived, 'broke to the wide,' with a malamute dog and dozens of stray cats. A visit from Barry and his wife set the wheels of a new writing project in motion, the memoir that would become *The Silent Screen and My Talking Heart*. Although she was spurred by reading the manuscript for *Lionhead Lodge* written by Lloyd Peters, her 'little ex-carpenter from Spokane days,'[13] Shipman took some persuading to write her own story: she had too much on her plate; she was just too busy. With two typewriters in the house '(in case one broke down), and reams of script and carbon paper,'[14] her writing schedule was dedicated to a 'borderline' series, 'Stories of the Northwest High Frontier.' Besides, she wrote, 'there have been too many [memoirs of the silent period] already and, I think, it's all so old hat. Who cares?'[15] Nevertheless, she started writing the manuscript, partly with the idea that she could sell along with it 'a reprint of the only thing [she] ever did like, a children's fairy story, based on a pitiful attempt ... to make a short film on zero-plus money. The last effort of the dying swan.'[16] When she got down to it, though, she mapped out three or four books, with the last two titled '"Tissue-Paper Tower" (come-back failures, complete loss, and the death of a partner) and, finally, "Naked on the Palisades."'[17] She got only the first volume finished, the chronicle that ends in 1925. *The Silent Screen and My Talking Heart* was finished by February 1969, although it was not published in her lifetime.

Nell Shipman died 23 January 1970.

'Your Nell heists [*sic*] one as Simka looks on' – 1969 snapshot, autographed for Gordon Sparling.

The Sound of the Silent Voice

This portrait of Nell Shipman at work is as close as I can get it. But still not quite, not quite complete.

Missing from this picture is her speaking voice. For although we have her body on the screen and in the holes in the paper, the cinema she inhabited was silent. She does not appear in her only extant sound movie. We have her 'voice,' of course, in the intertitles of the films, which serve invariably as her point of enunciation, and in the novels, letters, and autobiography. That literary voice is consistently as robust and vigorous as the body that she displays onscreen. Given to describing herself with heroic hyperbole as well as self-reflexive irony, she performs herself for the reader in colloquialisms and slang. She confesses to loving a smutty joke, and renders her own self-evaluation in parodic phrases, such as 'Head for the barn, Nellie!' She refers to herself as an 'outdoors gal' and contemplates her ample 'Barham bottom' with rueful and realistic indulgence. In the novels, the narrational voice is often that of melodramatic lyricism, while she takes on an exuberant diversity of direct address modes, from a Scottish burr or a Metis patois to a 'proper English' grammar. From her letters especially, full of short-form endearments – she addressed her son with variations of Barry such as Barax and pet names from Woozle to Woozlet – one has the sense of her being just like the character that she constructs for herself in the films: a kind of slangy, western, natural woman imbued with the forthright casual self-confidence of modernity.

It is rather a shock to hear her speaking voice, on an audio tape recorded by her son Barry – albeit when she was of considerable age and reciting a children's story for her great-grandchildren.[18] At the same time as one hears the careful enunciation of the actorish habit at the coming of sound, one remembers that she came from British stock of which she was immensely proud and was raised in Victoria, BC, a British enclave at the time and still the place to take high tea and a walk in the rose gardens.

Hearing her speak, her schoolmarmish well-modulated voice carefully enunciating every phrase, projects us into a new understanding. Her filmic, literary, and familial voice seems, retrospectively – in contrast to her speaking voice – to be a modernist self-construction. In her literary and filmic voice, she is performing herself in a new guise, departing from her Victorian heritage and throwing herself vigorously into a new world in a performance of modernity at its most optimistic measure.

In Nell Shipman's time, a little less than 20 per cent of automobile drivers were women. Still less than that proportion were the film producers/directors/writers who were women. Nevertheless, there was a critical mass of women doing those jobs, aware of each other – even if geographically isolated, as Nell Shipman was – and feeling 'ordinary' about their lives. They were not ahead of their time, unique, extraordinary, or superwomen. They were, I am convinced, like the many of us who are still confronting, even in 2003, the hopes and failures of modernity and the possibilities of a satisfactory life for women.

In 2003, only about 20 per cent of university professors are women. Nevertheless there is a critical mass of women scholars who are researching women filmmakers of the silent era. And the feeling among us is that we are not alone, that we are not unique or isolated, that we have friends and colleagues. In our domestic lives, we may make donuts, install light fixtures, raise children, build stone walls, and repair our cars, just as Shipman did.

And this is finally the body that we embrace – a body that braved the new world of modernity, took on technology, responsibility, solitude, and the vicissitudes of aspiration for reciprocity in partnerships, social equality, economic independence, and career satisfaction. Through her self-representation on the screen, through her voice on an audio-tape, through the archive, through those holes in the paper, Nell Shipman touches me.

appendix a

::   ::   ::   ::   ::

Biographical Timeline

1892 – 25 October, born Helen Foster Barham in Victoria, British Columbia
1904 – family moves to Seattle, Washinton
     – takes acting lessons at a local drama school
1905 – joins touring vaudeville group
1910 – 25 August, marries Canadian-born Ernest Shipman; moves to California
1912 – while pregnant, begins to write about films
     – 24 February, son Barry is born
     – begins to act in movies
1913 – writes and stars in *The Ball of Yarn*
     – writes *Outwitted by Billy* and *One Hundred Years of Mormonism*
1914 – directs her first one-reeler, possibly *Outwitted by Billy*
     – writes *The Shepherd of the Southern Cross*
1915 – writes scenarios for *The Widow's Secret, The Pine's Revenge,* and *Under the Crescent*
     – publishes a novelized version of *Under the Crescent*
1916 – stars in *God's Country and the Woman*
     – stars in *The Fires of Conscience* and *Through the Wall*
     – writes and stars in *The Melody of Love*
     – writes scenario for *Son o' the Stars*
1917 – stars in *The Black Wolf*
     – writes scenario for *My Fighting Gentleman*
     – turns down seven-year contract with Goldwyn
1918 – January, stars in *The Wild Strain*
     – May, stars in *Baree, Son of Kazan*
     – July, stars in *A Gentleman's Agreement*
     – stars in *The Girl from Beyond, The Home Trail,* and *Cavanaugh of the Forest Rangers*

1919 – adapts and stars in *Back to God's Country*
       – returns to California, living with Bert Van Tuyle and son Barry
1920 – 10 May, divorces Ernest Shipman
       – writes, stars in, and directs *Trail of the Arrow* and *Something New*
1921 – launches Nell Shipman Productions
       – writes, directs, produces, and stars in *The Girl from God's Country*
1922 – moves to Priest Lake, Idaho, with Barry, Bert, and the zoo of wild
         animals
1923 – writes, directs, produces, and stars in *The Grub-Stake*
       – writes, directs, produces, and stars in a series of short films, *Little Dramas
         of the Big Places*, of which only *Trail of the North Wind* and *The Light on
         Lookout* are extant
1924 – writes, directs, produces, and stars in another short film, *White Water*,
         which is also extant
       – separates from Bert Van Tuyle
       – Nell Shipman Productions goes bankrupt
       – leaves Priest Lake with Barry, first for Seattle and eventually for New
         York, where she meets artist Charles Ayers
1925 – marries Charles Ayers; goes to Spain
1926 – twins Daphne and Charles born 3 May in Spain
1931 – 7 August, Ernest Shipman dies in New York
1934 – separates from Charles Ayers
1935 – falls in love with Amerigo Serrao (aka Arthur Varney, Grover Lee, and
         Peter Locke)
       – writes story (uncredited) for *Wings in the Dark*
1947 – writes, directs, and produces (uncredited) *The Clam-Digger's Daughter* /
         The Story of Mr Hobbs in Charles Bay, Virginia
1950s – Nell and Amerigo Serrao separate
1960 – Amerigo Serrao dies
1964 – Charles Ayers dies
1970 – 23 January, Nell Shipman dies in Cabazon, California
1994 – 12 August, Barry Shipman dies in San Bernardino, California

⠃⠃   ⠃⠃   ⠃⠃   ⠃⠃   ⠃⠃

Known Nell Shipman Filmography

1913 – *The Ball of Yarn* (d. Norval MacGregor, sc. Shipman; stars Shipman)
  – *Outwitted by Billy* (d. Edward Le Saint, sc. Shipman; Selig Polyscope Company)
  – *One Hundred Years of Mormonism* (d. Norval MacGregor, sc. Shipman)
1914 – *The Shepherd of the Southern Cross* (d. Alexander Butler, sc. Shipman; produced in Australia)
1915 – *The Widow's Secret* (d. J. Warren Kerrigan, scenario by Shipman; cast includes Barry Shipman)
  – *The Pine's Revenge* (d. Joseph De Grasse, scenario by Shipman)
  – *Under the Crescent* (d. Burton L. King, scenario by Shipman, starring Ola Humphrey; Universal), a series of six two-reelers
1916 – *God's Country and the Woman* (d. Rollin S. Sturgeon, adapted from James Oliver Curwood novel by Agnes Christine Johnston; stars Shipman; Vitagraph;)
  – *The Fires of Conscience* (d. Oscar Apfel, sc. Henry Christeen Warnack; stars Shipman; Vitagraph)
  – *Through the Wall* (d. Rollin S. Sturgeon, sc. Marguerite Bertsch from Cleveland Moffett's novel; stars Shipman; Vitagraph)
  – *The Melody of Love* (d. J. Warren Kerrigan, sc. Shipman; stars Shipman)
  – *Son o' the Stars* (d. Jacques Jaccard, scenario by Shipman; cast includes Barry Shipman)
1917 – *The Black Wolf* (d. Frank Reichler; sc. Jean Barrymore; stars Shipman; Famous Players–Lasky)
  – *My Fighting Gentleman* aka *A Son of Battle* (d. Edward Sloman, sc. Doris Schroeder, scenario by Shipman)
1918 – *The Wild Strain* (January; d. William Wolbert; sc. George H. Plympton

and Garfield Thompson, based on story by George Randolph Chester and Lillian Christy Chester; stars Shipman; Vitagraph)

– *Baree, Son of Kazan* (May; d. David Smith; sc. James Oliver Curwood; stars Shipman; Vitagraph)

– *A Gentleman's Agreement* (July; d. David Smith, sc. Frederick Buckley; stars Shipman; Vitagraph)

– *The Girl from Beyond* (d. William Wolbert, sc. Donald I. Buchanan, based on a story by Cyrus Townsend Brady; stars Shipman; Vitagraph)

– *The Home Trail* (d. William Wolbert; sc. George H. Plympton; stars Shipman; Vitagraph)

– *Cavanaugh of the Forest Rangers* (d. William Wolbert, sc. Hamlin Garland, based on his novel *Cavanaugh, Forest Ranger*, stars Shipman; Vitagraph)

1919 – *Back to God's Country* (d. David M. Hartford, sc. Nell Shipman [uncredited], based on James Oliver Curwood's story 'Wapi, the Walrus,' p. Ernest Shipman, cin. Joseph B. Walker, Val Clawson; cast: Nell Shipman, Roy Laidlaw, Wheeler Oakman, Ronald Byram, Wellington Playter, Charles Murphy, Charles Arling, William G. Colvin, Brownie the bear, Tresore and Rex; Canadian Photoplays Production)

1920 – *Trail of the Arrow* (d., sc. Shipman; stars Shipman and Marjorie Cole)

– *Something New* (d., sc. Shipman; co-d. and co-sc. Bert Van Tuyle; p. B.F. Croghan, cin. Joseph B. Walker; cast: Nell Shipman, Bert Van Tuyle, L.M. Wells, William McCormack, Laddie the dog, the 1920 Maxwell; Nell Shipman Productions)

1921 – *A Bear, a Boy, and a Dog* (p., d., sc. Shipman, p. William H. Clune, cin. Joseph B. Walker; cast: Sunny Howard, Brownie the bear, Laddie the dog; Nell Shipman Productions)

– *The Girl from God's Country* (p., d., sc. Shipman, co-d. Bert Van Tuyle; cast: Nell Shipman, Edmund Burns, Al W. Filson, George Berrell, Walt Whitman, Cecil Van Auker, Boyd Irwin, Lillian Leighton, L.M. Wells, Milla Davenport; Nell Shipman Productions)

1923 – *The Grub-Stake* (d. Bert Van Tuyle, p., sc. Shipman, cin. Joseph B. Walker, Bobby Newhard; cast: Nell Shipman, Walt Whitman, Alfred Allen, Lillian Leighton, George Berrell, Hugh Thompson, C.K. Van Auker, Ah Winh, Brownie the bear; Nell Shipman Productions. Titled *The Romance of Lost Valley* in Great Britain, re-released as *The Golden Yukon*, 1927)

– *a series of short films, Little Dramas of the Big Places* (Nell Shipman Productions): *Trail of the North Wind* (p., d., sc. Shipman, cin. Bobby Newhard; cast: 'Daddy' Duffill, Barry Shipman, Nell Shipman, Ralph Cochner, Tex the malamute); *The Light on Lookout* (p., d., sc. Shipman, cin.

Bobby Newhard, Aubrey Overmeyer; cast: Nell Shipman, 'Daddy' Duffill, Ralph Cochner, Dorothy Winslow, Bert Van Tuyle, Brownie the bear)

1924 – *White Water* (d. Bert Van Tuyle, Nell Shipman, cin. Robert S. Newhardt; cast: Nell Shipman, Ralph Cochner, Ray Peters, Donald Winslow; Nell Shipman Productions)

1935 – *Wings in the Dark* (d. James Flood, sc. Philip D. Hurn, story Nell Shipman [uncredited]; cast: Cary Grant, Myrna Loy; Paramount)

1947 – *The Clam-Digger's Daughter*, aka *The Story of Mr. Hobbs* (d. Lorenzo Alagia and John M. McCool, sc. Nell Shipman; cast: Frances Helm, Arthur Varney [aka Amerigo Serrao])

Notes

Introduction

1 Nell Shipman, *The Silent Screen and My Talking Heart* (Boise, ID: Hemingway Western Studies Series, 1987) (hereinafter *Heart*).

2 Kay Armatage and Linda Beath, eds., *Women and Film International Festival Catalogue* (Toronto: Women and Film, 1973).

3 *Camille Claudel*, d. Bruno Nuytten, 1988.

4 *Artemisia*, d. Agnes Merlet, 1997.

5 Griselda Pollock, 'Introduction,' *Differences* 4, no. 5 (1992): x.

6 Jane Gallop, *Around 1981: Academic Feminist Theory* (New York: Routledge, 1992).

7 Yvonne Rainer, *The Films of Yvonne Rainer* (Bloomington: Indiana University Press, 1989).

8 Jeanne Betancourt, *Women in Focus* (Dayton, OH: Pflaum Publishing, 1974).

9 Karyn Kay and Gerald Peary, eds., *Women and the Cinema: A Critical Anthology* (New York: Dutton Press, 1977).

10 VeVe Clark, Millicent Hodson, and Catrina Neiman, eds., *The Legend of Maya Deren: A Documentary Biography and Collected Works*, vols 1 and 2 (New York: Anthology Film Archives, 1985, 1988).

11 Louise Heck-Rabi, *Women Filmmakers: A Critical Reception* (Metuchen, NJ: Scarecrow Press, 1984).

12 Anthony Blaché, ed., *The Memoirs of Alice Guy Blaché* (Metuchen, NJ: Scarecrow Press, 1986).

13 Ernest Ferlita and John R. May, *The Parables of Lina Wertmuller* (New York: Paulist Press, 1977).

14 E. Ann Kaplan, *Women and Film: Both Sides of the Camera* (New York: Methuen, 1983).

15 Kaja Silverman, *The Acoustic Mirror* (Bloomington: Indiana University Press, 1988).

16 Teresa de Lauretis, *Technologies of Gender* (Bloomington: Indiana University Press, 1987).

17 Lucy Ann Liggett Stewart, *Ida Lupino as a Film Director, 1949–1953: An Auteur Approach* (New York: Arno Press, 1980).

18 Lauren Rabinovitz, *Points of Resistance: Women, Power and Politics in the New York Avant-Garde Cinema, 1943–1971* (Urbana: University of Illinois Press, 1991).

19 Sandy Flitterman-Lewis, *To Desire Differently: Feminism and the French Cinema* (Urbana: University of Illinois Press, 1990).

20 An anthology of critical considerations of Wieland's films is now available: *Joyce Wieland: A Guide to the Film Literature*, ed. Kathryn Elder (Toronto: Cinematheque Ontario Publications, 1999). In addition, two new biographies of Joyce Wieland have recently been published: Jane Lind, *Joyce Wieland: Artist on Fire* (Toronto: Lorimer, 2001), and Iris Nowell, *Joyce Wieland: A Life in Art* (Toronto: ECW Press, 2001).

21 Janet Bergstrom and Mary Ann Doane, eds., *Camera Obscura: The Spectatrix* 20–1 (May–Sept. 1989).

22 In American television, less than 10 per cent of those in creative positions are women.

23 Laura Mulvey, 'Visual Pleasure and Narrative Cinema,' in *Visual and Other Pleasures* (Bloomington: Indiana University Press, 1989), 15. Originally published in *Screen* (1975).

24 Tania Modleski, *Feminism without Women: Culture and Criticism in a 'Postfeminist' Age* (New York: Routledge, 1991), 5.

25 Anthony Slide, *Early Women Directors* (New York: Da Capo Press, 1972; 2nd ed. 1984).

26 Janis Cole and Holly Dale, *Calling the Shots: Profiles of Women Filmmakers* (Kingston, ON: Quarry Press, 1993).

27 Kay Armatage, Kass Banning, Brenda Longfellow, and Janine Marchessault, eds., *Gendering the Nation: Canadian Women's Cinema* (Toronto: University of Toronto Press, 1999).

28 Tom Gunning, 'Film History and Film Analysis: The Individual Film in the Course of Time,' *Wide Angle* 12, no. 3 (1990): 5.

29 Ibid., 14.

30 Griselda Pollock, *Old Mistresses* (London: Routledge and Kegan Paul, 1981).

31 Irit Rogoff, 'Tiny Anguishes: Reflections on Nagging, Scholastic Embarassment, and Feminist Art History,' *Differences* 4, no. 5 (1992): 39–40.

32 Ibid., my emphasis.

33 B. Ruby Rich, 'Women and Film: A Discussion of Feminist Aesthetics,' *New German Critique* 13 (winter 1978): 87.

34 Rogoff, 'Tiny Anguishes,' 61.

35 Pollock, 'Introduction,' x.

36 Shipman, *Heart*, 40.

37 Ibid., 43.

38 Ibid., 50.

39 Fred Balshofer, 'Going into the Film Business,' in *The First Film Makers*, ed. Richard Dyer MacCann (Metuchen, NJ: Scarecrow Press, 1989), 37.

40 Robert C. Allen, 'Motion Picture Exhibition in Manhattan, 1906–1912: Beyond the Nickelodeon,' in *Film before Griffith* (Berkeley: University of California Press, 1983), 170.

41 Ibid., 177–8.

42 Garth S. Jowett, 'The First Motion Picture Audiences,' in *Film Before Griffith*, 201.

43 Balshofer, 'Going into the Film Business,' 38.

44 Paul C. Spehr, *The Movies Begin: Making Movies in New Jersey, 1887–1920* (Newark, NJ: Newark Museum, 1977).

45 Peter Morris, 'The Taming of the Few: Nell Shipman in the Context of Her Times,' in *Heart*, 216.

46 Peter Morris, *Embattled Shadows* (Montreal: McGill-Queen's University Press, 1978). See also Peter Morris, 'Ernest Shipman and *Back to God's Country*,' in *Canadian Film Reader*, ed. Seth Feldman and Joyce Nelson (Toronto: Peter Martin Associates, 1977), and Peter Morris, *The Film Companion* (Toronto: Irwin, 1984).

47 Shipman, *Heart*, 31.

48 Morris, 'Ernest Shipman,' 17.

49 David Clandfield, *Canadian Film* (Toronto: Oxford University Press, 1987), 4.

50 Ibid., 5.

51 ibid., 4.

52 Shipman, *Heart*, 31.

53 Ibid., 40.

54 The Museum of Modern Art, for example, featured Shipman in its tribute to Canadian cinema in the autumn of 1989.

55 James R. Mellow, *Charmed Circle: Gertrude Stein and Company* (New York: Praeger, 1974).

56 In the meantime, definitions of biography have undergone enormous transformations. We have seen biographies take many forms, and there are biographies of ideas, of God, and now of Jell-O (Carolyn Wyman, *Jell-O: A Biography* [New York: Harvest Books, 2001]).

57 Gertrude Stein's phrase.

58 See Joy Parr, *Domestic Goods: The Material, the Moral, and the Economic in the Postwar Years* (Toronto: University of Toronto Press, 1999).

59 Along with the turn of scholarly interest to cinema history, the increase in the numbers of women in the academy, brought about by the feminist revolution of the 1970s, has resulted in a more welcoming climate for women graduate students pursuing studies connected with women's concerns.

60 Shipman, *Heart*, 136.

61 Nell Shipman, *Get the Woman*, also known as *M'sieu Sweetheart* (New York: Dial Press, 1930).

62 Meaghan Morris, *The Pirate's Fiancee: Feminism, Reading, Postmodernism* (London: Verso, 1988), 16.

63 Rogoff, 'Tiny Anguishes,' 62–3.

64 Ibid., 61.

1: Women Directors of the Silent Era

1 Gwendolyn Foster, *Women Film Directors: An International Bio-Critical Dictionary* (Westport, CT: Greenwood Press, 1995), xiii.

2 Richard Henshaw, 'Women Directors: 150 Filmographies,' *Film Comment* 8, no. 4 (Nov.–Dec. 1972): 33–45.

3 Foster, *Women Film Directors*, xiii.

4 Andrew Sarris, *The American Cinema: Directors and Directions, 1929–1968* (New York: Dutton, 1968).

5 Peter Wollen, *Signs and Meaning in the Cinema* (London: Secker and Warburg, 1969).

6 Giuliana Bruno, *Streetwalking on a Ruined Map: Cultural Theory and the City Films of Elvira Notari* (Princeton, NJ: Princeton University Press, 1993), 234–5.

7 Ibid., 24.

8 Ibid., 235.

9 Ibid., 240.

10 Foster, *Women Film Directors*, xii–xiii.

11 Anthony Slide, *Early Women Directors* (New York: Da Capo Press, 1972), 9.

12 Ibid., 107.

13 Cleo Madison, Ruth Stonehouse, Lule Warrenton, Grace Cunard, Elsie Jane Wilson, Ruth Ann Baldwin, Jeanie MacPherson, Ida May Park.

14 Slide, *Early Women Directors*, 9–11.

15 Ibid., 13.

16 Judith Mayne, *Directed by Dorothy Arzner* (Bloomington: Indiana University Press, 1994).

17 Cari Beauchamp, *Without Lying Down: Frances Marion and the Powerful Women of Early Hollywood* (Berkeley: University of California Press, 1997).

18 Anthony Slide, *Lois Weber: The Director Who Lost Her Way in History* (Westport, CT: Greenwood Press, 1996).

19 Sandy Flitterman-Lewis, *To Desire Differently: Feminism and the French Cinema* (Urbana: University of Illinois Press, 1990).

20 Andrea Weiss, *Vampires and Violets: Lesbians in Film* (New York: Penguin, 1993).

21 Lynn Attwood, ed., *Red Women on the Silver Screen: Soviet Women and Cinema from the Beginning to the End of the Communist Era* London: Pandora, 1993).

22 Andrée Wright, *Brilliant Careers: Women in Australian Cinema* (Sydney: Pan Books, 1986).

23 Sharon Smith, *Women Who Make Movies* (New York: Hopkinson and Blake, 1975), 4.

24 Ibid., 4.

25 Ibid., 14.

26 Ibid., 92.

27 Louise Heck-Rabi, *Women Filmmakers: A Critical Reception* (Metuchen, NJ, Scarecrow Press, 1984), xii.

28 Ibid., xii–xiii.

29 Ibid., 67–8.

30 Claire Johnston, ed., *The Work of Dorothy Arzner: Towards a Feminist Cinema* (London: BFI, 1975). The book includes Pam Cook, 'Approaching the Work of Dorothy Arzner.'

31 Barbara Koenig Quart, *Women Directors: The Emergence of a New Cinema* (New York: Praeger, 1988), 18.

32 Ibid., 17.

33 Ibid., 18–19.

34 Incidentally, there is some controversy about Weber's poverty and the claim that Frances Marion paid for her funeral. Anthony Slide is sceptical; see *Lois Weber*, 150. Cari Beauchamp finds evidence in letters from Frances Marion about the event; see *Without Lying Down*, 346.

35 Quart, *Women Directors*, 20.

36 Ibid., 21.

37 Ibid., 21–2.

38 Ally Acker, *Reel Women: Pioneers of the Cinema, 1896 to the Present* (New York: Continuum, 1993), xviii.

39 Ibid., xxv.

40 Ibid., xx.

41 The note on Shipman, which is based on early and limited research, repeats some of the errors of previous scholarship.

42 Incidentally, Canadian director Patricia Rozema (*I've Heard the Mermaids Singing*, 1987) is accorded a lively and lengthy note (Acker, *Reel Women*, 315–17).

43 Annette Kuhn with Susannah Radstone, eds., *The Women's Companion to International Film* (London: Virago Press, 1990).

44 Ibid., vii.

45 Ibid., 391.

46 Foster, *Women Film Directors*, ix.

47 Ibid., xi.

48 Of course there are omissions. Like most American-based scholarship, Foster overlooks several important Canadian women feature filmmakers of the modern era. Anne Claire Poirier (*A Scream from Silence*, 1979; *Turning Forty*, 1982) has had a forty-year career in cinema, beginning with National Film Board documentaries and going on to dramatic features in the 1970s. Paule Baillargeon (*La cuisine rouge*, 1980) and Mireille Dansereau (*La vie rêvée*, 1972) represent a generation of important women feature directors in Quebec. Women directors from Quebec tend to be universally unknown, as little has been written in English about them; this perhaps explains their omission here. Of English-Canadian directors, perhaps the most significant omissions are Patricia Rozema (*I've Heard the Mermaids Singing*, 1987; *White Room*, 1990; *As Night Is Falling*, 1995; *Mansfield Park*, 1999) and Deepa Mehta (*Sam and Me*, 1991; *Fire*, 1996; *Earth*, 1998). Both Rozema and Mehta premiered their first films at Cannes, Rozema winning Le Prix de la jeunesse, so they are not unknown outside Canada.

Again, I do not mean to nit-pick. Foster does include a handful of Canadian women who have created significant bodies of work: Janis Cole and Holly Dale (*P4W: Prison for Women*, 1981; *Hookers on Davie*, 1984; *Calling the Shots*, 1988; *Dangerous Offender*, 1993); Laurie Colbert and Dominique Cardona (who made one film, *Thank God I'm a Lesbian*, 1992); Micheline Lanctôt (*The Handyman*, 1980; *Sonatine*, 1983; *The Pursuit of Happiness*, 1987; *Deux actrices*, 1993); Caroline Leaf (many short animated films, 1969–90); Marilu Mallet (a Chilean living in exile in Canada whose best-known film is *Unfinished Diary*, 1982); Alanis Obomsawin (*Incident at Restigouche*, 1984; *Kahnesatake: 270 Years of Resistance*, 1993); Léa Pool (*La femme de l'hôtel*, 1984; *Anne Trister*, 1986; *À corps perdu*, 1988; *Mouvements du désir*, 1994; *Emporte-moi*, 1999); Loretta Todd (a Native Canadian who has made two films); Anne Wheeler (*Loyalties*, 1985; *Bye Bye Blues*, 1989; *The Diviners*, 1993); and Joyce Wieland (an avant-garde filmmaker of over twenty short films as well as two features, *Reason over Passion*, 1969, and *The Far Shore*, 1976). With a few exceptions, these are the Canadians who were profiled in *The Women's Companion*, but Foster has not updated the filmographies from the earlier text. It appears that Foster has not delved further into Canada with her own original research.

49 Foster, *Women Film Directors*, 364–6.

50 Gloria Gibson-Hudson, 'Aspects of Black Feminist Cultural Ideology in Films by Black Women Independent Artists,' in *Multiple Voices in Feminist Film Criticism*, ed. D. Carson, L. Dittmar, and J. Welsch (Minneapolis: University of Missouri Press, 1994), 365–79.

51 Mary Dean and Theresa Leiniger, eds., *The Harlem Renaissance from A to Z* (New York: Facts on File, forthcoming).

52 Foster, *Women Film Directors*, xvii.

53 Slide, *Lois Weber*, 2–3.

54 Ibid., 8.

55 Ibid., 9.

56 Ibid., 127.

57 Ibid., 131.

58 Ibid., 138.

59 Ibid., 149.

60 Ibid., 142–5.

61 Beauchamp, *Without Lying Down*, 380.

62 Ibid., 56.

63 Ibid., 35.

64 Bruno, *Streetwalking on a Ruined Map*, 3.

2: Women with Megaphones

1 Nell Shipman, *The Silent Screen and My Talking Heart* (Boise: Idaho University Press, 1988), 40. In this chapter, further references to Shipman's memoirs are indicated in the text by page numbers only. An 'n' following a page reference refers to Tom Trusky's annotations in Shipman's published memoir.

2 Kalton C. Lahue, *Continued Next Week: A History of the Moving Picture Serial* (Norman: University of Oklahoma Press, 1964), 31.

3 That would put the date sometime in 1914, but Tom Trusky suggests in his note that this film might be the presumed lost three-reeler *Melody of Love*, copyright 17 June 1916 (Tom Trusky's notes, *Heart*, 169).

4 Nell Shipman, *Abandoned Trails* (New York: Dial Press, 1930), 52–3.

5 Tom Trusky, 'Nell Shipman: A Brief Biography,' *Griffithiana* 32/33 (1988): 252–8.

6 Gwendolyn Foster, *Women Film Directors: An International Bio-Critical Dictionary* (Westport, CT: Greenwood Press, 1995), 365.

7 Joseph B. Walker, *The Light on Her Face* (Hollywood: ASC Press, 1984), 89.

8 Cari Beauchamp, *Without Lying Down: Frances Marion and the Powerful Women of Early Hollywood* (Berkeley: University of California Press, 1997), 9.

9 Anthony Slide, *Early Women Directors* (New York: Da Capo Press, 1972), 90.

10 Beauchamp, *Without Lying Down*, 451–2. Incidentally, this is the first real evidence I have seen that supports the common feminist claim that women wrote or directed under male pseudonyms.

11 Foster, *Women Film Directors*, 94–7.

12 Quoted in Eldon K. Everett, 'The Great Grace Cunard–Frances Ford Mystery,' *Classic Film Collector* (summer 1973): 22.

13 Henry T. Sampson, *Blacks in Black and White: A Source Book on Black Films* (Metuchen, NJ: Scarecrow Press, 1977), 188–9.

14 Yvonne Lynn Welbon, personal communication: ywelbon@nwu.edu

15 Annette Kuhn with Susannah Radstone, ed., *The Women's Companion to International Film* (London: Virago Press, 1990), 277.

16 Lyell's career has been pieced together by Andrée Wright in *Brilliant Careers: Women in Australian Cinema* (Sydney: Pan Books, 1986).

17 Foster, *Women Film Directors*, 228.

18 Ibid., 319.

19 Cecile Starr, 'Lotte Reiniger's Fabulous Film Career,' *Sight Lines* (summer 1980): 17–19.

20 Sandy Flitterman-Lewis, *To Desire Differently: Feminism and the French Cinema* (Urbana: University of Illinois Press, 1990), 57.

21 Foster, *Women Film Directors*, 116.

22 Ibid., 116.

23 Kuhn and Radstone, eds., *The Women's Companion*, 164.

24 Vlada Petric, 'Esther Shub: Film as a Historical Discourse,' in *Show Us Life: Towards a History of Aesthetics of the Committed Documentary*, ed. Thomas Waugh (Metuchen, NJ: Scarecrow Press, 1984), 22. An early version appeared as 'Esther Shub: Cinema Is My Life,' *Quarterly Review of Film Studies* (fall 1978): 429–48.

25 Foster, *Women Film Directors*, 342.

26 Petric, 'Esther Shub.'

27 Lynne Attwood, 'The 1920s,' in *Red Women on the Silver Screen: Soviet Women and Cinema from the Beginning to the End of the Communist Era*, ed. Lynne Attwood (London: Pandora Press, 1993), 32.

28 Kuhn and Radstone, eds., *The Women's Companion*, 390.

29 Maya Turovskaya, 'Woman and the "Woman Question" in the USSR,' in *Red Women on the Silver Screen*, ed. Attwood, 142.

30 Stroeva began her career as a screenwriter, and continued to direct films

until 1959 (Sharon Smith, *Women Who Make Movies* [New York: Hopkinson and Blake, 1975], 136).

31 Foster, *Women Film Directors*, 311.
32 Ibid., 311.
33 Turovskaya, 'Woman and the "Woman Question,"' 142.
34 Attwood, 'The 1920s,' 49.
35 Smith, *Women Who Make Movies*, 135.

3: *Back to God's Country*

1 The adaptation of *God's Country and the Woman* was written by Christine Johnston, who had a career in movies that included seventy-four produced films and spanned the years 1915–48.
2 Remade later with the same title (d. William Keighley, p. Hal B. Wallis, 1937).
3 Remade in 1925, d. William Keighley.
4 Nell Shipman, *Abandoned Trails* (New York: Dial Press, 1932), 35 (hereinafter *Trails*).
5 Edward Everett Hale, *The American Year Book: Literature and Language Bibliographies from the American Year Book, 1910–1919* (Ann Arbor, MI: Pierian Press, 1970), 71.
6 Ibid., 91.
7 *The Prospector* (1904).
8 *Beautiful Joe* was republished countless times, including as a pamphlet distributed by the Unitarian Church. Heather Murray, University of Toronto, who has been promising a book about Margaret Marshall Saunders for some time, gave me the information about the pamphlet.
9 Hale, *American Year Book*, 135.
10 Ibid., 197.
11 Ibid., 111.
12 Other titles of films include *The Golden Snare* (1921), *Code of the Mounted* (1932), *Red Blood of Courage* (1935), *Call of the Yukon* (1938), *Call of the Klondike* (1950), *Northwest Territory* (1952), *Northern Patrol* (1953), *Yukon Vengeance* (1954).
13 Shipman, *Trails*, 35–6.
14 Tom Trusky's notes in Nell Shipman, *The Silent Screen and My Talking Heart* (Boise: Idaho University Press, 1988), 186n.
15 Joseph B. Walker, *The Light on Her Face* (Hollywood: ASC Press, 1984), 83–4.
16 Ibid., 88.
17 Shipman, *Heart*, 73.
18 Shipman, *Trails*, 29.

19 Ibid., 39.

20 Ibid., 31–2.

21 Ibid., 38–9.

22 Shipman, *Heart*, 41.

23 Ibid., 42.

24 Giuliana Bruno, *Streetwalking on a Ruined Map: Cultural Theory and the City Films of Elvira Notari* (Princeton, NJ: Princeton University Press, 1993).

25 Ibid., 18–19.

26 George F. Custen, *Bio/Pics: How Hollywood Constructed Public History* (New Brunswick, NJ: Rutgers University Press, 1992). Custen mentions only two Lincoln biopics, *Abe Lincoln in Illinois* (RKO, 1940) and *Abraham Lincoln* (United Artists, 1940), but there were many more. He discusses *The Story of Alexander Graham Bell* (Twentieth Century–Fox, 1939) and *Night and Day* (a biopic of Cole Porter; Warner Brothers, 1946).

27 Ian K. Easterbrook, *Canada and Canadians in Feature Films: A Filmography, 1928–1990* (Guelph, ON: Canadian Feature Project, University of Guelph, 1996).

28 Bruno, *Streetwalking on a Ruined Map*, 163.

29 Tom Gunning, 'Film History and Film Analysis: The Individual Film in the Course of Time,' *Wide Angle* 12, no. 3 (1990): 6.

30 Ibid., 11.

31 Ibid., 11–14.

32 Sandy Flitterman-Lewis, *To Desire Differently: Feminism and the French Cinema* (Urbana: University of Illinois Press, 1990), 3.

33 Ibid., 22.

34 Ibid., 26.

35 Ibid., 22.

36 Ibid., 21.

37 Ibid., 22.

38 Irit Rogoff, 'Tiny Anguishes: Reflections on Nagging, Scholastic Embarassment, and Feminist Art History,' *Differences* 4, no. 5 (1992): 38–9.

39 Shipman, *Heart*, 80.

40 Shipman, *Trails*, 78.

41 William K. Everson, 'Rediscovery,' *Films in Review* 40, no. 4 (1989): 231.

42 Shipman, *Heart*, 78. I do not intend to claim here that Shipman originated the double exposure, or indeed even the idea of a multiple montage to represent a dream. An early silent film, *Dream of a Rarebit Fiend* (Edison Films, d. Edwin S. Porter, 1906), had used a double exposure (albeit not nearly as complicated as the one in *Back to God's Country*) also to represent a 'mixture' of dream and reality.

43 Lev Kuleshov's term for the editing process that can make two shots from different locations appear to be contiguous.

44 Walker, *The Light on Her Face*, 95–6.

45 Shipman, *Heart*, 186.

46 Ben Singer, 'Power and Peril in the Serial-Queen Melodrama,' in *Melodrama and Modernity: Early Sensational Cinema and Its Contexts* (New York: Columbia University Press, 2001), 221.

47 A Nell Shipman Production, prod. B.F. Croghan, dir. Nell Shipman and Bert Van Tuyle, scen. Nell Shipman, cin. Joseph B. Walker, stars Nell Shipman, Bert Van Tuyle, L.M. Wells, William McCormack, Laddie the Dog, 1920. Although the title *Something New* does not signify its territorial regime, it remains a signifier of a sequel. In the eighteenth century, when three-volume novels repeated formulaic patterns, 'Something New' from the same publisher would signify in fact a variation on something old.

48 Singer, 'Power and Peril,' 117.

49 The Hays Office, run by William Harrison Hays. As president (1922–45) of the Motion Picture Producers and Distributors of America, Hays administered the motion-picture moral code (popularly called the 'Hays Code') that was promulgated in 1934 by agreement of the most prominent men of the industry.

50 Shipman, *Heart*, 79. Peter Morris, however, notes Annette Kellerman's nude scene in *A Daughter of the Gods* three years earlier. See 'Ernest Shipman and "Back to God's Country,"' in *Canadian Film Reader*, eds. Seth Feldman and Joyce Nelson (Toronto: Peter Martin Associates, 1977), 19.

51 *Moving Picture World*, 24 July 1920, 42.

52 Shipman, *Trails*, 66.

53 Ibid., 67.

54 Ibid., 68.

55 Ibid., 70.

56 Ibid., 75–6.

57 Ibid., 89.

58 See Axel Madsen, *Forbidden Lovers: Female Stars Who Loved Other Women* (Secaucus, NJ: Citadel Stars, 1995) for a rumour-laden, yellow journalism approach to this subject.

59 See Cari Beauchamp, *Without Lying Down: Frances Marion and the Powerful Women of Hollywood* (New York: Scribner's, 1997).

60 Shipman, *Trails*, 8.

61 Ibid., 92.

62 Ibid., 86.

63 Ibid., 9. Shipman was not so liberal that she embraced homosexuality, how-

ever. In her memoir, she notes that she was embarrassed to discover that the gay actors of whom she had been fond were ridiculed by others (*Heart*, 12–13).

64 Gina Marchetti, *Romance and the 'Yellow Peril': Race, Sex And Discursive Strategies in Hollywood Fiction* (Berkeley: University of California Press, 1993), 44.

65 Catherine Clement, *Opera, or the Undoing of Women*, trans. Betsy Wing (Minneapolis: University of Minnesota Press, 1988), passim.

66 Rogoff, 'Tiny Anguishes,' 61.

67 Ibid., 62.

68 Shipman, *Heart*, 70–83.

69 Shipman, *Trails*, 19.

70 Ibid., 22–3.

71 Ibid., 21.

72 Shipman, *Heart*, 72.

73 Shipman, *Trails*, 41.

74 Ibid., 43–4.

75 Shipman, *Heart*, 187n.

76 Ibid., 180n.

77 Ross Gibson, 'The Nature of a Nation: Landscape in Australian Feature Films,' in *South of the West: Postcolonialism and the Narrative Construction of Australia* (Bloomington: Indiana University Press, 1992), 65.

78 Ibid., 66.

79 Ibid., 69–70.

80 Ibid., 66.

81 Benedict Anderson, *Imagined Communities: Reflections on the Origin and Spread of Nationalism* (London: Verso, 1991), 36.

82 Gibson, 'Nature of a Nation,' 65.

83 After shooting the winter exteriors at Lesser Slave Lake, Alberta, the cast and crew had to return to California to shoot the interiors as well as the bucolic forest scenes featuring the wild animals.

84 Gibson, 'Nature of a Nation,' 66.

85 In the following year, Hudson had his first major success in a starring role in *Magnificent Obsession* (Universal, d. Douglas Sirk, 1954). For issues of stardom, extra-filmic information affecting the reception of a film, and Hudson as a 'central cultural symbol,' see Barbara Klinger, 'Star Gossip: Rock Hudson and the Burdens of Masculinity,' in *Melodrama and Meaning: History, Culture, and the Films of Douglas Sirk* (Bloomington: Indiana University Press, 1994), 97–131.

86 Nick Roddick, *A New Deal in Entertainment: Warner Brothers in the 1930s* (London: British Film Institute, 1983), 200.

87 *Moving Picture World*, 21 February 1920, 1243.

88 James Oliver Curwood, *Back to God's Country and Other Stories* (New York: Grosset & Dunlap, 1920).

89 Peter Morris, ed., *Canadian Feature Films, 1913–1969* (Ottawa: Canadian Film Archives, 1976).

4: Something New

1 Nell Shipman, *The Silent Screen and My Talking Heart* (Boise: University of Idaho Press, 1988), 88 (hereinafter *Heart*).

2 Ibid., 172n.

3 Joseph B. Walker, *The Light on Her Face* (Hollywood: ASC Press, 1984), 97.

4 Ibid., 106.

5 Shipman, *Heart*, 96.

6 Barry Shipman, 'Silent Star,' an unpublished screenplay registered 21 March 1988, 45. Barry Shipman gave me a copy; undoubtedly there is also a copy in the Shipman Archives at Boise University Library.

7 Walker, *Light on Her Face*, 112.

8 It is thanks to Tom Trusky's assiduous research that Walker's film is readily available for viewing.

9 William H. Drew, *Something New: Speeding Sweethearts of the Silent Screen, 1908–1921*. www.mindspring.com/~kallym/chap.10, copyright 1997.

10 Shipman, *Heart*, 88.

11 Timothy Corrigan, *A Cinema without Walls: Movies and Culture after Vietnam* (New Brunswick, NJ: Rutgers University Press, 1991), 143.

12 Shari Roberts, 'Western Meets Eastwood: Genre and Gender on the Road,' in *The Road Movie Book*, ed. Steven Cohan and Ina Rae Hark (London: Routledge, 1997), 45–67.

13 Ibid., 63–5.

14 Ibid., 66.

15 Shipman, *Heart*, 97.

16 Katie Mills, 'Revitalizing the Road Genre: *The Living End* as an AIDS Road Film,' in *Road Movie Book*, ed. Cohan and Hark, 322.

17 Plot summary from Patricia King Hanson, ed., *The American Film Institute Catalog of Motion Pictures Produced in the United States: Feature Films, 1911–1920* (Berkeley: University of California Press, 1988), 944. Quoted in Drew, *Something New*, chap. 10.

18 Mills, 'Revitalizing the Road Genre,' 321.

19 Roberts, 'Western Meets Eastwood,' 53.

20 Quoted in 'The Doctors' House Victorian Museum Presents the Nell Ship-

man Exhibit,' http://www.ci.glendale.ca.us/doctors_house/nell/
Page1.html.

21 Virginia Scharff, *Taking the Wheel: Women and the Coming of the Motor Age* (Toronto: Collier Macmillan, 1991), 8–9.

22 Ibid., 23.

23 Gloria Swanson, *Swanson on Swanson* (New York: Random House, 1980), 56–7.

24 Scharff, *Taking the Wheel,* 21.

25 Ibid., 24.

26 Ibid.

27 Ibid., 24–5.

28 'Review of New Films,' *New York Dramatic Mirror,* 24 October 1908.

29 Drew, *Something New,* chap. 3.

30 Scharff, *Taking the Wheel,* 16.

31 Ibid., 135.

32 Our only clue is the simple sleeveless dress Shipman wears, without a hat, in *Something New.*

33 Scharff, *Taking the Wheel,* 35–51.

34 Ibid., 47–57.

35 Drew, *Something New,* chap. 3.

36 Betty Harper Fussell, *Mabel* (New Haven, CT: Ticknor and Fields, 1982), 96.

37 Mabel Condon, 'Pacific Coast News,' *New York Dramatic Mirror,* 26 August 1916.

38 Jill Allgood, *Bebe and Ben* (London: Robert Hale, 1975), 51–7.

39 'Ormi Hawley,' 'The King of the Movies: Film Pioneer, Siegmund Lubin,' http://www.mc3.edu/gen/faculty/jeckhard/lubin.htm.

40 Quoted in Drew, *Something New,* chap. 3.

41 *Green Book Magazine,* April 1914, 844.

42 Newspaper interview with Florence Lawrence, 27 August 1920, courtesy of Kelly Brown.

43 'Natural Backdrop,' http://www.lightlink.com/jwrogers/thsept.htm, in 'Ithaca's Silent Movie History,' http://www.lightlink.com/jwrogers/wharton.htm.

44 Drew, *Something New,* chap. 3.

45 Mary Pickford, 'Answers to Correspondents, Daily Talks,' *Detroit News,* 11 December 1915.

46 Drew, *Something New,* chap. 3.

47 Ally Acker, *Reel Women: Pioneers of the Cinema 1896 to the Present* (New York: Frederick Unger, 1991), 253.

48 Robert Sklar, *Movie-Made America: A Cultural History of American Movies* (New York: Random House, 1975), 89.

49 'Helen's Daring "Stunt,"' *New York Dramatic Mirror*, 9 June 1917.

50 Drew, *Something New*, chap. 3.

51 Scharff, *Taking the Wheel*, 79–81.

52 Ibid., 87.

53 Gertrude Stein, *The Autobiography of Alice B. Toklas* (New York: Vintage Books, 1961), 172–80.

54 Scharff, *Taking the Wheel*, 102.

55 Ibid., 84.

56 Shipman, *Heart*, 112.

57 Ibid., 175n.

58 Walker, *Light on Her Face*, 77. Virginia Scharff provides an interesting footnote that relates Bert Van Tuyle to the history of women driving. The first auto clubs were formed just at the turn of the century. The elite Automobile Club of America (ACA), founded as an organization of auto owners in New York in 1899, immediately barred women from membership (*Taking the Wheel*, 68). Similar auto clubs appeared in the country over the next few years. However, the American Automobile Association, founded in 1902, was more democratic and included women members. We can only assume that the auto club of Philadelphia, according to Walker, or Rochester, the founding of which the anonymous author of the newspaper article quoted above attributes to Van Tuyle, belonged to the latter association, for all evidence suggests that he had no problem with Shipman's ownership and driving of her own car.

59 Shipman, *Heart*, 87.

60 Ibid., 89.

61 Ibid., 88–9.

62 Drew, *Something New*, chap. 3.

63 Ibid.

64 Ibid.

65 Eileen Bowser, *The Transformation of Cinema, 1907–1915*, vol. 2 of *History of the American Cinema*, ed. Charles Harpole (New York: Scribner's, 1990), 57.

66 Richard Koszarski, *An Evening's Entertainment: The Age of the Silent Feature Picture, 1915–1928*, vol. 3 of *History of the American Cinema*, ed. Harpole (New York: Scribner's, 1990), 164.

67 Miriam Hansen, *Babel and Babylon: Spectatorship in American Silent Film* (Cambridge, Mass.: Harvard University Press, 1991).

68 Janes Gaines, 'Fire and Desire: Race, Melodrama, and Oscar Michaux,' in *Black American Cinema*, ed. Manthia Diawara (New York: Routledge, 1993), 61–2.

69 Laura Mulvey, 'Visual Pleasure and Narrative Cinema,' in *Visual and Other Pleasures* (Bloomington: Indiana University Press, 1989).

70 Lynne Kirby, *Parallel Tracks: The Railroad and Silent Cinema* (Durham: Duke University Press, 1997), 107–8.

71 Gaines, 'Fire and Desire,' 61–2.

72 Kirby, *Parallel Tracks*, 105.

73 Bowser, *Transformation of Cinema*, 57.

74 Ibid., 183.

75 Ben Singer, 'Power and Peril in the Serial-Queen Melodrama,' in *Melodrama and Modernity: Early Sensational Cinema and Its Contexts* (New York: Columbia University Press, 2001), 222–4. Originally published as 'Female Power in the Serial-Queen Melodrama: The Etiology of an Anomaly,' *Camera Obscura* 22 (Jan. 1990).

76 Ibid., 253.

77 Kirby, *Parallel Tracks*, 114.

78 Ibid., 114.

79 Singer, 'Power and Peril,' 224.

80 Kirby, *Parallel Tracks*, 281.

81 Quoted in ibid., 230.

82 Ibid., 115.

83 Bowser, *Transformation of Cinema*, 206.

84 Kirby, *Parallel Tracks*, 116.

85 T.J. Jackson Lears, 'From Salvation to Self-Realization: Advertising and the Therapeutic Roots of the Consumer Culture, 1880–1930,' in *The Culture of Consumption: Critical Essays in American History, 1880–1930*, ed. Richard Wrightman Fox and T.J. Jackson Lears (New York: Pantheon, 1983), 26, quoted in Kirby, *Parallel Tracks*, 115–16.

86 Sarah Berry, *Screen Style: Fashion and Femininity in 1930s Hollywood* (Minneapolis: University of Minnesota Press, 2000).

87 Singer, 'Power and Peril,' 262.

88 Kirby, *Parallel Tracks*, 2.

89 Kathleen McHugh, 'Stopping Traffic: Women, Cars and the Cinema,' www.cmp.ucr.edu. n.p.

90 Ibid., n.p.

91 Ibid.

92 *The Biograph Bulletin*, quoted in Robert M. Henderson, *D.W. Griffith: The Years at Biograph* (New York: Farrar, Straus and Giroux, 1970), 134.

93 Barry Salt, 'The Early Development of Film Form,' *Film Form* 1, no. 1 (1976): 103.

94 Kirby, *Parallel Tracks*, 2.

95 Ibid., 7.

96 Ibid., 8. According to anecdotal evidence, on the contrary, the 'thrill of

instability' seems to be outweighed, for the women who drove cars in the early part of the century, by the thrill of velocity and the sense of control over the powerful machine. Even for women railroad passengers, confronting the dangers of a heterotopic space and making frequently unsanctioned decisions about personal and social motility, it seems probable that the 'thrill' resided in their sense of freedom, adventure, knowledge of new places, and independent agency, even if that Cartesian subjectivity was an illusory product of modernity.

97 Kirby is not alone in her technicist argument: it has been generated from decades of work on the apparatus and spectatorship, much of which remains convincing to me. However, it seems excessive to argue, for example, that as we move through the world we see it as 'a chain of essentially still images'; it makes as much sense to characterize walking as analogous to cinema. Furthermore, Kirby has described train travel as a heterotopic and dangerous space wherein bodies jostled and mingled. Even modern trains sway, bump, and pitch as they move along the tracks, and within them, passengers also move at will through the interior space with attendant collisions and falls. In a cinema, in contrast, the spectator sits, eyes fixed in one direction, in a chair bolted to the floor. Unlike the train, in the movie theatre jostling and mingling disrupts the cinematic experience. The analogy does not hold except as a simple metaphor generalized to its extreme. While the unstable subject of modernity – primarily characterized as a dualistic split subject – may have appealing resonance with the technical alternation of image and darkness through projection, the flickering presence/absence dialectic of cinema, it is not monolithically constructed by the cinematic apparatus.

98 Kirby attempts to argue further that train travel was constructed as dangerous for women by moralists who sought to contain female mobility, although she offers only one supportive anecdote as evidence, and does not address the popularity of representations of women on trains, driving cars, or piloting airplanes.

99 Roderick Nash, *Wilderness and the American Mind* (New Haven, CT: Yale University Press, 1967).

100 Kirby, *Parallel Tracks*, 150–64.

101 Ibid., 164.

102 Walker, *Light on Her Face*, 77–8

103 Ibid., 80–2.

104 Nell Shipman, *Abandoned Trails* (New York: Dial Press, 1932), 106.

105 Ibid.,107.

106 Shipman, *Heart*, 88.

107 Ibid., 88.

108 Ibid., 89.
109 Michel Foucault, 'What Is an Author,' in *Language, Counter-Memory, Practice*, ed. D. Bouchard (Ithaca, NY: Cornell University Press, 1977), 128.
110 Shipman, *Heart*, 117.
111 See, for example, Raymond Bellour, 'Hitchcock the Enunciator,' in *The Analysis of Film*, ed. Constance Penley (Bloomington: Indiana University Press, 2000), originally published in *Camera Obscura* 2 (fall 1977): 66–87.
112 Giuliana Bruno, 'Towards a Theorization of Film History,' *Iris*, 45.

5: *The Girl from God's Country*

1 Nell Shipman, *Abandoned Trails* (New York: Dial Press, 1932), 102.
2 Ibid., 103.
3 Quoted in Tom Trusky's editorial notes to Nell Shipman, *The Silent Screen and My Talking Heart* (Boise: Idaho University Press, 1988), 173n. In this chapter, subsequent references to Shipman's memoirs are referred to in the text by page number only.
4 Shipman, *Trails*, 90.
5 Advertising flyer in the manuscript collection at Boise State University Library.
6 Shipman, *Trails*, 87.
7 Ibid., 92.
8 Ibid., 93.
9 *Wid's Daily*, 18 September 1921, 9.
10 Quoted in Trusky's notes, *Heart*, 173.
11 Editor Tom Trusky, a meticulous researcher, was not able to find even one sample of the ad (*Heart*, 174n).
12 Lola Young, *Fear of the Dark: 'Race,' Gender and Sexuality in the Cinema* (London: Routledge, 1996), 95.
13 Eric Lott, *Love and Theft: Blackface Minstrelsy and the American Working Class* (New York: Oxford University Press, 1993), 77.
14 Following Daniel Francis, I will use the term 'Indian' to refer to what he calls 'the imaginary Indian' – 'the image of Native people held by non-Natives' – versus the terms Natives, Native people, or Aboriginals to refer to 'the actual people.' Daniel Francis, *The Imaginary Indian: The Image of the Indian in Canadian Culture* (Vancouver: Arsenal Pulp Press, 1992), 9.
15 Roberta E. Pearson, 'The Revenge of Rain-in-the-Face? Or Custers and Indians on the Silent Screen,' in *The Birth of Whiteness: Race and the Emergence of U.S. Cinema*, ed. Daniel Bernardi (New Brunswick, NJ: Rutgers University Press, 1996), 283.

16 Kevin Brownlow, *The War, the West and the Wilderness* (New York: Alfred A. Knopf, 1979), 261.

17 Ibid.

18 Gregory S. Jay, '"White Man's Book No Good": D.W. Griffith and the American Indian,' *Cinema Journal* 39, no. 4 (2000): 10.

19 Available credits are only for feature roles. They are: Nell Shipman as Neeka Le Mort and Marion Carslake; Edmund Burns as Owen Glendon; Al W. Filson as J. Randall Carslake; George Berrell as Pierre Le Mort; Walt Whitman as the Old Inventor; Cecil Van Auker as Otto Kraus; Lillian Leighton as Notawa; L.M. Wells as Sandy McIntosh; and Milla Davenport as Mrs Kraus.

20 Lloyd Peters, *Lionhead Lodge: Movieland of the Northwest* (Fairfield, WA: Ye Galleon Press, 1976), 131–2.

21 See especially Hartmut Lutz, '"Indians" and Native Americans in the Movies: A History of Stereotypes, Distortions, and Displacements,' *Visual Anthropology* 3 (1990): 31–49.

22 Jay, 'White Man's Book,' 7–10.

23 Pearson, 'Revenge,' 275.

24 Ibid., 283–5.

25 Francis, *Imaginary Indian*, 123.

26 Ibid., 146.

27 Pearson, 'Revenge,' 287.

28 Ian Angus, *A Border Within: National Identity, Cultural Plurality, and Wilderness* (Montreal: McGill-Queen's University Press, 1997), 128–9.

29 Ibid., 129.

30 Homi Bhaba, 'The Other Question,' *Screen* 24, no. 6 (1983): 18–36.

31 Francis, *Imaginary Indian*, 59–60.

32 Ibid., 61.

33 A popular poem written by a Mountie, quoted in ibid., 63.

34 Ibid., 63.

35 Ibid., 64–72.

36 Ibid., 74.

37 Ibid., 75.

38 Ibid., 64–82.

39 Steve Neale, 'The Same Old Story: Stereotypes and Repetition,' *Screen Education*, nos. 32–3 (1979–80): 33–7.

40 Shipman, *Heart*, 90.

41 Ibid., 102.

42 Ibid., 101–2.

43 Lott, *Love and Theft*, 140–2.

44 Nell Shipman, *Get the Woman*, also known as *M'sieu Sweetheart* (New York: Dial Press, 1930).

45 Peter Brooks, 'Melodrama, Body, Revolution,' in *Melodrama: Stage Picture Screen*, ed. Jacky Bratton, Jim Cook, and Christine Gledhill (London: British Film Institute, 1994), 16.

46 See the many texts originating from a feminist perspective, especially Christine Gledhill (ed.), *Home Is Where the Heart Is: Studies in Melodrama and the Women's Film* (London: British Film Institute, 1987); Tania Modleski, *Loving with a Vengeance: Mass-Produced Fantasies for Women* (New York: Methuen, 1982), Janice Radway, *Reading the Romance: Women, Patriarchy and Popular Literature* (Chapel Hill: University of North Carolina Press, 1984); Mary Ann Doane, *The Desire to Desire: The Woman's Film of the 1940s* (Bloomington: Indiana University Press, 1987).

47 Brooks, 'Melodrama, Body, Revolution,' 11.

48 Ibid., 17.

49 Ibid., 18.

50 Geoffrey Nowell-Smith, 'Minnelli and Melodrama,' in *Imitations of Life*, ed. Marcia Landy (Detroit: Wayne State University Press, 1991), 268–74.

51 Brooks, 'Melodrama, Body, Revolution,' 22.

52 Simon Shepherd, 'Pauses of Mutual Agitation,' in *Melodrama: Stage Picture Screen*, ed. Jacky Bratton, Jim Cook, and Christine Gledhill (London: British Film Institute, 1994), 27.

53 Shipman, *Get the Woman*, 47.

54 Shepherd, 'Pauses of Mutual Agitation,' 19.

55 Ibid., 27.

56 Shipman, *Get the Woman*, 48.

57 Brooks, 'Melodrama, Body, Revolution,' 13.

58 Shepherd, 'Pauses of Mutual Agitation,' 30.

59 Shipman, *Get the Woman*, 60.

60 Shepherd, 'Pauses of Mutual Agitation,' 25.

61 Jacky Bratton, 'The Contending Discourses of Melodrama,' in *Melodrama: Stage Picture Screen*, ed. Jacky Bratton, Jim Cook, and Christine Gledhill (London: British Film Institute, 1994), 38–49.

62 Shepherd, 'Pauses of Mutual Agitation,' 30.

63 Tom Gunning, 'The Horror of Opacity,' in *Melodrama: Stage Picture Screen*, ed. Jacky Bratton, Jim Cook, and Christine Gledhill (London: British Film Institute, 1994), 54–5.

64 Ibid., 51–2.

65 Ibid., 57.

66 Shepherd, 'Pauses of Mutual Agitation,' 30.

67 Shipman, *Get the Woman*, 248.

68 Lutz, '"Indians" and Native Americans in the Movies,' 33.

69 See Roderick Nash, *Wilderness and the American Mind* (New Haven, CT: Yale University Press, 1967).

70 Gunning, 'The Horror of Opacity,' 55.

71 Brooks, 'Melodrama, Body, Revolution,' 17.

72 Ibid., 18.

73 Ibid., 18.

74 Shipman, *Get the Woman*, 308.

75 Brooks, 'Melodrama, Body, Revolution,' 19.

76 Chuck Kleinhans, 'Realist Melodrama and the African-American Family,' in *Melodrama: Stage Picture Screen*, ed. Jacky Bratton, Jim Cook, Christine Gledhill (London: British Film Institute, 1994), 162.

77 Young, *Fear of the Dark*, 45–8.

78 Ibid., 88.

79 Angus McLaren, *Our Own Master Race: Eugenics in Canada, 1885–1945* (Toronto: McClelland and Stewart, 1990), 58.

80 See Young, *Fear of the Dark*, 46 on the former, and, for the latter, Gina Marchetti, *Romance and the 'Yellow Peril': Race, Sex and Discursive Strategies in Hollywood Fiction* (Berkeley: University of California Press, 1993), 10–27.

81 Marchetti, *Romance and the 'Yellow Peril,'* 109–76.

82 Young, *Fear of the Dark*, 48.

83 See Sylvia Van Kirk, *Many Tender Ties: Women in Fur-Trade Society, 1670–1870* (Winnipeg: Watson and Dwyer, 1981).

84 Francis, *Imaginary Indian*, 200–1.

85 Constance Backhouse, *Colour-Coded: A Legal History of Racism in Canada 1900–1950* (Toronto: Osgoode Society, 1999).

86 Jane Gaines, '*The Scar of Shame*: Skin Color and Caste in Black Silent Melodrama,' in *Imitations of Life: A Reader on Film and Television Melodrama*, ed. Marcia Landy (Detroit: Wayne State University Press, 1991), 340.

87 McLaren, *Our Own Master Race*, passim.

88 For a thoroughly researched documentary film on the subject of eugenics, see *Homo Sapiens 1900* (Sweden, directed by Peter Cohen, 1999).

89 Sander Gilman, *Difference and Pathology: Stereotypes of Sexuality, Race and Madness* (Ithaca, NY: Cornell University Press, 1985), 21–5. I have some discomfort with this respected view. If, as Gilman and others who use a psychoanalytic model argue, the construction of difference and otherness develops unconsciously during infancy as a component of identity, how the hell are we going to change anything?

90 Young, *Fear of the Dark*, 32.

91 'Mulatto, n. A child of two races, ashamed of both.' This definition is from Ambrose Bierce's *The Devil's Dictionary* (1911). An early study of the figure was Edward Byron Reuter's *The Mulatto in the United States Including a Study of the Role of Mixed-blood Races throughout the World* (1918). The term has been reappropriated in a variety of contemporary contexts. There is even a contemporary alternative rock band called Tragic Mulatto (Round Flat Records).

92 Sterling Brown, 'Negro Character as Seen by White Authors' (1933), reprinted in *Dark Symphony: Negro Literature in America,* ed. James A. Emanuel and Theodore L. Gross (New York: Free Press, 1968), 139–71.

93 Kathy Davis, 'Headnote to Lydia Maria Child's "The Quadroons" and "Slavery's Pleasant Homes,"' in *The Online Archive of Nineteenth-Century U.S. Women's Writings,* ed. Glynis Carr. Posted summer 1997. www.facstaff. bucknell.edu/gcarr/19cUSWW/LB/HNQSPH.html.

94 See Judith Berzon, *Neither Black Nor White: The Mulatto Character in American Fiction* (New York: New York University Press, 1978) and Victor Sejour, 'The Mulatto,' in *The Norton Anthology of African American Literature,* ed. Henry Louis Gates et al. (New York: W.W. Norton, 1997). For another respectable historical and literary discussion of 'passing,' see Werner Sollor, 'Passing; or, Sacrifice a Parvenu,' in Werner Sollor, ed., *Neither Black Nor White Yet Both: Thematic Explorations of Interracial Literature* (London: Oxford University Press, 1997).

95 Chon A. Noriega, 'Birth of the Southwest: Social Protest, Tourism, and D.W. Griffith,' in *The Birth of Whiteness: Race and the Emergence of U.S. Cinema,* ed. Daniel Bernardi (New Brunswick, NJ: Rutgers University Press, 1996), 207.

96 Ibid., 204.

97 Ibid., 208–9.

98 Young, *Fear of the Dark,* 108.

99 See for example, Karen Sanchez-Eppler, *Touching Liberty: Abolition, Feminism, and the Politics of the Body* (Berkeley: University of California Press, 1993).

100 Geoffrey Nowell-Smith, 'Minnelli and Melodrama,' 268–74.

101 Young, *Fear of the Dark,* 94–5.

102 Ibid., 113.

103 Veronica Strong-Boag and Carole Gerson, *Paddling Her Own Canoe: The Times and Texts of E. Pauline Johnson (Tekahionwake)* (Toronto: University of Toronto Press, 2000).

104 Gaines, '*The Scar of Shame,*' 336.

105 Marchetti, *Romance and the 'Yellow Peril,'* passim.

106 Ibid., 125.
107 Ibid., 49.
108 Shipman, *Get the Woman*, 51.
109 Ibid., 42.
110 Ibid., 7.
111 Ibid., 47.
112 Ibid., 45.
113 Shepherd, 'Pauses of Mutual Agitation,' 32.
114 Shipman, *Get the Woman*, 307.
115 Francis, *Imaginary Indian*, 106–7.
116 Jay, 'White Man's Book,' 12.
117 Lutz, '"Indians" and Native Americans in the Movies,' 37.
118 Shipman, *Get the Woman*, 46–7.
119 Ibid., 227.
120 Kleinhans, 'Realist Melodrama and the African-American Family,' 160.
121 Jacky Bratton, 'The Contending Discourses of Melodrama,' *Melodrama: Stage Picture Screen*, ed. Jacky Bratton, Jim Cook, and Christine Gledhill (London: British Film Institute, 1994), 39.
122 Shipman, *Get the Woman*, 55.
123 Ibid., 59.
124 Ibid., 174.
125 Ibid., 199.
126 A remark in Shipman's memoir suggests that this also was the ending of *The Girl from God's Country*: 'in the plot [the two women] didn't know of their relationship and the dark one thought herself Injun until that moment when, immersed in water, the color line down under showed pink' (Shipman, *Heart*, 90).
127 Shipman, *Get the Woman*, 310.
128 Bratton, 'The Contending Discourses of Melodrama,' 47–8.
129 Jane Shattuc, 'Having a Good Cry over *The Color Purple*,' in *Melodrama: Stage Picture Screen*, ed. Jacky Bratton, Jim Cook, and Christine Gledhill (London: British Film Institute, 1994), 154.

6: *The Grub-Stake*

1 Nell Shipman, *The Silent Screen and My Talking Heart* (Boise: Idaho University Press, 1988), 109. In this chapter, further references to Shipman's memoirs are referred to in the text as *Heart*.
2 Lloyd Peters, *Lionhead Lodge* (Fairfield, WA: Ye Galleon Press, 1976), 22–5. Further references to this book are referred to in the text as *Lionhead*.

3 Nell Shipman, *Abandoned Trails* (New York: Dial Press, 1932), 112.

4 Shipman, *Heart*, 115. Although other directors may not have edited their own films, it must be remembered that Shipman was here working to finish the film well after the entire production budget had been spent. It seems also that Shipman was not a particularly expert editor. Her comments on the improvement in her splices over those of the previous film, as well as the continued re-editing of *The Girl from God's Country*, offer some evidence of her level of achievement in editing.

5 Shipman, *Trails*, 112.

6 Ibid., 113–14.

7 Ibid., 116.

8 Ibid., 115–16.

9 In an unpublished paper presented at the Women Film Pioneers conference, Santa Cruz, November 2001, Tom Trusky insinuated that the construction of Jeb's character as an artist indicates effeminacy and perhaps homosexuality. I would argue, on the contrary, that his character is another Shipman effort to decentre gender dualities.

10 Naomi Scheman, 'Missing Mothers / Desiring Daughters: Framing the Sight of Women,' *Critical Inquiry* 15, no.1 (1988): 62–87.

11 E. Ann Kaplan, 'Mothering, Feminism and Representation: The Maternal in Melodrama and the Woman's Film, 1910–1940,' in *Home Is Where the Heart Is: Studies in Melodrama and the Woman's Film*, ed. Christine Gledhill (London: BFI Publishing, 1987), 123.

12 Ibid., 125.

13 Linda Williams, '"Something Else Besides a Mother": *Stella Dallas* and the Maternal Melodrama,' in *Home Is Where the Heart Is: Studies in Melodrama and the Woman's Film*, ed. Christine Gledhill (London: BFI Publishing, 1987), 300.

14 Ibid., 301.

15 Ibid., 314.

16 Ibid.

17 Mary Ann Doane, 'The "Woman's Film": Possession and Address,' in *Home Is Where the Heart Is: Studies in Melodrama and the Woman's Film*, ed. Christine Gledhill (London: BFI Publishing, 1987), 283–98.

18 See Shipman, *Heart*, 12–13.

19 Williams, '"Something Else Besides a Mother,"' 320.

20 E. Ann Kaplan, *Motherhood and Representation: The Mother in Popular Culture and Melodrama* (London: Routledge, 1992), 125–6.

21 Ibid., 135.

22 Ibid.

23 Ibid., 137.

24 Ibid.

25 Scot D. Ryersson and Michael Orlando Yaccarino, *Infinite Variety: The Life and Legend of the Marchesa Casati* (London: Pimlico, 1999).

26 Patricia Hill Collins, 'Shifting the Center: Race, Class and Feminist Theorizing about Motherhood,' in *Representations of Motherhood*, ed. D. Bassin, M. Honey, and M.M. Kaplan (New Haven: Yale University Press, 1994), 56–74.

27 Mary Odem, 'Single Mothers, Delinquent Daughters and the Juvenile Court in Early 20th Century Los Angeles,' *Journal of Social History* 25 (fall 1991): 27–43.

28 Kaplan, *Motherhood and Representation*, 138.

29 Kaplan 'Mothering, Feminism and Representation,' 126.

30 Ben Singer, 'Power and Peril in the Serial-Queen Melodrama,' in *Melodrama and Modernity: Early Sensational Cinema and Its Contexts* (New York: Columbia University Press, 2001), 221–62. Originally published as 'Female Power in the Serial-Queen Melodrama: The Etiology of an Anomaly,' *Camera Obscura* 22 (January 1990): 91–128. Shelley Stamp, *Movie-Struck Girls: Women and Motion Picture Culture after the Nickelodeon* (Princeton, NJ: Princeton University Press, 2000).

31 Doane, 'The "Woman's Film,"' 285.

32 Ibid., 288.

33 Ibid.

34 ibid., 289.

35 Shipman, *Trails*, 174. Hereafter, this book is referred to in the text as *Trails*.

36 Janey Place, 'Women in Film Noir,' in *Women in Film Noir*, ed. E. Ann Kaplan (London: British Film Institute, 1978), 35–67.

37 Christian Metz, *The Imaginary Signifier: Psychoanalysis and the Cinema*, trans. Celia Britton, Annwyl Williams, Ben Brewster, and Alfred Guzzetti (Bloomington: Indiana University Press, 1977), 54–7.

38 Laura Mulvey, 'Visual Pleasure and Narrative Cinema,' in *Visual and Other Pleasures* (Bloomington: Indiana University Press, 1989).

39 Mary Ann Doane, 'The Woman's Film: Possession and Address,' in *Home Is Where the Heart Is: Studies in Melodrama and the Woman's Film*, ed. Christine Gledhill (London: British Film Institute, 1987), 283–98.

40 Tom Gunning, *D.W. Griffith and the Origins of American Narrative Film: The Early Years at Biograph* (Urbana: University of Illinois Press, 1991). The cinema of attractions in Gunning's formulation, as Charlie Keil points out, has been too rigidly aligned with common descriptions of modernity; its use and usefulness are compromised and distorted by its appropriation as a model of spectatorship, both 'modern' and 'postmodern.' See Charlie Keil, 'Fatal Attractions: Modernity versus Integration,' in *American Cinema's Transitional*

Era: Audiences, Institutions, Practices, ed. C. Keil and S. Stamp (Berkeley: University of California Press, forthcoming).

41 Laura Marks, *The Skin of the Film: Intercultural Cinema, Embodiment and the Senses* (Durham, NC: Duke University Press, 2000), 333.

42 Ibid.

43 Ibid., 336.

44 Ibid., 343–4.

45 Vivian Sobchack, *The Address of the Eye: A Phenomenology of Film Experience* (Princeton, NJ: Princeton University Press, 1992), 103.

46 Ibid., 122.

47 Ibid.

48 In the sense of subject of research. I refuse to call her an object.

49 Ashley Montagu, *Touching: The Human Significance of the Skin* (New York: Columbia University Press, 1971), 110.

50 Roland Barthes, *Camera Lucida* (New York: Farrar, Strauss and Giroux, 1981; orig. published Paris: Editions du Seuil, 1980), 26–7.

51 Marks, *Skin of the Film*, passim.

52 Sobchack, *Address of the Eye*, 122.

53 Walter Benjamin, 'The Work of Art in the Age of Mechanical Reproduction,' reprinted in Leo Braudy and Marshall Cohen, ed., *Film Theory and Criticism: Introductory Readings*, 5th ed. (New York: Oxford University Press, 1999).

54 Marc Vernet, 'The Fetish in the Theory and History of the Cinema,' in *Endless Night: Cinema and Psychoanalysis: Parallel Histories*, ed. Janet Bergstrom (Berkeley: University of California Press, 1999), 89.

55 Ibid.

56 Jean Beaudrillard, *The System of Objects*, trans. James Benedict (London: Verso, 1996).

57 Susan Stewart, *On Longing: Narratives of the Miniature, the Gigantic, the Souvenir, the Collection* (London: Johns Hopkins University Press, 1984), 160.

58 Ibid., 154.

59 Ibid., 164–5.

60 C. Nadia Seremetakis, ed., *The Senses Still: Perception and Memory as Material Culture in Modernity* (Oxford: Westview Press, 1994), 7.

61 Claire Denis filmography: *Vendredi soir* (2002), *Trouble Every Day* (2001), *Beau travail* (1999), *Nénette et oni* (1996), *À propos de Nice, la suite* (1995), *Boom-Boom* (1994), *Le Chêne et le roseau* (TV, 1994), *US Go Home* (TV, 1994), *J'ai pas sommeil* (1994), *Contre l'oubli* (1991), *Keep It for Yourself* (1991), *Jacques Rivette, le veilleur* (1990), *S'en fout la mort* (1990), *Man No Run* (1989), *Chocolat* (1988).

62 Question period after screening of *Trouble Every Day*, Toronto International Film Festival, September 2001.

7: Bits and Pieces

1 Nell Shipman, *The Silent Screen and My Talking Heart* (Boise: Idaho University Press, 1988), 103.
2 Ibid., 188n.
3 Nell Shipman, *Abandoned Trails* (New York: Dial Press, 1930), 94–5.
4 Shipman, *Heart*, 96–7.
5 Ibid., 99.
6 Shipman, *Trails*, 77–8.
7 Ibid., 55.
8 Ibid., 60.
9 Ibid., 55–6.
10 Ibid., 56.
11 Shipman, *Heart*, 100.
12 Shipman, *Trails*, 78.
13 Ibid., 82–3.
14 Ibid., 84–5.
15 Shipman, *Heart*, 196n.
16 Joseph B. Walker, *The Light on Her Face* (Hollywood: ASC Press, 1984), 111.
17 Shipman, *Heart*, 196n.
18 Ibid., 117.
19 Ibid., 175n.
20 Walker, *Light on Her Face*, 111–12.
21 Charles Musser, *Before the Nickelodeon* (Berkeley: University of California Press, 1991), 173.
22 Ibid., 429.
23 Derek Bouse has written a PhD dissertation that examines the influence of nineteenth-century landscape painting on wilderness documentaries: 'The Wilderness Documentary: Film, Video and the Visual Rhetoric of American Environmentalism' (University of Pennsylvania, 1991).
24 Shipman, *Heart*, 137. An example of the 'not so real' can be found in one of Shipman's typical star turns in *The Trail of the North Wind*, a somewhat comic and lyrical scene in which Dreena drags baby skunks and their grown-up parents out of their nest and plays with them. Her star credentials as the girl from God's country, at home with creatures of all kinds, are on spectacular display here. She lifts – by the tail, carefully – each skunk in turn, pets and coos to it, and even dresses one baby in a little sweater. Shipman was 'acting' caution in this scene, as the skunks were 'fixed and scentless' (*Heart*, 91).
25 Ibid., 137.
26 Ibid., 124.

27 Ibid., 119.
28 Alexander Wilson, *The Culture of Nature* (Toronto: Between the Lines, 1991), 124.
29 Musser, *Before the Nickelodeon*, 42.
30 Ibid., 50.
31 Edison films catalogue description, Library of Congress on-line: http.//memory.loc.gov./cgi-bin/query/r?ammen/papre:@field [edmp+0951]
32 Quoted in Musser, *Before the Nickelodeon*, 426.
33 Gregg Mitman, *Reel Nature: America's Romance with Wildlife on Film* (Cambridge: Harvard University Press), 11.
34 Ibid., 6.
35 Charles G.D. Roberts, 'The Animal Story,' in *The Kindred of the Wild: A Book of Animal Life* (New York: Blue Ribbon Books, 1932; first published 1896), 15.
36 Ibid., 16.
37 Mitman, *Reel Nature*, 7.
38 Edison catalogue description, quoted in Musser, *Before the Nickelodeon*, 169.
39 Ibid., 164–5.
40 Ibid., 15.
41 Ibid., 25.
42 Ibid., 351.
43 Onno Dag Oerlemans, 'The Meanest Thing That Feels: Anthropomorphizing Animals in Romanticism,' *Mosaic* (Winnipeg) 27, no. 1 (1994): 1–32. Online article, no page numbers. See also, among many others, Myrna Milani, *The Body Language and Emotion of Cats* (New York: Quill, 1993); George Page, *Inside the Animal Mind: A Groundbreaking Exploration of Animal Intelligence* (New York: Doubleday, 1999); Joyce Poole, *Coming of Age with Elephants: A Memoir* (New York: Hyperion, 1996); Lesley Rogers, *Minds of Their Own: Thinking and Awareness in Animals* (New York: Westview, 1998).
44 Musser, *Before the Nickelodeon*, 349.
45 Mitman, *Reel Nature*, 9–11.
46 Ibid., 7.
47 Ibid., 9–10.
48 Wilson, *Culture of Nature*, 121.
49 Mitman, *Reel Nature*, 13.
50 Ibid., 14.
51 Quoted in Ibid., 16.
52 Oerlemans, 'Meanest Thing That Feels,' n.p.
53 Roberts, 'The Animal Story,' 20–2.
54 Wilson, *Culture of Nature*, 122.

55 Kevin Brownlow, *The War, the West and the Wilderness* (New York: Alfred A. Knopf, 1979), 440–1.

56 Ibid., 441.

57 Ibid., 466–8.

58 Although credit is routinely given to Martin Johnson as cinematographer and director, it is clear that Osa Johnson played a large part in the productions. She seemed equally at home with the gun or with the camera (cf. ibid., 470).

59 Mitman, *Reel Nature*, 28–9.

60 Ibid., 30.

61 Ibid., 32.

62 Roberts, 'The Animal Story,' 17.

63 Mitman, *Reel Nature*, 33–4.

64 Wilson, *Culture of Nature*, 122.

65 Mitman, *Reel Nature*, 35.

66 Wilson, *Culture of Nature*, 124.

67 Brownlow, *The War, the West, and the Wilderness*, 466.

68 Ibid., 525.

69 Mitman, *Reel Nature*, 38–9.

70 Ibid., 40.

71 Brownlow, *The War, the West, and the Wilderness*, 529.

72 Mitman, *Reel Nature*, 40.

73 Ibid., 40–50.

74 Wilson, *Culture of Nature*, 155.

75 Ibid., 125.

76 Shipman, *Heart*, 100.

77 Jonathan Auerbach, '"Congested Mails': Buck and Jack's "Call,"' *American Literature* 67, no. 1 (1995): 51.

78 Ibid.

79 Oerlemans, 'The Meanest Thing That Feels,' n.p.

80 Wilson, *Culture of Nature*, 118–20.

81 Oerlemans, 'The Meanest Thing That Feels,' n.p.

82 Mitman, *Reel Nature*, 11.

83 Wilson, *Culture of Nature*, 120.

84 Oerlemans, 'The Meanest Thing That Feels,' n.p.

85 Roberts, 'The Animal Story,' 23–34.

86 Oerlemans, 'The Meanest Thing That Feels,' n.p.

87 Wilson, *Culture of Nature*, 124.

88 Ibid., 155.

89 Oerlemans, 'The Meanest Thing That Feels,' n.p.

90 Roberts, 'The Animal Story,' 27.

91 Ibid., 28.

92 Ibid., 27.

93 On the other hand, in *Trail of the North Wind* as well we find Shipman indulging in one of the most egregious forms of anthropomorphism – for many scientists and/or humanist culture critics – in the scene in which she plays with the skunks. Not only does she fondle and snuggle them, but she dresses one of the babies in a little woolly sweater.

94 Rod Preece, *Animals and Nature: Cultural Myths, Cultural Realities* (Vancouver: UBC Press, 1999), 64–5.

95 Wilson, *Culture of Nature*, 127.

96 Brownlow, *The War, the West, and the Wilderness*, 281–3.

97 Preece, *Animals and Nature*, 33.

98 Ibid., 126.

99 Barry Holstun Lopez, *Of Wolves and Men* (New York: Charles Scribner's Sons, 1978), 203–4.

100 Ibid., 230.

101 Ibid., 209.

102 Erwin A. Bauer, *Wild Dogs: The Wolves, Coyotes and Foxes of North America* (San Francisco: Chronicle Books, 1994), 15–16.

103 Diane Antonio, 'Of Wolves and Women,' in *Animals and Women: Feminist Theoretical Exploration*, ed. Carol J. Adams and Josephine Donovan (Durham: Duke University Press, 1995), 220.

104 Wilson, *Culture of Nature*, 127.

105 Lopez, *Of Wolves and Men*, 210–11.

106 Farley Mowat, *Never Cry Wolf* (Toronto: McClelland and Stewart, 1963).

107 Lopez includes an extensive interdisciplinary and multilingual bibliography up to 1978.

108 Marian Engel, *Bear* (Toronto: McClelland and Stewart, 1976).

109 For a discussion of Engel's novel as a pastoral and the dangers of romanticizing nature, see Margaret Gail Osachoff, 'The Bearness of *Bear*,' *University of Windsor Review* 15 (1979–80): 1–2, 13–21.

110 Josephine Donovan, 'Animals Rights and Feminist Theory,' *Signs* 15, no. 2 (1990): 350–75. Ned Noddings, 'Response to Josephine Donovan,' *Signs* 16, no. 2 (1991): 418–22. Donovan, 'Response to Ned Noddings,' *Signs* 16, no. 2 (1991): 422–5.

111 For an excellent meta-theoretical critique of this work, see Catriona Sandilands, *The Good-Natured Feminist: Ecofeminism and the Quest for Democracy* (Minneapolis: University of Minnesota Press, 1999).

112 Carol A. Adams and Josephine Donovan, eds., *Animals and Women: Feminist Theoretical Explorations* (Durham: Duke University Press, 1995).

113 A third approach, it must be said, challenges animal rights feminists as diverting attention from the more pressing issues of human needs such as violence against women, homelessness, and health crises. Eco-feminists see this argument as participating in the same anthropocentric species hierarchy that was the basis for discrimination against women throughout the centuries. A contemporary postmodern approach finds Donna Haraway's *Primate Visions: Gender, Race, and Nature in the World of Modern Science* (New York: Routledge,1989) to be a central text. Haraway's famous cyborg metaphor points to the degree to which all elements are partly 'machine' or cultural construction.

114 Mary Ann Elston, 'Women and Anti-vivisection in Victorian England, 1870–1900,' in *Vivisection in Historical Perspective*, ed. Nicolaas A. Rupke (London: Croom Helm, 1987), 259–73.

115 Ibid., 280.

116 Ibid., 285.

117 Lawrence Finsen and Susan Finsen, *The Animal Rights Movement in America: From Compassion to Respect* (New York: Twayne Publishers, 1994), 42–54.

118 See Reginald Abbott, 'Bird Don't Sing in Greek: Virginia Woolf and the Plumage Bill,' in *Animals and Women: Feminist Theoretical Exploration*, ed. Carol J. Adams and Josephine Donovan (Durham: Duke University Press, 1995), 263–89. Woolf's newspaper article is reprinted in the Appendix of *Animals and Women*.

119 Shipman, *Heart*, 189n.

120 Sandilands, *Good-Natured Feminist*, 208.

121 Ibid.

122 Shipman, *Heart*, 136. The quotes in the balance of this chapter are all taken from Shipman's memoir.

8: Tissue-Paper Tower

1 Nell Shipman, *The Silent Screen and My Talking Heart* (Boise: Idaho University Press, 1988), 156–9. Many years after their relationship had ended, Shipman described Van Tuyle as the 'Top Top Banana': 'Here was a man! A ready laugh, an ability to face down discomforts and the anthills of problems built up in all moving picture productions. Once a star driver in the days when thundering motorcars went out for Century Runs over roads which were practically nonexistent, he was capable and owned a pair of hands able to build things, as my father had built them ... Such was Bert, very much loved, admired, obeyed for many moons. The thing undermining his drive, coiled and waiting the evil hour, was that foot frozen on the

night in Canada when he toiled for a movie far beyond the line of duty' (*Heart*, 112).

2 Barry Shipman, Afterword, in *Heart*, 180.

3 Ibid., 181.

4 Shipman, *Heart*, 159.

5 Ibid.

6 Author's interview with Barry Shipman, 1993.

7 Ibid.

8 Barry Shipman, Afterword, 205.

9 Ibid., 207.

10 Ibid., 208.

11 According to 'Film Actress Is Noted for Literary Work,' *Sarasota Examiner*, 27 November 1927.

12 Shipman interview, 1993.

13 Shipman, Afterword, 208.

14 Lillian C. Ford, 'Hollywood Favorites Prove Their Versatility,' *Los Angeles Times*, 12 June 1932, 14.

15 Shipman, Afterword, 208.

16 Shipman interview, 1993.

17 He wrote serials such as *Durango Kid, State Trooper,* and *Soldiers of Fortune* at Republic as a head writer earning $85 per week. After 1938, he left Republic for Universal, where he wrote *Flash Gordon, Dick Tracy,* and *The Lone Ranger.* In 1956 Republic produced his 'serious' screenplay, *Stranger at My Door* (directed by William Witney, starring Macdonald Carey and Patricia Medina). His credits as a 'B' movie writer include four or five movies a year, from *Robinson Crusoe of Clipper Island* (1936) to *Purple Death from Outer Space* (TV, 1966). He was 'always in the $200–$500 per week group,' he told me in the interview in 1993.

18 Shipman interview, 1993.

19 Ibid.

20 She seems to have written a number of projects in collaboration with or for Putnam, including *Hot Oil,* a vehicle for Will Rogers, who died before the film was able to be produced. Tom Fulbright, 'Queen of the Dogsleds,' *Classic Film Collector* 25 (autumn 1969): 30–1, 39.

21 Letter from Nell Shipman to Barry Shipman, 29 December 1933. This and all subsequent letters are quoted with the kind permission of the Nell Shipman Archive Special Collections Department, Boise State University Library.

22 Letter from Nell Shipman to Barry Shipman, 11 July 1934.

23 Hurn and Shipman got credit for the story but not screenplay.

24 Letter from Nell Shipman to Barry Shipman, 11 February 1935.

25 Letter from Nell Shipman to Barry Shipman, summer 1934.

26 Letter from Nell Shipman to Barry Shipman, 7 November 1934.

27 Letter from Nell Shipman to Barry Shipman, 6 October 1935.

28 In a letter to Barry Shipman, Serrao gives his credentials at length: 'In the eight years I was in Hollywood, from 1920 to 1929 I don't [think] I had over six months of inactivity ... in three years in London I made two pictures on salary, and eleven for myself via Paramount and Fox release. In 33 I made two pictures in Fort Lee, N.J. and in 34 I had a fairly good income from serving in an advisory capacity on production at Pathe, for H.E.R Laboratories, and directing for our beloved friend, the late Mr. Glett, who then called himself Regent Pictures, or something like that; I forget' (letter to Barry Shipman, late November 1938).

29 Shipman, Afterword, 208. Tom Trusky's view is quite different. In a letter, he wrote, 'I guess one major thing that affected my new view of Nell was her head-over-heeldom with Serrao. Barry really put me off on the guy and while I'm too well-versed in the nature of FreudianLand (i.e., well aware of Barry's dislike of all the men who stole his mum away), Serrao always seemed pretty dubious or suspect to me. Then you read Nell's letters about him. And I got his scrapbooks from Daphne's [Shipman's daughter] husband. The guy has an estimable career in England – he was not just poseur or flake. The fact that they were together over twenty years should have been clue enough. Although what's also clear in the letters, I think, was that by the mid-50's Nell had had enough of him. She stayed on the West Coast while he watched his body rot away in Hotel Fleabag in NJ, for crissakes, pleading with her to come to him to go make movies in France. Right' (e-mail to author from Tom Trusky, 26 October 2000).

30 According to Tom Fulbright, who based his information on interviews with Shipman, this was Amerigo Serrao's family name. Fulbright, 'Queen of the Dogsleds.'

31 As Arthur Varney, he is credited as director of *Winds of the Pampas* (1927), *The Road to Fortune* (1930), *The Wrong Mr Perkins* (1931), *Immediate Possession* (1931), *The Eternal Feminine* (1931), and *Almost a Divorce* (1931). Fulbright adds that Varney was once an assistant to D.W. Griffith. Ibid.

32 Shipman, Afterword, 208.

33 Shipman interview.

34 Letter from Nell Shipman to Barry Shipman, 27 July 1935.

35 Letter from Serrao to Barry Shipman, late November 1938.

36 Shipman, Afterword, 208–9.

37 [9 January 1939], handwritten. I have placed dates in square brackets when

there were no dates on the letters and I have had to work out the chronology through the contents. Unless otherwise indicated, all letters are from Nell to Barry.

38 20 January 1939.
39 [28 January 1939].
40 The only match I can find for this name is Harry Haskins, an assistant director from the silent period. He worked on *Forbidden Paths* (1917), *The Secret Game* (1917), *Jules of the Strong Heart* (1918), and *Risky Business* (1926) (www.imdb.com).
41 Shipman invariably spells her husband's nickname this way, with an 'e' – Seeley. Both Seely and Barry spell it without the 'e' – Seely.
42 10 February 1939.
43 She may be referring to the producer of *The Devil and Daniel Webster* (1941) (www.imbd.com).
44 10 February 1939.
45 Ibid.
46 Ibid.
47 Ibid. The film with Maurice Chevalier is *Avec le sourire* (d. Maurice Tourneur, 1936).
48 Ibid.
49 Serrao to Barry Shipman, 24 February 1939.
50 Ibid.
51 Ibid.
52 25 February 1939.
53 Ibid.
54 [25 February 1939].
55 Ibid.
56 [2 March 1939].
57 Ibid.
58 [15 March 1939].
59 Ibid.
60 Ibid.
61 Barry Shipman, Afterword, 208.
62 30 March 1939.
63 Ibid.
64 Ibid.
65 [18 April 1939].
66 Ibid.
67 Ibid.
68 Ibid.

69 [22 April 1939].

70 [April(?) 1939, possibly 23 April].

71 Ibid.

72 Ibid.

73 Ibid.

74 [18 April 1939].

75 [28 April 1939].

76 Ibid.

77 Serrao to Barry Shipman, [7 May 1939].

78 Ibid.

79 Ibid.

80 [8 May 1939].

81 Ibid.

82 Ibid. She is referring to *Only Angels Have Wings*, with Cary Grant and Jean Arthur, 1939, directed by Howard Hawks.

83 Ibid.

84 Ibid.

85 Serrao to Barry Shipman, [14 May 1939].

86 Ibid.

87 [1 June 1939].

88 [June 1939].

89 Ibid.

90 Serrao to Barry Shipman, [summer 1939].

91 [3 July 1939].

92 Ibid.

93 Ibid.

94 Ibid.

95 6 July 1939.

96 [8 July 1939].

97 [15 July 1939].

98 Ibid.

99 Ibid.

100 Ibid.

101 Ibid.

102 [23 July 1939].

103 Ibid.

104 Ibid.

105 Serrao to Barry Shipman, [26 July 1939].

106 Ibid.

107 Sunday; possibly 6 August 1939.

108 Serrao to Barry Shipman, headed 'Same day – Same Place'; possibly 6 August 1939.
109 [13 August 1939].
110 Sunday, September(?) 1939.
111 Headed 'Friday'; sometime in September,1939.
112 Ibid.
113 Ibid.
114 1 October 1939.
115 Ibid.
116 Ibid.
117 Ibid.
118 Ibid.
119 Headed Saturday night; it must have been 21 October 1939. Her birthday was 25 October, which fell on Wednesday in 1939.
121 [October 1939].
121 Ibid.
122 [28 October 1939].
123 Ibid.
124 Ibid.
125 Headed Wednesday; it must have been 1 November 1939.
126 Headed 'Sunday nite'; it must have been 5 November 1939.
127 Headed Thursday; it must have been 9 November 1939.
128 Ibid.
129 Headed Armistice; 11 November 1939.
130 Ibid.
131 Headed Thursday; it must have been 23 November 1939.
132 Ibid.
133 Headed 1 December.
134 20 December 1939.
135 20 April 1940.
136 Shipman first mentions *Jungle Ship* in a letter to Barry Shipman, 21 May 1935.

9: Naked on the Palisades

1 Letter to Barry Shipman, 19 December 1941. This and all subsequent letters are quoted with kind permission of the Nell Shipman Archive, Special Collections Department, Boise State University Library.
2 *The Story of Mr Hobbs*, the British title of *The Clam-Digger's Daughter*, first came to the attention of British National Film Archive cataloguer Luke

McKernan in 1988. The British print puzzled McKernan. A 1981 gift to the British Film Institute from the late and controversial silent film collector Raymond Rohauer, the British film was missing the final (seventh) reel. This final reel perplexes Rohauer Estate officials as much as do the first six. They have no record of Rohauer donating the print to BFI, or of the film ever having been in the Rohauer Collection. The first reel of *The Story of Mr Hobbs* is mysterious for other reasons. Credits on this reel state the film was 'recompiled for release by Anthony A. Termini.' Not only have McKernan and Trusky been unable to locate information about Termini, but also unidentifiable are the film's director ('Lorenzo Alagia') and producer ('John McCool'). Only after inquiries by William Neville of Cape Charles in 1992, did McKernan learn that his *The Story of Mr Hobbs* was Cape Charles's *The Clam-Digger's Daughter* and that Shipman and Varney, Serrao, Locke, and Lee were responsible for the film. From Tom Trusky's undated Press Release.

3 A pseudonym for Amerigo Serrao?

4 One of the actors, Frances Helm, did become a professional. Helm's first film role was playing Timmy Hobbs, the heroine of *The Clam-Digger's Daughter*. Helm's later studio film credits include *The Ugly American* (with Marlon Brando) and the made-for-television movie *Love and Betrayal: The Mia Farrow Story* (playing Farrow's mother, Maureen O'Sullivan).

5 Letter from Nell Shipman to Beatta Quinn, Motion Picture Relief Fund, 12 June 1963.

6 Ibid.

7 Letter from Barry Shipman to Nell Shipman, 30 June 1963.

8 Letter from Beatta Quinn to Nell Shipman, 19 July 1963.

9 The California town where she was living.

10 'Southern Pacific Centennial' proposal, 10 October 1967, held in the Boise State University Archives.

11 Letter from Georgia Burre McManis to William Morris, 20 September 1967.

12 Letter from Georgia Burre McManis to Nell Shipman, 4 November 1967.

13 Barry Shipman, Afterword, in Nell Shipman, *The Silent Screen and My Talking Heart* (Boise: Idaho University Press, 1988), 203.

14 Ibid., 201.

15 Letter from Nell Shipman to Gordon Sparling, 3 June 1968. Quoted in Shipman, Afterword, 203.

16 Shipman, Afterword, 203.

17 Ibid., 204.

18 Audio tape, held in the Boise State University Archives.

Illustration Credits

Index

temporary work on, 23–4; contradictory nature of, 31; defiance of social convention, 104; disappointments of, 124; eugenics, 194; femininity, 154–6; Hollywood landscapes, 117; identity of women culturally, 13; melodramatic conventions, 190; optimism of, 126, 140, 155, 160; unstable subject of, 375n97; wilderness as antidote to, 275, 277; and women, 127–8, 146, 152, 271–2

Modleski, Tania: *Feminism without Women: Culture and Criticism in a 'Postfeminist' Age,* 10–11

Mojave Desert, 114; setting for *Trail of the Arrow,* 123

monopoly: vertical integration, 18

Montagu, Ashley, 255

Montaigne, Michel de, 189

morality, 103–4; and animals, 184, 276–7; and hierarchy of gender, 230; and melodrama, 185–7, 189–90, 208–10; publication of *Abandoned Trails,* 306; and regulation of gender, 142. *See also* Hays Office (William Harrison)

Morris, Meaghan, 31

Morris, Peter, 18; on Ernest Shipman, 19–21; 'The Taming of the Few: Nell Shipman in the Context of Her Times,' 19

Morris, William, 348

Mothering Heart (d. D.W. Griffith), 226

mothers: Native women, 231; and role in melodrama, 226–8; in Shipman's films, 223–4, 226; single, 231

Motion Picture Producers and Directors of America, 369n49; and miscegenation, 193

Motion Picture Relief Fund: Shipman not eligible, 346–7

Motion Picture World: review of wildlife film, 277

Motor magazine: 'The Wonderful Monster,' 127

Mounties: 178–81; as the embodiment of the Law, 185; generic film character, 86; popular in film, 180; race and representations of villainy/heroism, 178–80, 207.

Movieola, 171, 217

movie theatres: conversion from theatres, 18

Moving Picture World: James Oliver Curwood Productions, 119

Mowat, Farley: *Never Cry Wolf,* 293

M'sieu Sweetheart: serial in *McCall's,* 306

mulatto. *See* 'tragic mulatta'

Mulvey, Laura, 10; and the history of the gaze, 249; 'Visual Pleasure and Narrative Cinema,' 142

Musidora, 48, 70–1

Musser, Charles, 273; 'teddy' film, 276

Muybridge, Eadweard, 272

narrative: and animal scenes, 90, 92–3; captivity tale, 202; destabilizing force of automobile, 147; driven by the heroine, 229; and geography of wilderness, 87, 93; and ideological imperative, 107–8; influence of landscape, 115–16; miscegenation, 200–1; nature as active agent of, 190–1; and parallel editing, 142–3; parallel love affairs, 201; plot-driven, 239; and privileging of consciousness, 209–10; racial identity and villainy/heroism,